"Better for man
Were he and nature more familiar friends."

# ON FOOT

# THROUGH THE PEAK:

OR,

## A SUMMER SAUNTER AMONG THE HILLS AND DALES OF DERBYSHIRE.

By JAMES CROSTON, F.S.A.,

*Fellow of the Royal Historical Society of Great Britain; Member of the Architectural, Archæological, and Historic Society of Chester; Member of the Council of the Holbein Society.*

AUTHOR OF
"A HISTORY OF SAMLESBURY;" "OLD MANCHESTER AND ITS WORTHIES;"
"HISTORICAL MEMORIALS OF THE CHURCH IN PRESTBURY;"
"BUXTON AND ITS RESOURCES," &c., &c.

> " There is a pleasure in the pathless woods,
>   There is a rapture in the lonely shore,
> There is society where none intrudes,
>   By the deep sea—and music in its roar :
> I love not man the less but nature more.
> From these our interviews, in which I steal
>   From all I may be, or have been before,
> To mingle with the universe, and feel
> What I can ne'er express, yet cannot all conceal."
> BYRON.

NEW EDITION.

E. J. MORTEN (Publishers)
Didsbury, Manchester, England

*First Printed by*
JOHN HEYWOOD
141 & 143 Deansgate, Manchester

*Republished 1973 by*
E. J. MORTEN (Publishers)
10 Warburton Street, Didsbury
Manchester, England

*Printed in Great Britain by*
Scolar Press Limited, Menston, Yorkshire

# PREFACE TO THE FIRST EDITION.

This volume owes its existence to no pre-arranged plan of travel for the purpose of writing a book, the excursion, of which it is a record, having been undertaken solely with the desire of combining healthful recreation with intellectual amusement, and to cultivate a more close acquaintance with the charms of nature. It is hoped, however, that, without claiming to rank as a guide to the Peak District of Derbyshire, it may be found an agreeable and useful companion to the tourist, by facilitating his progress and enhancing his enjoyment while visiting that romantic region.

A few of the earlier chapters have already appeared in the columns of the *Manchester Courier*, under the title of "A Ramble in the Peak of Derbyshire," and the approval they met with at the time has induced the Author to extend his labours, and to offer the narrative in its now complete form. He has taken no pains to amuse by relating imaginary adventures, his aim having been rather to portray scenes as they appeared to him at the time he witnessed them—to

give, as far as he has been able, a true presentment of nature
in her various and ever-changing aspects, with such historical
notices as might be applicable or add to the interest of the
places described. At the same time he is conscious of
having failed in conveying to the reader more than a limited
idea of the loveliness and beauty of the country he has
traversed.

The matter is derived from notes and observations made
during the rapidity of the journey, frequently in a brief style,
and without any immediate view to their publication. Had
time and other avocations permitted, many of these hasty
sketches might have been re-arranged and improved. To do
so, however, though it might have rendered them in some
respects more complete, would have deprived them of whatever freshness, precision, and circumstantiality may attach
to them in their present form.

In conclusion, the Author would bespeak the indulgence
of the reader for any defects or shortcomings which may
appear ; and in deprecation of any harsh criticism he would
observe that the text has been written hastily in his leisure
hours—oftentimes in those brief moments which he has
been enabled to snatch from other and more legitimate
pursuits.

# PREFACE TO THE THIRD EDITION.

THE call for another edition has enabled the Author not only to revise his work and bring down the information to the present time, but to make such additions as appeared to improve the accuracy and completeness of the narrative.

In addition to the Itinerary, which it is hoped will be found serviceable to the tourist, a new feature in the present volume is the catalogue of mosses and ferns found in the neighbourhood of Castleton for which he is indebted to Mr. John Tym. His thanks are also due to several friends for information communicated, and especially would he take the opportunity of acknowledging the renewed kindness of the eminent antiquary, Llewellynn Jewitt, Esq., F.S.A., of Winster Hall, to whom he is indebted for the loan of several of the illustrations which add interest to his pages.

UPTON HALL, PRESTBURY, CHESHIRE,
AUGUST, 1876.

# CONTENTS.

## CHAPTER I.

## CHAPTER II.

## CHAPTER III.

## CHAPTER IV.

## CHAPTER V.

## CHAPTER VI.

## CHAPTER VII.

## CHAPTER VIII.

## CHAPTER IX.

## CHAPTER X.

## CHAPTER XI.

## CHAPTER XII.

## CHAPTER XIII.

## CHAPTER XIV.

## CHAPTER XV.

## CHAPTER XVI.

## CHAPTER XVII.

## CHAPTER XVIII.

## CHAPTER XIX.

## CHAPTER XX.

## CHAPTER XXI.

## CHAPTER XXII.

## CHAPTER XXIII.

## APPENDIX.

# ILLUSTRATIONS.

# CHAPTER I.

INTRODUCTORY.

" England, thou hast within thy wave-girt isle
Scenes of magnificence and beauty rare,
Too often scorn'd by thy ungrateful sons,
Who leave, unseen, thy lovely hills and vales,
And seek for pleasure 'neath a foreign sky."

ROGERSON.

" KNOW most of the rooms of thy native country before thou
goest over the threshold thereof; especially, seeing England
presents thee with so many observables." This was the
advice given by quaint old Fuller a couple of centuries ago—
advice that would not be out of place even now-a-days,
when summer after summer so many pleasure-seekers betake
themselves to the Continent, rambling over hill and valley,
among glaciers, and through mountain passes, that they may
be enabled to utter a few worthless commonplaces on the
charms of scenery—a glorifying of nature that has dege-
nerated into a mere sentimental adoration of the picturesque
features of particular countries—whilst localities nearer home,
where nature presents herself in a garb not less beautiful
and romantic, are passed by with indifference, oftentimes
for no other reason than that they are more conveniently
accessible.

It is true the mountains of our own country many not
exhibit the wild desolation of Mont Blanc, or compare with
the savage grandeur of Alpine scenery ; but there are features
and characteristics peculiarly their own that amply compensate for the stern rigidness and lofty magnificence of their
foreign rivals.

It is the soft and graceful beauty, and the happy proportion of the component parts, that constitutes the great
charm of our home scenery : there is in it an endless variety
of form and outline, a blending together of hill and dale, of

B

wood and water, with a diversity in the colouring of the
foliage and vegetation, with which that of no other country
can compare.

But he who would thoroughly appreciate the rich stores of
England's beauty must leave her iron roads and beaten
highways and wander lovingly over her green hills, and
explore the mazy windings of her secluded dales—in the
early greyness of the morning, when the mists linger in the
vales, and the dew lies heavy upon the grass—at mid-day,
when the landscape is bathed in brilliant sunlight—and at
eventide, when the declining sun fills the glowing west with
gorgeous beauty, when the shadows lie in lengthened lines
upon the grassy slopes, and the woods and valleys are wrapped
in a rich glow of golden light. He must follow the sweet
meanderings of her mountain streams, winding hither and
thither through shady nooks, fringed and festooned with
greenery, where the tributary rills come trickling down
from the mossy heights, gladdening the ear with their tiny
melodies. He must loiter in her by-lanes, between banks
rife with ferns, foxgloves, and blooming harebells, where the
thick hedgerows and the nodding trees mingle and form a
bower overhead, and the bright sunbeams, playing through
the leaves, dapple the greensward with their restless and
ever-changing shadows. And so pace from hamlet to hamlet,
and from village to village, inhaling the fragrance of the
flowery meads, and listening to the joyous warblings of the
birds, the mingled harmony of dancing leaves, the lowing of
the kine, and the gentle murmuring of sunny music. If he
will do all this, he will understand something of the charms
of English scenery, and will learn that travelling at home is
not less enjoyable than travelling abroad.

Though the listless idler may pronounce such outdoor
wanderings dull and wearisome, the man of active and
inquiring mind will find in them a never-failing scource of
interest and amusement. To him every turn of the road,
every sudden gleam of sunshine, and every flitting cloud-
shadow that sweeps across the landscape, is a pleasure; and
the constantly-recurring changes of scene that travel opens
up, and the numerous individualities and circumstances that
are brought objectively before him, afford equal enjoyment

and gratification. If, with a keen perception of the beautiful, he unites a knowledge of some branch of natural science—if he is prepared to take as his lesson-book the works of God in nature, and to derive instruction from the mute preachers he meets with by the wayside—then his walk will become still more pleasurable and attractive. He will be led to look "through nature up to nature's God;" and in every object around him, however trivial and seemingly insignificant, he will recognise the evidence of a divine Being, the witness of a divine power, and the outward and visible sign of a divine and inapproachable glory.

How much enjoyment may be derived from things that seem trifling in themselves! The naked lifeless-looking rock—the shattered crag—the fragment of limestone with its conglomerate of primeval shells—even the tiny pebble that we kick before us—all bear some evidence of the inner life of nature, and reveal something of the history of a pre-Adamite or an antediluvian age, showing how worlds are constructed upon the wreck and ruin of preceding worlds, and how closely the waxing and waning of living races are bound up and associated with each other. The simple daisy with its elegant fringe-like petals—the lily of the valley that breathes forth its balmy essence—the common harebell with its azure flowers hanging in graceful clusters from its slender thread-like stem—the waving ferns which throw out their drooping fronds—the wild flowers that spring from the crevices of the rocks—the leaves of the forest—the grasses of the field—and the multitudinous variety of plants that our great Creator has scattered over the earth—have each their individual forms, and are invested with a beauty peculiar to themselves. To descend lower in the scale of nature, the various forms of life that are ever germinating and springing up on every hand, all busy in the fulfilment of their offices of absorption or reproduction—the trailing lichen that clings so fondly to the weather-beaten rock—the green moss that wreathes itself round the decayed stump of some old, withered, and blasted tree—the green, dust-like *confervæ*—all these, with a host of others, unfold their beauteous forms and are suggestive of curious thought to the lover of nature. Even the commonest fungus that grows in the dreariest out-of-the-way spot is possessed of a charm which, though unknown to the superficial observer, is at once manifest to the intelligent and inquiring eye.

Of all the many beautiful localities in this our all-beautiful land, there is none more abundant in natural charms, or that possesses a greater diversity of objects to interest and attract, than that section of England which is comprised within the limits of what is usually designated the Peak District of Derbyshire—a district that is as interesting from its historical associations, as it is remarkable for its geologic structure, its mineral wealth, and its picturesque beauty ; and where the many crumbling and time-stained monuments of the past —the memorials of ancient chivalrous splendour—which remain, are scarcely less striking and attractive than the quiet pastoral beauty of its romantic vales, or the bold and rugged grandeur of the precipitous rocks that bound the course of its mountain streams.

The singularly undulating character of the surface, and consequent variations of temperature, which prevail, produce a corresponding change in the character of the scenery, so that whilst in the high lands we have a region of heathy moors and wild and rugged rocks, with intervening glens and ravines, in the valleys the country assumes a more soft and pastoral character, exhibiting a rich fertility of soil, with an abundance of foliage and the most luxuriant vegetation—the contrast presented being at once striking and impressive ; whilst not unfrequently these distinct characteristics closely combine, when we have the stern grandeur of rock scenery united with the calm and placid beauty of a well-wooded and thoroughly cultivated country.

We know of no district that better repays investigation than the Peak of Derbyshire, and to those in search of novel and rational sources of amusement, or who desire to cultivate a more intimate acquaintance with the charms of nature, there are few that offer a greater fund of exciting interest, or to which an excursion can be made with more pleasurable results.

With us Derbyshire has long been a favourite theme. On its moorland wastes our first lessons in peripatetics were learned. We have scaled its loftiest hills and explored the labyrinthine passages of its cavernous recesses ; we have admired the wild scenery of its bleak moors and the charming beauty of its pastoral vales ; we have roamed with delight over its heathery heights and plucked the wild flowers in its secluded dells ; we have looked down upon the sweet vale of Castleton, and viewed the still more beautiful Hope Dale, from the brow of Mam Tor ; with light and cheerful step we have climbed the steep acclivities of the rock, from the verge of which, for centuries past, the great stronghold of the Peverels has frowned upon the vale below—

> " The fierce and haughty Peverel's tower,
> The tower which Scott hath hallowed by romance,
> Standing in ruins on its lofty cliff."

At Hathersage, which is said to have given birth to and where rest the bones of famous " Little John," we have renewed the darling theme of our boyhood, listening to the ballad history of Robin Hood and his followers—

> " Merry and free
> Under the leaves so green."

> " In this our spacious isle I think there is not one
> But he hath heard *some* talk—of him and Little John ;
> And, to the end of time, the tales shall ne'er be done
> Of Scarlock, George-a'-Green, and Much, the miller's son,
> Of Tuck, the merry friar, which many a sermon made
> In praise of Robin Hood, his outlaws and their trade."

Eyam, with its melancholy history, has long been familiar to us, and there, in the quiet eventide, seated on the high-backed settle in the chimney nook, we have listened to its tale of suffering and woe, and heard recounted the acts of Christian fortitude and heroic zeal displayed by its faithful pastor, William Mompesson ; we have gazed with wondering eye upon the gorgeous splendour of the " Palace of the Peak," and wandered with fond delight through the silent courts and deserted halls of dear old Haddon, conjuring up bright visions of a far back age, when

> " Tapers shone, and music breathed,
> And beauty led the ball ; "

we have mused in the ruined and roofless apartment at Wingfield which once formed the prison house of Scotia's hapless queen, and, while contemplating its tottering walls

and desolated chambers, we have been reminded of the
mutability of earthly grandeur and human greatness; we
have gazed upon the bewildering beauty of Matlock Dale,
and followed the devious windings of Cotton's "beloved
nymph, fair Dove;" we have walked over fields where the
hardy Briton and his invading foe have rushed to the deadly
onslaught, and where Cavalier and Roundhead have met in
fiercest conflict; we have lingered in spots memorable alike
in the history of the county and the kingdom, and have
made acquaintance with places, hallowed by associations that
can never be dissevered from them, which have erst been
the abiding places, and have inspired the genius, of some of
the brightest intellects of which England can boast.

The recollection of our former rambles made us long to
renew acquaintance with a district fraught with so many
pleasing reminiscences. It was therefore with feelings of
hopeful anticipation of coming pleasure that we started
upon the excursion which forms the subject of our narrative.

# CHAPTER II.

JULY, the richest, gayest month of all the year—the month
when Nature arrays herself in her grandest robe, and flowers
in rich abundance bedeck the emerald meads—when the trees
display all the fulness of their exuberant foliage, and the
orchards bend beneath the weight of their blushing fruit—
when the water-flags begin to droop by the river's brink, and
the changing colour of the ripening grain tells of the coming
of the joyous harvest time—bright July was drawing near
its close, the sun was circling towards the ruddy west, and
the lengthening shadows that lay upon the ground, whilst
denoting the near approach of evening, gave unmistakable
evidence that the summer days were beginning to draw
in, when with light heart and bounding step, and in the
pleasant companionship of cheerful friends, we bade adieu to
the busy bustling manufacturing metropolis of the north,
and some few minutes later were seated in the train and
darting along over a mazy labyrinth of house-tops and mill-
roofs, and through clouds of murky vapour, on our way to
the health-inspiring hills and valleys of the Peak.

After passing through, or rather over, Stockport, with its
smoke-begrimed mills, its countless factory chimneys and
almost suffocating atmosphere, the country assumes a more
picturesque and interesting character. On the left we have
an uninterrupted view of the long chain of Derbyshire
hills—Kinder Scout, the highest point of the Peak range,
looming mistily in the distance. Ere long the prospect opens
over the valley of the Goyt ; and a charming valley it is,
with its deep wooded glens and green undulating hills,
chequered with stone walls, and feathered here and there

with clumps of trees and patches of plantation. On the
right the eye takes in the broad flat meadows and rich
pasture-lands of Cheshire, and as the train speeds along we
catch glimpses of modern red-brick dwellings and quaint
old-fashioned cottages with low-thatched roofs, and smiling
farmsteads that lie scattered here and there. Every few
minutes we stop at a roadside station, where there is sure to
be some show of life and bustle, and something worth noting
or remembering ; then we hurry on—rattling over viaducts,
tumbling through deep sandy cuttings, and darting past
straggling hamlets, past fields of waving grain, and acres of
cultivated greenness.    Everywhere the haymakers are at
work, and as the playful breeze sweeps through the carriage
it loads the air with the rich perfume of the new-mown hay.
There are plenty of cattle grazing in the meadows, and, as we
thunder past, now and then a solitary horse throws up his
heels, and with a loud snort scampers off, scared at the sound
of our fiery iron steed ; and so we steam along, the changing
scenes coming and going, and following each other in quick
succession.

Now and then the bright beams of the declining sun come
streaming upon us, and as we turn aside to avoid the glare,
we get a passing glimpse of a deep hollow or woodland dell,
at the bottom of which a narrow by-path winds beneath the
shadowing trees to some hidden retreat, where "fays and
fairies love to dwell ; " and the charm is heightened by a
little brook that ripples merrily along, tumbling over the
stony ledges and prattling cheerfully to the mossy boulders
that bestrew its shallow bed.    Anon we catch a glimpse of
Disley Church, a quaint old structure crowning a wooded
eminence on the right ; then, emerging from the tunnel a
little beyond the station, the line enters a deep cutting,
where precipitous rocks, almost destitute of vegetation, shoot
boldly up on each side, their fronts mapped and streaked
with brown and grey and red, as if to make up for the lack
of verdure, whilst a dark shaly streak, a few feet above the
ground, evidences the nature of the strata, and our close
proximity to the coal formation.    Passing through this
cutting, we again come upon the open country, the railway
for some distance running parellel with the Peak Forest

Canal, which here forms a pleasing feature in the landscape. Approaching Whaley Bridge, after passing the well-wooded grounds of Lyme Park, we have a charming retrospective view of the valley of the Goyt, the eye, as it ranges into the far distance, passing over a variety of scenery of the most diversified character.

When we reached the station the sun was sinking in the western horizon, gilding with bright tints the highest peaks of the distant hills; the clouds were beginning to assume a ruddy burning tinge, suffusing a warm roseate tint over the scene; a purple gauze-like vapour hung over the valley, softening the outline of distant objects, yet so transparent as not to exclude the slightest undulation from the sight, so tender, so pure, so soft, that it conveyed the idea of atmosphere to perfection. The play of light and shade was admirable, the different gradations of colour beautifully harmonizing together—the bright green of the new-mown fields contrasting with the brown colouring of the heathy moors and the more sombre tints of the distant woods. The river, sparkling in the warm sunlight, pursued its course through a succession of fertile meadows, its banks clothed with luxuriant foliage; and the little groups of cottages and quiet homesteads that studded the green hill sides gave an air of quietude and tranquillity to the scene. Bugsworth lay on the opposite side of the valley, and before us the little hamlet of New Mills, romantically situated on the mountain slope, was dimly discernible through the evening mist, whilst in the far distance the tower of Marple Church, standing out in high relief against the evening sky, formed a prominent object in the view. The whole scene was one that might vie in beauty with anything which the most florid imagination of the artist could create.

Within a short distance of the Whaley Bridge station there is an interesting memorial of bygone times, called the Roosdyche, which some antiquaries believe to have been a *Rhedagua*, or racing-ground, in the Anglo-Roman period. The chariot-course, which still remains in a tolerably perfect state, appears to have been artificially formed by excavating along the side of the hill. It is enclosed on each side by steep embankments of earth, the slopes of which are partially wooded with oak, elm, birch, and other trees, whose spreading boughs, as they reach across, impart a verdurous shade that well accords with the ancient character of the place.

At Whaley the extension line of the London and North-Western Railway commences. Here the Goyt, which separates the counties of Derby and Chester, is crossed, and a little further on the line sweeps round the head of the Comb's valley, near the reservoir that supplies the Peak Forest Canal. In constructing the railway embankment and bridge at this point considerable difficulty was experienced in consequence of the treacherous nature of the soil. Again and again the embankment slipped, and eventually the original route had to be slightly deviated from. Popular suggestion attributed the impediment to other than natural causes, the general belief in the neighbourhood being that it was caused by the miraculous " Dickey," the ghostly owner of the skull which from time immemorial has had an abiding place in the window of a cottage at Tunstead, a little hamlet close by—a relic of mortality that is said by tradition to have belonged to a female, one of two co-heiresses who resided at the cottage, and who, having met with a violent death during the Commonwealth period, declared in her dying moments that her skull should remain there for ever. Another and more reliable authority, however, tells us that it belonged to a trooper, Ned Dickson by name, who went

> " For a soldier across the salt sea,
> To serve Henry-quatre with Lord Willoughby :
> At Ivry he fought in the Huguenot war,
> And followed the white plume of him of Navarre ;
> Of Henry le Roi, when he burst like a flood
> Through the ranks of the Leaguers in glory and blood ;"

and who, returning from the wars to his home at Tunstead, was strangled by his kinsman for the sake of his inheritance. Half-a-mile beyond the scene of " Dickey's " vagaries is the station for Chapel-en-le-Frith, the point where our railway journey terminates—the town itself being some three-quarters of a mile distant.

Chapel-en-le-Frith is a respectable looking little town, pleasantly situated on the slope of a hill which rises from a deep valley, shut in by lofty eminences that environ it on every side. The houses are, for the most part, built of grit-stone, and though somewhat old-fashioned in aspect, have an air of comfort about them that speaks much for the domestic thrift of their occupants. The principal street is steep and somewhat indifferently paved, with passages leading off on either side to queer little out-of-the-way places. The shops abutting upon the principal thoroughfare put on an air of business, and there is no lack of accommodation for tipplers, if we may judge from the number of signs that hang invitingly across the way. The church—a comparatively modern structure, without any pretensions to architectural excellence—occupies the site of an earlier foundation, which gave name to the place. An ancient stone coffin may still be seen in the graveyard; and a cross, with the date 1637 inscribed upon it, occupies an elevated position in the Market Place, contiguous to which are the stocks, a terror to evil-doers in days gone by.

As we had purposed staying the night at Castleton we proceeded on our journey, taking the way that leads along the side of Rushup Edge. At the end of the town the road separates. Keeping to the left we cross the tramway, and then, passing an iron foundry, continue along a pleasant rural highway, bordered by stone walls that alternate now and then with grassy banks, whereon grow clumps of thorns and brambles. The road soon leaves the open valley, and for some two or three miles beyond is one continuous ascent. As we journey on many a pretty view is afforded us. The patches of stone wall—all grey and jagged and weather-stained—that skirt the wayside are grown over with mosses and lichens, and well-nigh hidden from view by the ferns and brambles that thrive in rich profusion; while plantations of spruce and larch here and there impart a sense of shelter, and occasionally a dwarf oak or ash flings its branches across the road, and chequers the sunny pathway with the shadows of the rustling leaves. Gradually the prospect widens, and on the right we obtain glimpses of green meadows and swelling uplands, with little rustic cottages hiding away in green cloughs and shady dells, and dotting the grassy knolls and moorland heights. Ere long we reach the high ground, from whence we can overlook the valley. Fields and meadows lie upon each side, bounded by steep hills ; and deep in the hollow, where a little rivulet meanders freakishly through the glade, cultivated enclosures, green lawns, and gravelled paths, show where wealth and taste have encroached upon the wild and untrimmed beauties of nature.

Daylight was now fast fading from the landscape, and as we neared Slack Hall, an old-fashioned stone building, erected, as the date over the door testifies, in the early part of last century, we paused to look back upon the valley through which we had passed, and a scene of varied loveliness met our view— undulating eminences, partially covered with plantations of larch and mountain pine, surrounded us on every side ; Chapel-en-le-Frith lay beneath us, its presence indicated by the smoke curling upwards through the trees, and the tower of its church, a fitting object to adorn the landscape, rising over all ; Bowdon Hall and Bowdon Edge, with Chinley-Churn and cloud-capped Kinder, lay upon the right, and on the left a valley, at the bottom of which a tinkling rill, that rippled cheerfully through the meadows, separated us from a long chain of hills which stretch away in the distance in the direction of Tideswell and Buxton ; before us, Eccles Pike reared its lofty head, and a vast amphitheatre of mountains closed in the scene beyond.

We lingered some time watching the changing effects of the expiring day. Twilight was coming on apace, and the shades of evening were beginning to close around. A few faint streaks of golden light which yet lingered in the western heavens showed where the sun had gone down behind the darkening hills ; and, as these gradually died away, a train of black vapoury clouds stretched across the horizon, and gathered themselves in strange weird shapes round the fading light. A deepening gloom crept stealthily across the hillsides, and spread itself over the fair green meadows ; the distant landscape now slowly faded from the sight, and more prominent objects began to assume a shadowy indistinctness ; mists were accumulating in the valleys, from which wreath after wreath ascended, like incense to the skies ; the last smiles of day that lingered upon the tops of the mountains had died away, and, as they vanished from the sight, a low murmuring breeze that arose swept across the valley, and rustled through the branches of the trees with a strange mournful sound. The bold and jutting headlands that in the dim uncertain light seemed to increase in magnitude, gradually melted away in gloomy indistinct masses, and the shadows of objects became blended in undistinguishable darkness. A quiet stillness reigned around— all nature seemed hushed in repose—night gathered round her sable curtain and gently let down the canopy of mystery and darkness—earth and sky softly blended together—and the world appeared wrapped in impenetrable gloom.

After passing Slack Hall the country assumes a more wild and moorland character, and for a distance of about three or four miles is as dreary as can well be imagined. Though not positively sterile, it exhibits an almost entire absence of cultivation, and is totally devoid of picturesque beauty. Bleak moorland wastes extend as far as the eye can reach, everywhere intersected by stone walls, with here and there a tree planted, as if for no other purpose than to remind the wayfarer of their general absence and the barren and cheerless character of the land.

Bleak and barren, however, as this region is, the thoughtful mind will find ample food for observation and inquiry. Half-a-mile beyond Slack Hall a large quarry has been opened in the millstone grit, and a little further on the road enters upon the limestone formation. Here the book of Nature opens its pages, which, like the prophet's roll, are written within and without in characters of the sublimest significance. The stone walls on either hand are built up of limestone blocks, every fragment of which presents an almost bewildering profusion of fossiliferous remains, the entombed types of living creatures that floated about in the carboniferous seas long ages before that

> "Awful shock
> Which turned the ocean bed to rock,
> And changed its myriad living swarms
> To the marble's veined forms."

The limestone hereabouts presents one vast aggregation of extinct organisms that thronged the waters with life long ere the "Spirit of God had moved upon the face of the deep." Here a huge *productus* is seen mingling with the long jointed stems of the *encrinite*—there the delicate feather-like *retepora*, the *spirifera*, and the *orthocera*, with a host of others, are lying matted together—the silent though eloquent witnesses of pain and pleasure, of suffering mingled with enjoyment, and the twin but opposing mysteries of life and death—life, that barrier of the Creator's secret which we may never overpass, and death, the work of the pale King of Terrors, effected millenniums of ages before man's first transgression.

The entrance to the vale of Castleton is by a steep and winding road, carried round the foot of Tray Cliff and along the base of Mam Tor, commanding at different points some fine scenic views of the country in and around Hope Dale, the beauty of which is rendered more apparent by contrast with the barrenness of the neighbouring moors, and the suddenness with which the prospect breaks upon the sight. This road was cut about the beginning of the present century, previous to which the approach was by a narrow precipitous descent through the vale of the Winyates or Winnats.

We preferred the latter route to that by Tray Cliff, and striking off suddenly to the right followed the Buxton Road for a distance of about a quarter of a mile, then turning to the left we passed through a gate and entered the rocky ravine of the Winnats, one of the most imposing scenes to be met with in the High Peak.

This chasm, which has been named the *Wind-gates* or *portals of the wind*, from the breezes that constantly sweep through and gather in every hollow and angle, has the appearance of having been at some remote period rent asunder by a convulsion of nature. Wildness and rugged grandeur are the characteristics of this gloomy pass, and to us the effect was heightened by the sudden transition from the bleak and barren waste we had just traversed. On each side the limestone cliffs rise to an immense altitude, their summits split and rent into a variety of fantastic forms; in some places huge shapeless masses jut out over the narrow causeway without any apparent support, menacing with destruction anyone who may venture beneath, whilst fragments of rock, which, having become detached, have been hurled down from the mountain tops, lie scattered about in wild profusion. Not a tree or a shrub is to be seen, the only sign of vegetation being a few patches of scant herbage thinly scattered about the fissures of the crags and upon the rocky slopes, affording pasture to a few sheep that skip about from cliff to cliff with marvellous agility. As the traveller advances the rocks seem to gain additional elevation, and to increase in the interest they excite. Near the further end of the dale the road takes a sudden turn to the left, where a huge mass of limestone, rising abruptly to a prodigious height, seems to oppose a barrier to further progress. Winding round the base of this a vista opens, and the vale in which reposes the village of Castleton comes suddenly upon the view, presenting the appearance of a wide-spread panorama, broken into picturesque undulations, and dotted over with snow-white cottages and little clustered folds, whose presence was only revealed to us by the lights that twinkled through the evening gloom.

To us, accustomed to the turmoil and bustle of a crowded city, the effect of this rocky gorge was rendered more than ordinarily striking by the time and circumstances under which we viewed it. Shut out apparently from the world, not a habitation or the sign of any living creature could we discern, not a sound could we distinguish save the soughing of the wind through the fissures of the mountain and the sharp echoes of our footsteps ringing upon the flinty footpath. Havoc, ruin, and desolation were everywhere apparent. A few stars glistened in the firmament, and the moon, partially obscured by a bank of clouds, shed a feeble and uncertain light upon the scene—sufficient only to make the darkness visible. The dark and rugged cliffs, frowning grimly on each side, seemed, in the dim and shadowy light, to increase in magnitude, and, as it were, to grow up and prop the clouds. A feeling of awe took possession of the senses, and the mind, conscious of the deep solitude that prevailed, became oppressed with melancholy. We passed onwards in silence, as if afraid that even the sound of our voices might break the charm and bring down the incumbent masses of rock like an avalanche upon us.

The Winnats is not without its tale of blood. Tradition asserts that, about a century ago, a lady and gentleman, travelling on horseback, were waylaid and murdered in this mountain pass, The attendant circumstances are related by the villagers with much minuteness, though who the victims were, and whence they came, has never been satisfactorily established. It is believed, however, that they were upon a matrimonial excursion to the neighbouring hamlet of Peak Forest.

As illustrative, though by no means confirmatory, of the story, it may be stated that at the period alluded to Peak Forest, distant about three miles from the scene of the murder, was extra-parochial, and enjoyed much the same privileges as until lately pertained to Gretna Green, for which reason it was frequently resorted to for the solemnisation of runaway matches.

Immediately on leaving the vale of the Winnats we passed on our right a little white-washed cottage, the entrance to the Speedwell Mine, one of the wonders of the Peak, and a few minutes later entered the village of Castleton.

The open doorway of the *Bull's Head* and the lights twinkling through the windows were a welcome sight, and being hungry and weary we were nothing loth to accept the kindly offices of the good-humoured hostess of that comfortable little hostelry.

# CHAPTER III.

CASTLETON, distant about 25 miles from Manchester, and 10 from Buxton, is one of the most interesting villages in Derbyshire, presenting to the mineralogist and geologist, as well as to the antiquary and the lover of nature, an assemblage of objects of curiosity and attraction such as few other places can show. Mawe, in the preface to his "Mineralogy of Derbyshire," observes that, "for the purpose of obtaining mineralogical information, Castleton seems to be the best situation, where such a variety of strata, mines, and minerals occur, as perhaps no other situation in the kingdom can boast."

The village stands at the head of one of those romantic valleys which Derbyshire, more than any other English county, abounds in. This valley is about two miles in breadth, and extends eastwards as far as Hathersage, a distance of about seven miles. A noble amphitheatre of mountains, of varied form and elevation, environ it on every side— Bamford Edge, Winhill, Losehill, and Mam Tor, rising prominently above the rest, the latter attaining an elevation of about 1,300 feet above the general level of the plain. A number of lesser dales open into it, and several hamlets and villages are included within the limits.

It derives its name from an ancient stronghold built upon the extreme edge of a lofty eminence on the south, the ruins of which still remain. The village itself is of considerable antiquity, and was at an early period, to protect it from the attacks of wandering marauders, surrounded by a defensive ditch or fosse, which extended in a semicircular course round the town from the Castle Rock, traces of which may yet be discerned in certain directions.

C

Respecting the early history and antiquity of this castle antiquaries are at issue. Mr. King, who has minutely described it in his "Observations on Ancient Castles" (Archæologia, vol. vi., pp. 247-254), contends for its Saxon origin, and assumes it to have been a fortress and place of royal residence during the Heptarchy. An able article from the pen of the Rev. Charles H. Hartshorne, which appeared in the "Journal of the Archæological Institute of Great Britain and Ireland" for 1848, assigns a much later period as the date of its erection, the opinion of the writer being that it is a Norman structure. So far as our own observation went we could not discover a trace of Anglo-Saxon work, the archways, shafts, capitals, and other details being unmistakably Norman. It is true an example of "herring-bone" masonry still remains below the basement of the keep, but this, though evidencing considerable antiquity, would not in itself afford indisputable proof of its Saxon origin. That a military fortification existed here anterior to the Conquest is not improbable ; for at a time when the art of war was but little understood, and the means of attack comparatively few, it is not likely that a position offering so many natural advantages, and which must then have been almost impregnable, would be over-looked. The tradition of the place is that the castle was built by William Peverel, a natural son of William the Conqueror, and its ancient appellation of "Peverel's Place in the Peke," would seem to countenance this opinion. Certain it is, that at the time of the Domesday survey, which was begun in 1081, and completed in 1086, twenty years after the landing of the Norman invader, and after he had extended his sovereign authority over the entire kingdom, the place was held by William Peverel—the entry in the survey being, "*Terra Castelli Wi. Peverel. in Peche fers,*" an expression which Lysons says seems to import that the castle was built by him.

The name of Peverel is closely identified with the early history of Derbyshire. William Peverel, the supposed founder of Peak Castle, was a natural son of William the Conqueror, by Maud, the daughter of Ingelric, a Saxon nobleman related to Edward the Confessor, and the founder of the Collegiate Church of St. Martin's-le-Grand, in the city of London. This

lady, who is represented as possessing great personal attractions, afterwards became the wife of Ranulph Peverel, of
Hatfield Peverel, in the county of Essex, a son of Payne
Peverel, standard-bearer to Robert Duke of Normandy, the
father of William I. ; and the use of surnames becoming
common amongst the Norman barons about this time, the
king's son by his concubine adopted the name of Peverel,
that of the family into which his mother had subsequently
married.

As in all probability the connection between William of
Normandy and the daughter of Ingelric took place on the
occasion of the visit of the former to his kinsman, King
Edward the Confessor, in 1048, William Peverel must have
been approaching manhood at the time of his father's successful
expedition to this country, and very shortly after this event
he had conferred upon him, by the favour of the king,
immense possessions in the newly acquired territory—the
Castle of Peke, with the honour and forest,* being included.
After the death of his father, and on the accession to the
throne of his half-brother, William Rufus, Peverel continued
in favour at Court ; and in 1094, on the breaking out of
hostilities between the king and his elder brother, Robert
(Curthose), he, with eight hundred men, held the Castle of
Helme, in Normandy, on the king's behalf, but being closely
besieged was compelled to surrender it, and is supposed to
have died shortly afterwards.

Peverel was succeeded in the honours and estates by his
son William, who, in the reign of Henry I., founded the Priory
of Lenton, near Nottingham, for Cluniac Monks, endowing it
with lands in Derbyshire and Nottinghamshire, together with
the whole tithe of his lead and venison in the Peak, and to
which his knights and great tenants made considerable additions. He gave to the Abbey of St. Mary, in York, founded by

* An old Inquisition in the possession of the Norfolk family gives the following
as the metes and bounds of the Forest of Peak : "It beginneth at the head of
the river Goyte, and so down to the river Edewe (Ederowe or Etherow), and so to
a place called Ladycross, at Longdendale, and from Longdendale head to the head
of the river Derwent, and so to a place called Masham (Mytham) Ford, and so to
Bradwell Brook, and to the Great Cave of Hazlebage, and from thence by Poynton
Cross to Tideswell Brook, and so down to the river Wye, and so ascending up the
river Wye to Buxton Town, and from thence to the head of Goyte again." This
would give a circumference of about 60 miles, but within the limits were included
several manors that appear to have been held direct from the king in *capité*,
though within the honour and forest.

Allan, Earl of Brittany, eight carucates of land in Rudstan; and having founded an abbey of Black Monks near the town of Northampton, died, according to the register of that abbey, on the 5th of the calends of February, 11 Henry I. (1113).

William Peverel, by his wife Aveline, or Adeline, left a son, bearing the same baptismal appellation, in whom the name and honours of the family terminated, he having been accused of administering poison to the Earl of Chester whilst in prison, intriguing and confederating with his countess, Aloisa, daughter of the Earl of Gloucester, in the nefarious fact. This circumstance occurred in 1152, or, according to Simeon of Durham and some other authorities, in 1154, and so skilfully and adroitly was the deed accomplished, that the earl lingered for a considerable time before death put an end to his sufferings—the ignorance and superstition of the age attributing his sickness to "sorcery and devilish enchantment." The accounts given of this transaction by ancient historians are very brief and unsatisfactory. Gervase of Canterbury says, "The noble and famous Earl Ranulph of Chester, by a certain William Peverel, according to report, being poisoned *(per quendam Will. Peverel, ut fama fuit veneno infectus)* After suffering many torments, this man, distinguished for military glory and insuperable boldness, hardly to be alarmed or conquered but by death, finished his temporal life and was committed to the grave." This atrocious act is mentioned by the Monk of Waverley, and other writers.

Peverel, dreading the severity of the king, from whom he could expect no mercy, sought refuge in the monastery at Lenton, of which he was patron, and which, as already stated, had been founded by his father, and, relinquishing everything he possessed, assumed the tonsure and cowl of a monk. He was not, however, able to remain long in his seclusion, for in the month of February, 1155, the king, journeying to York, passed through Nottinghamshire, when the conscious criminal was compelled to cast aside his monkish habit and quit the country to escape the consequences of his act, forfeiting the whole of his rich and valuable possessions.

From the foregoing narrative it will be seen that the fief of Castleton, with its adjacent wastes and forests, was enjoyed by the great feudal house of the Peverels for only three generations, having passed from their hands within a century of the time it was conferred by the Conquerer upon his illegitimate son, the first baron.

Pilkington gives the following account of a grand tournament which is said to have been held at Peak Castle during the time it was in the occupancy of the Peverels: "Pain Peverel, a half-brother of William, Lord of Whittington, in the county of Salop, had two daughters, one of whom, named Mellet, was no less distinguished by a martial spirit than her father. This appeared from the declaration she made respecting the choice of a husband. She firmly resolved to marry none but a knight of great prowess; and her father, to confirm her purpose, and to procure and encourage a number of visitors, invited all noble young men who were inclined to enter the lists to meet at Peverel's Place in the Peak, and there decide their pretensions to the use of arms, declaring, at the same time, that whoever vanquished his competitors should receive his daughter and his castle at Whittington as a reward for his skill and valour. Guarine de Metz, a branch of the House of Lorraine, and an ancestor of the Lords Fitz-Warrine, hearing this report, repaired to the place above-mentioned, and there engaged with a son of the King of Scotland, and also with a Baron of Burgoyne, and, vanquishing them both, obtained the prize for which he fought." Were it not for spoiling so pretty a story we should be almost inclined to doubt the authenticity of Pilkington's statement, for within so circumscribed an area as the court of Peak Castle it is difficult to understand how sufficient space could be found for such a "grand" display of knightly pageantry.

Sir Walter Scott has thrown the halo of romance over Peak Castle by making it the scene of one of the most popular of the Waverley Novels, "Peverel of the Peak," though to suit the purpose of his story the great necromancer of the north has dealt somewhat unceremoniously with history and dates, things, it must be confessed, he did not at all times stand greatly in awe of.

Henry II., to avenge the death of the Earl of Chester, seized the entire of the possessions of William Peverel, including the castles of Nottingham, Bolsover, and the Peak, which thenceforward became vested in the Crown. At this time the forest of Peak was frequently resorted to by the Norman sovereigns and their successors, who were passionately fond of the pleasures of the chase. From the sheriff's accounts, contained in the great Pipe Roll of the Exchequer, it would appear that the king paid a visit to the castle in 1157 ; the official for the county returning in his account for that year : Corrodies for the king at Pech, the amount of £4 1s. 5d., and corrodies for the king of Scotland at Nottingham and Pech, £38 12s. 3d., and payment for wine (*apud Pech*), £3 12s. There is also a well authenticated tradition current in the neighbourhood that Edward I. was engaged in the pastime of hunting here when news of the death of his queen, Eleanor, reached him. After the exile of the Peverels the castle was given by Henry II. to his youngest and favourite son, John Earl of Montaigne, afterwards king. Edward II. conferred the governorship upon his favourite, Piers Gaveston, and after his banishment the office was held by John Earl of Warren for life. Subsequently, in 46 Edward III., it was given, with the honour and forest of Peke, by the king to his son, the Earl of Richmond, commonly called John o' Gaunt, who, having married Blanche, youngest daughter of Henry Duke of Lancaster, in 1359, his father, in 1362, created him Duke of Lancaster, when the Castle of Peak became parcel of the Duchy of Lancaster.

The Duke of Devonshire, who is the present lessee under the Duchy of the honour and forest of Peak, has the nominal appointment of constable of the castle, and holds a court-leet and court-baron half-yearly at Easter and Michaelmas.

The morning succeeding our arrival at Castleton we awoke with a happy and joyous feeling. The church clock was chiming the hour of six, and as we looked out from our chamber window to our pleasurable surprise the ivy-covered walls of the old castle and the roofless keep crowning the top of a steep grassy hill appeared full in view. As the bright sunlight fell upon its scathed towers and streamed through its broken archways it looked indeed utterly lonely, a picture of abject ruin and desolated grandeur, so strangely in contrast with what it must have been in those fierce feudal ages with which its history is so intimately associated. There had been a slight fall of rain during the night, but the breeze which followed had dried up the pavement, a still rapture lay upon the green hills, and everything from earth to sky looked fresh and cheering. The good folks of the *Bull's Head* were not yet astir, so we quietly let ourselves out, resolved to have a climb to the top of the castle rock before breakfast.

When we strode forth into the open air the little village seemed to have hardly awoke from its slumber; all was quiet and still, and, with the exception of the lowing of the cattle as they wended their way to the rich pastures, or the snatch of a ballad trolled forth by some hardy brown-hued miner on his way through the sunshine to his daily labour, there was nothing to break the stilly reign of sleep and silence.

It was a lovely summer's morn, and there was a cool and invigorating freshness in the atmosphere that gave a buoyancy and elasticity to the spirits. The mists, which during the night had accumulated in the valleys, were creeping lazily up the mountain sides and gradually disappearing under the genial influence of the morning sun, and every object seemed redolent with smiles, as if welcoming the return of day.

The first object that engaged our attention was the castle ; and bending our steps in that direction we soon reached the foot of the rock, on the summit of which stand the decayed ruins of what was once the great stronghold of the Peverels. Viewed from certain positions, the old castle, and the eminence on which it is seated, forms a not unpleasing object in the landscape, but seen in the distance, and contrasted with the loftier hills that surround it, much of the effect is lost, and it has, comparatively, but an insignificant appearance. A better position, however, for a fortress, or one offering greater security in case of attack, cannot well be conceived, and before cannons were known,

> " And villainous saltpetre had been dug
> Out of the bowels of the harmless earth,"

it must have been almost impregnable. The rock, which appears to have been uplifted from the plain by some great convulsion of nature, is almost insulated, being connected with the adjoining hill only by a narrow strip or tongue of

land, with a bold escarpment on each side, so rugged as to
be only accessible in one direction, and that is so steep that
a traverse or zigzag course is necessary to reach the summit.
We began the ascent, and a weary and toilsome work we
found it, the difficulty being increased by the slippery nature
of the short thick grass with which the slope is overgrown.
Success at length crowned our efforts, and amply were we
rewarded for our exertions by the magnificent views of
country that were afforded.

The ruins of the old fortress, though by no means extensive, are deserving of careful examination. The ballium, or
castle yard, occupies nearly the entire area of the summit,
and is enclosed by a curtain wall partially destroyed and
overgrown with ivy. The plan is in the form of an irregular
parallelogram, with a donjon or keep at the south-west angle,
immediately over the entrance to the great cavern, and at
the extreme edge of the rock, which on this side is quite
perpendicular, and upwards of 260 feet in height. Flanking
the eastern and western angles of the north side were two
square towers, now in part destroyed, and between them are
the remains of what appears to have been a sallyport. The
postern, or entrance gateway, some traces of which yet exist,
was on the east side, and here was stationed the porter,
whose annual allowance is entered upon the great Pipe Roll
of the Exchequer. The keep is quadrangular in plan, being
about 21 feet from north to south, and 19 feet from east to
west, internal admeasurement, with walls 8 feet thick, the
height from the basement being about 55 feet. The masonry
is of a very substantial character, and strongly grouted, the
heart of the walls being composed of broken and irregular
pieces of limestone, cemented together with a mortar of such
excellent temper as to render the whole almost as hard as
adamant. The walls have been faced on the outer surface
with finely-wrought ashlaring, set in regular courses, and the
south and south-west sides (those least accessible) remain in
a tolerably perfect state, but the north and east sides have
been denuded of nearly the whole, the stone having been
appropriated by some Vandalistic churchwarden to repair
the church at Castleton. Enough of the outer walls yet
remain, however, to give a tolerably accurate idea of the

general features and characteristics of the building. From these it would appear that there was originally a broad pilaster-like buttress placed rectangular-wise at each corner of the keep, with a plain torus moulding or small cylindrical shaft worked on the angle, an addition frequently met with in buildings erected during the later period of the Norman style ; buttresses, similar in design, were also disposed against each face of the building. The entrance is at the south-east angle, in which is a narrow winding staircase, much dilapidated, giving admission to the upper story. The interior of the keep is a complete vacuity, and remarkable only as exhibiting an almost entire absence of ornament, and an equal want of accommodation. It originally consisted of two chambers in addition to the basement, the floor that once separated them no longer existing. The lower story, about 14 feet in height, is lighted by a semicircular window on the north and east sides; the one above is 16 feet high, and lighted by three windows ; this was originally approached by a flight of steps on the outside, but these no longer remain, though they are said to have existed until within a comparatively recent period. The doorway that leads to this staircase still remains, and has a curious double archway.

Peak Castle was evidently erected at a very early period, but there is nothing in its present aspect to favour the idea that it has been a Saxon fortress. The general appearance, the peculiar character of the masonry, and the various details, all exhibiting the same Norman characteristics, lead to the supposition that it was commenced in the time of the first Peverel, and completed within about a century of that period. The existence of " herring-bone " work has been adduced in proof of its antiquity ; but this style of masonry is not unfrequently met with in Norman erections, and cannot, therefore, be implicitly relied on as evidence of its earlier origin. In fact, it was often adopted as a matter of convenience, to enable the workman to level off his work at each course, which, with stones of irregular shapes and sizes, could not well be done in any other way ; whilst, by varying their inclination, it was easy to preserve the required evenness and regularity. The Saxons were but little acquainted with the science of architecture ; and, judging from the few examples of Anglo-Saxon work that remain at the present day, there can be little doubt but that their fortresses were of the most rude and imperfect kind, and very inferior both in size and in the mode of construction to those erected by the Normans, or even those built during the period of Roman occupation. The probability is that such fortifications were confined to the enclosure of an advantageous site by walls, and the erection of earthworks, where necessary. Indeed, the genius of our Saxon forefathers, like their descendants of the present day, seems to have been better adapted to *field* warfare than the defending of a fortified position; for it is a singular fact that, amid those internal wars which ravaged the country from the time of their arrival until the Conquest, during which the number of battles fought was almost incredible, we have scarcely a single instance recorded in history of a protracted siege.

The Peverels are represented as having resided here in great pomp and splendour; but when we remember the circumscribed area of the castle yard, and the fact that no remains of any building except the keep have been discovered, it is difficult to imagine how sufficient accommodation could be afforded for the numerous retinue of a great feudal chieftain. The probability is that the fortress was designed more as a place of refuge to flee to in times of extreme danger, and also as a place for the reception of prisoners, such hapless creatures we know, from the Hundred Rolls and other sources of information, having been incarcerated within its walls. In 2 Edward I. (1273) John de Nedham, a companion of Hubert the Robber, who was afterwards hung, was immured within its walls, and Henry the clerk took from the said John, whilst he was in prison, an acre of land worth 40s., that he might assist him in his delivery. Upon his release he paid a fine of five marks for being allowed to dwell in the district. At a later period, 4 Henry IV. (1402), Godfrey Rowland, a poor and simple squire of the county of Derby, as he styles himself, petitioned the Parliament against the injuries that had been inflicted on him by Thomas Wandesby, Chivaler, and others, who came and besieged his house at Mickel-Longsdon, and having pillaged the same carried him off to the castle of the High Peak, where they kept him six days without meat or drink, and then, cutting off his right hand, sent him adrift.

The old stronghold of the Peverels scarcely retains a feature of its former consequence, and is now nothing but a heap of ruins, fitted only to adorn the landscape. To the thoughtful mind, however, these decayed memorials of fallen grandeur, rude and unshapely though they be, are, from their historical associations, objects of great and powerful interest. They serve as a link to connect the present with the far-off past, so pregnant with mighty thoughts and great and illustrious acts. In the contemplation of them the mind reverts to a period of remote antiquity, and the scenes of centuries gone by float before the imagination with a rapidity and indistinctness like figures in a dream. A feeling almost of sadness stole over the senses as we stood within that time-worn tower and thought of the changes that had come over the fortunes of the place. What scenes of "antique pageantry" have been witnessed beneath the shadow of those walls. That rampart that once stood out in haughty strength and echoed only the measured tread of the armed sentinel is now broken and crumbling to decay, and the mantling ivy spreads its roots and clings with fond tenacity, as if flourishing in its ruin; that spot on which once encamped the followers of the haughty Peverel is now covered with moss and weeds, and the dock and the nettle grow up together in wild luxuriance; that tower, from whose portal oft hath issued the mailed warrior in all the pride and pomp of power to lead his vassals to the fight, is now roofless, silent, and deserted, the bat and the owl its sole occupants, and, as if in mockery of its former greatness, a few sheep skip about in peaceful security and crop the green herbage that thrives upon its threshold.

From the castle yard a delightful view is obtained of the vale of Castleton, better known to travellers by the name of Hope Dale. The prevailing character of the scenery is that of soft and graceful beauty, and whilst shrinking from approaching that wildness and sublime grandeur which distinguish some other parts of the Peak, it challenges admiration as affording a scene which, for varied pastoral beauty and fertile loveliness, will be rarely met with in the same limits. The valley is of considerable extent, and includes the villages of Castleton, Hope, Brough, Bamford, and Hathersage—the Nowe, a pleasant stream of some pretensions, flowing through the entire length, and receiving in its course several tributary rills that meander pleasantly down from between the lonely hills.

Standing close by the north wall of the castle you may scan the whole circle of the horizon, from Mam Tor in the west to the bleak ridges of Bamford Edge and the moorland wastes beyond Hathersage in the east, the scene within the limits giving you the idea of a wide-spread panorama. In whichever direction you gaze the prospect is equally imposing. At the foot of the rock, and immediately in front, lies the village of Castleton, clustering picturesquely round its ancient church. Following the course of the Nowe to its confluence with the Derwent, the eye, as it ranges into the far distance, passes over a large extent of country, embracing bleak hills and sheltered vales, green fields and pleasant pasture lands, with fertile meadows whose greenness outvies the verdure of nature. The well-cultivated lowlands, and the graceful uplands studded here and there with snow-white cottages and farmsteads, that shine brightly in the morning sunlight, add their charms to the general beauty. The wreaths of smoke curling upwards in places from amid clumps of trees show where unseen habitations are lurking within their shady retreats ; and the white roads and winding pathways leading over the green hill slopes tell how even these can beautify a landscape. On the left the rocky entrance to the vale of the Winnats, through which we passed so recently, appears in all its picturesque beauty. In the middle distance the broad spire of Hope Church is seen rising like a landmark above the sombre foliage. Further on the little hamlet of Bamford may be discerned, seated upon the slope of a barren mountain, whose dark and rugged outline cuts sharply against the eastern sky ; and beyond the view takes in the shadowy form of the hills that environ the village of Hathersage. From this point a chain of moorlands, rising grandly in ridges and knolls and peaks, sweeps round in an irregular circle towards the west, Mam Tor and Tray Cliff shutting in the view and giving a finish to the scene. Like the vale of

Tempé, all seems tranquillity and peace. The unceasing hum of insects and the lowing of the kine in the distant meadows are the only sounds that break upon the prevailing quietude, mingled now and then with the bleating of a sheep or the caw of some solitary rook as he stretches his jetty wings and, rising high in the air, gives warning to his brethren of the presence of intruders.

Perhaps the most striking object in the landscape is the steep eminence on the left, Mam Tor, or the Shivering Mountain—one of the wonders of the Peak—which lifts its huge form above the neighbouring hills, rising to the height of 1,300 feet above the plain. This mountain is situated at the western extremity of Hope Dale, and is distant about a mile and a half from Castleton. It presents a singular aspect, the face to a considerable extent appearing as if it had been scooped out. Mam Tor is the ancient British name signifying the mother hill, the term Shivering Mountain being a more recent appellation, derived from the circumstance of the crumbling substance of which it is composed continually trickling down the slopes. It is composed of silicious sandstone and shale, in alternate stratification, the latter impregnated with the oxide of iron, which, on being exposed to the action of the atmosphere, becomes disintegrated, and gradually slides down into the valley below, where it forms a regularly increasing mound.

From this point the peculiarities of the several formations, and the marked difference which geological structure produces on the scenery, is clearly manifested. On the northern side the gritstone predominates, and here we have the deepest valleys and the widest moorlands, which in the autumn time are purpled o'er with flowering heather ; whilst on the south we have the limestone in dark frowning masses, bare and barren in places, with its craggy summits and narrow glens and gorges, decked with ferns and clothed with a scant covering of herbage, but without a trace of mountain heather, and therefore lacking that fresh wildness and glorious colour which the millstone-grit possesses.

The summit of the hill appears to have been the site of a Roman fortification, which extended along the ridge, and included an area of upwards of sixteen acres of ground ; the greater part of the rampart, and a double trench that surrounded it, still remaining in a tolerable state of preservation. Within the lines of the encampment a spring of water issues into day, and finds its way down the side of the hill into Edale, a secluded valley with a tiny rivulet flowing through its midst; and the quaintly-named hamlets of Over Booth, Nether Booth, Barber Booth, and Lady Booth look down from the steep bluffs and tufted slopes upon a miniature old church, with a tiny bell-cot, all looking so primitive and "unimproved" that you might fancy the world to have stood still for centuries.

As already stated, the rock on which stands the ruined fortress of the Peverels is almost insulated, being connected with the adjoining mountain only by a narrow tongue of land. On the western side the view is singularly impressive. Standing upon the extreme edge of a stupendous rock, which rises perpendicularly to a height of upwards of 260 feet, the beholder looks down into a deep chasm, at the bottom of which yawns the dark and gloomy entrance to the Devil's Cavern. The crest of the rock for several feet is covered with small trees and underwood of various foliage, in the branches of which a number of loquacious rooks and daws have fixed their habitation in undisturbed security, but the lower part is one broad mass of limestone rock, cold and grim and lifeless looking, save where a few ferns and mosses and a scattered growth of brambles have attached themselves to the clefts and ledges, softening the otherwise naked and weather-beaten surface. Near the mouth of the cavern a brawling stream breaks through the side of the cliff and rushes merrily onwards over its stony bed, throwing up the white foam bubbles on its way, as if rejoicing at having once more gained the light of day after its passage through the dark and cavernous recesses of the earth. A little further on it receives the waters of the Russet Well, a clear spring of great power that rises from beneath the rock on which the castle stands. After heavy rains an immense volume of water is discharged, and it will eject with considerable force any article that may be thrown into it.

Nearly an hour had slipped away whilst we had been loitering about examining the ruins of the castle, and contemplating the beauties of the surrounding landscape. Then turning to depart we followed the same zigzag course by which we had ascended, and soon reached the valley, from whence a pathway leads to the rocky glen called Cave Dale.

The approach to this narrow defile has a rather forbidding appearance, the entrance being by a cleft in the mountain, not more than five or six feet in width. Passing through this portal we were at once struck with the widely different character of the prospect assumed. Just before, we had been gazing upon a scene almost unequalled for its calm and placid beauty, when suddenly, as if by a stroke of the magician's wand, the scene was changed, and all before us was dreary solitude and barren desolation.

The dell is rather more than a mile in length, and closely hemmed in on every side by steep and inaccessible rocks, partially clothed with scant herbage, through which the grey limestone occasionally protrudes; here and there a solitary tree or hardy shrub endeavours to obtain sustenance from the rocky soil, but their stunted growth and blighted appearance only renders the place more cheerless and uninviting. Further on, the crumbling and ivy-covered walls of Peverel's castle are seen, with the dilapidated and roofless keep standing, sentinel-like, upon the very verge of a precipitous crag that hangs beetling over the pathway. Looking back from this point through the narrow portal we discern the village church, with the clustering homes around, and beyond the fertile valley backed by a range of lofty hills and shadowy eminences that stretch far away in perspective.

Immediately under the keep of the castle is a small opening or cavernous recess, in which Mr. Rooke Pennington has at different times discovered various animal remains, flint implements, and fragments of pre-historic pottery, leading to the supposition that it has been occupied from time to time during a lengthened period, probably commencing in the neolithic age, and extending into those of bronze and iron; whilst in historic times it has been the refuge of badgers and foxes, man now and then resorting to it for temporary purposes. A little way higher up a clear spring, to which the name of the Lady's Well has been given, is seen bubbling through the grass; presently it loses itself again, in the earth, and is supposed to supply the shower which is perpetually falling in " Roger Rain's House," in the Peak, Cavern, that penetrates the mass of limestone beneath.

PEAK CASTLE FROM CAVE DALE.

For a distance of half-a-mile the dell gradually expands, then again it becomes contracted. On either side of the onward path the ground rises in precipitous slopes, the surface smooth and green, through which the naked rock occasionally protrudes. Wild plants and mosses grow in rich abundance on the moist and slippery crags, and the botanist will have no difficulty in beguiling the hours away. Further on, a regular basaltic column, of hexagonal form, is seen cropping up above the green turf—part of a basaltic mass that ranges north and south for a considerable distance, and which in texture and hardness closely resembles the columnar masses at Staffa and the Hebrides. Then the road winds on until the summit of Long Cliff is reached, from whence a charming prospect is obtained.

After a pleasant ramble we returned to our quarters with an appetite sharpened by the keen mountain air, and a determination to do full justice to good fare which had been provided for us.

D

# CHAPTER IV.

AFTER breakfast we strolled through the village in the direction of the church. The living of Castleton is a vicarage in the diocese of Lichfield and Coventry, the patronage of which is vested in the Bishop of Chester. In 1269 the church, then described as the Church of Peak Castle, was given by Prince Edward, afterwards Edward I., to the Abbey and Convent of Vale Royal, Cheshire. After the dissolution of religious houses in the reign of Henry VIII., the great tithes and the advowson of the vicarage were given by that monarch to the Bishop of Chester and his successors, in whose hands it has continued to the present time.

The church, dedicated to St. Edmund, was erected at a very early period, and exhibits traces of almost every style of ecclesiastical architecture, from the early Norman to the late perpendicular or debased Gothic. It includes a nave, chancel, and south porch, with an embattled tower at the western end adorned with crocketted pinnacles that spring from each angle, and intermediately from the centre of each face of the parapet. The exterior was repaired some forty years ago, when, with execrable taste, nearly the whole of the body of the church was covered with cement—for which we are indebted, doubtless, to the individual who denuded the keep of Peak Castle of so much of its outer stonework. The interior is worthy of inspection. The pews are all of dark oak, curiously carved, many of them with the names of their former owners, and in the centre aisle there is an ancient stone font of octagon form. The nave is separated from the chancel by a fine semicircular Norman archway, enriched with chevron and billet mouldings. Over the altar is a small cabinet picture, said to be by Vandyke, representing the adoration of the Magi. The chancel is lighted by a triplet window filled with stained glass, placed there some few years ago by the parishioners as an affectionate tribute to the memory of their former vicar. The subject of the design is Christ's charge to Peter, and at the foot is the following inscription : " Dedicated by the grateful affection of the parishioners of Castleton to the memory of the Rev. Charles Cecil Bates, M.A., for thirty-five years the faithful vicar. Lost to them 4th January, 1853." The church contains but few monuments. On the south side a marble tablet records the decease of John Mawe, the mineralogist, whose remains are interred in the Church of St. Mary-le-Strand, London ; but by his desire this monument was erected in the church of the place where he commenced his mineralogical labours. On the north side of the nave is a monument to the memory of an eccentric attorney, who received his education at the Free Grammar School at Manchester, and afterwards amassed considerable property at Castleton, his native place. The inscription is said to have been written by himself, and its doubtful theology would seem to bear out the somewhat indifferent professional reputation of the author which still floats in the memories of the older inhabitants to whom his name is not unknown. It is as follows :—

> To the Memory of
> Micah Hall, Gentn.
> Attorney-at-Law,
> who died on the 14th of May, 1804,
> Aged 79 years.
> Quid eram, nescitis ;
> Quid sum, nescitis ;
> Ubi abii, nescitis ;
> Valete.

In the church there is, we believe, a brass, which we did not observe, to the memory of the Rev. Edward Bagshawe, M.A., for 46 years the vicar of Castleton, who died the 12th April, 1769, at the age of 79.

In the vestry there is a library, the gift of a former vicar, the Rev. Frederic Farran, to which additions have been made by his daughter, Miss Farran, and Captain Hamilton.

It contains upwards of 1,000 volumes, chiefly in divinity, history, and biography. They are lent to the parishioners at the discretion of the vicar for the time being, a provision which tends to ensure their preservation. On the table we noticed two curious old folio Bibles, one a copy of Cranmer's, or the "Bishop's Bible," in black letter, the imprint bearing date 1539; the other a Genevan translation of the Scriptures, made by the English refugees who had been driven to Geneva by the fierce persecutions in Queen Mary's days, and is more generally known by the name of the "Breeches Bible."

Before leaving the churchyard we visited the grave of a Derbyshire worthy, Elias Hall, the fossilist and mineralogist. Mr. Hall was an instance of genius in the humbler walks of life. He was emphatically a self-taught man, and for whatever mental attainments he possessed he was indebted solely to that indomitable perseverance and stern self-reliance which formed so remarkable a trait in his character. At an early age he imbibed a taste for natural science, in the study and cultivation of which he devoted nearly the whole of a long and active life. As a practical geologist he attained to a considerable degree of eminence, and was favourably known as the author of several productions having reference to the structure of the earth. His most important work, and that on which perhaps more than any other his reputation is founded, is a geological and mineralogical map of the great coalfield of Lancashire, with parts of the neighbouring counties of Derbyshire, Cheshire, and Yorkshire, coloured stratigraphically. In this map, which is dedicated to Professor Sedgwick, the vice-president of the Geological Society, the physical geography of the district is delineated with considerable minuteness of detail and admirable graphic power. It must have been an exceedingly difficult undertaking, and those only who have been similarly engaged can form an adequate idea of the care and labour required in its preparation. After its publication he issued a sectional view, showing the various strata from the Irish Sea to the German Ocean, through Lancashire, Derbyshire, Yorkshire, Nottinghamshire, and Lincolnshire, to which he subsequently appended a key or introduction, and with the assistance of Mr. Francis Looney, F.G.S., gave a list of the organic remains found in the different beds. He afterwards commenced a geological map of the central part of the kingdom, and on this work he was employed up to within a short period of his death. In addition to the works already enumerated, Mr. Hall completed several carefully-executed models of portions of the earth's surface, including the Peak of Derbyshire, and parts of the Lake district of Cumberland and Westmorland, in which, with the aid of colour, the stratification and other geological details are indicated with admirable clearness and accuracy. Two of these models were, at the instance of the late Sir Joseph Banks, purchased by the trustees of the British Museum, and are now deposited in the geological gallery of that institution. Another, a model of the district around Manchester, is preserved in the museum of Owens College in that city. When the celebrated French naturalist, M. Faujas St. Fond, visited this country, Mr. Hall accompanied him through Peak's Hole, and showed him the wonders of that remarkable cavern ; and some fifty years ago, when Mr. Farey was collecting information for his " View of the Agriculture and Minerals of Derbyshire," he rendered him considerable assistance, revising and correcting those parts of his work which relate to the stratification and minerals of the county.

Mr. Hall may fairly claim to rank as the father of geology in Derbyshire. He first directed his attention to the subject at a time when geology, as a science, had made but little progress, and in this country was comparatively unknown, and he continued his investigations with unceasing application for more than seventy years. We remember him in the later years of his life, a fine hale and hearty old man, with an energy and restless activity remarkable in one of his advanced age ; plain, homely, and unaffected, with a cheerful and social disposition, and a kindliness of manner that secured for him the friendship of all with whom he came in contact. He was ever ready to afford information, and to communicate unreservedly the results of his investigations to those who desired to possess them. He retained his mental faculties to the last, and died on the 30th December, 1853, in the ninetieth year of his age. He is buried in the churchyard at Castleton, on the south side, with nothing but the upheaved turf to mark his last resting-place. Some other members of his family are interred near the south-west corner of the church, and we are told that it was intended to remove the stone from their grave and place it upon that of poor Hall. We should hope not. Surely amongst the geologists of this district there is sufficient public spirit to raise some memorial to keep alive the remembrance of one who did so much for science, receiving so little pecuniary reward!*

Among the places of attraction in the village we must not omit to mention the museum that has recently been opened, with the view of illustrating the archæological, geological, and mineralogical productions of this part of the Peak district. It is situated behind Mr. Tym's spar manufactory, and contains : (*a*) A series of articles of the Bronze and Neolithic periods from Switzerland, Denmark, Cissbury, Yorkshire, with a large number of the prehistoric remains from the tumuli, &c., near Castleton, the result of the explorations of Mr. Rooke Pennington, F.G.S., and Mr. John Tym, during the last few years. (*b*) Palæolithic implements. (*c*) A magnificent series of the Pleistocene animals of the Derbyshire district—bison, grizzly bear, reindeer, rhinoceros, hyæna, &c. (*d*) A good geological series, of about 1,500 species of fossils, numbering about 3,500 specimens, from Crag to Laurentian, and including a good icthyosaurus, plesiosaurus, crag, and eocene mammals, some good fish, &c. Most of the formations are well represented, but particularly those prevailing near Castleton (mountain limestone, Yoredale series, and coal measures). (*e*) A series of minerals and rocks, the Derbyshire minerals being specially good ; and some educational sets of fossils and minerals. All the above are properly arranged with explanatory notes, so as to be useful

* Since this notice of Mr. Hall was written, a few of his admirers in Manchester and the neighbourhood have caused a neat headstone, bearing the following inscription, to be erected over his remains :

IN MEMORY OF
ELIAS HALL, THE GEOLOGIST,
Who died on the 30th day of December, 1853,
Aged 89 years.

Born of parents in humble life, and having a large family to provide for, yet he devoted himself to the study of geology for 70 years with powers of originality and industry rarely surpassed.

To mark the last resting-place of one who had worked so long and so hard for the public, a few of his friends and admirers living at a distance have placed this stone.

to the uninitiated, and to teach geological rudiments, whilst affording advanced students opportunity of comparing their "finds" and naming them. (f) A series of the fauna and flora of North Derbyshire, including mammals (stuffed), birds, and their nests and eggs, ferns and mosses, &c. (g) Collection of old china, entirely obtained from the older houses in the neighbourhood, with old books, ornaments, coins, &c. (h) Set of archaic mining tools from the old lead mines of Castleton. (i) The natural and commercial productions of the neighbourhood. (k) Geological maps and sections, guidebooks, and a small scientific reference library. Mr. Pennington's collections are all included in the museum. Mr. Tym, who acts as curator, is the lessee of the Speedwell Mine, and may be considered as the botanist and geologist of the neighbourhood. He is a very worthy person, civil, intelligent, and possessing withal a sufficiently intimate knowledge of geological and mineralogical science to make him a desired companion for anyone wishful to investigate the natural products of the locality.

Peak's Hole was the next place that claimed our attention, and as a signpost on the roadside pointed the way to this "grand natural curiosity," we followed the path indicated.

The caverns at Castleton are naturally its chief attraction. To the ordinary tourist they are an unfailing source of wonder, and to the geologist they are especially interesting. There are three in all—the Peak Cavern (or Devil's Hole, as it is sometimes called), the Speedwell Mine, and the Blue John Mine, all of which should be seen by the visitor; for though they have many features in common, there is a speciality and distinctness in their appearance that renders each equally worthy of inspection.

These subterranean cavities have long engaged the attention of scientific men, among whom there exists a diversity of opinion respecting their origin. Their formation is generally attributed to the shrinking and contraction of the limestone during the process of sub-crystallisation or consolidation subsequent to the deposition of the beds, and probably at the time they were upheaved into their present angle of dip, and the same agency is supposed to have caused the perpendicular fissures and horizontal cracks which form

so remarkable a characteristic of the carboniferous or mountain limestone. Some geologists have expressed an opinion
that the streams of water which channel their way through
the rock have produced these great excavations; but this is
hardly likely. The erosive power of water, surcharged with
carbonic acid, passing through the various rents and fissures,
may have enlarged original openings or carried away the soft
beds of clay or loose sand that were interposed between the
hard strata, and thus have contributed to the enlargement
of these subterranean cavities; but there are openings and
chasms that show no evidence of having been water-channelled
at any time, and which could therefore only have been
formed by the shrinkage of the limestone during the process
of hardening or by disruption, the immediate consequence of
volcanic action—an agency that has at some remote period
of time been in active operation in this district, as evidenced
by the igneous rocks that have in some places overflowed the
strata, and which may be seen covering or underlying the
ordinary strata that has not been acted upon by fire.

Our first subterranean expedition was to explore the
recesses of the great Peak Cavern—or, to speak more correctly, caverns, for what is usually designated a cavern is
nothing less than a series of internal chambers or openings,
communicating with each other by means of connecting
passages that have either been naturally formed, or have
been driven through the rock, to render the approach more
accessible.

Following the course of a small stream which issues from
near the mouth of the cavern, we soon reached a narrow
ascending path that forms the approach to this extraordinary
work of nature. A high projecting bank on the right pre-
vents a distant view of the entrance being obtained, and it is
only when close upon it that you become fully conscious of
its vast proportions and the imposing character of the scene
which then for the first time bursts upon the sight. It is
situated near the termination of a narrow and gloomy ravine,
the sides of which are formed by immense limestone rocks,
that rise perpendicularly to a height little short of three
hundred feet, their sides, for a considerable distance upwards,
sparingly clothed with foliage and underwood that seems to

grow out of the very stone, affording an inaccessible retreat
for countless rooks and daws, who keep up a continual clatter.
Seated upon the extreme verge of a precipitous crag, high
impending over the abyss, the grey and ruined keep of
Peverel's Castle forms a striking object in the view, the effect
being increased and rendered more imposing by the commanding position it occupies amid the rocks and precipices
that surround it.    Some thirty feet below the footpath a
stream of water issues from the side of the mountain, and
pursues its onward course, murmuring and sparkling over its
pebbly bed.    After heavy rains the force of this current is
considerably increased, and the effect of the scene proportionately augmented.    It then seems to boil up from beneath
the rock, rushing onwards with impetuosity, and throwing up
the whitened foam as it breaks over the fragments of rock
that continually impede its progress.

PEAK CAVERN.

The entrance is by an archway in the rock, one hundred
and twenty feet in width, about forty-two feet in height,

and in receding depth about ninety feet,* the outline of which is very regular, assuming a depressed or segmental form. Passing through this Cyclopean porch we entered a vast subterranean cavity, the full extent of which, in the dim and uncertain light, it was impossible to discern. Here we found a number of twine makers established, who appear to have carried on their occupation from time immemorial, though every person of taste must regret their presence. Their rude apparatus covers nearly the whole area, and the discordant noises they create sadly impairs the effect which the character of the place is calculated to produce. We walked in a few yards, and entered a small hut, where we obtained the services of a guide. Depositing our hats, and receiving each in exchange a felt cap, similar to those worn by the miners, we set forward on our expedition.

As we advance the light fades softly away and the outlines of objects, rendered more shadowy and indistinct, at length become lost in obscurity. About thirty yards from the entrance the sides gradually contract, and the roof becomes lower until a small door-way is reached, through which we pass. Here the last gleam of daylight disappears, and the remainder of the journey has to be accomplished with the aid of candles. Assuming a stooping posture we follow the guide along a narrow descending path that conducts to a spacious opening called the Bell House, so named from the number of round or spherical holes which appear in the roof. Here a stream of water is met with which formerly it was necessary to cross in a small flat-bottomed boat, the visitor lying upon his back whilst he was being propelled beneath a massive archway of solid rock. The voyage, though short, was not altogether free from danger ; for if he happened to raise his head the chances were in favour of its being caught against the sharp inequalities of the superincumbent mass, which, in some places, descends to within a few inches of the water. For the convenience of explorers another passage has been made by blasting through the limestone, and this part of the journey can now be accomplished with comparative comfort. The next point we arrived at was the Grand Saloon, an apart-

* For the principal dimensions of this cavern we are indebted to the description given by the guide. They are, no doubt, a near approximation ; if anything, perhaps, rather over than understated.

ment of considerable magnitude, the full extent of which the sickly glare of our candles failed to illuminate. This cavern is said to be about 220 feet square, and in some places 120 feet in height. It is traversed by a number of steps cut in the ground, leading to the "second water." An involuntary exclamation broke from us as we entered. Huge masses of rock bulge out on every hand and glisten in the feeble light, where the moisture oozes over them, rippling their surface with countless crystallised convolutions, between which the water trickles in tiny threads. Near the further extremity a group of broken rocks have become detached from the parent mass, to which the appellation of Roger Rain's House has been given, from the circumstance that the moisture which escapes through the crevices of the mountain is continually trickling down the sides. The noise, as each drop falls to the ground with a dull leaden sound, that reverberates from the ample roof and sides of the subterranean vault and breaks upon the death-like silence that prevails, exercises a peculiarly depressing influence upon the senses.

Leaving Roger Rain's House we reach next the Chancel, a naturally formed opening or gallery, at a considerable elevation in the rocks, access to which is obtained by a steep and rugged pathway on the right. Incrustations of stalactite spread over the surface and depend from the more prominent parts of the rocks ; curiously formed growths adhere to the roof ; and, as you stand aside in the gloom, you may see the smooth glittering surface and the brightness that flashes from every projection and inequality. From the Chancel the road gradually descends, until another opening is reached, called the Devil's Cellar, where you are startled by a loud rumbling resembling the falling of a distant cataract, caused, as the guide informs you, by the rushing of water through various unexplored recesses in the mountain. The next halting-place is the Half-way House, to reach which we have to follow a toilsome and difficult path, some 150 feet in length, strewn with stones and fragments of broken rock, and in some places so low that we are compelled to adopt a stooping posture to avoid knocking our heads against the roof. On the way we come across a stream of water that has to be crossed and recrossed several times, either by means of stepping-stones, conveniently placed for the purpose, or on the ready shoulders of the guide. Then we meet with a singular example of Nature's handiwork, a passage running beneath a succession of immense semicircular archways formed in the solid rock, not unlike the groined crypt of an ancient cathedral. From the bold and graceful curves, and the regular outline of the arches, you might almost imagine that the chisel of the mason had been employed in their formation. Traversing this natural colonnade we arrive successively at Gloucester Hall and Great Tom of Lincoln, the latter an ample cavernous expanse, so designated from its having a regular concavity in the roof resembling the form of a bell. The distance from this point to the termination of the cavern is but short, the sides gradually contract, and the roof descends until barely sufficient room is left for the passage of the water, when all further progress is precluded. As we returned we found that a little *coup de théâtre* had been provided for our entertainment. Whilst we had been exploring the inner recesses of the cavern a number of children, who had been trained to act the part they have to play, had ascended to the Chancel, and as we approached this part of the cavern, the sound of their voices broke suddenly upon the ear. The harmonious strains issuing thus unexpectedly from the heart of the mountain, where all around is silent as the tomb, produced an agreeable surprise.

A very remarkable effect is experienced in returning, as, emerging from the blackness, you see the light of day gradually illuminating the mouth of the cavern. The visitor is generally stayed at a point commanding a distant view of the entrance. At this spot all that he can discern is a faint glimmer, like the first streaks in the eastern sky heralding the return of day; advancing, the light becomes more and more intense, the weird forms and shadowy outlines of objects assuming a more clear and distinct appearance, until, emerging through the immense orifice into open day, the light bursts upon him with dazzling, almost blinding brilliance.

The total length of the Peak Cavern, from the mouth to the furthest extremity, is estimated at 2,300 feet, and the depth from the surface of the mountain 600 feet. It is intersected in different parts by a current of water, which it is necessary for the visitor repeatedly to cross. This water first enters the ground by what is termed a swallow-hole at Perry-foot, about four miles distant, on the Buxton Road, and after pursuing its course through a succession of subterranean caverns, including the Speedwell Mine and Peak's Hole, finds an outlet near the mouth of the latter, and finally loses itself in the Nowe at a point a little beyond Hope Church. In rainy seasons this stream is often very much swollen, when access to the interior is rendered difficult, and sometimes altogether impossible.

The Speedwell Mine is distant about half-a-mile from Castleton, on the left of the old Buxton Road, and close to the entrance to the Winnats. It was originally excavated by a company of proprietors in search of lead ore, but the result proved unfortunate ; and, after eleven years' fruitless toil, and an expenditure of £14,000, it was finally abandoned, the principal shareholder, a Mr. Oakden, of Staffordshire, having been ruined by the undertaking. It now remains only an object of attraction to the curious, and a monument of mining skill and patient industry unhappily unrewarded.*

The entrance is mean and unpretending, in this respect contrasting unfavourably with the magnificent approach to Peak's Hole—a low white-washed cottage, with the name painted over the door, being the only outward indication of its existence.

Descending by a flight of upwards of a hundred steps, we arrived at a "level," or subterranean canal, some six or seven feet in breadth, that has been hewn out of the limestone, where we found a long narrow boat, capable of seating about twenty persons, in readiness, in which we embarked, the guide impelling us along by pushing against the sides of the rock. There was just sufficient room to sit upright in the boat without knocking our heads against the top, the channel being not more than eight or nine feet from the roof to the bottom of the water—the latter being about three or

---

* Three sets of workmen were employed in this undertaking—five to each set—by which means the work was constantly carried on night and day (Sundays excepted) for eleven years. Each man used one pound of gunpowder per day (for the whole excavation was effected by blasting). The quantity used amounted to 51,645 pounds.—*Moore's Excursions in the Peak.*

four feet in depth. At the commencement of the journey our conductor placed a lighted candle against the side, and others again at short intervals as we went along, and so straight is the excavation that, looking back, they could be distinctly seen the entire length—the reflection upon the still water presenting, as may readily be imagined, a very pleasing effect. As the boat glides along, several veins of lead ore are seen, though none sufficiently rich to repay the cost of working. In places sudden breaks and fissures appear at right angles with the passage that look as if nature had begun a series of transepts, and then abandoned the design ; and here and there huge rents are seen, caused by the cooling of the vast limestone mass in primeval days. Then we come to the Half-way House, where a tunnel branches off to the right. For a time the stillness was almost unearthly, then the echoes were awoke by our companion playing Luther's grand old hymn upon the bugle, the tones reverberating back through the long watery vault, producing an effect that will leave an echo in the memory to life's latest day. As the sounds died away we became conscious of a hollow murmuring in the distance, the sound of which increased as we proceeded on until it became a loud roar, caused as we learned by the water falling into the " Bottomless Pit."

We had traversed a distance of seven hundred and fifty yards and had now reached the Grand Cavern, a vast opening fashioned by nature in the heart of the mountain, the height and depth of which have never yet been ascertained. Huge bulging masses of rock stand out on either hand as if they were about to topple down upon us, and everywhere the roof and sides are intersected by fissures that have been either formed or enlarged by the erosive action of water passing through them for successive ages. Across the opening a broad archway or platform, protected by an iron railing, has been erected for the accommodation of visitors. Mooring our boat to the rock, we ascended this, the better to survey the abyss beneath ; and strange indeed must be the feeling, and firm the resolution, of the man who could stand upon this spot and look down into the unfathomable gulf in which the seething waters plunge night and day into the deep darkness, without experiencing a sensation of the profoundest awe.

As we leaned over the railing and gazed into the immense void, the feeble and sickly light of our candles, overpowered by the impervious gloom, whilst they failed to illuminate, served to render the surrounding darkness still more striking and apparent. Miners have been let down this chasm a distance of ninety feet, at which point commences a pool of water that is said to have swallowed up 40,000 tons of rubbish, produced in driving the level from 600 to 700 yards beyond the cavern, without making any perceptible difference either in extent or depth. The so-called pool is, however, nothing more than an underground current communicating with other caverns, along which the rubbish has no doubt been carried by the force of the stream.

The height of the dome has never been determined, but the distance to the surface of the mountain has been computed at eight hundred and forty feet, and nearly the whole of the intervening space is believed to be one vast cavity. We peered into the darkness, but our candles were too feeble to illuminate the lofty roof, and the gloom was more palpable from the absence of ornament—no gleaming stalactites or glittering crystallisations giving back the dim candle flame. Steps have been formed by placing wooden pegs across a cleft in the rocks for a considerable way upwards, and up these the guide climbed and fired a blue-light which revealed to us for a few moments some of the hidden recesses of this magnificent cavern, but there was still a space above which the light failed to penetrate. Some idea of the altitude of this cavern may be formed from the fact that rockets of sufficient strength to ascend 450 feet have been discharged, and have risen unimpeded to their highest elevation, exploded, and thrown out their brilliant coruscations as freely as if they had ascended beneath the vault of heaven.

The visitor is generally entertained with a "blast" before leaving the cavern, for which a trifling additional charge is made. A small quantity of gunpowder is wedged in the rock and fired, the sound of the explosion reverberating from side to side with fearful intonation.

Having completed our examination of the Speedwell Mine, we lost no time in visiting the Blue-John Cavern, another, and certainly not the least interesting of the Derbyshire wonders. This cavern is situated near the foot of Tray Cliff, immediately opposite the shivering front of Mam Tor. By the carriage road it is distant about a mile and a half from Castleton; but pedestrians will find a much shorter route by following a narrow track that leads across the edge of the cliff.

This cavern is the grand depository of the amethystine or topazine fluor of mineralogists, locally designated Blue-John, a name given by the miners to distinguish it from Black Jack, a species of zinc ore found in the neighbourhood. This substance is composed of lime and fluoric acid—the most penetrating and corrosive of any acid known—the blue colouring matter being oxide of manganese. It is found in different parts of Derbyshire and Saxony; but it is only in Tray Cliff that it can be obtained in sufficient abundance to repay the cost of working, and even here it does not appear to exist in any considerable quantity, and is said to be less plentiful than formerly, the annual product of the mine being ten or twelve tons; the price at the present time is about £40 per ton in the "rough." It appears in detached masses, in veins three or four inches thick, running in various directions, separated from the limestone rock by a lining of cawke or sulphate of barytes, and by a thin layer of unctuous clay. Sometimes it is found adhering to loose rocks and "riders," and other adventitious substances. The crystallisations generally assume the figure of a cube, with its modifications, the octahedral or dodecahedral form being rarely met with. The exquisite richness and sudden contrasts which occur in the colouring of this beautiful material have occasioned it to be worked in a variety of forms, as brooches, vases, obelisks, &c. The largest vase ever made from the fluor spar is in the possession of the Duke of Devonshire, and may be seen in the sculpture gallery at Chatsworth.

Antiquaries have established the fact that fluor spar was known to the Romans, who found it probably whilst seeking for lead in the Tray Cliff. It is supposed that the famous *vasæ murrhina* were made of this material, and certainly Pliny's description of those vases would answer as well to the fluor spar productions of the present day.

In a geological point of view this cavern is perhaps the most interesting of any in the Peak, and being comparatively easy of access, it may be explored without inconvenience. The entrance, which is at base of Tray Cliff, and within a short distance of the road, has nothing attractive in its outward appearance, or at all indicative of the wonders below.

Descending by a flight of steps we reached a narrow confined passage that winds between stupendous rocks which appear to have been rent asunder by some convulsive effort of nature. From the roof of this passage stalactites are pendant, and all along, the sides are coated with crystals of carbonate of lime, and embedded with fossil shells, entrochi, coralloids, madrepores, and a host of others that have not seen the light since these rocks were deposited as calcareous mud upon the bottoms of the carboniferous seas. In some places huge masses of detached rock project into the pathway, threatening a barrier to all further progress; in others the limestone is dislocated and broken into a diversity of forms, rugged as chaos, then the pathway gets rougher, and we go twining between damp slimy walls of rock, and a little further on we come to a crystalline spring in a hollow on the left, so transparent as to be treacherous in the uncertain light. After proceeding some distance a spacious opening is reached one hundred and fifty feet in height and about sixty feet in diameter, called Lord Mulgrave's Dining-room, from the circumstance of its having been used as such by the Marquis of Normanby and the miners who accompanied him on his three days' subterranean expedition in the endeavour to discover another outlet.

Continuing our journey along a vaulted and circuitous pathway that leads through a succession of clefts and cavities, which ramify and extend far away into the heart of the mountain, widening and narrowing as they run along, we come to the Variegated Cavern, a noble apartment, said to be upwards of one hundred feet in height, but the full extent of which our lights failed to disclose. The scenery here is most impressive. Great rocks bulge out on either hand, making us feel like pigmies at their feet, and raising our candles high above our heads, we perceive a mighty cavern, the roof of which is lost in the blackest darkness. Suddenly

E

the guide fires a Bengal light, and the effect is then brilliant
and dazzling in the extreme—the overhanging masses are
thrown out in bold relief, contrasting with the opposing
rocks, the sides of which are incrusted with myriads of
crystals that reflect the dazzling light in countless coruscations.    The beautiful spars and metallic substances with
which this cavern abounds render it especially interesting to
the mineralogist.

> " Here, ranging through her vaulted ways,
>    On Nature's alchemy you gaze ;
>    See how she forms the gem, the ore,
>    And all her magazines explore."

The Variegated Cavern is the farthest part of the mine
usually shown to visitors, and a railing has been placed
across to prevent them wandering beyond and becoming lost
among the labyrinth of passages that radiate from it.   Our
curiosity being excited by what we had already seen, we
felt a strong desire to still further explore the recesses of
this interesting cavern, a desire the guide obligingly con-
sented to gratify.   In undertaking this part of the journey,
however, we had little calculated upon the difficulty and
danger attending it.   From the entrance of the cavern to this
point the pathways are everywhere smooth and pleasant to
walk upon; but beyond, everything is in the wildest disorder,
loose pointed stones and fragments of rock of every conceivable size and shape, that by some violent concussion have
become detatched from the superincumbent mass, lying
scattered about in the greatest confusion.

Leaving the less venturesome of the party behind, we
set forward on our toilsome march, picking our way over
the rugged and uneven surface as best we could—now clam-
bering over a broken crag, and now dropping down a
precipice.   Our progress was necessarily slow, for, owing
to the slippery nature of the ground, it required the
utmost circumspection to keep from falling; everything
being covered with a thick slimy deposit it was almost
impossible to obtain a firm footing, and in the deep gloom
that prevailed every step was attended with the risk of
sliding away—we knew not exactly whither.   In some places
the passages were so confined that we had to crawl on our

hands and knees, in others we had to squeeze through narrow openings in a cramped doubled-up posture that was anything but agreeable. To add to our discomfort we were in danger of being left in utter darkness, a predicament anything but pleasant to contemplate, but rendered more than probable, as every now and then a drop of water falling from the roof into the flame of our miserable candle, with a hissing sputtering sound, seemed to threaten its extinguishment. Having penetrated for a considerable distance into the heart of the mountain without meeting with anything to compensate for the labour of investigation, we returned to the friends we had left waiting in the Variegated Cavern, and set about exploring the more accessible parts of the mine.

After wandering awhile amid these gloomy avenues the eye becomes more accustomed to the surrounding darkness, and objects, that at first were either totally obscured or presented only a shadowy and indistinct form, become more clearly discernable. For this reason the guide generally reserves his descriptions until the return.

A singular stalactitic formation that had escaped our notice on entering was now pointed out : a group of slender columns or shafts of unsullied purity depending from the roof, and which have in the course of time become connected with the stalagmites below, forming a series of fairy-like pillars that seem to give support to the overhanging rock. These columns, which have received the name of the Organ, from their supposed resemblance to that instrument, have a delicate waxen appearance, and when reflecting the lights of visitors have a pleasing effect. Some of the stems have unfortunately been broken off by the careless handling of sightseers, or in sheer wantonness, and the place is now fenced off to prevent further injury being sustained.

These stalactitic incrustations occur in almost all caverns in the limestone districts, but in none of those in the Peak range do they assume more varied or graceful conformations than in the Blue-John Mine. They are caused by water charged with carbonic acid gas percolating through the pores of the limestone. On reaching any cleft or cavity the moisture becomes evaporated by the air, when the lime previously held in solution is deposited in a thin layer upon the surface of the rock. Each succeeding drop leaves a fresh coating of solid matter, and, this process continually going on, in time these successive additions assume the form of an irregular elongated cone, called a *stalactite*, or (locally) *water icicle*. If the supply of water is too rapid to admit of its evaporation at the end of the stalactite, it drops to the ground, and then, in like manner, forms a mass of calcareous matter rising upwards; this, to distinguish it, is called a *stalagmite*. Sometimes the stalactite and the stalagmite immediately beneath continue increasing in length until the points become united, when a natural pillar is formed, and in this way the delicate columns of the Organ have been fashioned.

If not the largest, certainly the most beautiful of the caverns in this mine is that known as the Crystallised Cavern. The height of this subterranean chamber is estimated at 100 feet, and the area midway up about 50 feet. It is exhibited by means of a rude kind of chandelier, garnished with lighted candles, which is hoisted to the top by a windlass. The spectator is generally placed in an angle in the pathway, and when seen from this point the effect is very imposing. A dark mass of intervening rock hides the chandelier from view, whilst a flood of light is thrown upon the roof and sides, which are everywhere adorned with stalactites, that hang like countless icicles from every projection and inequality, and when thus illuminated gleam and sparkle "like a firmament of stars." In the upper part of the cavern these incrustations assume more regular forms, and depend in graceful circles round the dome, presenting the appearance of elaborately-feathered mouldings rising one upon another, until lost in the dim obscurity of space. The variegated colours and beautiful crystallisations here displayed have a brilliant effect, and it requires little stretch of the imagination for the visitor to conceive himself conveyed by some powerful but unseen agency to the regions of fairyland. Bakewell, in his "Introduction to Geology,"* says "the crystallisations and mineral incrustations on the roof and sides of the natural caverns which are passed through in this mine far exceed in beauty those of any other cavern in England; and," he adds, "were the descriptions of the

* Introduction to Geology. Edition 1833 p. 424.

grotto of Antiparos translated into the simple language of truth, I am inclined to believe it would be found inferior in magnificence and splendour of mineral decoration to the natural caverns in the Fluor Mine."

Returning from the Blue-John Mine by the new road that skirts the base of Mam Tor, we passed on the left the Odin Mine, one of the oldest lead mines in Derbyshire, believed to have been worked by our Saxon forefathers, at a period anterior to the introduction of Christianity, they having honoured it with the name of one of their heathen divinities. Though it has been in operation for so many ages, the supply of ore has scarcely yet been entirely exhausted. The vein runs from east to west, heading, or underlying to the south; the quality, it is said, varying in different parts of the mine, the best kinds yielding about three ounces of silver to the ton weight of lead. The entrance is within a short distance of the road, and, as the levels are driven in a nearly horizontal direction, it may be explored with comparatively little inconvenience.

The lead and the caverns all belong to the limestone, and it is in this formation that nearly all the so-called " wonders of the Peak" are found. Some three miles from Castleton, on the way to Sparrow Pit, there is on the side of a bleak bare mountain one of these chasms, called Eldon Hole, about the unfathomableness of which many tales used to be told ; and how, in Elizabeth's days, the Earl of Leicester's man who tried to find the bottom was rendered speechless, and died before he could reveal the mysteries he was supposed to have seen. Cotton, the poet of the Peak, tried to ascertain the depth but failed, as he tells us :—

> " For I, myself, with half the Peak surrounded,
> Eight hundred fourscore and four yards have sounded ;
> And though of these fourscore returned back wet,
> The plummet drew and found no bottom yet ;
> Though when I went to make a new essay,
> I could not get the lead down half the way."

Mr. Lloyd, F.R.S., who descended in 1780, was more successful, and a narrative of his adventures published in the " Philosophical Transactions" (v. lxi., p. 250), induces the conclusion that he found the bottom at a depth of 180 feet.

In 1873 another descent was made by Mr. Rooke Pennington, LL.B., in company with Mr. John Tym, of Castleton, and a descriptive account of what they saw is given in the "Manchester Literary and Philosophical Magazine," 1875, from which we make the following extract :—

"On the 11th of September, 1873, we explored the chasm for ourselves. A number of stout beams and planks had been brought up the day before, and of these a rude platform was constructed. We found it was impossible to make this platform and place our windlass so as to obtain a descent plumb to the bottom, or rather to the first landing-place in the chasm, insomuch as the northern end is the only part where such a drop can be obtained, and there the gulf was much too wide to be bridged over. Having made all our arrangements, we commenced our descent. My friend, Mr. J. Tym, of Castleton, was the first to go down. He was let down for about 15 or 20 yards before coming in contact with the projecting side of the gulf. For about another 10 or 12 yards he slipped over the rock, which was, however, perfectly smooth, so that there was no risk of cutting the rope. He sustained no further injury than that which befell those of us who followed him, viz., a complete rolling in mud derived from the damp and slippery rocks. As the pioneer, however, he ran great danger from stones which had lodged on ledges of rock, and which there was risk of disturbing. When a little more than half way down he came clear of the rock again, and there was a sheer descent to the bottom, the rope continuing to run over the smooth projecting sides. Three of us followed him, one at a time, each of us being tied to the rope so as to have the hands free to guide the body. The effect of being lowered into the dark abyss, with the blue sky above and the green ferns and creepers around, was very fine, but the knocking one got against the rock a few yards down soon distracted the attention from scenic effect. At a distance of 180 feet from the top a landing place was reached, although not a very secure one, as it was inclined at an angle of about 45 degrees. Thence a cavern ran downwards towards the south or south-east. The floor was entirely covered with loose fragments of limestone, probably extending to a considerable thickness.

This is no doubt to some extent natural, but principally artificial, being the result of the favourite amusement of visitors, the throwing down of loose stones from the protecting wall which surrounds the top. The farmer told me that during his time two or three walls had disappeared and been replaced. No doubt it had been the same in the time of his predecessors. There was quite sufficient light at this point to enable one to sketch or read. Having refreshed ourselves we left daylight behind, and scrambled, or rather slipped, into the cavern for some few yards, during which we descended a considerable distance. It was of a tunnel-like shape; then it suddenly expanded into a magnificent hall about 100 feet across and about 70 feet high. The floor of this hall sloped like the tunnel, and like it was covered with *débris*. At the lower side we were about 60 feet below our landing-place, and therefore about 240 feet beneath the surface. The entire roofs and walls of this cavern were covered with splendid stalagmitic deposits. From the roof were hung fine stalactites, whilst the sides were covered with almost every conceivable form of deposited carbonate of lime. In some places it was smooth and white as marble, in other places like frosted silver, whilst the rougher portions of the rock were clothed with all sorts of fantastic shapes glistening with moisture. When we had lighted some Bengal fire I need hardly say the effect was exquisite. From this cave we could find no opening of any length or depth save the one by which we had entered it, although we very carefully explored it. There is an absurd local tradition of an old woman's goose which flew down, and was given up as lost, but which subsequently re-appeared at the mouth of the Peak Cavern, at Castleton. The sagacious and enterprising bird must have been much cleverer than we were. There can be no doubt that this chasm has been formed by the chemical action of carbonic acid in water, and that it has attacked this particular spot either from the unusual softness of the rock originally situated here, or because there was here a joint or shrinkage in the strata. There is nothing, however, in the position of Eldon Hole to lead one to suppose that any stream has ever flowed through it; no signs of such a state of things appear anywhere around. In this it differs

from the numerous water swallows of the neighbourhood,
and from the pot-holes of North-West Yorkshire. It is not
related to any valley or ravine, or to any running water, and
there is, as observed, an absence of any well-defined exit for
water at the bottom. No mechanical action of a flowing
stream can therefore have assisted the process of enlargement.
That so deep a chasm should be entirely isolated is certainly
remarkable, because it cannot be said to represent a 'weak
point towards which the rainfall has converged.' It must
therefore be due to the gradual silent solvent properties of rain
water falling on the surface, and escaping through jointings
and insignificant channels in the hard rocks below. Whether
the excavation took place from above or below is uncertain.
Applying the rule, 'a ravine is a cavern open to the sky,'
such an abyss is simply a perpendicular cave whose roof has
at length fallen in. But there are many shallow funnel-
shaped depressions in the limestone to which this rule will
not apply, and which have been begun from the top, and
there are also holes of very irregular shape, apparently of
downward origin. So far as the perpendicular shaft of Eldon
Hole is concerned, it is not at all unlikely that the excavation
descended from the surface. On the other hand, there are
many underground chasms which have probably been excavated upwards, and which, when uncovered, will present very
much the appearance of Eldon Hole. For example, the
upper part of the great chasm in the Speedwell Mine bears
a strong resemblance to it, though the process is not there
yet complete; and could sections of the district south of
Castleton be made these hollow mountains would probably
reveal many such a cavity."

For the following lines upon Castleton, we are indebted to
John Leigh, Esq., of Manchester, the author of "Sir Percy
Legh, a Legend of Lyme, and other Ballads."

### CASTLETON.

Thy castled crags, their pinnacles uprearing,
  Fling their long shadows o'er the winding pass ;
And towering rocks, their rugged summits nearing,
  Make deeper gloom within the hollowed mass ;

And from their caverned deeps the rushing sound
  Of falling waters comes upon the ear,

In hidden cataracts the rivers bound,
 Then foam up from the mountain bright and clear.

Through the wide fissures made by earthquakes' might
 For ages have they won their wat'ry way,
Traversed the mountain depths in blackest night,
 Then bubbled up to meet the glare of day.

And in the hills have scooped out caverns vast,
 Whose glittering roofs fantastic forms display,
In pendant stalactites of snowy cast,
 Which sparkle in the flambeau's feeble ray.

The humble swain his humour here indulging,
 Hath named these palaces that nature made,
The splendid pillars from their sides out-bulging,
 And gem-bespangled roof that will not fade.

The proud nave's soaring height in thought he sees,
 And noble organ, though for ever mute,
Yet through whose columns white the whispering breeze
 Sighs for a response to his gentle suit.

Who shall tell how deep that vast abyss
 From whence comes up the river's sullen roar !
We hear the boiling waters seethe and hiss—
 In vain into the dark profound we pore.

The Norman keep, that on the green-clad hill
 Stands sentinel before these chasms wide,
Full many a tale of wonder yet could fill
 Of marvels wrought by the outpouring tide.

Thou lonely relic of the feudal past,
 In the long centuries that thou hast stood,
How many a grim defiance hast thou cast,
 How many a siege and stern assault withstood !

The Peverel here once kept his regal state,
 And in thy halls a princely rule maintained :
Broken and dismantled, no worse fate
 Is thine than nobler structures have sustained.

The lovely Mellet, warlike as her sire,
 Called here the youth of Europe to her feet,
That in the onslaught fierce—and in the fire
 Of battle—she might find a suitor meet.

But gone thy splendour, and thy halls no more—
 One shattered tower, and at its feet the fane
Wherein thy warriors worshippèd of yore,
 And left their impress, now alone remain.

So when the grandeur of the past is fled,
　　And stately walls are levelled with the sod,
The humble church still lifts its lowly head,
　　Still hymns of praise rise to the throne of God.

Aye, when the pomp of chivalry lies low,
　　And frowning castles crumble into dust,
Still at the humble shrine the knee we bow,
　　Still raise the sounds of hopefulness and trust.

In earlier times the Briton here pursued
　　His noble quarry over hill and fell,
Chasèd the antlered game with weapons rude,
　　And faithful dog whose bay was heard to swell

And wake the echoes in these dark defiles.
　　With steady pace he pressed the circling deer,
With well-trained cunning met his many wiles,
　　Till sank the prey beneath the unerring spear.

Deep in the leafy gloom of oaken wood
　　That canopied the valley's winding length,
With dauntless step the hunter oft hath trod,
　　To brave with well-nerved arm the savage strength

Of wolf or boar, that in the cave had found,
　　Or in the close-set thicket each his lair,
Ready to meet the sudden rush or bound
　　With conscious skill, and breast that knew not fear ;

Or in the river sought his glistening prey,
　　The silver greyling and the speckled trout ;
Or from the whimpering brook the sprawling cray
　　Furnished his simple meal—a prayer devout

His Druids taught him.　Rising from the feast,
　　His drink the purling stream or crystal well,
That, fed with dewy drops that still increased,
　　Lay hid in shady covert of the dell.

A simple circle on the lofty plain
　　Of rude unshapen stones from mountain riven,
Open alike to sun, and wind, and rain,
　　The roof alone the star-gemmed vault of heaven,

Served him for temple.　Here with awe-struck soul
　　He listened to the Druid's solemn voice,
Saw from the pyre arise the vaporous scroll
　　Of incense from the blood-stained sacrifice.

With reverent breast he worshipped here the cause
 Of life and light—the Giver of all good ;
Heard from sacred lips proclaimed the laws
 By which was ruled his scattered brotherhood.

Upon the barren moorland, bleak and lone,
 Where soughs the night-wind in a fitful tide,
Beneath an earthen mound with turf o'ergrown,
 Still rest his bones, his weapons by his side.

Let no irreverent hand disturb his rest,
 Nor scatter his poor relics o'er the plain :
His brethren laid him here in simple trust—
 Here let his humble sepulchre remain.

The Roman, too, once made these wilds his home,
 Bringing his legions from the distant south,
From the world's capital, imperial Rome,
 Thirsting for conquest with unquenchèd drouth.

The hardy Briton struggled with his foe,
 Dared him to battle on the neighb'ring height,
And dusky streamlets reddened with the flow
 From heroes dying for their country's right.

Their simple weapons 'gainst the serried ranks,
 Full disciplined in war, were hurled in vain,
Well greaved and helmeted the firm phalanx
 Received their fierce attack in proud disdain.

The length'ning road that stretched o'er hill and dale,
 Straight as the arrow's flight, the Roman laid,
And fortress strong that overlooked the vale
 He raised against the Brigant's sudden raid.

These teeming mountains, touched by Roman skill,
 Gave up the hidden treasures to his hands,
Rich veins of lead repaid his venturous will,
 And fluor begirt with amethystine bands ;

The darkling blende, concealing in its breast
 The shimmering zinc of pale cerulean hue,
And earthy calamine reward his quest—
 The golden orichalcum well he knew

From these to fashion ; and the silver bright
 Forth from its dross of lead he also drew—
Wrapped in a sullen robe, its beauteous light,
 Till cleared by fire, lay hidden from the view.

What wondrous shapes, to his astonished gaze,
  His tools reveal as he pursues his toil—
Corals and shells of various forms amaze,
  That in profusion fill the rocky soil.

In countless ages past, when earth was young,
  And ocean brooded o'er these mountain peaks,
The waters swarmèd with a living throng
  That played and sported in its bays and creeks ;

Or in the ocean depths lived out their time,
  Leaving their relics on their growing bed,
Till stretched the vast remains from clime to clime,
  A continent built of unnumbered dead.

Time—that in God's works hath no account,
  Illimitable as the space he fills—
Rolled on its eons from a ceaseless fount,
  As rose from darkness these once living hills.

What time the Raven flapped his gory wing,
  And scoured the White Horse o'er this harried realm ;
His crowded galley brought the dread Viking,
  Lust at his prow, and rapine at the helm.

A conquering rabble ravaged o'er these lands,
  Urged by Valhalla's maidens to the strife ;
Joyfully they left their yellow strands,
  That in the battle they might yield up life.

Opening the portals wide, with reddened hands,
  Of Odin's halls, they see the bright-haired race,
The fair Valkyria wait, in lovely bands,
  To fold their heroes in a fond embrace.

On Winhill's sloping brow the Saxon thane
  Unfurled his banner to the sweeping gale,
Waited the onset of the fiery Dane,
  And drove him vanquished back into the vale ;

But fate, alas ! too soon reversed the day :
  Again they met on the adjacent hill,
The Raven glutted on his dying prey,
  And steeped in carnage his insatiate bill.

Thus Roman, Saxon, Norman, ruthless Dane,
  Each in his turn a baleful part here played,
Carrying havoc o'er the fertile plain,
  And dark oppression marking all they swayed.

Yet suffering oft brings blessings in its train—
  No ill that hath not some attendant good :
The evil of the past is present gain—
  Fair liberty springs from the martyr's blood.

See now the race, of all the rest combined,
  Hardy and brave, enduring, patient, wise,
Holding to freedom with a common mind,
  Ready for this all else to sacrifice.

Eagle and Raven from these lands are fled ;
  With peaceful skill we cultivate the soil,
Nor more the devastating hosts we dread,
  Whilst teeming harvests compensate our toil.

These lovely valleys, with rich herbage spread,
  A verdant landscape, set with many flowers,
That from their opening buds a perfume shed
  And scent the gale that brings the fresh'ning showers.

Smiling in plenty, nestled lie 'midst hills
  Upon whose flanks the purple heather blooms,
Whose misty summits form the leaping rills,
  And flash in vivid gold as evening looms.

The lichen creeping o'er the rugged rocks
  Makes beauty-stains of every shade and hue—
Purple and orange, green and brown, whilst locks
  Of silvery grey drip with incessant dew.

The ruby chalice of the tiny moss
  In diamond-studded grotto hides away,
Rimmed with a fringe of gold to keep from loss
  The nectar treasured for the wandering fay.

Or in the dingle weaves a velvet pile
  Where plumy ferns shut out the fervid day,
On which beneath the moonbeam's flickering smile
  The elfin feet delight to trip and play.

The gaudy pansy on the terraced height
  Opens her bosom to the rising sun,
Basks in his rays till fades the waning light,
  Closes her leaves, and droops when he is gone.

Mounting in ether, hark the lavrock sings,
  Soaring aloft above the mountain peaks ;
How cheerily his matin song now rings,
  As, bathed in light, refulgent, still he seeks

To reach the nearer heaven—his glad wings
  Beating the tenuous air in gleesome time,
Then sinking down to earth, his music brings
  To where his mate sits in the fragrant thyme.

# CHAPTER V.

IT was about mid-day when, resuming the satchel and the
staff, we left our comfortable quarters at the *Bull's Head*,
and bade adieu to Castleton with its wonders—its castle and
caverns, its mines, minerals, and museums, and all the other
objects of interest and attraction which serve to engage the
attention or beguile the time of the tourist.

Eyam was the next place we purposed visiting. This
romantically-situated village lies about six miles to the
south-east of Castleton, the most direct way being through
Bradwell, Windmill, and Foolow; but as this road is, for the
most part, dreary and uninteresting, we gave preference to
the more circuitous but pleasanter route by Hope and
Hathersage. This road runs the entire length of Hope Dale,
and as the traveller proceeds some delightful views are
obtained of the charming scenery of this far-famed valley.

About a mile from Castleton, close to the road side, a
cupola smelting furnace has been erected, the huge circular
brick chimney of which forms a conspicuous object, and may
be seen from almost every part of the dale. Great heaps of
shining ore and mounds of ground spar, dross, and rubbish,
lay about in various directions, and here and there were
piled-up stacks of leaden pigs ready for carting away.

Continuing our journey, a few minutes' walk brought us
to Hope. The parish—one of the largest in the county—
comprises the parochial chapelry of Fairfield, with eighteen
townships, besides the villages of Alport, Coplow Dale, and
Small Dale, and a part of the town of Buxton.

The village is of very modest dimensions, the parsonage, a blacksmith's shop, and two or three public-houses, constituting the major portion. Hope Hall, now occupied as an inn, bearing the name of the Hall Hotel, was formerly the seat of the Balguys, who possessed considerable estates in this part of the county for many generations. The ancient and widely-spread family of Eyre, ancestors of the present Earl of Newburgh, date their connection with Hope so far back as the reign of Henry III., when William le Eyre held lands of the king *in capite* by service of the custody of the forest of High Peak.

Hope, Dugdale tells us, was given by Prince John to the canons of Lichfield, along with his turquoise ring : " *Quod donum non solum sigilli mei impressione, sed a proprii annuli appositione roboravi.*

The church, dedicated to St. Peter, stands on a gentle elevation, close to the roadside, and is nearly surrounded by tall and widely-spreading lime trees. Ascending a few steps, we entered the churchyard by a narrow quaint-looking opening between two upright stones. The building is a venerable structure, erected, apparently, about the early part of the fifteenth century, with additions of a later period. It consists of a nave, with clerestory and side aisles, chancel, south porch, and western tower, the latter supporting a broad and singularly heavy-looking octagonal broach spire ; the want of altitude in the superstructure (a defect common to many of the churches in Derbyshire) detracting greatly from the appearance of the edifice. The roof of the clerestory, side aisles, and choir, is surmounted by an embattled parapet, relieved at intervals with crocketted pinnacles. The eastern end of the chancel is lighted by a large pointed window of four lights, trefoiled, the head filled with perpendicular tracery, of good design. Near to this window is the following inscription, now almost obliterated :—

REPARED BY
THE D & C OF L. ;

and adjoining, the date " 1620." The building having probably been restored in that year at the cost of the Dean and Chapter of Lichfield. The entrance porch, on the south side, is supported by buttresses, placed on the angles. Above is an ancient porch-chamber, and on the external face of this is a triplet opening, with a crocketted canopy, intended originally to contain a small statue, probably the patron saint of the church. A number of grotesque gargoyles, for carrying off the water from the roof, are disposed round the building, some of which, it must be confessed, hardly accord with our modern sense of decency, much less with the sacred character of the fabric they are intended to adorn. In the interior are a few mural tablets, and near one of the arch-ways is a monumental brass to the memory of Henry Balguy, of Rowlee, in Hope Parish, who died 17th March, 1685.

In addition to some local charities left by benevolent individuals, there is an endowed school of ancient foundation. On the master's old oak chair, which bears date 1664, is carved the following inscription : " *Ex torto ligno non fit Mercurius*" ("An Apollo is not made out of a twisted log ")— an aphorism the truth of which we are not inclined to dispute.

Leaving Hope, we crossed the river Nowe, a busy little stream that takes its rise among the hills in the vicinity of Edale, whence it continues its snake-like course through a succession of meadows of the most vigorous green, receiving, as it progresses, several smaller rivulets, until it becomes lost in the Derwent, at Shatton, about midway between Hope and Hathersage.

At Brough, a mile further on, the Nowe is joined by a little brook called the Bradwell, and in the angle formed by the confluence of these two streams (a situation that would seem to have been invariably preferred), is the site of an ancient Roman station. The ground is slightly elevated, and bears the name of the Halsteads. There have been dug up, at different times, urns, bricks, stone columns, a bust of Apollo, a gold coin of the reign of the Emperor Augustus Cæsar, and various other articles, undoubtedly of Roman origin. From this station there appear to have been two ancient Roman roads ; one, called the Bathway or Bathom-gate, leading to Buxton, the other over the moors to Melandra Castle, in the township of Gamesly, near Glossop. A tradition also prevails that the Peverels had a residence at Brough, in addition to their stronghold at Castleton.

Brough Mill belonged to the family of Strelley in the reign of Edward III., who held it by the singular service of attending the king on horseback whenever he should come into Derbyshire, carrying an heron-falcon. If his horse should die in the journey, the king was to buy him another, and to provide two robes and *bouche* of court.

From Brough, a pleasant walk of a mile along the northern bank of the river, brought us to Mytham Bridge, a structure of three arches, spanning the river Derwent—as sparkling and brilliant a stream as ever imparted grace and animation to landscape scenery.

Here the changing aspect of the scenery becomes manifest. The country gradually loses its pastoral character, and assumes at every step a more bold and picturesque appearance. The Derwent forms a pleasing feature in the scene, its silvery waters coursing merrily along through a well-wooded and richly-pastured foreground, backed by a succession of eminences which descend almost to the river's brink, their sloping sides clothed to the summit with trees. Further on a charming view of Derwent Dale is afforded, and beyond the bleak and barren slopes of Hathersage Moor and Froggatt Edge fill up the background, their harsh and rugged outlines, softened by distance, meeting the sky and forming an admirable perspective.

The Derwent, or *dwr gwent*, as our Celtic forefathers called it, may fairly claim to rank as the principal of Derbyshire rivers, and from its source to its junction with the Trent—a distance of about forty miles—its course lies through some of the most richly-diversified scenery in the county, itself contributing not a little to enhance the beauty of the country through which it flows. It takes its rise in one of the wildest regions of the Peak, its main source being at a place called the Trough, in that mountainous gritstone ridge which separates the counties of York and Derby. Taking a southerly direction it receives in its course the waters of the Westend, and after passing the quiet little hamlet of Derwent, to which it gives name, becomes united with the Ashop, a gathering of numberless rills that come down from the wild cloughs and dingles in the hill country around Kinder Scout ; half-a-mile further on the Ladybower Brook

F

comes prattling down with noisy glee from the deep-wooded glen on the opposite side; then the river winds sweetly onwards through the pleasant vale of Bamford to Mytham Bridge, where the Nowe meets it with gladsome greeting. Leaving Hathersage about half-a-mile to the eastward, it pursues an indented course through the beautiful valley between Froggatt Edge and Eyam Moor, approaching within a short distance of Stoney-Middleton, receiving on its way the outpourings of the bordering hills. After passing the little village of Baslow it flows by the west front of Chatsworth and through the park to Rowsley, at which place it is joined by the winding Wye. From Rowsley the river gracefully serpentines through the rich pastoral vale of Darley, at the further extremity of which the sylvan character of the scenery changes, and tranquil beauty is succeeded by magnificence and grandeur. Here, as it enters Matlock Dale, the current flows rapidly over its rock-strewn bed, washing the foot of the majestic High Tor, then sweeping round the broad base of the stupendous Masson, and again hiding from view as it glides stealthily along beneath the pendant woods which shadow darkly its translucent bosom. Leaving the romantic dale of Matlock it flows through Cromford and Belper to Derby, and some ten miles beyond falls into the Trent, near the village of Wilne, on the confines of Leicestershire.

Though not possessing the queenly dignity of the Trent, nor those wild features that characterise and give interest to the Dove, the Derwent may, nevertheless, challenge comparison with any river in the kingdom for the rich and varied character of the scenery along its course. Generally its banks are well wooded—the oak, the elm, and the widespreading sycamore mingling their rich verdure with the more light and graceful foliage of the ash and the birch; whilst here and there, from amid the luxuriant masses of underwood that adorn its sloping sides, the delicate stems of the osier, and the slender branches of the wild honeysuckle, hang down to the water's edge, breaking its glassy surface into innumerable ripples. The beauty of the stream is increased by the ever-changing character of the currents: sometimes it bounds hurriedly on, leaping from crag to crag in little fairy-like cascades, throwing up the sparkling foam-bubbles as it breaks over the fragments of rock which have been toppled down from the overhanging cliffs; anon the troubled waves subside, and the current glides smoothly and leisurely along its surface, scarcely broken by a ripple. But, though often gentle, it is never languid, never sluggish. In some places it meanders pleasantly onwards over its pebbly bed, its gentle murmurs blending harmoniously with the rustling of the overshadowing trees.

We lingered for some time upon the bridge watching the broad clear stream as it meandered onwards over the moss-clad stones which nature, with a careless hand, has strewn along its channel, its rippled surface the while decked with a thousand silvery gleams. Then turning off to the left near the tollbar, we pursued our course, keeping beneath the friendly shade of the spreading trees to avoid the scorching beams of the meridian sun.

As we sauntered leisurely along we fell into company with a farmer's son, a lithe, active young fellow, on his way to a neighbouring village. We got into conversation about the beauty of the river and the surrounding scenery. He knew the country well, and related many a scrap of legendary lore. We soon found out that he had made good use of his eyes, as well as his ears, for he showed us all the choice bits of scenery, and pointed out the most interesting objects in the view, discoursing the while upon their merits with all the earnestness of one who felt that he had a personal interest in their reputation. We learned, too, that he was an enthusiastic botanist, and had spent some time in endeavouring to master the science of geology, though the subject, he said, he had found to be a very dry one.

Half-a-mile brings us to Bamford, as pleasant a little village as any in the Peak, delightfully situated on the slope of a bold gritstone ridge, with a charming vicinity that is sure to win the admiration of the wayfarer. Many of the houses have a comfortable well-to-do appearance about them; some have their gardens bright with flowers; and even the humblest has its window enlivened with some pretty plant or other. The hills rise on either side in lofty and picturesque masses, and all along, encroaching upon their broad slopes, spread meadows of luxuriant grass, while deep in the leafy

hollow below the Derwent ripples merrily onwards, gurgling
and splashing over its rock-strewn channel, delighting the
ear with the pleasant music of its babbling waters. A branch
of the cotton trade has extended itself even to this out-of-
the-way place, giving employment to a large portion of the
surrounding population, who are occupied in the doubling of
fine threads for lace manufacture, and now all is activity and
diligence where previously the quiet operations of husbandry
were carried on with no stimulus for the mind, and but little
increase of industrial wealth. The mill stands away down in
the valley by the river's brink, its harsher features concealed
by a mantle of foliage that has been trained to spread over
its walls. Altogether it looks so unobtrusive in its screen of
leaves that one can hardly object to its neighbourhood. The
proprietor, Mr. William Cameron Moore, is the principal
landowner in the district, and to his liberality the inhabitants
are indebted for many of the social privileges they now enjoy.
With a kindly feeling towards those whose labour has contributed to his wealth, he has spared no efforts in the
promotion of their moral and intellectual as well as physical
interests. The village schools are maintained principally at
his expense ; and within the last few years he has at his own
cost erected a handsome church, endowed it, and built a
commodious house for the clergyman, the nearest place of
worship previously being the mother church of Hathersage,
some three miles distant. May the noble example of liberality
and singleness of heart which he has shown find many
imitators among his class, that so our "traffickers" may be
truly called "the honourable of the earth."

The church, dedicated to St. John, is a very pretty structure, and from its elevated position forms a conspicuous
object in the landscape for miles around. It is built in the
decorated style, from designs by Mr. Butterfield, the details
exhibiting a closer adherence to the pure English-Gothic than
is usually met with in the creations of this architect. The
plan comprehends a nave, chancel, and north aisle, with a
tower, in which is a peal of bells, flanking the north-west
angle, surmounted by a spire that rises to the height of one
hundred and eight feet. The interior is very effective. The
floors are laid with tiles, and the chancel is adorned with

foliated panels worked in Derbyshire marble. The windows are filled with stained glass—that in the chancel is of three lights, trefoiled, with an elaborately foliated rose in the head. The subjects expressed are the Resurrection and the Ascension; and beneath them are the inscriptions, in black letter characters :—

𝕿𝖍𝖎𝖘 𝕵𝖊𝖘𝖚𝖘 𝖍𝖆𝖙𝖍 𝕲𝖔𝖉 𝖗𝖆𝖎𝖘𝖊𝖉 𝖚𝖕, 𝖜𝖍𝖊𝖗𝖊𝖔𝖋 𝖜𝖊 𝖆𝖑𝖑 𝖆𝖗𝖊 𝖜𝖎𝖙𝖓𝖊𝖘𝖘𝖊𝖘, and

𝕿𝖍𝖎𝖘 𝖘𝖆𝖒𝖊 𝕵𝖊𝖘𝖚𝖘 𝖘𝖍𝖆𝖑𝖑 𝖘𝖔 𝖈𝖔𝖒𝖊 𝖎𝖓 𝖑𝖎𝖐𝖊 𝖒𝖆𝖓𝖓𝖊𝖗 𝖆𝖘 𝖞𝖊 𝖍𝖆𝖛𝖊 𝖘𝖊𝖊𝖓 𝕳𝖎𝖒 𝖌𝖔 𝖎𝖓𝖙𝖔 𝖍𝖊𝖆𝖛𝖊𝖓.

BAMFORD CHURCH.

A window of three lights on the south side of the nave bears testimony to the liberality of a former vicar of Hathersage. The centre light represents the baptism of Christ, and in the side lights are the figures of Zacharias and Elizabeth. beneath is the inscription :—

𝕬𝖓𝖓𝖔 𝕯𝖔𝖒𝖎𝖓𝖎 1860. 𝕵𝖓 𝖍𝖔𝖓𝖔𝖚𝖗 𝖔𝖋 𝕲𝖔𝖉 𝖙𝖍𝖎𝖘 𝖜𝖎𝖓𝖉𝖔𝖜 𝖎𝖘 𝖌𝖎𝖛𝖊𝖓 𝖇𝖞 𝕳𝖊𝖓𝖗𝖞 𝕮𝖔𝖙𝖙𝖎𝖓𝖌𝖍𝖆𝖒, 𝕸.𝕬., 𝖘𝖔𝖒𝖊 𝖙𝖎𝖒𝖊 𝖛𝖎𝖈𝖆𝖗 𝖔𝖋 𝖙𝖍𝖊 𝖕𝖆𝖗𝖎𝖘𝖍 𝖔𝖋 𝕳𝖆𝖙𝖍𝖊𝖗𝖘𝖆𝖌𝖊.

The western gable is pierced by a large wheel window, the centre foil containing the letters I.N.R.I. The font is circular in form, of Derbyshire marble, and an inscription on the minister step records that it was given by Thomas Eyre, of Moorseats, Hathersage. The church is entered by a doorway in the west face of the tower, communicating with a covered vestibule that extends across the end of the nave. Within the entrance at the north end is a single-light window, in which is a shield charged with the arms of the founder—azure a swan with wings expanded argent, membered and beaked or; on a chief of the second a lion passant gules between two trefoils slipped vert; impaling or, on a bend sable, three chevronels of the first between two lions rampant of the second. Immediately underneath is the inscription:—

𝔉or the glory of 𝔊od and the good of 𝔥is people this 𝔠hurch was founded by 𝔚illiam 𝔠ameron 𝔐oore, A.D. MDCCCLX;

and graven upon the wall hard by, a text of Scripture reminds the worshipper, as he enters, that, "This is none other but the House of God." To the people of this same pleasant village of Bamford it is indeed the "House of God," and we are sure that we but echo the feeling of the benevolent founder in the wish that to them it may become "the gate of heaven."

The scenery around Bamford is boldly featured, and with its wild accompaniments of rock and wood presents much to delight the eye. On the right a lofty sweep of blackened crags overshadows the village, and seems to frown everything into silence. The lower slopes swell down in bold grassy sweeps into the vale, through which the Derwent flows in freakish windings, and above nothing is seen but mimic forests of pine and broad patches of scrub and brushwood, through which, here and there, the bare rock protrudes in gaunt unshapen masses, while high up, on the very verge of the precipitous cliffs, a grim and lifeless-looking crag, which the imaginative fancy of the villagers has likened to old Vulcan's bellows, juts out from the parent rock, like a stony coronal, all bleached and weather-worn, imparting a touch of savage grandeur to the scene.

On the opposite side of the valley the bleak cone of Winhill rises, with solemn and imposing aspect, the scattered group of dwellings that go to make the little hamlet of Thornhill, resting in peaceful seclusion upon its broad flank, half-hidden by the clumps of trees that spread about. Patches of plantation fringe the banks of the stream, and for some distance upwards signs of cultivation are seen, but all beyond is one broad tract of untrodden moorland sterility. The summit commands a wide expanse of country, and well repays the labour of ascent. On the further side, and separated from it by a secluded vale, through which the busy little Nowe murmurs with many-mooded cadences, there rises another eminence of almost equal elevation, bearing the name of Losehill—part of a steep rocky ridge that extends on from Mam Tor, forming the northern boundary of Hope Dale.

Tradition hovers about the place, and tells us that in the dim antiquity of the past, while Edwin ruled Northumbria's land, the armies of two Saxon kings here met in deadly conflict, and the now peaceful valley echoed to the bloody strife and clang of arms. Long and furiously the battle raged, nor ceased the combatants until the waters of the Nowe were crimsoned with the blood of the slain. The victorious army, it is said, encamped where Winhill lifts its stony diadem, the vanquished, on the opposing heights of Losehill.*

A story prevails that Winhill was, many years ago, the scene of a dark deed of blood, a peddler and his wife having, it is said, been barbarously murdered whilst crossing over the bleak summit on their way to a neighbouring town. The two were known to have ascended from the Ashopton side, but were never seen or heard of more. The hand of justice failed to reach the perpetrators of this fearful crime, though in the locality a few dark hints were now and then dropped respecting the supposed guilty persons. Some forty or fifty years ago a farmer, whilst removing earth from the summit of the hill, found human bones, and on making further

* Between Bradwell and Brough, about two and a half miles distant, and near the line of the old Roman road, the site of another battle, said to have been fought during the Saxon Heptarchy, is pointed out, at the close of which a king or military chief named Edwin was captured and hanged upon a tree that grew upon the spot, which still bears the name Edden tree—a corruption of Edwin's tree.

search the skeletons of a man and woman were discovered, which were generally supposed to be those of the murdered pair ; a few glass beads were found with them, but nothing else by which they could be identified.  The remains were gathered together and decently interred in the neighbouring churchyard of Hope.

Evening was creeping on when we entered the village of Bamford.  The rosy hues of the declining sun fell grandly upon the moorland hills, and tinged the rugged fringe of rocks with golden light, that softened into beauty every seam and furrow that time and tempest has ploughed down their hoary fronts.  There was yet half-an-hour or more of day-light, so we rambled on by the river's brink towards Yorkshire Bridge, lingering oftentimes in cool nooks to chat and watch the play and sparkle of the water as it came and went in many a silvery fall.  Hereabouts the river tumbles over the ledges of its stony channel in numberless cascades, presenting, with its accompaniments of rock and foliage, as many pleasing "bits" in one short mile as would store an artist's portfolio.  The soft warm haze of a summer's eve came stealing down into the vernal shade, brightening the shaggy scrub with golden radiance.  All was peaceful, calm, and still, nothing sounded audibly but the clear gurgling of the river and the sleepy rustling of the leaves overhead, save that now and then the distant baying of a shepherd's dog and the plaintive bleat of scattered sheep came from the opposite slopes of Winhill, mingled occasionally with the "clucking" cry of a startled grouse as it winged its way over the lonely waste.

Near the bridge we left the margin of the stream, and crossing a few green upland pastures regained the road at the point where it separates, Wood Lane leading down on the left to Ashopton, and thence through the woodlands to Glossop, and the other tending to the right until it enters the Ladybower, a deep secluded glen shut in by precipitous cliffs, clothed from base to summit with copsewood and spreading trees, between which the road winds on towards Sheffield.

At Ashopton, where the Ashop, the Derwent, and the Ladybower Brook unite, there is a comfortable inn resorted to by sportsmen and the votaries of the rod and line; and two miles further on is a secluded hamlet that takes its name from the Derwent, with a picturesque little church erected in recent years, and an ancient mansion that formerly belonged to the old family of the Balguys, but is now owned by England's premier duke—His Grace of Norfolk. From the Crook Hill, a gentle elevation that rises behind the Ashopton Inn, a charmingly picturesque scene meets the eye; and from the summit of Derwent Edge, the lofty eminence beyond, one of the best mountain views in all Derbyshire is obtained, comprising Kinder Scout, Fairbrook Naze, Winhill, Losehill, Madwoman's Stones, Lord's Seat, and Mam Tor, with an innumerable succession of ridges that stretch away into the remote distance, forming that vast and varied mountain group which geographers persist in designating the "Peak" of Derbyshire.

When we returned the sun had gone down behind the western hills, and the dreamy shades of night were falling softly upon the landscape, wrapping the moorland heights in their dusky embrace. Mam Tor had disappeared in the shadowy distance, and day's curtains were closing gently over the scene. No sound broke the stillness of the summer night, save the faint whispers of the evening breeze and the silvery tricklings of some distant rill that filled the air with its dreamy music. The hum of life from the village had died away, and everything seemed to have lulled itself to rest.

It was a cloudless summer morning when we awoke. The sun's broad disc was just peeping over the edge of the eastern hills, and his slant rays shot across the vale in arrowy gleams, bathing the broad front of Winhill in golden splendour, and lighting up the lingering dewdrops that hung upon the "pointed thorns;" the birds twittered blithely about the house-tops, and everything seemed to rejoice in the beauty of the awakening morn.

On leaving the quiet little village we turned off by a by-road that leads up through a tree-shaded hollow, along the side of which a moorland rill trickles over its well-worn bed of rock. By-and-by we come to Hurst Clough, a lonely dingle among the hills traversed by a tiny rivulet that channels its way round the mossy stones in many a freakish winding, at times half-hidden by the dwarf oaks and brambles that fringe its banks. Anon we ascend by a wild old wandering lane, grown over with moss and ferns, and full of deep ruts and water-holes ; high banks of hazel and thorn rise on each side, over-topped with trees that spread across and half exclude the light, producing a sort of chequered day and night. Here and there the native rock has been laid bare by successive rains, and we have to stride from one stony lump to another to avoid plunging into the slushy gullies that meet us at every stride. Quitting the miry highway we betake ourselves to the fields, following a beaten path that leads on past the Nether Hurst, a quiet little homestead, standing in a green nook at the foot of a grassy knoll, and presently reach the top of an eminence called the Ridgway, whence we get the first view of the town of Hathersage, resting upon the mountain slope—its fine old Gothic church crowning the top of a green knoll in front, and wooded hills encircling it on nearly every side. Delightful is the view that meets the eye. Thick woods mark the course of a stream that winds through the vale below the trees, thinning off where they meet the well-tilled uplands; thick plantations clothe the hills in rear, and beyond the wild moorlands stretch away in dim perspective. Moorseats stands out upon the opposite slope, and higher up the vale we catch a glimpse of North Lees, the old castellated home of the Eyres, peeping above its screen of trees. With more time we might ramble up and trace out its quaint antiquities, or loiter about the ruined walls and broken arches of its ancient chapel, in which the wild birds now flit to and fro, and weeds and brambles thrive with untrimmed prodigality.

From the high ground the road tends to the left, and we descend towards Brookfield, a pleasant mansion standing by the margin of the stream. A wooded eminence shuts out the view upon the left, and upon the right the way is bordered by tall trees through which the sunshine comes in fitful gleams, brightening the rugged stems with touches of golden light. At the bottom of the valley we cross the stream by a little bridge, whence the pathway leads off on the right over some pastures, and a few minutes later we enter the town of Hathersage.

Hathersage occupies a commanding position, overlooking the valley of the Derwent, the houses being for the most part built upon the rocky front of a lofty eminence, a part of that great alpine ridge that forms the eastern boundary of the county. Formerly the manufacture of metal buttons was carried on here to some extent, but this branch of industry would appear to have died out, the inhabitants being now employed chiefly in the manufacture of steel wire and needles, a trade that appears to have been more successful, if we may judge from the numerous manufactories in the place.

The church stands at the upper end of the town. It is an ancient structure, dedicated to St. Michael, and justly considered one of the handsomest edifices in Derbyshire. The style is that denominated the decorated Gothic, the purest and most beautiful in English ecclesiastical architecture, and which may be said to have prevailed from the close of the thirteenth to the latter part of the fourteenth century, or during the reigns of the first three Edwards. The plan includes a nave, chancel, and side aisles, clerestory and south porch, with a handsome embattled tower flanking the western end, of three stages, supported by buttresses placed rectangularwise, terminating in grotesque gargoyles, and surmounted by a lofty octagon spire, enriched at the angles with crocket work.

A writer who visited the place some years ago, describing the church, says : " The interior is in the most despicable order, the ' Commandments ' are broken, the pavement is damp and dislocated, the monuments are ill kept, and the very whitewash appears of the earliest ' Gothic ' application." However true this description may have been when written, it certainly no longer applies to Hathersage. Now everything is maintained with the utmost care and neatness, and decency and order prevail throughout—an improved state of things that is owing in a great degree to the active exertions of a former vicar. In 1851-2 the church underwent a thorough restoration, at a cost (exclusive of the beautifully stained glass windows, which have been furnished by private liberality) of upwards of £1,700. A considerable portion of the external masonry has been renewed, and in the several details the original character of the design has been carefully adhered to. The interior has a very effective appearance, the whole of the fittings being in keeping with the exterior, and throughout the same correctness of taste is everywhere apparent.

The nave is separated from the aisles on each side by three octagon columns, and deeply moulded capitals and bases, supporting four pointed arches, above which rises the clerestory. The roof is of open timber-work, supported by bracing ribs springing from angel-corbels and spanning the body of the church in the form of cinquefoiled archways. The floors are laid with Minton's tiles, those in the chancel being of an elegant geometrical pattern; and near the south entrance is an ancient octagon stone font with a carved oak cover. The most attractive feature is the rich stained glass with which nearly all the windows are filled, shedding a soft mellow light that gives increased sublimity and devotional character to the building.

From the time of the Reformation until within a comparatively recent period the art of painting on glass had fallen almost into disuse in this country, but of late years it has been revived, and attained to great perfection. Certainly there is no ecclesiastical ornament that can be more strictly appropriate, or more conducive to the due solemnity and splendour of the house of God, than the "storied window;" and as a memorial to perpetuate the pious deeds of departed worth it must be confessed that it is infinitely preferable to the heathen trash of painted cupids, sculptured urns, inverted torches, sarcophagi, *et id genus omne*, with which a barbarous taste has disfigured so many of our ancient parish churches.

The principal window, lighting the chancel, was given by voluntary subscription. It has three foliated lights, and illustrates the Nativity and Crucifixion, including figures of the Virgin Mary and St. John. At the western end of the nave is a large memorial window, also of three lights, by Warrington, of London, the gift of George Eyre, Esq., and his three sisters. The centre light contains a representation of Daniel interpreting the handwriting on the wall—in the two side lights are Noah constructing the ark, and Job—and beneath the following inscription, in black letter :—

To the glory of God, and to the memory of William Eyre, of North Lees, of Mary his wife, and John his son. A.D. 1856.

In the south side are two square-headed windows, with coupled lights, each light containing the figure of one of the Evangelists. At the east end of the same aisle is a window of similar design, with the figures of the apostles SS. Peter and Paul. This was subscribed for by the working people of Hathersage. There is another window on the south side of the chancel, the gift of the Rev. H. Cottingham, the vicar under whose superintendence the restorations were effected.

On the north side of the chancel, beneath a crocketted ogee canopy, is the altar-tomb of Robert Eyre, who fought in the battle of Agincourt, and his wife Joanna, daughter and sole heiress of Robert Padley, lord of the manor of Hather-sage. On the tomb is an incised brass, on which is depicted the figure of a knight in plain armour, with his long sword by his side, and his lady, habited in the costume of the reign of Edward IV., with a long robe and veiled head-dress. At the head is a shield charged with (what appears to be) the arms of Padley, arg. three horse-barnacles sable ; and at the feet is a label with the following inscription in black letter characters :—

Hic jacet Robertus Eyre armiger qui obiit xxi. die mensis Marcii. Anno dni Mill'mo cccclix. et Johne uxor ejus qui obiit ix. die mensis Marcii. Anno dni Mill'mo cccclxib. ac pueri eorundem quor animis p'picietur Deus Amen.

Beneath the legend are the effigies of their fourteen children, ten sons and four daughters. The Robert Eyre who is here represented, by his marriage with the heiress of Padley, acquired the Padley and Hathersage estates. The Eyres, as already stated, have been located in this neighbourhood from a very early period, and it is said, on the authority of an old pedigree still preserved at Hassop, that one of them saved the life of William the Conqueror at the battle of Hastings, in return for which service he received considerable grants of lands in Derbyshire.* To this once powerful family, whose name in days of yore was so prominently associated with the annals of the Peak, but little has been preserved beyond their monuments, their records, and their traditions. The lands they owned have passed from their possession, and the ancient halls in which they dwelt have become the abode of strangers, and will now "know them no more." There are several other monuments of the Eyre family in Hathersage Church, and also some memorials of that of Ashton.

A simple and affecting custom formerly prevailed here, as at Ashford, Matlock, Glossop, Tissington, and many other villages in the county, but which has of late years fallen into disuse. When a young maiden died it was usual for her companions to weave chaplets composed of wreaths of flowers and other emblems of youth, purity, and loveliness. These tokens of affection were borne before the bier, and afterwards hung up in the chancel, or some other conspicuous part of the church, in memory of the departed, where they remained suspended until they fell from age and decay.

> "To her sweet memory flow'ry garlands strung,
> On her now empty seat aloft were hung."

Several of these simple but graceful memorials of early dissolution are said to have existed at Hathersage within a recent period, but they have now all disappeared, not even a remnant remaining.†

Hathersage claims the twofold honour of having given birth to and being the last resting-place of John Nailor, Robin Hood's giant henchman, familiarly known to our childhood by the *sobriquet* of Little John. The cottage in which he is said to have been born, and to which he wearily returned to die, is evidently of great antiquity. It is a low

---

* According to the Hassop pedigree the founder of the family, whose name was Truelove, seeing William unhorsed in the battle of Hastings, and his helmet beat so close to his face that he could not breathe, pulled off his helmet and horsed him again. The King said, "Thou shalt hereafter from Truelove be called 'Air' or 'Eyre,' because thou hast given me the air I breathe." After the battle, the King called for him, and being found with his thigh cut off, William ordered him to be taken care of, and after his recovery gave him lands in the county of Derby, in reward for his services. The seat he lived at was called "Hope," because he had hope in the greatest extremity, and the King gave the leg and thigh cut off in armour for his crest, and which is still the crest of all the Eyres in England.

† An interesting paper on this beautiful custom, from the pen of Mr. Llewellyn Jewitt, F.S.A., is contained in the "Reliquary," vol. i., pp. 5-11.

thatched building, standing within a few yards of the church, and now partially overgrown with ivy and screened by lofty spreading trees. We remember in our earlier visits the house being tenanted by an aged widow, who appeared to place implicit faith in the whole tradition. We have heard her say that she had a distinct recollection of having, in her youth, seen Little John's green cap suspended by a chain in Hathersage Church.* She also remembered his grave being opened, by order of Captain Shuttleworth, when a thigh bone, measuring 32 inches in length, was dug up. The grave is on the south side of the church, nearly opposite the porch, and is distinguished by two small upright stones, one placed at the head and the other at the foot, the intervening space being about ten feet.

Apart from the traditions attaching to it, Hathersage derives especial interest from the numerous antiquities existing in its immediate neighbourhood. On the north side of the church is an ancient earthwork called Camp Green, believed to be of Danish origin, and on the surrounding moorlands there are several rock-basins and curious remains attributed to our Celtic forefathers, the most remarkable being the Higgar Rocks, and that singular structure called "The Carl's Work."

To these we directed our steps after visiting the church and Little John's grave, following a path that leads up through a deep hollow to the east. After traversing a mile or so we come upon the open ground, where the country looks barren and deserted, and the bleak moors are seen rolling away in the distance in long dark undulating lines. Striking off upon the right we have to cross a broad swampy patch, and then labour up a craggy steep, the summit of which is crowned by the Higgar Rocks, a chaotic mass of gritstone blocks, piled confusedly together, in some places

---

* In addition to the cap, Mr. Ashmole records that in 1652 the bow of the merry outlaw's companion was suspended in the church. This has now disappeared, but a writer in the *Derbyshire Times* recently gave some particulars respecting it. He says : "It may not be generally known that the bow of Little John, the companion of Robin Hood, now hangs in Canon Hall, near Barnsley, where it has been more than a century. Previous to that time it was in Hathersage Church, Derbyshire, when it was removed by Mr. John Spencer, of Canon Hall and Hathersage, whose mother, Miss Ashton, was heiress of that property, which has descended to the present Mr. Ashton-Shuttleworth through his grandmother, Miss Spencer, the eldest co-heiress of that family."

apparently so slightly connected that you almost fear to approach, while all around the base is strewn with detached masses that have toppled down from the parent heap. The sombre mass of blackened crags standing out upon the lonely moor looks primevally wild and forbidding, and you can hardly wonder at the superstitious belief that here the Druid priests of old performed their sacrificial rights before the wild and fiery Britons.

We sat down upon the dry ling in a kind of recess, with our backs resting against the weather-beaten stone, gazing upon the barren solitude that spread around. Wherever we looked the view was bounded by an infinity of moors and mountain tops that looked impressively sterile and aboriginal —vast untrodden wastes that have retained their desolate character through centuries of revolution and change. Grand and still and almost oppressive to the eye and the ear was that lonely landscape, in which the heavens and the earth seemed to gaze upon each other in silent serenity. Now and then a predatory bird winged its way over the lone expanse, lessening and lessening slowly in the distance, but no human being could anywhere be discerned—the lonely plover's wailing cry and the wild "hech-hech" of the startled grouse being the only sounds that broke upon the silent solitude.

We sat and talked and afterwards clambered up the rocks to the summit, then we struck across the moor, picking a way as best we could through the heath and ling that spreads about, and in a few minutes reached the Carl's Work—a rude fort built upon the brow of the hill by the skin-clad warriors of old Britain, looking like an irregular mound of rough unshapen stones, with walls, fences, and enclosures, that open into one another.

We walked round the old weather-worn monument of Celtic skill, and then came down by Millstone Edge, where an extensive quarry has been opened in the gritstone measures. Great masses of rock of every conceivable shape and size lay scattered about in wild disorder, some grey with clinging lichens and others furrowed and weather-worn. The lower slopes were strewn with millstones in various stages of formation, the general wildness being in some degree relieved by a scattered growth of brambles and a few dwarf oaks that have taken root and found sustenance in the stony soil.

The view from the Edge is one of almost surpassing loveliness. On the south it commands an uninterrupted view of the valley of the Derwent, with its dark rocks and wooded hills, its deep cloughs and shady dingles, its little hamlets and scattered folds, and the river far below with its perpetual lapse flashing and glittering in the sunlight as it winds its way through the rich pastures—a scene so rich and varied, so different from the weird and wild and dusky landscape that lies in the rear. Up the valley the town of Hathersage is seen basking in the warm sunshine. Then as the eye roves across the country new beauties successively reveal themselves. Hope Dale, with its verdant meadows and picturesque undulations, comes in view, with the shadowy outline of Mam Tor forming the horizon, from which a chain of hills sweep round to where Sir William lifts his lofty brow, frowning with haughty mien upon the wooded bluffs and knolls and peaks that gather like humble vassals round. How beautiful the grey old farmsteads look, with their quaint gables and clustering chimneys, each standing in its patch of green that has been won by years of patient toil from the barren wastes around, or sheltering in sequestered hollows where the tiny brooklets go singing along through the summer sunshine with prattling glee. The woods blend their hues with the purple heather, and the brown scrubby wastes through which the naked rock occasionally protrudes, show where pasturage becomes scant, and tillage altogether impossible.

Having leisurely surveyed the extended landscape we resumed our onward course. The descent from the top of the Edge we found to be no easy task. The rock near the summit rises almost perpendicularly, and we had to step from one stony ledge to another, pausing occasionally to take breath and steady ourselves; anon struggling among scrub and brushwood and prickly briars, clinging for support wherever a branch could be found to offer its friendly aid— the difficulty being nothing lessened by the sense of danger as each now and then a loose fragment of rock would become displaced and bound down the precipitous slopes, falling with a crashing sound into the thicket below. Presently we came to sloping patches of turf where the footing is easier; then a short run brought us to the highway near where two roads

G

meet; and a few minutes later we again entered the village of Hathersage nearly at the point at which we had quitted it a few hours before.

After a brief rest we resumed our journey, Eyam being the next halting-place. From Hathersage to Eyam is a long walk, but, fortunately for the lover of the picturesque, it is an exceedingly pleasant one—the scenery along the entire way presenting a rich combination of rock and wood, and meadow and water, with hills and dales and breezy moorlands that stretch away as far as the eye can reach.

As we left Hathersage the sky, which had hitherto been bright and clear, became overcast, and a few slight showers fell, but they were only of short duration, for soon the sun sent forth his rays again in all their former strength and brilliancy. The rain was an advantage rather than otherwise, as it served to refresh the soil and cool the overheated atmosphere, giving to the turf a livelier hue and to the foliage a brighter green, so that our walk was rendered the more agreeable. At every step the signs of fertility and cultivation were manifest. Our route lay through one of those old-fashioned country lanes, with tall embowering hedges hung with ferns, foxgloves, and wild roses, and many a charming view of well-tilled fields and distant uplands did we obtain as the windings of the road brought us to wider openings between the over-arching trees that here border the path. At Hazleford Bridge we crossed the Derwent, and shortly afterwards left the high-road, following a narrow lane that skirts the edge of Leam Woods. A little way up the hill we passed a Gothic stone dwelling, bearing the euphonious name of Hog Hall. On reaching the top of the eminence we sat down awhile to rest and enjoy the pure air and healthy breeze, so refreshing in comparison with the sultry atmosphere of the road we had left behind, gazing in lazy mood upon the wide extent of country that lay stretched before us like a panorama, bounded by an interminable range of lofty hills and canopied by the soft deep blue of infinite space. As we lingered upon the summit the sound of distant bells came borne upon the breeze, and the gladsome warbling of birds and the busy hum of insects were mingled in concert with the lowing of the cattle and the bleating of the sheep in the distant meadows.

Reluctantly at length we left our seat and started on foot, taking the path that runs along the undulating slope of the hill until we came to a farmhouse near Leam Hall. It happened to be a busy time—all hands were at work, for they were leading the hay, and the farmer was anxious to get it housed before sunset, and as the work went on many an anxious look was cast at the passing clouds and the distant hills.

Directly after leaving the farm we scaled a stone fence, intending to make a short cut over the moors and drop down into Eyam. At first we made but slow progress, for there was no path, and we had to stride through the tall grass and tough ling, now sinking in the soft wet turf and now splashing through a patch of boggy swamp. As we ascended the hill the ground became less treacherous, and we were enabled to make better headway. Still, however, we had to struggle through the deep heather and tangled gorse, picking our way over masses of naked rock which here and there crop out above the surface. A few sheep were browsing on the slope, and as we passed by them a black-faced ram would now and then stand and stare at us with a defiant air, as if about to dispute our further progress. These heathery wastes abound with game, and frequently a pheasant, disturbed by the sound of our footsteps, would start from the cover with "whirring" flight, or the moor-fowl would take wing with sudden flutter, uttering their peculiar wild "clucking" cry.

The ascent was long as well as steep, and difficult withal; but amply were we repaid for the toil by the magnificent views of scenery that met the eye every time we paused to look around us. At length we gained the summit, and selecting a good resting-place beneath the shadow of a stone wall, lay down, listlessly enjoying the glory of the summer day, and thankful that we had got beyond the reach of the tormenting flies.

But how shall we describe or do justice to the scene? The air was clear, and the sun, having passed the meridian, gave breadth and shadow to the different objects in the view; while the soft blue ether above, broken only by the fleecy cirrus cloud that sent its feathery streamers across the zenith, seemed to look down upon the earth with benignant smile.

The prospect viewed from this high point is indeed a glorious one—hill and dale, mountain and moor, dark woods and flashing streams, and lofty eminences rising one above another in seemingly endless succession, stretching away upon the horizon as far as the eye can reach. Everything seems to charm by the very order of nature's disorder. Below are the woods and plantations of High-low, Leam, and Sheriff, and beyond may be traced the Derwent as it serpentines for many a mile through the vale, now hidden beneath the dark foliage with which its banks are fringed, and now flashing in the bright sunlight like a gleam of silvery light. To the left, on the opposite side of the river, can be discerned the little town of Hathersage, seated upon the mountain slope, the light tapering spire of its handsome church a conspicuous object for miles around. Carrying the eye southwards we have a succession of woods and meadows, intermingled with green slopes of pasture, and farms and cottages that nestle among the trees, looking so contented and happy, with their smiling orchards and patches of garden, giving evidence of rural comfort and prosperity. Then we have undulating eminences chequered with dark shady lanes, and intersected by winding roads that look whiter by contrast with the sombre foliage. In the distance is Padley, for generations the family seat of the Eyres; and, beyond, the picturesque group of cottages forming the little hamlet of Grindleford Bridge. The eye, following the course of the stream, passes over the village of Froggatt, and near it is Stoke Hall, embowered in woods. Turning to the right the prospect takes in the hills and plantations forming the boundary of Chatsworth Park, the old hunting tower, with its four circular turrets, rising above the woods and basking in the glorious sunlight. Eastward the scenery is in perfect contrast to the foreground, a magnificent range of hills, looking primevally wild, filling up the background, their craggy summits tossed into every variety of fantastic form and figure, like the troubled waves of a tempestuous sea. Looking across the valley, in a northerly direction, we see the moors above Hathersage, with Bore Edge, Millstone Edge, and Booth's Edge, their sloping fronts descending almost to the margin of the river. Carl's Work and Higgar loom grandly in the distance; then comes a wide expanse of rock and heather, bounded by a charming valley, through which Burbage Brook, a busy little stream, winds its sinuous course between dark waving woods; and, beyond, Froggatt Edge rears aloft its dark and rugged crest, abrupt, bold, and stern, looking more bleak and desolate by comparison with the rich and varied greenery of the foreground. Looking again towards the south the eye takes in Curbar Edge and Baslow Edge, with a succession of eminences that rise one above another until they grow dim upon the distant edge of the horizon.

How we longed to lengthen the moments into hours, as we lay among the heather dreaming of the past and thinking of the future! What strange reminiscences do these old hills awaken! Through all the varying vicissitudes of time they alone have passed unchanged! How many dynasties have they outlived! How many shall they survive? Empires and kingdoms have risen and passed away—generation after generation has come and gone, like swathes of grass before the mower's scythe. These hoary hills, "the stern and bleak companions of the mist and cloud," present a type of almost every period of our history. On these heights, far back in the mist of ages, when the hardy woad-stained Briton roamed at large among his native woods, the Druid built his altar, worshipping his gods with superstitious rites and barbarous sacrifice within those mysterious circles of stone, the rude remains of which yet exist, having through countless ages withstood the wasting hand of time;[*] and here, in later days, the followers of Augustine raised the sacred symbol of our faith, and taught our Saxon forefathers the saving truths of Christianity, giving them in exchange for their heathen paganism the gospel of love and purity and peace, with all its humanising and civilising influences.[†] On these trackless wastes the martial Roman and the predatory Dane have left indelible traces behind them. Padley

---

[*] At a place called Wet-withins, on Eyam Moor, is a Druidical circle, consisting of sixteen stones, enclosing a space about ninety feet in diameter, in the centre of which there existed, until within a recent period, a large upright stone.

[†] The beautiful Runic cross now standing in Eyam churchyard is said to have been found upon these moors.

reminds us of the Norman barons and the days of chivalry ; and yonder wood-crowned hill, that overlooks " the princely Vernon's banner'd hall," carries the mind back to the days of the " King of the Peak," and the rude abundance and lavish hospitality of " Merrie England " in a feudal age ; while there, reposing in the soft and mellow sunlight, the fair and stately hall of Chatsworth gives us a picture of life in the present day, with all the comfort, the elegance, and the refinement, that wealth and ingenuity and art, aided by the most consummate taste, can supply, presenting a strange contrast to the roystering revelry which characterised the social existence of our forefathers.

The age of feudalism, with all its prejudices and cruelties— when men ruled by the stern will and the strong arm—has for ever passed away ; but amid the bigotry and intolerance that overclouded it there were frequent flashes of glorious heroism, and no lack of brave hearts and noble minds. Although there is much that we must deprecate and condemn there is also much that is morally good and dear and honoured to our every feeling of existence. While we rejoice that our lot is cast amid happier days, we look back with fond affection to the past, and delight to dwell upon the memories of those great and glorious spirits whose noble acts and illustrious deeds have elevated England to the position she occupies among the nations of the earth. It is the many time-stained memorials of the past which bestrew the soil—the foot-prints of time evidencing the mighty changes that have been wrought and the onward progress of our land, and on which the nation's history is written in characters imperishable—that perhaps, more than anything else, tend to cause and strengthen the love of country so deeply implanted in the breast of every Englishman.

The lengthening shadows reminded us that it was time to depart, for we had yet much ground to get over before the day closed; and, not without regret, we turned our backs upon the charming prospect.

At the further extremity of the moor we passed through a gate and crossed the road from Great Hucklow to Grindleford Bridge, called Sir William Road, taking the path that leads by the Lady Wash Lead Mine, then

winding round a deep hollow planted with shrubs and
trees, beyond which the view opens upon the grassy slopes
and undulations in the neighbourhood of Stoney Middleton ;
here we turned to the right, following a rough and broken
road that descends abruptly, and in a few minutes reached
the village of Eyam, just as the church clock chimed the
hour of six.

# CHAPTER VI.

EYAM is one of the most interesting places in Derbyshire—
interesting from its antiquity, the beauty of its situation, as
the birth-place and abode of genius, and, more than all, from
the melancholy associations connected with it.

It occupies an elevated position on the declivity of a hill,
part of a range that extends westward from Bradwell Edge
to the Valley of the Derwent, overlooking the romantic dale
of Middleton, with which it is connected by two precipitous
openings, called Eyam Dale and the Delf, or Cucklet Dell, of
which latter we shall have more to say by-and-by. On the
north side it is screened by a lofty eminence called Eyam
Edge, partially covered with rich green turf, and crowned
with plantations of larch and fir.

It is, take it altogether, a pretty-looking little mountain
village, consisting of one long straggling lane or street, with
dwellings of somewhat primitive aspect bordering either side,
and a few groups of cottages, with a scattered homestead or
two perched picturesquely upon the summit and upon pleasant
ledges of the mountain slope, whilst prominent over all the
pinnacled tower of its ancient church is seen peeping above
the spreading limes that encircle it, imparting an air of
importance and respectability to the scene.

Like most villages in the Peak the houses are built of
stone, and, although humble, are generally clean, and have a
comfortable and cheerful appearance. The inhabitants are
employed chiefly in lead mining—a branch of industry that
has been carried on here from the time of the Romans. Silk

weaving is also followed to some extent, and the cheerful song, mingling with the "clack" of the loom, we heard repeatedly as we passed through the village.

Eyam owes its celebrity to the melancholy circumstance of its having been almost depopulated by the plague, in 1666, and the more than Roman fortitude and self-sacrifice then exhibited by its pastor amidst scenes of unexampled suffering and woe.

Towards the end of the month of November, 1664, the plague, which had previously been ravaging the continent of Europe, made its appearance in London. As the winter of that year had passed over without any striking variation in the bills of mortality, it was hoped that the disease might have become exhausted; but those hopes were soon dispelled, for with the return of summer it again manifested itself, and continued with increasing fatality throughout the season. For a time the distemper was confined to the metropolis and its immediate vicinity, but it gradually extended into the country, and in the month of July, 1665, broke out in this unfortunate village.

The circumstance of its introduction to Eyam is related by Dr. Mead, in his " Narrative of the Great Plague in London," and by other writers. The infection, it is said, was conveyed in a box containing clothes and tailors' patterns sent from London. A journeyman named Vicars, who opened the box, was seized with violent sickness; the neck and other parts of his body became swollen, and soon the character of the disease revealed itself by that fatal token, the plague-spot, appearing upon his breast. This was the first person who fell a victim. "The whole of the family, with the solitary exception of one, shared the same fate. The disease spread rapidly, and almost every house was thinned by the contagion. The same roof, in many instances, sheltered at the same time both the dying and the dead. Short indeed was the space between health and sickness, and immediate the transition from the death-bed to the tomb. Wherever symptoms of the plague appeared, so hopeless was recovery that the dissolution of the afflicted patient was watched with anxious solicitude, that so much of the disease might be buried and its fatal influence destroyed. In the churchyard, on the neighbouring hills, and in the fields bordering the village, graves were dug ready to receive the expiring sufferers, and the earth, with an unhallowed haste, was closed upon them even whilst the limbs were yet warm, and almost palpitating with life."*

Some idea of the virulence of the disease may be formed from the fact that out of a population of about 350, 260 fell victims, being nearly four-fifths of the inhabitants.

The Rev. William Mompesson, who at the time held the living of Eyam, was the means, under Providence, not only of alleviating the agonies of those who suffered from the disease, but also by his prudence and forethought was mainly instrumental in preventing the contagion speading into the surrounding country. Like a faithful pastor he determined to remain in the midst of his people, and, with Christian fortitude and resignation, share with them the danger of the pestilence. He endeavoured, as far as was possible, to confine the disease within the limits of his own village, knowing that were the inhabitants instinctively to flee to the surrounding country they must of necessity carry the seeds of death with them. With a desire to devote himself alone to the hazardous service he urged upon his wife, then only in her twenty-seventh year, the necessity of seeking a temporary home for the safety of herself and their two children; but he addressed a spirit as noble and devoted as his own. She resolutely refused to leave him—he with whom she had sworn to live, and to love and cherish "until death do part," she would not desert in the hour of trial. The children were sent to a distance, but she heroically remained, preferring to share with her husband the painful duties of his office.

Summoning his parishioners Mompesson announced to them his determination to remain faithful at his post, showing them the consequence of fleeing from their homes, and of communicating to others the malady which was then sweeping those around them into the grave, and the little probability of escaping the contagion by flight. His resolution and Christian devotion elevated the hopes of his flock, and his example, the love he was held in, and the influence he possessed over the minds of his people, induced them to adopt and cheerfully carry out those salutary measures which he propounded.

* Rhodes.

His first step was to write to the Earl of Devonshire, then staying at Chatsworth, acquainting him with his intention and asking for assistance, pledging himself that if supplies of food and other things necessary to mitigate the horrors of the disease were daily deposited in certain places indicated, not a single inhabitant would transgress the boundary. The earl entered cordially into the views of the rector, and, undeterred by the fear of contagion, remained at Chatsworth during the whole time the plague raged, superintending the supply, and by his influence and example assisting Mr. Mompesson in his benevolent work.

From this time Eyam, with its little community of sufferers, was cut off from the outer world, none attempting to pass beyond the limits prescribed. With a view to prevent, as far as possible, the spread of the distemper, pest-houses were opened in the village, and there the dying and the dead were huddled together in horrible confusion. Provisions were left at stated spots along the boundary line of communication, where troughs or reservoirs of water were placed to receive and purify the money deposited in exchange. A small stream that supplied these reservoirs is pointed out by the villagers, which still bears the hallowed name of Mompesson's Brook.

The malady continued throughout the winter, and when summer again came round its virulence only increased. Feeling more than ever the necessity of spiritual advice and consolation, and yet fearing that the assemblage of a number of persons under a confined roof would only be to woo the embraces of death, Mompesson determined upon closing the church, and collecting the scattered remnant of his flock in the Delf, a narrow romantic dell lying between the village and Middleton Dale; on the west side of this dell, on a steep acclivity, is an opening fashioned by nature in the face of the rock, and from beneath this rude archway, Sunday after Sunday, and thrice during the week, did this good and faithful man administer the simple services of the Church, addressing words of comfort and religious consolation to his fear-stricken parishioners, enforcing upon them the obligation of obedience and Christian resignation to the affliction with which a Divine Providence was then visiting them. The place is still venerated by the inhabitants, and is known by the name of Cucklet Church and the Pulpit Rock.

> " Contagion closed the portal of the fane
> In which he wont the bread of life to deal ;
> He then a temple sought, not made with hands,
> But reared by Him amidst whose works it stood
> Rudely magnificent."

As the summer advanced the plague became still more fatal in its ravages. As yet, the pastor's house had been mercifully preserved, but the time was at hand when one was to be taken and the other left—when his home was to be visited by the angel of death, and his hearth made desolate. In the second week of the month of August his noble-minded wife was stricken with the pestilence, and fell a victim to her own disinterestedness and self-devotion. His anguish under this sad bereavement appears to have been of the most poignant character, and it will hardly be expected that under so severe a trial his fortitude should have remained unshaken. As it has been truly remarked, " he did his duty like a man, but he also suffered like a man." It would seem that even the hope of his own life now failed him. His letters written at this time are among the most simple and affecting compositions in our language. That to his children announcing the death of their mother is peculiarly touching. In a letter addressed to Sir George Saville, then patron of the living of Eyam, dated 1st September, 1666, he says : " This is the saddest news that ever my pen could write. The destroying angel having taken up his quarters within my habitation, my dearest wife is gone to her eternal rest, and is invested with a crown of righteousness, having made a happy end. Indeed, had she loved herself as well as me, she had fled from the pit of destruction with the sweet babes, and might have prolonged her days ; but she resolved to die a martyr to my interest. My drooping spirits are much refreshed with her joys, which, I think, are unutterable." " Sir," he afterwards writes, " I have made bold in my will with your name as executor, and I hope that you will not take it ill. I have joined two others with you, who will take from you the trouble. Your favourable aspect will, I know, be a great comfort to my distressed orphans. I am not desirous that they should be great, but good; and my next request is that they be brought up in the fear and admonition of the Lord" "Dear sir," he concludes, "I beg the prayers of all about you, that I may not be daunted by the powers of hell, and that I may have dying graces. With tears I beg that when you are praying for fatherless orphans you will remember my two pretty babes."

August appears to have been the most fatal month, the number who then fell victims being 78—nearly one-third of the entire population. From this time the disease began to abate, and in October it had entirely ceased. In a letter dated the 20th November, 1666, addressed to John Beilby, Esq., Mr. Mompesson says : "The condition of this place has been so sad that I persuade myself it did exceed all history and example. I may truly say that our place has been a Golgotha—the place of a skull; and had there not been a small remnant of us left, 'we had been as Sodom, and been like unto Gomorrah.' My ears never heard such doleful lamentations, and my eyes never beheld such ghastly spectacles. Now, blessed be God, all our fears are over, for none have died of the infection since the 11th of October, and all the pest-houses have been long empty."

It was not to be expected that such self-devotion as that exhibited by Mr. Mompesson would pass unrecognised. His noble disinterestedness procured for him many friends, and, had he been at all desirous, the highest ecclesiastical preferment might have been attained. He was shortly afterwards presented to the rectory of Eakring, but such was the terror felt by the inhabitants of that place, after the terrible scourge at Eyam, that they dreaded his coming amongst them, and a hut had to be erected at Rufford Park, where he remained until all fear had subsided. He afterwards obtained the prebends of York and Southwell, and, subsequently, the deanery of Lincoln was offered to him ; but that he generously declined in favour of his friend Dr. Fuller. He died in 1708.

It has been well remarked by a writer, from whose work we have already quoted, that "a fervent piety, a humble resignation, a spirit that, under circumstances peculiarly affecting, could sincerely say, 'not my will, but thine be done,' a manly fortitude, and a friendly generosity of heart, were blended together in the character of Mompesson."*

During the whole of this trying period Mr. Mompesson was ably seconded in his benevolent and self-denying labours by the Rev. Thomas Stanley, a Nonconformist minister then residing at Eyam.

Eyam, the Athens of the Peak, as it has been called, has long been celebrated as the abode of talent. The Rev. Thomas Seward, who succeeded Mr. Bruce in the rectory of Eyam, was the author of several poems printed in Dodsley's Collection. He also published an edition of Beaumont and Fletcher's plays, and a treatise on the conformity between the Pagan and Romish Churches. His daughter, Anna Seward, the intimate friend and contemporary of Dr. Darwin, Lovell Edgeworth, and Thomas Day, the eccentric and accomplished author of Sandford and Merton, was born at Eyam in 1742, and at an unusually early age evinced a strong poetical tendency. Her writings are remarkable for their chasteness and purity of style. In 1782 she published her poetical novel, "Louisa," which met with immense success, and rapidly exhausted three or four editions. In 1799 she gave to the world a collection of "Sonnets," intended to "restore the strict rules of legitimate sonnet." In 1804 she published the life of her friend, Dr. Darwin, in which she lays claim to the authorship of the first fifty lines of the "Botanic Garden." After her death, which occurred in 1809, Sir Walter Scott, to whom she had bequeathed her literary productions (including the works she had herself intended for the press), issued an edition of her poems and three volumes of literary correspondence, with a biographical preface; and about the same time Mr. Constable published her "Letters" in six closely printed octavo volumes.

The Rev. Peter Cunningham, who held the curacy under Mr. Seward, and afterwards, on that gentleman's preferment to the canonry of Lichfield, became the rector, was a man gifted with a refined poetic taste. He spent the greater part of his life at Eyam, and it was here he wrote his "Chatsworth," "Russian Prophecy," and "Naval Triumphs," poems possessing considerable literary merit.

* Rhodes's Peak Scenery.

Richard Furness, a native of Eyam, and a self-educated man, was distinguished for his literary genius and poetic power. For many years he held the appointments of master of the Free School and vestry and parish clerk of Dore, a little village about six miles from Hathersage, on the confines of the county. His writings contain many passages of considerable beauty and poetic excellence, and his descriptions are vigorous and life-like. Throughout there is evidence of a strong independence of thought, and an abhorrence of everything like oppression. His first production, and that most favourably known, was a satire in three cantos, entitled the "Rag Bag." This he published in 1832; and four years afterwards he issued his "Astrologer," a work of somewhat inferior merit. He was also an occasional contributor to the "Poet's Corner" of the *Sheffield Iris* during the time that paper was under the management of Montgomery, the poet. He died December 13th, 1857, and was interred in Eyam churchyard. After his death his miscellaneous poems, with the "Rag Bag" and "Astrologer," were published in a collected form, under the editorship of Dr. G. Calvert Holland, to which was prefixed a biographical sketch of the author.

Among the writers and poets who have conferred such classic pre-eminence on this lowly mountain village we must not omit the name of its historian, William Wood. Of humble parentage, Mr. Wood, by his own unaided efforts, acquired for himself considerable reputation as an author, and secured the friendship of many literary friends. He first became known as a writer by the publication, in 1837, of an unpretending little volume entitled, "The Genius of the Peak, and other Poems." Five years later he gave to the world his "History of Eyam," with a particular account of the Great Plague—a work which has already gone through four editions, and by which his name will be best remembered. In 1862 he published his "Tales and Traditions of the High Peak," and besides these, his more important works, he was a frequent contributor to the pages of the *Reliquary*, his papers being all characterised by patient research, and evidencing a vigorous and intelligent mind. Mr. Wood died on the 27th June, 1865, in his 61st year, and he now rests within the church-yard of Eyam, where a monument has been erected by his neighbours and friends to mark their appreciation of his virtues and intellectual worth.

On entering the village of Eyam we ordered tea at a small public-house, and, whilst it was being prepared, made a short pilgrimage to the Riley graves. Leaving the high road we struck off to the left, following an ascending path that leads through a plantation, until we came to an eminence over-looking the village, called Riley Side. This, at the time the plague was depopulating Eyam, was the burial-place of the Hancock family, who then resided at a house near the top of the hill. The graves are situated in the middle of a cultivated field, and surrounded by a low stone fence. In this humble enclosure there are six headstones and one square tomb, recording the last resting-place of an entire family who, with one exception, were swept away by the plague. The inscriptions, though much worn, may yet be traced. On the tomb which contains the ashes of the father of this family of sufferers are the words—

> " Here lies buried the body of
> John Hancock, Gent.,
> Who died Aug. 7, 1666.
> Remember, man, as thou go'st by,
> As thou art now, even so was I.
> As I lie now, so thou must lie :
> Remember, man, that thou shalt die."

On the four sides of the tomb are the words, " *Horam,*"
" *Nescites,*" " *Orate,*" and " *Vigilate.*" The several headstones
are inscribed as follows :—

> " John Hancocke, jun., bur. Aug. 2nd, 1666."
> " Mary Hancocke, bur. Aug. 3rd, 1666."
> " Oner Hancocke, bur. Aug. 7th, 1666."
> " William Hancocke, bur. Aug. 7th, 1666."
> " Alice Hancocke, bur. Aug. 9th, 1666."
> " Ann Hancocke, bur. Aug. 10th, 1666."

What a saddening picture do these stones present. The
words are, indeed, few—but what an amount of human
suffering and woe do they imply ! Within a period of eight
days seven persons in one family swept away in the full
vigour of the spring-tide of life ! *
But little respect appears to be paid by the inhabitants to
these sad memorials. They are now overgrown with nettles
and weeds, and, with an unpardonable indecency, the wall
which surrounded them has been broken down, and in this
neglected state they have been permitted to remain for
years. The timely expenditure of a few shillings would have
preserved for generations to come these sepulchral mementos
of one of the most mournful episodes in connection with the
desolation of Eyam.†
Within the last twenty years many similar memorials of
dissolution were to be seen in the fields and on the hillsides
in the immediate vicinity of the village, but they are fast
disappearing. Some have been destroyed, and others, with an
unseemly indifference, have been appropriated to baser uses.
After tea we visited the church, which stands near the
centre of the village, surrounded by a row of fine old stately
limes that look almost as venerable as the fabric itself. It
is an ancient structure, in that peculiar style of architecture
which it would puzzle an antiquary to define—a kind of
Gothic-composite, if we may so term it, containing a little of
every style that has prevailed from the time of the second
Henry down to the golden days of the " Virgin Queen "—

---

\* A descendant of this family, Mr. Joseph Hancock, was the originator, in
1750, of the art of plating copper with silver, which he practised at Sheffield, and
which gave " Sheffield plate " an European celebrity, and the town employment
and wealth ever since.

† The repairs here suggested have since been effected.

H

addition upon addition, and repairs upon repairs, without any attempt at uniformity of outline. The north aisle appears to be the most ancient part of the building, and probably dates as far back as the twelfth century ; the south aisle is some four centuries later. The chancel, now overgrown with ivy, and the tower, were rebuilt about the year 1600—the latter at the expense of a maiden lady of the name of Stafford, and the same munificent individual gave the bells. The principal entrance is on the south side, over the doorway of which is a complex sundial, on which the parallel of the sun's declination for every month in the year, a scale of the sun's meridian altitude, an azimuthal scale, the points of the compass, and a number of meridians, are delineated.

The interior is sadly disfigured by low projecting galleries and high-backed pews, but there are some details we should have been glad to have examined more at leisure. At the east end of the north aisle we noticed an ancient piscina, and near to it an oblique aperture or narrow opening in the pillar, through which in times past the people assembled in the aisle were enabled to see the elevation of the host at the high altar. There is also an ancient stone font, some curiously carved bosses, fragments of stained glass, and other objects of interest. An effort is now being made to raise sufficient funds to carry out the much required work of restoring and enlarging the ancient village church, and in this way it is proposed to commemorate the bi-centenary of the " Mighty Woe " of Eyam.*

On the south side of the churchyard, near the entrance

* Since this was written the work of restoration has been effected, and with such good taste that it would be difficult to meet with a church in better order throughout. The north aisle has been entirely rebuilt and enlarged, and the columns and archways of the nave have been renewed. The heavy galleries have been removed, and the unsightly box-like pews have also disappeared, their place being supplied with open benches of pitch pine. The floors have been laid with tiles, and the triplet lancet window which lights the chancel has been enriched with stained glass, the subjects being illustrative of the Passion and Death of the Saviour, and erected, as the inscription testifies, by Charles Gregory, of Hampstead, in memory of his wife, a native of Eyam. A brass affixed to the wall of the north aisle bears the following inscription : "This Memorial Aisle was erected by voluntary contributions obtained in 1866 to commemorate the Christian and heroic virtues of the Rev. Wm. Mompesson (rector), Catherine, his wife, and the Rev. W. Stanley (late rector). When this place was visited by the plague in 1665-6 they steadfastly continued to succour the afflicted and to minister among them the truth and consolations of the Gospel of Jesus Christ." The rebuilding and enlarging of the aisle led to the restoration of almost the entire church in 1868-9, at a cost of £2,160.

to the chancel, is an ancient Runic or Scandinavian cross. This relic of antiquity is supposed to be of early Saxon origin, and to be nearly one thousand years old. The face and back are carved with curiously interlaced knots; on the arms are figures of angels with trumpets and other symbolic devices; and in the centre a representation of the Virgin and Child. In style and appearance it bears a strong resemblance to the cross at Bakewell, but it is superior in form, and the carvings are more elaborate. This relic of early Christianity has suffered from time and neglect. It was originally some ten feet in length, but about two feet of the upper portion of the shaft has been broken off and destroyed. Of its early history but little is known. A tradition prevails that it was found on one of the neighbouring hills. For a considerable period it lay in a corner of the churchyard, nearly overgrown with weeds. From this state of degradation it was rescued and set up on the spot where it now stands, when the upper part of the cross was replaced upon the imperfect shaft.

RUNIC CROSS, EYAM.

Within a few feet of the old cross is the tomb of Mrs. Mompesson, nearly hidden among rank weeds and nettles. On one end is sculptured a winged hour-glass, and the inscription, "*Cavete, nescitis, horam;*" and on the other a death's head, and the words, "*Mors mihi lucrum.*" On the top slab is the following inscription :—

> CATHERINA VXOR
> GVLIELMI MOMPESSON
> HVIVS ECCLESIÆ RECTS.
> FILIA RADVLPHI CARR
> NVPER DE COCKEN IN
> COMITATV DVNELMENSIS
> ARMIGERI
> SEPVLTA VICESSIMO
> QVINTO DIE MENSIS AVGTI
> ANO. DNI. 1666.

At each corner of the tomb is placed a small stone pillar, chamfered at the edge.

Near the north-west corner of the churchyard, beneath the shadow of a wide-spreading lime, a monument records the last resting-place of Richard Furness. The spot is alluded to in the concluding canto of his poem, "The Rag Bag:"

> "Near those tall elms, in that sequestered spot,
>  There all these rags in quietness shall rot,
>  With their poor bard, who never sung for fame
>  (Since rags, and shrouds, and mortals are the same)."

The monument consists of a plain square plinth, resting upon a basement, and surmounted by a sculptured urn. On the face is this inscription :—

> "Richard Furness.
> Born at Eyam, August 2nd, 1791 ;
> Died at Dore, Dec. 13th, 1857.

> Land of my fathers ! how I love to dwell
>   On all thy scenery !  Barren as thou art,
> Still hast thou genuine charms, or some sweet spell
>   That binds thy beauties to my ravished heart ;
> That spell will never break, till death's sure dart
>   Shall reckless strike this penetrable crust.
> And oh ! 'tis sweet to think my baser part
>   Shall then be mingled with my mountain dust ;
>   Rocks, hills, my monument to be—no chiselled bust.

"This monument, originally erected by the poet to the memory of his wife, was elevated and enclosed by numerous attached friends, in order that they might record their high opinion of the genius of the poet, and worth of the man, whose remains rest here."

The lines are taken from one of his poems, entitled, " The Tomb of the Valley."

On the same side of the churchyard a monument has been erected over the remains of William Wood, the historian of Eyam, on the front of which is the following inscription :—

In
Memory of
William Wood,
Who died June 27th, 1865,
Aged 60 years ;
Author of the " History and Antiquities of Eyam,"
" Tales and Traditions of the Peak," &c., &c.

Men but like visions are,
Time all doth claim ;
He lives who dies and
Leaves a lasting name.

The obverse side of the monument is inscribed as follows :—

This monument was
erected by his neighbours and friends to
record their high opinion of his upright and faithful character,
and their admiration of his genius and
literary attainments.

Eyam is rich in churchyard literature, few places possessing so many or such a variety of epitaphs as are here to be met with. Some convey serious lessons of mortality, and others are remarkable for their quaint and simple pathos. We select the following as an example of the better class. It is believed to be from the pen of the Rev. Mr. Cunningham, and is inscribed on the tomb of a youth of the name of Froggatt :—

" How eloquent the monumental stone
Where blooming modest virtues prostrate lie,
Where pure religion from her hallow'd throne
Tells man it is an awful thing to die.
Is happiness thy aim ? or death thy fear ?
Learn how their path with glory may be trod,
From the lamented youth who slumbers here,
Who gave the glory of his youth to God."

The bump of veneration would appear to be not over-prominently developed in the good people of Eyam, if we may judge from the state in which the churchyard is permitted to remain. In most country villages we find that, though even the church itself may sometimes be neglected, there is yet an affectionate regard and loving care shown for the place which contains the ashes of departed relatives or dear friends. In Eyam, however, no such simple homage is paid to the depository of the dead. The graveyard is in a state of disorder, affording evidences of heedless indifference and unseemly disrespect enough to " sear the eye and grieve the heart." The little mounds of earth, where sleep "the rude forefathers of the hamlet," are overgrown with docks and nettles ; the tombs are broken and dislocated ; and the very headstones, leaning in every direction, appear as if about to sink into the graves of those they commemorate. We could not help contrasting the indifference exhibited by the inhabitants to that feeling so beautifully expressed in the following lines :—

" Encircled by trees, in the Sabbath's calm smile,
    The church of our fathers, how meekly it stands !
O villagers, gaze on the old hallow'd pile—
    It was dear to their hearts, it was raised by their hands !
Who loves not the place where they worshipped their God ?
    Who loves not the ground where their ashes repose ?
Dear even the daisy that blooms on the sod,
    For dear is the dust out of which it arose."

On leaving the churchyard we saw a number of miners congregated at a corner of the road, discussing the affairs of the State amidst the obscuring clouds of tobacco-smoke. We inquired of one of them the most direct way to Cucklet Church. After some hesitation he exclaimed, as if suddenly recollecting himself, " Oh, why, yo mean't Delf ; yo mun go forrard and past are hoise, an' o'er th' steel (stile), an' across th' fields, an' yul be theere directly." We thanked him kindly for the information, though we must confess that to us it was not very intelligible.

Taking the direction indicated we crossed a stile, and followed a narrow footpath that leads through the fields. After proceeding some distance, and when, as we thought, we were about to enter the Delf, we found ourselves unexpectedly upon the verge of a precipitous rock overlooking Middleton

Dale, and some 300 feet above the roadway. The place is one commanding a fine view of the dale, and at another time and with more daylight, we should have enjoyed the prospect ; but it was now getting late, and the night was rapidly closing upon us. To attempt a descent was out of the question, so we had no alternative but to retrace our steps. After wandering about for some time we came upon the Pulpit Rock, almost hidden among the dark umbrageous foliage that surrounds it. Here we found a number of sheep congregated, which, at our approach, beat a hasty retreat, the noise, as they scampered through the bracken and underwood, disturbing a colony of rooks who had taken up their abode for the night, and who expressed their disapproval of the intrusion by a loud and incessant cawing—the noise of the birds and the bleating of the sheep producing a concert certainly not of the most harmonious character. From the Pulpit Rock a steep and difficult descent brought us to the bottom of the valley.

The Delf, or Cucklet Dell, by which latter name it is more familiarly known to tourists, has become almost classic ground, from the circumstance, as already stated, of its having been selected by Mr. Mompesson as the place where to assemble his parishioners at the time the plague was devastating Eyam ; and assuredly a spot better fitted by nature for the hallowed purpose could hardly be conceived. It is a deep secluded dell, formed by a cleft in the limestone, which descends from the village towards Middleton Dale, and from its romantic and fertile beauty presents an admirable contrast to the grim and savage character of the scenery in the adjoining dale. The sides are clothed with the softest turf, from which here and there jut out grey masses of rock, all mottled and chequered with mosses, lichens, and wild flowers. On each side the grassy acclivities are adorned with a thick growth of underwood, brambles, and wild roses, from amid which rise the tall stems of the stately ash and the pensile birch, their light and graceful verdure mingling with the more sombre foliage of the oak and the elm. Near the north end is a chasm in the rock, called the Salt Pan, from which issues a small crystalline stream that trickles along the bed of the valley, finding an

outlet at the opposite extremity.  On the west side, and about
midway down the dell, is the Pulpit Rock, now overgrown
with ivy, and nearly obscured with shrubs and trees—a bold
limestone crag jutting out from the parent mass, and rising
almost perpendicularly to a considerable altitude.  Near the
top is a singularly-formed archway, naturally excavated in
the rock, from which during the visitation of the plague the
good pastor of Eyam was wont to address the words of life
and hope to his suffering flock, seated upon the opposite slope,
at distances a yard apart from each other.  The place is
admirably adapted for the purpose, being sufficiently high to
command a view of the entire length of the valley, whilst
the covered archway would serve to concentrate and throw
forth his voice to his hearers opposite.

It is impossible to conceive a scene more deeply affecting
or more solemnly impressive than that of this good and holy
man in the discharge of the sacred duties of his office,

CUCKLET DELL.

administering the consolations of religion to his afflicted parishioners, who, cut off from all communion with the outer world, had in their solitude become familiarised with death in its most harrowing and repulsive form.

We conclude our notice of Eyam and its mournful history with the following lines, from the pen of Mr. E. Rhodes, the accomplished author of " Peak Scenery :"

> " In a deep dell, with pendant ash trees crowned,
> Where wild-briar roses creep along the ground—
> Where rock and mossy verdure intervene,
> And the tall elm, and hazel freshly green,
> And the dark yew, their varied tints unite,
> Rich with the gay vicissitudes of light—
> There, a rude arch, not formed by mortal hands,
> The unconsecrated Church of Cucklet stands.
> To this sequestered spot, where all might seem
> The sweet creation of a poet's dream,
> Mompesson saw his suffering flock repair,
> Duly as tolled the Sabbath bell for prayer.
> When through th' afflicted village, wild with dread
> And lost to hope, the plague contagion spread,
> There, from a rocky arch with foliage hung,
> Divinest precepts issued from his tongue.
> To all his kindly aid the priest affords—
> They feel his love, and live upon his words :
> The soothing words, the heavenly truths he spoke,
> In every breast divine emotions woke.
> He taught that suffering was our lot below,
> And how religion mitigates the blow—
> Points the bright path, by pilgrim footsteps trod,
> That leads the pure in heart to rest with God—
> Assures the contrite soul, the feeble cheers,
> Reanimates their hopes and calms their fears—
> Strives to estrange the heart from earthly ties,
> And fix its hopes of bliss beyond the skies,
> Where sin ne'er enters, and where sorrows cease :
> They hear, and to their homes return in peace."

We had some trouble in finding our way into Cucklet Dell, and we had no less difficulty in making our way out of it again. Near the further end the valley is covered with nettles of the most luxurious growth, and through these we had to struggle, at times nearly breast deep. At length we reached the termination of the dell, and scaling a stone wall came upon the highroad that runs through Middleton Dale. Our troubles, however, were not yet at an end. The darkness had come upon us, and we were in uncertainty as to which direction to take, whether to turn to the right or to the left. We climbed up to look at a neighbouring guide-post in the hope of thus obtaining information, but the old weather-beaten friend of the traveller had lost a wing, and was therefore mute to our inquiries. With the aid of a lighted match, a piece of paper, and the Ordnance Map (a companion which, by the way, no tourist ought ever to be without), we managed to solve the problem, and turning to the left proceeded down the dale.

From the Delf to Stoney Middleton the distance is only about a mile, but the scenery along the road is eminently picturesque, and for wildness and stern grandeur is hardly equalled in the Peak. When we started the light of day was gone, and the soft twilight of a summer eve was rapidly deepening into gloom, the last golden streaks that lingered in the western heavens had disappeared, and the shrouding shadows of night were gathering thick and fast around. A few stars gemmed the firmament, and night's fair queen, now

" Riding near her highest noon,"

shed a soft and silvery lustre, lighting with delicate touches the fringe of foliage upon the rocks, and faintly illuminating the distance, casting the while broad shadows across the deep recesses of the dale that gave vastness and immensity to the scene. Now and then a few flying clouds swept across the heavens, shrouding the moon from view and creating a dim obscurity through which we could faintly trace the rugged forms of the half-concealed mountains. The sudden gleams of weird light added to the savage grandeur of the scene, and gave to it an air of romantic beauty which the most brilliant sunshine would have failed to create.

The rocky chasm through which winds the road from Tideswell to Stoney Middleton has evidently, at a remote period, been rent asunder by some convulsive effort of nature. On the left hand side of the dale rugged and weather-beaten crags, abrupt and vast, rise to the height of 300 or 400 feet, their cold grey colour agreeably harmonising with the mosses and lichens that chequer their channelled sides. The lower part, in some places, is partially covered with brushwood, mountain ash, and other hardy trees; but the upper portion is one solid and compact mass of naked perpendicular rock, the horizontal lines marking the different strata being clearly defined, presenting the appearance of having been laid on in successive layers. At the entrance to Eyam Dale is a little public-house called the *Golden Ball*, beyond which, on the same side, is a huge pile of limestone, rising tier on tier to an immense altitude, called the Castle Rock, the craggy pinnacles and regular bastion-like projections which hang lowering over the base, giving it the appearance of some ancient castellated building. Lower down the dale is the celebrated Lover's Leap, a rocky cliff that rears its bold and naked front almost perpendicularly to an immense elevation, and from the summit of which it is said that, about the year 1760, a love-stricken damsel, of the name of Baddeley, finding that her affections were not returned by a youth to whom she was fondly attached, threw herself into the chasm below, and, incredible as it may appear, sustained but little injury from her rash attempt at self-destruction.

The opposite side of the dale is less precipitous, and the shrubs that cover its sloping sides present an agreeable contrast to the whitened fronts of the neighbouring rocks. Along the side of the road a series of limekilns have been erected, from which the smoke issues, curling fantastically about the rocks in light blue vapoury clouds, and adds greatly to the effect of the wild scenery around.

As we wended our way through the gloom the stillness was suddenly broken in upon by the creaking of wheels and the clattering of hoofs—sounds that echoed with strange effect in the dreamy silence. A farmer's cart was returning from some neighbouring market, and the driver was singing blithely as he went along. He passed us with a cheery " Good night," and then, resuming the burden of his song, disappeared in the shadowy darkness. Close to the entrance to the village of Stoney Middleton is the *Moon Inn*, unpretending, but clean and comfortable, with good fare and moderate charges, where, weary and fatigued, we took up our quarters for the night, and soon afterwards retired to rest.

# CHAPTER VII.

SOUNDLY did we sleep beneath the shadow of the *Moon*.
The morning dawned with a grey and hazy appearance,
giving promise of a glorious day. We had a short stroll
before breakfast, intending to explore the immediate locality,
and take a daylight survey of the wild and romantic dale
through which we had passed the previous evening. The
air was deliciously cool, and the dewdrops sparkled upon the
grass, and upon every leaf and flower. The time, however,
was not the most favourable for our purpose—the atmosphere
was too thick to admit of an extended prospect being obtained,
and the misty exhalations that ascended from the earth
lingered about the summits of the rocks, hiding their more
elevated peaks from view.

Stoney Middleton wears quite an air of bustling importance. There are a goodly number of shops in the place, a
respectable roadside inn, two or three public-houses, a church,
one or two dissenting chapels, and, of course, that establishment so essential to every country town—the blacksmith's
forge. It is a singularly quaint and picturesque looking
village, built as if with studied irregularity. The inhabitants
are chiefly miners and people employed at the neighbouring
limekilns, and their cottages are erected along the side of
the dale, and above one another up the steep acclivities
of the rock, sometimes standing upon the shelving ledges
of limestone, and frequently placed on the most seemingly
inaccessible and out-of-the-way spots, where approach would
be deemed almost impossible—hanging upon the abrupt hill

sides like martins' nests against a wall, with their whitewashed gables gleaming in the sunshine. The church, a comparatively modern erection—having been rebuilt about a century ago—stands near the eastern end of the village. It is an octagonal building, in the Grecian style, with a square tower on the north side. Within a short distance of the church are the tepid baths, dedicated to St. Martin, which are said to have been established at the time the Romans were occupiers of the soil. The temperature of these springs is 70°, or two degrees higher than those at Matlock. A little stream that takes its rise among the neighbouring hills, after running the length of the dale, flows through the village. In one place an archway has been thrown across, on which stands a discarded Gothic tollgate house.

After breakfast we started on our excursion to Chatsworth. Almost the first house that meets the eye after leaving the village is Middleton Hall, a gabled stone building, the seat of Lord Denman, standing within a short distance of the road, on the left hand side. This place was formerly the parsonage, but afterwards became the residence of Dr. Denman, one of the Court physicians of George III., and father of the late Lord Chief Justice of that name. It was enlarged and greatly improved by the late Lord Denman, who generally passed his legal vacations, and principally resided here after his retirement from the Bench.

As we descend into the valley of the Derwent, the country loses much of its wild and rugged character, and assumes at every step a more rich and fertile appearance. The huge precipitous rocks that bound the road at the upper end of the dale now give place to low stone walls and patches of hedgerow; beyond which the view is made up of broad smiling meadows, woods, and plantations, and acres of cultivated verdure; whilst, through the interlacings of the trees, pleasant glimpses are obtained of the blue uplands that stretch away in the far distance.

Presently we meet a long train of carts returning from the limekilns, the drivers of which are seated upon the shafts, each whistling or humming some popular air, and looking as contented and happy as if thought and care were alike unknown. They are Derbyshire carts, we can tell at a glance, for all hereabouts are of the same diminutive size, in fact not much larger than an ordinary wheelbarrow.

A few minutes' walking brings us to Calver, a little straggling hamlet, abounding in limekilns, from which the pale blue smoke ascends, wreathing itself into a variety of fantastic looking clouds.

The limestone obtained from the hills which surround Calver is admirably adapted for making and repairing roads, and also for agricultural purposes. Here some very extensive furnaces have been built, and others are in course of erection. Cotton spinning is also carried on to some extent in the neighbourhood.

Leaving Calver we pass through the tollgate and cross the Derwent, where, from the bridge, we have a good view of the Calver Cotton Mills, a substantial pile of stone, standing in the midst of a prettily laid out flower garden, near to which a neat Gothic church, with a parsonage house and schools, has lately been erected, and then turning to the right take a southerly direction. From this point to Baslow, a distance of about two miles, the road is continued along the east side of the river, and as we advance the scenery becomes still more beautiful and diversified.

The day is delightful—everything which a pedestrian could desire—bright and clear, without being at all sultry or oppressive. The hazy mists, which at an earlier hour obscured the distant headlands from view, have disappeared before the genial influence of the sun, and the eye is enabled to range over a wide extent of country. The air is fragrant with the odours of the many-tinted flowers, and from every copse and thicket the feathered tribes send forth a song of gladsome melody. The sturdy oaks, all mantled with ivy, and the noble beech trees which line the way, spread their leafy boles across, dappling the whitened road with their restless and ever-changing shadows. To the right the stately Derwent sweeps along in graceful curves, now reflecting upon its clear and placid bosom all the charms by which it is surrounded, and now, as it falls over the broken ledges of rock, its crystal waves flash brilliantly in the glorious sunlight. Beyond we have a rich combination of scenic beauty— emerald meads with gentle wood-crowned eminences sometimes rising into bold and swelling hills, between which lie innumerable dells and ravines. Before us we see the circular turrets of the old hunting-tower at Chatsworth peeping out from amid the thick umbrage, the grey hue of the stone-work contrasting beautifully with the foliage of the woods beyond. To the left the scenery is of a more abrupt and striking character, lofty ridges of unbroken rock ascending from the valley, their brown heathy summits looming against the sky, making the azure above look still more intense.

We meet but few people upon the road, and there are still fewer habitations; but the signs of industry and cultivation are everywhere apparent. It is the season for getting in the hay, a time of hurrying and bustling excitement in these parts. A whole population seem to have turned out— young, middle-aged, and old: the rosy-cheeked maiden and the hardy sun-browned labourer are here, all ready to lend a helping hand to hasten and secure the safe ingathering of the crop. The mowers are at work, and the haymakers are busy spreading out the fresh-cut swarths. A delicious odour comes floating on the breeze from the clover and the new-made hay. On every side we hear the sharp "chick, chick," as the mower whets his scythe, and the creaking of the wagon as it bears its fragrant load to the barn or stack-yard; and social mirth and light-hearted glee, the merry song and the cheerful laugh, resound on every hand.

Baslow is a pretty little rural village, consisting of a few irregular groups of cottages standing on the slope of a hill that rises from the eastern bank of the Derwent. The church is an ancient structure, occupying a position near the angle formed by the junction of the Chesterfield and Bakewell roads. It is built in the later style of English architecture, with a tower, surmounted by a low octagonal spire, flanking the western end of the north aisle. In the churchyard are some ancient stone coffins, and a few curious stone slabs.

The building was thoroughly repaired some few years ago at the expense of the late Duke of Devonshire, and a handsome stained glass window was about the same time added to the chancel.

Near the entrance to the village the river is crossed by an old-fashioned bridge of three arches. Looking up the valley from this point some pleasing views occur—Bubnell Hall, an antiquated structure partially hidden in wood, an old corn mill with its dripping wheel, the rushing stream, the foaming weir, the bridge, and two or three cottages which form the foreground of the picture, are exceedingly pretty in their grouping, whilst beyond the eye passes over a succession of wooded eminences and rugged hills that stretch away to the farthest point of distance.

Visitors approaching Chatsworth from Matlock and the south are admitted by the Edensor lodge, but those coming from Chesterfield, Sheffield, and the north, generally enter by the Baslow gate ; consequently in the summer season the place has quite a busy appearance.  There are two good inns in the village—the *Peacock* and the *Wheat Sheaf*—where excellent accomodation can be had at reasonable charges, and at one or other of these visitors generally leave their vehicles before entering the park.

Chatsworth—or, as it was anciently written, *Chetesourde*—boasts considerable antiquity.  At the Domesday survey it was held under the Crown by William Peverel.  For several generations it was the property of a family of the name of Leche, or Leech, one of whom, named John, was chirurgeon, or, as a medical attendant was then termed, leech to King Edward the Third.  The family became extinct in the male line about the middle of the sixteenth century, previous to which the manor of Chatsworth had been sold by Francis Leech to the family of Agard, of whom it was afterwards purchased by Sir William Cavendish, who married Elizabeth, daughter of John Hardwicke of Hardwicke—the celebrated " Bess of Hardwicke"—who afterwards became the wife of the Earl of Shrewsbury, and in the illustrious family of Cavendish the estate of Chatsworth has ever since continued.

The family of Cavendish is one of the oldest and most illustrious in the county of Derby.  They trace their descent from one of the branches of the de Gernons, whose ancestor, Robert de Gernon, served under William of Normandy at the battle of Hastings, and was afterwards rewarded by that monarch with considerable grants of land in Hertfordshire, Gloucestershire, and other counties. His descendant, Geoffrey, who lived in the time of Edward the First, and who is

described as of Moor Hall, near Bakewell, had a son, Roger
de Gernon, of Grimston Hall, in Suffolk, who married Mary,
daughter and heiress of John Pottin, or Potkins, lord of the
manor of Cavendish, in the same county, and whose children,
in accordance with the custom of that age, assumed the
surname of Cavendish, in compliment to their mother. Robert
de Gernon died in 1334, leaving four sons, John, Roger,
Stephen, and Richard. John, the eldest son, became Lord
Chief Justice of the King's Bench, and Chancellor of the
University of Cambridge; and was beheaded by the insur-
gents at Bury St. Edmunds, in 1381, when returning from
suppressing an insurrection at York. Roger, the second son,
was ancestor of the famous circumnavigator, Sir Thomas
Cavendish, who undertook the third voyage round the world.
The third son became an eminent merchant, and was Lord
Mayor and twice M.P. for the city of London. Sir John
Cavendish, son of the Lord Chief Justice, was knighted for
slaying the rebel leader, Wat Tyler, in 1379. He was one of
the esquires of the body to Richard II. and Henry V., and
was present at the battle of Agincourt.

From Sir John Cavendish, the fourth in direct descent
was William, who attained to great distinction in the reign
of Henry VIII., through the influence of Cardinal Wolsey,
to whom he had been appointed gentleman usher. After the
death of the great cardinal he was retained in the service of
the king. In 1530 he was appointed one of the commissioners
for visiting religious houses, and was made one of the Court
of Augmentation, which was instituted for the extinction of
monastic establishments. He subsequently obtained from
the Crown, as a reward for his services, grants of lands in
Hertfordshire. He also had conferred upon him the honour of
knighthood, and was appointed treasurer of the chamber to
the king, which office he continued to hold in the reigns of
Edward VI. and Queen Mary, when he was made a Privy
Councillor. Sir William Cavendish was married three times,
having issue by each marriage. His third wife was Elizabeth,
daughter of John Hardwicke of Hardwicke, and widow of
Robert Barley of Barley, in the county of Derby. This lady
brought a very considerable property to the Cavendish family.
In addition to the large estates she acquired under settlement

I

from her first husband she inherited, as co-heiress of her brother John, the manor of Hardwicke. At her instigation Sir William exchanged his Hertfordshire manors for lands belonging to the dissolved priories and abbeys in Derbyshire, &c., and commenced the building of Chatsworth, which he did not live to see completed. His widow afterwards became the wife of George Talbot, Earl of Shrewsbury, to whose keeping Mary Queen of Scots was committed a prisoner, an unenviable charge, for the unhappy earl had to keep his prisoner continually moving between Sheffield, Wingfield, Hardwicke, and Chatsworth, of which last-named place Burleigh remarks : " It is a very mete house for good preservation of his charge, having no town of resort where any ambushes might lye."

It is difficult to say whether this remarkable woman had greater *penchant* for building or matrimony. She possessed great personal attractions, and was married no less than four times, always contriving to obtain possession of her husband's estate, either by direct demise or by intermarrying the children of her former marriages with those of her former husbands. By this means she brought together an enormous property, and laid the foundation of four dukedoms. At the age of fourteen she became the wife of Robert Barley; next she married Sir William Cavendish ; her third husband was Sir William St. Lo, captain of the guard to Queen Elizabeth ; and subsequently she married the Earl of Shrewsbury. She built Chatsworth, Hardwicke Hall, and Oldcotes, three of the finest mansions ever raised by one person in the same county, and these were transmitted to her son, Sir William Cavendish, who was afterwards created Earl of Devonshire. Tradition asserts that it was foretold to her that so long as she kept building so long would her life be spared, and that the moment she ceased would be the moment of her death. She therefore continued to build house after house. At length, while erecting some almshouses at Derby a severe frost set in. Every means was resorted to to enable the men to continue their work. Their mortar was dissolved in hot water; and, when that failed, hot ale was employed. But the frost triumphed, the work ceased, and " Building Bess " died.

Lodge, in his " Illustrations of British History," gives the following character of this celebrated lady : "She was a woman of masculine understanding and conduct—proud, furious, selfish, and unfeeling. She was a builder, a buyer and seller of estates, a money-lender, a farmer, a merchant of lead, coals, and timber. When disengaged from these employments she intrigued alternately with Elizabeth and Mary, always to the prejudice and terror of her husband. She lived to a great old age, continually flattered but seldom deceived, and died immensely rich and without a friend." Her death occurred 13th February, 1607, and about the 87th year of her age.

Henry Cavendish, the eldest son, married Grace, third daughter of George, Earl of Shrewsbury (his mother's fourth husband) ; but, dying without issue, the estates descended to the second son, Sir William Cavendish, who was elevated to the peerage, as Baron Cavendish of Hardwicke, 4th May, 1605, and advanced to an earldom, as Earl of Devonshire, 2nd August, 1618. He died in 1625, and was succeeded by his second son, William, a nobleman distinguished for his classical knowledge and mental attainments. He travelled over the continent of Europe, having for his tutor and companion the celebrated Thomas Hobbes of Malmesbury, the author of "Leviathan," and friend of Descartes, Galileo, Gassendi, and other learned men. On the return of his lordship to England, Hobbes was retained in the capacity of private secretary, and on the death of his patron he undertook the education of the young earl, with whom he also made a Continental tour. After his return, the renowned philosopher resided for some time at Chatsworth ; but, on the breaking out of the civil wars, he retired to Paris, and became mathematical instructor to Charles, Prince of Wales, afterwards Charles II., then residing in the French capital. After the Restoration, Charles conferred upon him an annual pension of £100, and he finally took up his abode with the earl's family, at Chatsworth, where he spent the remainder of his days in comparative comfort and retirement. It was at Chatsworth he wrote his "Wonders of the Peak," and the "Behemoth, or a History of the Civil Wars from 1640 to 1660." He died in 1679, at the advanced age of 92.

The second Earl of Devonshire died in 1628, having

enjoyed the title and estates for three years only. He was succeeded by his son William, then in his eleventh year, who married Elizabeth, second daughter of William Cecil, Earl of Salisbury, and died in 1684, when the family honours descended to his eldest son, William Cavendish, who succeeded as fourth Earl of Devonshire. He was distinguished as a wit, a scholar, and a soldier. While a commoner he served as a knight of the shire for the county of Derby in the Parliament, immediately after the Restoration; and in 1665 accompanied the Duke of York in the expedition against the Dutch. Shortly after the accession of James II., his lordship having, in the king's presence-chamber, met Colonel Colepepper, by whom he had been insulted, took him by the nose and led him out of the room, for which act a prosecution was commenced in the Court of King's Bench, and his lordship was committed to prison and condemned to pay a fine of £30,000. He gave bond for the payment of the fine, which, fortunately for himself, was remitted in the succeeding reign. On his retirement from the Court the earl turned his attention to architecture, and built the whole of the present mansion at Chatsworth, with the exception of the north wing.

The old mansion, erected under the direction of the celebrated Countess of Shrewsbury, mother of the first earl, was a quadrangular pile of buildings in the Elizabethan style, enclosing a spacious court-yard, and flanked at each corner by massive square towers or turrets. During the unhappy troubles between Charles the First and his Parliament, the house shared the fate of nearly all the old baronial mansions. It was alternately garrisoned by the Royalist and Parliamentarian forces, and became the theatre of important military operations. In 1643 it was held on behalf of the Parliament by the forces commanded by Sir John Gell, of Hopton, a soldier distinguished for his bravery and military skill. In December of the same year the Royalists, under the Earl of Newcastle, having previously stormed and taken Wingfield Manor House, made themselves masters of Chatsworth, and placed a garrison there under the command of Colonel Eyre. In September, 1645, it was again held for the king by Colonel Shalcross, with a garrison from Welbeck, and a skirmishing force of 300 horse, and was besieged by Major Mollanus, but the siege was raised by command of Colonel Gell, who ordered the major to return with his forces to Derby.

It would appear from documents in the possession of the Duke of Devonshire that the rebuilding of Chatsworth was commenced in April 1687, under the direction of William Talman, an architect of considerable reputation, who, in the reign of William III., held the office of Comptroller of the King's Works. The south front was the first part completed ; the great hall and staircase were covered in about the middle of April, 1690, and in May, 1692, the works were surveyed by Sir Christopher Wren. The east front was finished in 1700. In the same year the west front was taken down, and the whole was completed about the year 1706, being nearly twenty years from the commencement.

Kennet gives the following account of the building of this magnificent mansion : "The duke," he says, " contracted with the workmen to pull down the south side of the good old seat, and to rebuild it on a plan he gave to them, for a front to his gardens, so fair and august that it looked like a model only of what might be done in after ages. When he had finished this part he meant to go no further, till, seeing public affairs in a happier settlement, for a testimony of ease and joy, he undertook the east side of the quadrangle, and raised it entirely new, in conformity with the south, and seemed then content to say he had gone half-way through, and would leave the rest for his heir. In this resolution he stopped about seven years, and then resumed courage, and began to lay the foundation for two other sides, to complete the noble square ; and these last, as far as uniformity admits, do exceed the others, by a west front of most excellent strength and elegance, and a capital on the north side that is of singular ornament and service ; and though such a vast pile (of materials entirely new) required a prodigious expense, yet the building was his least charge, if regard be had to his gardens, waterworks, statues, pictures, and other, the finest pieces of art and of nature that could be produced at home or abroad."

During the period that Chatsworth was being rebuilt, the earl took a prominent part with other patriots in bringing

about the Revolution of 1688, which resulted in the abdica-
tion of the misguided monarch, James II., and the placing of
William Prince of Orange upon the throne of England.   His
lordship was honoured with the favour and confidence of
William III., and on the accession of the king he was made
a member of the Privy Council, and at the coronation he
served as lord high steward.   In May, 1694, he was created
Marquis of Hartington and Duke of Devonshire, and installed
a Knight of the Garter.   During the king's absence he was
repeatedly named in the royal commission for conducting the
business of the Crown.   After a long and active political life,
spent in the service of his country, he expired at Devonshire
House, London, on the 18th of August, 1707, in the 67th
year of his age.   It has been well said that " he united to a
liberal mind great political foresight, and was considered a
wise and resolute statesman.   He possessed an elegant and
discriminating taste, which he had much enriched by observation and reading.   Chatsworth remains a monument of his
love of the fine arts, and the Revolution of 1688 is an
historical proof of his attachment to the liberties of his
country."

His grace was succeeded by his eldest son, William
Cavendish, Marquis of Hartington, who, like his father,
enjoyed many considerable offices at Court, and took an active
part in the administration of the affairs of the kingdom.   In
1710 he was admitted a Knight of the Garter; four years later,
on the accession of George I., he was appointed one of the
regents of the kingdom, and in 1716 was made Lord President
of the Council.   He died on the 3rd June, 1729, and was
buried at All Saints', Derby.

The third in direct descent from the second duke was
William Cavendish, who inherited the barony of Clifford of
Lanesborough, in right of his mother.   His grace, who united
a stern probity of character with a cold and apathetic
demeanour, that was all but incapable of emotion, married in
1774 the beautiful and gifted Lady Georgiana, daughter of
John Earl Spencer, the " beautiful duchess," as she was afterwards called, one of the most celebrated women of her day,
the friend of Fox, and the lady paramount of that aristocratic
Whig circle in which rank and literature were blended with

political characters. Possessing a high sensibility, a vivacious spirit, and a generous and impulsive disposition, her cordial and high-souled nature recoiled within itself from the calm and inert automaton to whom she was so unequally yoked, and whose love was at best but the semblance of affection. Having but little domestic sympathy at home she appears to have sought relief by plunging into the vortex of politics, in which she played a conspicuous part ; and, forgetful of her position and her sex, even went so far as to mingle in the tumult of Parliamentary elections.

It is recorded that in the election for Westminster, in 1784, when Lord Hood, Sir Cecil Wray, and Fox, were candidates, after three weeks' polling, when the list of voters was supposed to be nearly exhausted, and Fox remained at the foot of the poll, the duchess, laying aside rank and dignity, and sacrificing her feminine delicacy in the cause of party, undertook with her sister, the Lady Duncannon, personally to solicit the votes of some of the more obstinate of the outlying electors, and it was humorously remarked at the time that two fairer portraits had never before been seen on *canvass*. Among those waited upon was a butcher, named Steel, who stoutly refused his vote, except on one condition— " Would her grace give him a kiss ? " The request was granted, and the vote was one which helped to place Fox above his opponent on the poll.

> " Condemn not, prudes, fair Devon's plan,
>     In giving *Steel* a kiss :
>   In such a cause, for such a man,
>     She could not do amiss."

Three children of rare promise were the fruit of this marriage, the eldest of whom, Georgiana-Dorothy, became the wife of the Earl of Carlisle, and was mother of the present Dowager-Duchess of Sutherland. Henrietta Elizabeth, the second daughter, married Granville Earl Granville ; and William Spencer Cavendish, the only son, born May 21, 1790, who succeeded to the title and estates.

The " beautiful duchess " died in 1806 ; and in 1809 the duke espoused the Lady Elizabeth Foster, widow of John Thomas Foster, and daughter of the fourth Earl of Bristol, who was also a distinguished beauty and the reigning toast in her day, but by her, who died in 1824, had no issue. His grace died July 29th, 1811, and was succeeded by his son, the late illustrious William Spencer Cavendish, sixth Duke and ninth Earl of Devonshire, Baron Cavendish of Hardwicke, and Baron Clifford of Lanesborough, D.C.L., a nobleman distinguished for his munificence and hospitality, his pure and refined taste, and an amiability of disposition and benevolence of heart that endeared him to all who came within the range of his influence.

His grace was born at Paris, in the dawn of that revolution in France which shook the foundations of all social life. He received his education at Cambridge, and on the 29th July, 1811, two months after he had attained his majority, he succeeded, on the death of his father, to the title and estates. On the accession of the late Emperor Nicholas to the throne of Russia he was nominated ambassador extraordinary from His Britannic Majesty to assist at the coronation, and the splendour and magnificence displayed by his grace on that occasion surpassed, in costliness and elegance, all previous embassies of a similar character. It is said that his retinue cost £50,000 more than the allowance made by Government. He was received with great favour by the Emperor, and had conferred upon him the Russian Orders of St. Andrew and St. Alexander Newski. The friendship engendered on the occasion of his visit to St. Petersburg was never relaxed, and when the emperor visited this country in 1844 he was entertained by the duke, at Chatsworth, with princely hospitality. The year succeeding his visit to Russia his grace was made a Knight of the Garter, of which illustrious Order he was, at the time of his death, the senior knight. In the same year he was admitted a member of the Privy Council; and about the same time was appointed lord chamberlain to George the Fourth's household, an office which he also held in the following reign. He took but little part in the conduct of public affairs, though he always retained the traditional politics of his ancestors, assisting the old Whig party by his influence and silent vote in the House more than by any other means, for he never spoke upon any of the great questions advocated or opposed by his party.

The magnificent mansion of Chatsworth was greatly improved, and important additions were made to it, during the lifetime of the duke. By his direction the great northern wing, a chaste and elegant structure, between 300 and 400 feet in length, was erected from designs by and under the superintendence of Sir Jeffrey Wyatville, the architect of the improvements at Windsor Castle. These additions, though differing slightly from the original style, harmonise well with the general character of the building. In their construction the Doric, Ionic, and Corinthian orders have been employed, and they will long remain a monument of the wealth, liberality, and taste of the sixth Duke of Devonshire. At Chatsworth the duke exercised unbounded hospitality, and the new wing was intended chiefly for the accommodation of his numerous and distinguished visitants. As already stated, the Emperor of Russia was entertained here in 1844; in 1832 Her Majesty (then Princess Victoria), accompanied by the Duchess of Kent, visited Chatsworth; and again, in 1843, she, with her late illustrious consort, was the guest of his grace. It is worthy of remark that the last festive entertainment given by the Duke at Chatsworth, was to the Executive Committee of the Manchester Exhibition of Art Treasures, 1857.

Possessing a liberal and cultivated mind, his grace expended a princely fortune in the encouragement of literature and the patronage of the fine arts, and his refined sensibility, his strict probity of character, and his kindness of heart, caused him to be held in general esteem. By the tenantry of the estate he was greatly beloved, and his many acts of private benevolence will long be held in remembrance by those who were the recipients thereof.

The following anecdote, related to us by a resident, deserves recording, as illustrating the kindly and unaffected disposition of the duke. When residing at Chatsworth he spent a considerable portion of his time in comparative retirement, frequently walking about the neighbourhood, as any country gentleman might do, inspecting personally the alterations and improvements going on upon the estate. One day a negligent carter was driving along a field road, when one of the wheels of his cart got fast in a drain. Looking round for someone to help him, he observed an elderly gentleman in a loose morning coat, to whom he called, "Heigh! mestur, will you come and put your shouder (shoulder) here, and give us a lift?" The person appealed to rendered all the help he could, and by dint of much pushing and pulling, the two succeeded in getting the cart righted again, when the carter, with more candour than gratitude, quietly remarked, "Well, thee are about as awkurd a chap as ivir I seed." A servant of the estate who had witnessed the affair from a distance, soon afterwards came up, and inquired of the carter what the duke had been saying to him. "The Duke!" replied he in amazement. "Aye," said his interrogater. "Don't you know that that was the duke hissel?" "Why, whativer mun I do?" exclaimed the man. "Shuld I go an' ax his pardon?" But the duke had disappeared, and the carter was left to meditate upon his own politeness.

His grace expired suddenly at Hardwicke Hall, near Chesterfield, on the evening of Sunday, the 17th January, 1858, in the 68th year of his age, and was interred, in accordance with his previously expressed desire, in a grave in the open churchyard of Edensor, over which a simple tomb, surmounted by the emblem of the Christian faith, has been erected. By his death the barony of Clifford fell into abeyance between his sisters the co-heiresses, the Dowager Countesses of Carlisle and Granville, and the dukedom, with the other honours, devolved on his grace's cousin, William Earl of Burlington, the present illustrious possessor of the title.

# CHAPTER VIII.

WE reached Baslow about half-an-hour before the time for opening the gates at Chatsworth, and rested awhile at the *Peacock*. Carriage after carriage, laden with sightseers, rattled up to the door, and the numerous visitors sauntering about betokened something more than ordinarily attractive.

On leaving we passed by the beautiful gardens and bowling-green at the rear of the house, taking a narrow footpath that leads through some pleasant fields, along which a few minutes' walk brought us to one of the numerous gates which mark the boundaries of the park that environs the ancestral home of the Cavendishes—the "Palace of the Peak."

The park is about eleven miles in circumference, and abounds in scenery of a rich and exquisitely diversified character, the beauty being increased by the natural irregularities of the surface. The ground, for the most part, is undulating—gentle eminences occasionally rising into bold and swelling hills, chequered with luxuriant woods, and smooth-shaven slopes adorned with clumps of trees, and dotted here and there with huge weather-beaten oaks—very patriarchs of their kind—looking so old and venerable, that we imagine them to have been planted ages before the time when Bess was queen. The park abounds with deer, and as we sauntered along we noticed several fine-looking herds with their graceful antlers; some butting playfully against each other, and others reposing quietly beneath the shade of the wide-spreading beeches. Now and then the sound of merry laughter would break upon the ear, and we could hear the gladsome voices of the numerous excursionists, who, like ourselves, were bent upon viewing the splendours of Chatsworth. Presently we overtook a picnic party who had come from the murky town of Sheffield to enjoy a happy holiday. There were two families of them—husbands and wives, and lads and lasses. The youngsters romped and chased each other over the smooth-shaven grass, evidently enjoying the pure air and the wide prospect quite as much as they would the wonders they had come professedly to see.

Crossing a little rivulet on the confines of the park we came to a broad gravelled path that leads from the Baslow lodge to the hall. Proceeding along this we passed on the right the extensive fruit and vegetable gardens, close to which is Barbrook Hall, a villa in the Anglo-Italian style, built as a residence for the late Sir Joseph Paxton; and soon afterwards the towers and terraces, the columns and balustrades, of Chatsworth, with all their beautifully-varied features, came upon the sight. It is difficult to find language sufficiently expressive to convey an idea of the beauty of the scene which now for the first time bursts upon the visitor : nature and art seem to have indeed both combined to render this elegant mansion worthy of its title as the "Palace of the Peak."

Chatsworth is in every sense magnificent. The house stands on gently rising ground, the western or principal front overlooking the Derwent, which flows within 200 or 300 yards of the house, and is here crossed by a stone bridge of three arches, supposed to have been designed by Michael Angelo, and adorned with figures in statuary marble from the chisel of Cibber. In the intervening space between the hall and the river, and separated from the park by a dwarf balustrade, is the Italian garden, laid out in neat and trim parterres, the centre of which is ornamented by a *jet d'eau.* The view from the west is of uncommon beauty, the effect of the building itself being increased by its situation, the delicate cream colour of the masonry being happily relieved by the dark and sombre woods which form the background.

The exterior of the mansion at once arrests the attention. As already stated, it has been erected at two distinct periods. The oldest portion is a square pile of building enclosing a quadrangular court, the principal entrance being on the west

CHATSWORTH.

side, the approach to which is by a flight of steps to a terrace extending the entire length of the building. The style of architecture adopted is the Ionic. The western front is arranged in three divisions, the centre being advanced slightly forward from the side compartments, and relieved by four fluted columns, resting upon a rusticated base, that gives support to an ornamented frieze and pediment, in the tympanum of which is a shield, surrounded by military trophies carved in stone, charged with the arms of the Cavendish family—sable, three harts' heads, caboshed arg., surmounted by the crest; a snake nowed ppr., and having beneath the motto, " *Cavendo tutus*," the supporters being two harts ppr. attired or, each gorged with a garland of roses, arg. and az. barbed ppr. The side compartments are relieved by fluted Ionic pilasters, supporting light and elegant balustrades surmounted by vases and allegorical figures. The south and east sides, though not so elaborate in their details, present the same characteristics as the west front. The more modern part of the building is the north wing, erected during the lifetime of the late duke. It differs slightly from the older portion, being a combination of the different classic styles, and is more elaborate in appearance than the western *façade*, the outline being more varied and broken, yet presenting an assemblage of parts well harmonising together. At the northern extremity of this wing is an Italian tower or open temple, surmounted by a balustrade, adorned at the angles with vases, from the summit of which some fine views are obtained of the bold and romantic scenery in and around the park.

The west front of Chatsworth has a very fine effect; but decidedly the best view of the mansion is obtained from the opposite bank of the Derwent, on the ascending ground between the river and the Edensor Road. From this point the view takes in the south and west sides of the old mansion, with the elegant additions of Sir Jeffrey Wyatville at the north end, and includes the magnificent pleasure grounds, with the fountains and great cascade, backed by the wood-clothed heights of Beeley, and the hills extending towards Baslow and Hathersage.

On presenting ourselves at the entrance lodge—a neat

Doric structure forming three archways, ornamented with carved roses, and having richly gilded gates of wrought-iron —we are admitted, with other visitors, through the centre archway, and conducted along a broad gravelled path that runs parallel with the kitchens and domestic offices in the north wing, and terminates in a square plot, in the centre of which is planted a magnificent weeping ash that formerly ornamented the grounds of Messrs. Wilson, of Derby. Passing under the colonnade attached to the semi-circular north front we enter the sub-hall, the first apartment to which strangers are admitted. Here we are transferred to the care of a female domestic, and as we pass through the hall we linger to admire the beautiful tesselated pavement and the not less beautiful painted ceiling, the latter adorned with a copy of Guido's "Aurora," the work of an accomplished lady artist, Miss Curzon.

Proceeding along the north corridor we reach the great hall, an apartment 60 feet by 29 feet, in every way worthy as the entrance to the magnificent suite of rooms which follow. Here it is customary to enter the name in the visitors' book. The effect of this hall is singularly good, and at once strikes the beholder with an air of grandeur. The floor is of mosaic work, the material being of black and white marble, and was laid in 1779 by Mr. Henry Watson, son of the celebrated carver. The north and south ends assume the form of triplet archways, one communicating with the north corridor and the other leading to the south gallery and state apartments. A gallery, protected by an open balustrade, has been carried round three sides, and above the walls glow with the productions of Verrio and Laguerre, two of the most eminent decorative painters of their day, and whose fame has been celebrated by Pope in verse. The subjects are taken from the life of Julius Cæsar. The side panel illustrates the sacrifice before going to the Senate after the closing of the Temple of Janus. In one of the oval compartments the warrior is crossing the Rubicon, and in the other he is voyaging across the Adriatic to join his army at Brundusium. Over the door he is represented as falling before the dagger of Brutus at the foot of Pompey's statue, as described by Akenside in the following lines :—

"When Brutus rose,
Refulgent from the stroke of Cæsar's fate,
Amid the crowd of patriots, and, his arm
Aloft extending like eternal Jove,
When guilt brings down the thunder, called aloud
On Tully's name, and shook his crimson steel,
And bade the father of his country hail !
For lo ! the tyrant prostrate in the dust,
And Rome again is free."

On the ceiling we have the apotheosis or deification, where, surrounded by a host of cupids, he is depicted as soaring through clouds of glory to join the immortal gods. In the centre of the hall is a beautifully-carved and richly-gilt table, the top of which is formed of one immense slab of highly-polished fossil marble from the Derbyshire quarries. On this is placed a magnificent candelabrum, and near it is an ornamental canoe, presented to the late duke by the Sultan of Turkey. Over the fireplace we noticed a simple tablet, on which is cut the following Latin inscription, the English translation of which we have added :—

"Ædes has paternas dilectissimas,
Anno libertatis Anglicæ MDCLXXXVIII. institvtas,
Gvl. S. Devoniæ Dvx, Anno MDCCCXI. Hœres accepit,
Anno mœroris svi MDCCCXL. perfecit."

"These well-loved ancestral halls,
Founded in the year of English freedom 1688,
William Spencer, Duke of Devonshire, inherited in 1811,
And perfected in the year of sorrow 1840."

A "year of sorrow" truly for the noble duke, the year which witnessed the completion of these "ancestral halls" being that in which his niece, the lady Blanche-Georgiana, Countess of Burlington, and wife of the present owner of Chatsworth, died.

Leaving the great hall, we pass along the south corridor, containing some cabinet pictures, a few Swiss views, a painting, said to be by Hogarth, of the interior of an ancient clubhouse at Rome, and other objects of interest, to the chapel, occupying the south-west corner of the building. This room is elaborately ornamented—painting, sculpture, and carving having been profusely employed in the decoration. The floor is laid with black and white marble in mosaic work, and the walls are wainscoted with cedar-wood, which emits a most agreeable fragrance in the room. The first object that arrests the attention on entering is a painting over the altar, by Verrio, "The Incredulity of St. Thomas," in which the risen Saviour is represented as addressing the unbelieving disciple. This is generally considered as Verrio's masterpiece, and is unquestionably a fine work of art— the figures are well drawn, vigorous, and life-like, and free from those defects and absurdities noticeable in many of the other productions of the same artist.

The other subjects that adorn the walls of the chapel are chiefly illustrative of passages in the life of our Saviour. On one side of the room are depicted the miracles of Christ; on another "Bartemeus Restored to Sight;" over the doorway, "Christ and the Woman of Samaria;" and on the ceiling is the "Ascension." The altar is composed of some of the finest fluors and marbles of Derbyshire, and adorned with sculptured figures of "Faith" and "Hope," the work of Caius Gabriel Cibber, the father of the well known laureate, Colley Cibber. The chapel contains some excellent specimens of ornamental wood carving, representing fruit, flowers, &c., which are said to have been executed by Grinling Gibbons, but are more probably the work of Thomas Young—who was engaged as principal carver in wood during the rebuilding of Chatsworth—and his pupil, Samuel Watson, a native of Heanor, in Derbyshire.

From the chapel we ascend to the third or state-room story, passing by the south gallery, which contains a valuable and extensive collection of original drawings, outlines, and sketches, by the most eminent masters, arranged according to the different schools, including sketches by the hand of Raffaelle, Rembrandt, Da Vinci, Titian, Rubens, Claude Lorraine, Poussin, and Salvator Rosa. If there is one part of this mansion more than another where we would wish to linger, it is here, among the creations of those great masterminds who have made art immortal.

The state apartments occupy the entire of the upper story of the south front, extending about 200 feet in length, and form the most magnificent part of the old mansion at Chatsworth. These rooms are frequently pointed out as those occupied by the unfortunate Mary Queen of Scots during the

K

period of her long sojourn here. This is not strictly correct —as already shown, this portion of the mansion was rebuilt in the reign of William III. Some of the original furniture, however, remains, and some examples of needlework worked by the hand of the famous "Bess of Hardwicke;" and there is a tradition that these apartments occupy the site of those actually appropriated to the use of the unfortunate queen during her captivity—a captivity rendered more than ordinarily painful by the jealous bickerings of the Countess of Shrewsbury, who openly complained to Queen Elizabeth of Mary's intimacy with her husband, a charge for which, it is hardly necessary to say, there was not the slightest foundation, and which the countess was afterwards obliged to retract.

The view from the state apartments is one of almost unexampled loveliness. Immediately in front are seen the smooth shaven lawns and terraces, with the cascades and glistening fountains throwing up their shining showers in the glorious sunlight, and flashing refreshingly upon the eye ; the tastefully-laid-out walks and richly-coloured parterres, adorned with statues and busts, and backed by almost impenetrable woods. In the middle distance is seen the beautiful valley through which winds the Derwent, with the quiet little villages of Edensor and Beeley ; and beyond the wooded heights overlooking the far-famed Haddon Hall, with a succession of eminences that stretch away towards Darley Dale and Matlock, the entire prospect comprising an assemblage of hills and valleys, fertile plains, with rock, wood, and water, than can hardly be equalled for variety and beauty.

This suite of rooms contains some admirable specimens of ancient and modern art. The ceilings are splendidly adorned with a series of paintings, chiefly of a mythological character, the production of Verrio and Sir James Thornhill. The carvings are exquisite, and for delicacy of execution and fidelity to nature unsurpassed by anything of the kind in the kingdom. The door-cases are all of Derbyshire marble, enriched with foliage and flowers; and the floors are of polished oak, parquetted. The rooms are furnished with articles of comfort and luxury, and in them are preserved many articles of interest and curiosity, which have been presented to the late duke or his ancestors. Amongst them we may mention " Watson's Feather," the *chef d'œuvre* in carving of this artist, so truthfully rendered that it seems as if a breath almost would ruffle it. In one of the rooms we noticed a quaint conceit. Behind a side door is painted the representation of a violin suspended by a cord, and so close is the resemblance that it is only upon a near approach that the counterfeit is discovered. The door is generally left half open, and in the subdued light the deception is rendered more perfect, visitors frequently being prompted to touch to assure themselves that it is not a reality.

The first room we enter is the state or scarlet bedroom, on the ceiling of which is painted the allegorical figure of " Aurora " as the morning star chasing away the shadowy night. This room contains the bed in which George II. expired. The bed and hangings are of crimson silk damask, much decayed and faded by age. Here also are the chairs and footstools used at the coronation of George the Third and Queen Charlotte. Adjoining the scarlet bedroom is the state music-room, in which we noticed a fine full-length portrait of the first Duke of Devonshire in his robes of state, said to be by Paul Vansomer. Amongst the furniture there are two gilt chairs, in which William the Fourth and Queen Adelaide were crowned. These became the perquisites of the late Duke of Devonshire by virtue of his office as lord chamberlain of the household. The state drawing-room is the next in succession. The walls of this apartment are hung with Gobelins tapestry, now much faded. The subjects are of an allegorical character, representing Jupiter and Antiope, and the Muses on Parnassus. The ceiling is elaborately painted, the subject being Phaeton, with loose rein and fiery steeds, taking charge of the chariot of the sun. In this room is a model of a Russian farm, and an excellent bust in bronze of Louis XIV. of France. From the drawing-room we enter the state dining-room, the last of the suite on this story. This chamber is beyond comparison the most elegant of the entire range. The ceiling is adorned with a series of allegorical paintings by Verrio. What, however, most attracts the attention of visitors are the exquisite wood carvings, which excel in beauty anything of the kind even at Chats worth. They are believed to have been produced by the magic hand of Watson and others, though Walpole—without adducing any evidence of the fact—assumes them to be the work of Gibbons : " There is no instance," he observes, " of a man before Gibbons who gave to wood the loose and airy lightness of flowers, and chained together the various productions of the elements with a free disorder natural to each species." Over the fireplace is a representation of dead game, fish, fruit, flowers, &c., grouped together in the most natural manner. We noticed in particular a bird-net containing partridges, pheasants, quails, grouse, and snipe, looking as if they had just been brought in by a sportsman from the field—the different attitudes of the birds, the softness of the plumage, the drooping of the wings, are all so truthfully depicted that we imagined them almost to flutter with the last quivering of life ; whilst the flowers, in their fragile delicacy, wanted only the varied tints of nature to render the illusion complete. In this room is a magnificent table of polished malachite, a gift to the late duke from the Emperor Alexander the First of Russia. On it is placed an elegant timepiece of the same material, presented by the late Czar Nicholas. Here are also, on brackets arranged against the wall, busts of the fifth Duke of Devonshire, Lord George and Lady Cavendish, the Duke of Bedford, and others.

After viewing the state apartments at Chatsworth we descend by the south staircase, and are conducted along the south gallery, passing on the way a very effective picture, " The Monks at Prayer," a masterly work of art by Granet, which originally formed part of the collection of the Duchess de Berri. The subject represents a number of monks in the solemn attitude of prayer. The figures are painted in high relief, the broad deep shadows and the reflected light from the tapers being rendered with marvellous fidelity and power.

The first apartment we enter is the music-room, adjoining the chapel, through which we pass to the red velvet or billiard room, containing some choice pictures, chiefly of the modern school of art, among the most prominent of which we may mention Landseer's well-known picture of " Bolton

Abbey in the Olden Time," a fine composition, and which may fairly claim to rank as the *chef d'œuvre* of the artist. The scene is laid in the court of the refectory at Bolton Abbey, in Yorkshire—one of the seats of the Duke of Devonshire—and represents a present of game for the abbot's table ; the principal figure is the abbot himself, a portly-looking personage, with a broad expressive forehead and dignified mien, holding under his arm an ancient breviary, and in the act of reading a letter, which we may suppose to have accompanied the tribute of fish, fowl, and game lying at his feet. By his side is an attendant monk, holding a salver with a wine flask and glass. The other figures in the group are a gamekeeper, with a couple of dogs in leash, and a peasant girl offering a basket of trout. The whole is a masterpiece of composition ; the figures are admirably delineated ; and the dogs, the dead buck, and other accessories, are depicted with wonderful power. We first saw this picture a few years after it was painted. It was then hung in the dining-room, and the colours were fresh and brilliant, with, perhaps, the slightest tendency to obtrusiveness. The tones have since become softened and mellowed by age, and the appearance is greatly improved thereby. In the same room is another example of the works of our modern artists, the "Spartan Isidas," by Eastlake. The subject is taken from Grecian history, and represents the youthful Isidas, sword and spear in hand, dealing death and destruction among the Theban soldiery. Here is also a charming piece by Collins, entitled "Rustic Civility," and a small picture by Liverseege The ceiling of this room has been decorated by Sir James Thornhill.

The next in succession is the great drawing-room, occupying the south-east angle of the building, and the last of the range of rooms extending along the south front of the library story. It is a magnificent apartment, splendidly furnished, and contains a fine collection of works of art. The decorations are chaste and beautiful ; the style of ornament adopted is the Louis Quatorze ; and the colours employed chiefly white and gold. From this apartment we are ushered into the great library, the second of the suite of rooms extending along the east side of the mansion, and which command some fine prospects of the waterworks, the spacious conservatory, and the beautifully-wooded eminences immediately behind the pleasure grounds. The doors of these rooms are so arranged as to open opposite to each other, thus presenting a magnificent vista 560 feet in length. The great library is one of the most elegant appartments in the suite. It measures ninety-two feet by twenty-two feet, and was originally constructed for dancing. The decorations partake much of the same character as the drawing-room. The ceiling is of pure white, relieved by ornamental work in basso-relievo, forming five circular compartments, adorned with paintings of a mythological character, by the celebrated French artist, Louis Charon. The floor is parquetted, and the doors are of Spanish mahogany, highly polished and enriched with carving ; the bookcases, which are of the same material, are divided into compartments by light semicircular pilasters, terminating in foliated capitals forming cantilevers, that give support to a gallery carried round three sides of the room. This gallery is protected by an ornamental baluster, enriched with dead and burnished gold, and gives access to the upper range of shelves. On one side of the room, opposite the window, is a marble chimney-piece, supported by columns adorned with carved foliage, over which is placed a mirror, six feet by four feet six inches.

This library contains a fine collection of books, among which, in addition to those forming the old library of Chatsworth, are several that formerly belonged to the celebrated Hobbes ; the library of Henry Cavendish has also contributed to swell its stores. Here are some of the first editions of Shakspere, several volumes of old poetry, and curious pamphlets by early printers ; but the greatest attraction of all is the celebrated *Liber Veritatis* of Claude, containing drawings and sketches of all the pictures painted by that great master, a fac-simile of which was printed for private circulation some years ago, under the direction of the late Duke of Devonshire.

The next apartment is the anti-library, the ornamentation of which is in the same style as the great library itself. On one side of the room a doorway communicates with the north corridor and staircase leading to the great hall already

described. The staircase was designed by Sir Jeffrey Wyat-
ville ; the details are good, and the effect is very imposing.
On the first landing are hung full-length portraits of the late
Emperor and Empress of Russia, by Dawe; there is also a
portrait of Richard, third Earl of Burlington, and one of
George IV. in his coronation robes, painted by Sir Thomas
Lawrence.

Adjoining the anti-library is the cabinet library, much
smaller than either of the other two. The roof is of a domi-
cular form, divided into compartments, richly decorated,
and supported by columns of alabaster and Italian marble,
surmounted by sculptured Corinthian capitals, ornamented
in dead and burnished gold.

From the cabinet library we enter the dining-room. This
is, without question, the most beautiful and the most splendidly adorned of any of the modern entertaining rooms, and
may be considered as an example of the perfection to which
the art of decoration has been carried in the present day ;
everything that ingenuity could suggest, or wealth and art,
aided by the purest taste, could supply, having been provided
for. The ceilings are of pure white, panelled and slightly
coved. The deep plinth which surrounds the apartment is of
Hopton marble, of a beautiful colour and highly polished.
The pediments surmounting the doorways are supported by
columns of African marble and Siberian jasper, with Ionic
capitals of the same materials. The fireplaces are of noble
dimensions, and the chimneypieces are splendid examples of
the sculptor's art, the two, it is said, having cost the late duke
not less than two thousand guineas. They are executed in
Carrara marble, and are most elaborately ornamented—one,
executed by the younger Westmacott, is adorned with
sculptured figures, life-size, of "Bacchus" and a "Bacchante;"
and the other (the work of Sievier) is equally beautiful,
the supporting figures being Bacchus crowned with vine
leaves, and an attendant priestess in the act of replenishing
the wine cup. The side tables, six in number, are
arranged against the walls. They are composed—two
of hornblende, two of porphyritic-siennite, and two of
Siberian jasper, the latter being a gift from the late
Emperor Nicholas to the late duke. It is needless to say

that the furniture of this room is in a style corresponding
with the magnificence of the decorations.  The walls are
hung with family portraits, amongst which are those of the
first Earl and Countess of Devonshire, said to be by Vandyke;
the second Duke of Devonshire, by Sir Godfrey Kneller; the
Countess of Devonshire, and her family, &c.

From the dining-room we are conducted through a small
ante-room to the Sculpture Gallery—the pride and glory of
Chatsworth.  This apartment was erected by the late duke
as the depository of the magnificent collection of art treasures
which he succeeded in bringing together, a collection not
surpassed by that of any mansion in Europe.  The lighting
is artistically arranged, and the colouring of the walls, which
are of polished gritstone, forms an agreeable background to
the delicate white of the statuary.

It will be obvious that in a work of this kind it would be
impossible to give anything like a detailed account of all the
chiselled forms of classic beauty here beheld—to enumerate
them even would occupy more space than can be afforded.
Canova, Thorwaldsen, Bartolini, Schadow, and many others
have contributed to swell this rich galaxy of talent.  Our
native school of sculpture is also well represented.  Here
we find the names of Gibson, Westmacott, Wyatt, Campbell,
and others, who made art illustrious.  Among the more
notable specimens, we may mention the recumbent figure of
" The Sleeping Endymion," with his dog watching at his feet,
by Canova; an exquisite piece of sculpture, admirably conceived, and executed with all the delicacy and grace of the
artist.  Here, also, is Canova's "Hebe," descending from the
skies, and just touching, with one foot, the throne of imperial
Jove; in her left hand she holds a cup, and in the right a
pitcher, from which she is pouring out nectar for the immortal
gods.  The gem of the collection is, undoubtedly, the famous
statue of " Madame Letizia Ramolini," the mother of him who
"made a million mothers childless"—the first Napoleon.
This statue ranks as one of the grandest efforts of Canova's
genius.  The figure is seated, or rather reclines, in an attitude
of pensive composure, with one arm resting upon the back of
an antique chair.  The head is remarkably fine, and the expression of the countenance dignified and commanding.  The

figure is almost covered with drapery, which has been very successfully treated, and so arranged as to fall in graceful and flowing lines. Near to this statue is a colossal bust of the warrior emperor himself, also by Canova—a gloriously fine head, with an expression at once calm, intellectual, and dignified. The "Filatrice, or Spinning Girl," by Schadow, is a beautiful conception. It represents a young girl apparently amusing herself with a ball of thread and a kind of spindle. The attitude is easy, natural, and life-like; and there is an ideal grace and loveliness about the figure which at once bespeaks it the production of a master mind. The pedestal on which it is placed is granite, a fragment from one of the columns of Trajan's Forum at Rome. A copy of this statue is preserved in the royal collection at Berlin. Thorwaldsen is represented by a "Venus" and his famous bas-reliefs "Night" and "Morning," two exquisitely poetical conceptions—the one typified by a female figure full of calm repose, winging her shadowy flight through the air; the other, representing Morning, is full of life and motion, clothed with flowing drapery, and

"Scattering bright flowers on the jewelled earth."

Wyatt's "Venus Musidora" is a very successful effort of the artist's skill; the figure is full of loveliness and purity, and presents an excellent model of female form and feature. The sculptor has endeavoured to embody the poetic conception of the author of the "Seasons," and this he has singularly well expressed. The figure is that of a young girl preparing for the bath, but hesitating before she plunges in.

"With fancy blushing at the doubtful breeze,
Alarmed and startling like the fearful fawn,
So stands the statue that enchants the world.
Her full proportions such, and bashful so,
Bends ineffectual from the roving eye."

Among the other works are Gibson's colossal group, "Mars and Cupid;" Westmacott's "Cymbal Player;" "Achilles Wounded," by Albicini; "Cupid and Psyche," by Finelli; and Tanerani's group, "Cupid Extracting a Thorn from the Foot of Venus." There are other artistic works which yet remain to be noticed before we leave the gallery. In the centre of the room is the gigantic Mecklenburg Vase, by Canteen, measuring twenty feet in circumference, and sculptured out of one solid block of granite. Near to this are two tables resting upon gilt stands—the one nearest the door composed of Labrador feldspar, bordered with Elfdalen porphyry; the other Plasma Verde, enriched with ornamental mosaic work in different-coloured Derbyshire marbles. This table was manufactured by Mr. Mills, of Ashford-in-the-Water, near Bakewell. On it is placed the beautiful fluorspar, or Blue-John vase, alluded to in our notice of the Blue-John Mine at Castleton. In addition to this work there are some beautiful Corinthian columns in Oriental porphyry and Verde Antique. At the further end of the gallery, placed one on each side the doorway, are two colossal lions in Carrara marble—one by Rinaldi, and the other by Benaglia. They are from Canova's monument to Clement XIV., in St. Peter's, at Rome, and their united weight is said to exceed eight tons.

On quitting the Sculpture Gallery, we enter the Viridarium or Orangery, well stored with orange trees, araucariæ, rhododendrons, and camelias, with other choice exotics, and a variety of shrubs and flowers, including a magnificent rhododendron imported from Nepaul, which has been known to bear more than two thousand blossoms at one time. Many of the plants were brought from Malmaison, once the residence of poor Josephine, the divorced wife of the Emperor Napoleon.

In this conservatory there are some fine pieces of sculpture and bas-relief in marble, the delicate whiteness of which forms an admirable relief to the varied greenery of the plants and shrubs. At the northern end a door communicates with the gardens; and here, our conductress having reached the limits of her jurisdiction, we were transferred to the charge of one of the gardeners.

After wandering for more than an hour, with a crowd of other visitors, through the gorgeous saloons and magnificent apartments of Chatsworth House, it becomes quite a relief, on again reaching the open air, to breathe the balmy atmosphere and drink in the fresh fragrance of the flowers, to saunter along the shady avenues or sit beside the cooling fountains watching the clear and sparkling drops descending through the gorgeous sunbeams like showers of liquid silver.

The gardens and pleasure-grounds are among the chief attractions of Chatsworth, and for extent and beauty are worthy of all the eulogiums that have been pronounced upon them. In their arrangement great judgment and taste have been employed, and in the most trifling details the presence of a master mind is evident. They occupy the south and east sides, extending round to the west front of the mansion, and exhibit a curious blending of the antique and the modern with the classical and the rustic. They are laid out in walks, terraces, lawns, and parterres, diversified by numerous fountains and cascades, with vistas opening themselves on every side, adorned with busts and statues of the purest marble, that form admirable contrasts to the dark umbrageous foliage above and around.

On leaving the Orangery we cross the broad carriage road and ascend a few steps leading to what is termed the French Garden. Here the refinements of art are blended with the fairest productions of nature. The ground is laid out in gay parterres, adorned with the rarest and most beautiful flowers, their tints as brilliant as the rainbow, and their forms as varied as the ever-changing figures of the kaleidoscope. Along the sides of the walks are placed a number of classic columns, six or seven feet in height, supporting busts and vases sculptured in white marble, and wreathed and entwined with the graceful tendrils of the hop, the woodbine, and the ivy. Some of these columns are connected by training the delicate creepers across the walks in hanging festoons, forming a sort of *berceau*, an arrangement which seems hardly in accordance with good taste. It is said that the plan of this garden was brought by the late duke from France, and that it formed one of his most favourite retreats. The figures which adorn the columns were removed from the inner court of the old mansion of Chatsworth.

Following the route usually taken by visitors, we proceed along a path running parallel with the east front of the mansion, passing on the way a noble ash tree, one of the largest we remember to have seen, and presently reach the great cascade. Looking towards the top of the hill we see a long succession of steps between lines of lofty woods, straight and looking somewhat stiff and formal, reminding the spectator of "Jacob's ladder." These steps are terminated at the top by a stone water temple, with a metal cupola, adorned with columns and pilasters, and ornamented with heads of dolphins, sea nymphs, &c. Our attendant made a sign, and water began to gush forth from the cuploa, pouring through the urns at the sides and springing up in fountains from underneath ; gradually it began to fall from step to step, wave succeeding wave, until the whole was covered with a sheet of foam, that danced and sparkled in the mid-day sun. At the foot the water loses itself among the grass and fragments of broken rock, whence it is conveyed in pipes under the garden to the Derwent.

Standing close by the great cascade and looking across the country in a westerly direction, the view struck us as being eminently beautiful. The position is extremely favourable, affording a general view of the house and grounds, with the exquisitely diversified park, containing in itself every variety of picturesque scenery. In front is seen the stately " Palace of the Peak," standing out in all its magnificence, with its ample terraces, its lawns and groves, and its glistening fountains, adorned with tritons and sea-horses, flinging abroad their shining showers ; further on the placid Derwent sweeps along with sparkling ripples through the level meadow breadths ; in the middle distance we see the village of Eden-sor, with here and there a cottage or a village happily disposed upon the nearer eminences ; and beyond the view is made up of a seemingly endless succession of hills, clothed almost to the summit with thick woods, whose dark outlines form an agreeable contrast to the richly-varied scenery of the foreground.

Continuing our walk, we come next to the ornamental gardens, abounding in scenery of a wild and romantic character, and which, perhaps from their very seclusion, form one of the most agreeable retreats that even Chatsworth can show. Here art seems to have been most successful. In every direction masses of grey rock are strewn about in the most picturesque and unstudied disorder. In some places the blocks have been piled up one above another to a considerable height, and so skilfully has this been accomplished that their rugged and broken outline would lead you to believe they had occupied their present position for centuries. They are for the most part covered with indigenous plants and shrubs, and adorned with a variety of mosses and lichens intermixed with ferns and wild flowers. Some of the blocks have been brought from a considerable distance, and a great amount of labour as well as taste and skill has been employed in their arrangement.

In the middle of this rocky valley is an hydraulic curiosity— the model of a weeping willow in copper, presenting the appearance of a living tree, in which every branch is a pipe and every sprig and leaf a syringe, whilst among the grass which surrounds it are concealed innumerable jets, all ready to shed a flood of tears upon the unsuspecting wight whose curiosity may induce him to come within their range. We remember on one occasion passing through the grounds with a party of visitors from Sheffield, when one of the company, an amateur botanist, usurping the gardener's office, volunteered to describe and give the technical names of the different plants and shrubs. When we reached the willow the gardener, with a mischievous smile, appealed to our amateur for the name. "Certainly, he would just examine the formation of the leaf, and then tell him the particular class." No sooner said than done ; he unsuspectingly stepped on to the grass, and in an instant a thousand jets were pouring their united streams upon his devoted head. He contrived to make his escape, all dripping and drenched, and, disappearing among the shrubberies, we saw him no more.

Passing beneath a rustic archway and through a narrow opening in the rocks, the entrance to which is blocked by an immense piece of gritstone balanced upon a pivot so as to turn with the slightest pressure of the hand, we enter the drive and continue our walk, winding through a labyrinth of rockwork abounding in scenery of a broken and rugged character. In some places we notice hugh piles of gritstone rising to a great elevation, their precipitous fronts clothed with mosses and creeping plants, and over which the water has been made to descend in beautiful cascades. Some of these towering masses have received the appellation of the

Victoria, Albert, and Wellington Rocks, so designated in honour of the visits of the distinguished persons whose names they bear.

ROCKWORK—CHATSWORTH.

A few paces further on we reach a second archway in the rocks, emerging from which we come suddenly upon an open garden, in the centre of which stands the great conservatory.

This garden is of an oblong form, surrounded by a steep embankment crowned with a thick hedge of yew, and environed by lofty forest trees which shelter it from the inclemency of our northern climate. The open ground is planted with a number of prickly Sicilian firs, a tree popularly known by the designation of the monkey's puzzle, and the slopes of the embankment are laid out in beds, adorned with flowers of the most beautiful forms and colours—geraniums, verbenas, and calceolarias of the most ornamental and varied kinds, and some rare and beautiful specimens of roses. A broad gravelled path has been formed along the top of the embankment, communicating with the lower level at each corner by a flight of steps with ornamental stone balusters.

The Chatsworth Conservatory may be considered as the prototype and precursor of the Hyde Park palace of industry, and before the erection of that edifice it was the finest structure of the kind in the world. The merit of having first suggested such a building is due to the late Sir Joseph Paxton, of whose skill and genius it will long remain a monument. The effect is at once imposing and magnificent, presenting the appearance of a vast mountain of glass, its channelled sides, when reflecting the rays of the sun, giving it quite a brilliant and fairy-like appearance. Some idea of its extent may be formed from the fact that it covers nearly an acre of ground. The form is that of a parallelogram, including a centre and two side compartments; the length being 276 feet, and the width 123 feet; the height of the centre roof is 67 feet, and the transverse span 70 feet. The basement consists of a substantial stone plinth, three or four feet in height, resting upon arches fitted with ventilators, and from this plinth springs the main structure—a wall of glass rising 40 feet in height, and having an inward curve of an elliptical form, supported by a framework of iron resting upon a double range of light and elegant columns. From the framework springs a second series of ribs, 35 feet in height, supporting a lofty dome, which assumes the form of a square cone. It has been calculated that the surface contains 70,000 square feet of glass, disposed in zigzag rows, presenting a series of angular projections—an arrangement which, it is said, enables it better to withstand the force and violence of storms.

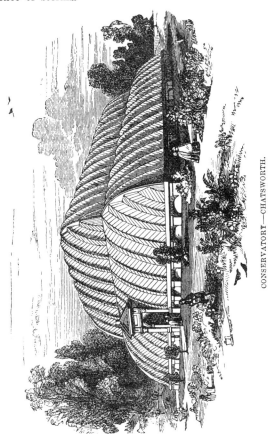

CONSERVATORY—CHATSWORTH.

The entrance is by a neat Grecian doorway, surmounted by a cornice and pediment, supported by pilasters.    On entering we at once feel the deliciously warm temperature, and almost fancy ourselves transported by some unseen agency into southern lands, the sight that greets the eye being one of rare and dazzling beauty—a broad carriage-drive runs through the centre, and on each side of this are arranged the choicest and most beautiful of nature's productions, growing as freely and as luxuriantly as if in their own native climes. Here we see the tall and stately banana, with its gorgeous array of scarlet flowers; the lotus, and the Egyptian papyrus, their broad green leaves mingling with the delicate tracery of the fern; palms of almost every kind, with a variety of plants, shrubs, and other tropical productions that have been brought hither from the prairies of America, the banks of the Nile, and from the farthest Ind. A gallery supported by light iron brackets has been carried round the dome, the approach to which is by a flight of steps formed in the ornamental rockwork. From this gallery the *coup d'œil* is magnificent. It is impossible, however, for words to convey an idea of the glories of the scene, and the most florid picture which the imagination could create would only shadow forth a faint resemblance of the gorgeous beauty displayed.

The scene has been thus described by a recent writer : " The view from this gallery is, perhaps, more striking than that which is obtained below. You gaze in speechless rapture upon a glowing assemblage of all that is most beautiful in nature's productions. Every shade of exquisite colour, brilliant and almost dazzling in their combined effect—every form of foliage in its most endless variety, and every shade of green, softening from its reposing qualities the otherwise too gorgeous mass of bright colours—every curious berry and wondrous production that hitherto one was contented to read about, without aiming at anything beyond—are all to be seen here growing in such luxuriance and profusion that you might be in the country belonging to each variety and not see them to greater advantage. Large pools of water are provided for the cultivation of the rare specimens of water plants. The beautiful blue water lily from the rivers of South America is here, seeming as if it had stolen the colour of the deep blue sky above it; together with the matchless crimson lily, reflecting itself in the transparent water, and looking as though it blushed at its own gorgeous beauty. Every brilliant variety of the cactus, and the varied forms of ferns, adorn the rockwork as you ascend to the gallery, now and then affording you glimpses, through their luxuriant growth, of the beauty above, below, and around you, till at the top nearly the whole of the interior bursts at once upon the view."

Among the floral productions at the further end of this tropical garden are some marble fragments from Minerva's Temple, at Sunium, brought to this country some years ago by Sir Augustus Clifford, then in command of H.M.S. Euryalus. On the pedestal which supports them are inscribed the following lines from the pen of the Earl of Carlisle :—

> " These fragments stood on Sunium's airy steep,
>      They rear'd aloft Minerva's guardian shrine ;
>   Beneath them roll'd the blue Ægean deep,
>      And the Greek pilot hail'd them as divine.
>
> " Such was e'en their look of calm repose,
>      As wafted round them came the sounds of fight,
>   When the glad shout of conquering Athens rose
>      O'er the long track of Persia's broken flight.
>
> " Though clasp'd by prostrate worshippers no more,
>      They yet shall breathe a thrilling lesson here ;
>   Though distant from their own immortal shore,
>      The spot they grace is still to freedom dear."

Leaving the Conservatory by the opposite door to that by which we entered we pass under an arch overgrown with ivy, and descend towards the lower garden, passing some clumps of magnificent trees, through the openings of which we occasionally obtain delightful views of the surrounding country. Almost the first object that meets the eye is a circular fountain, in the centre of which a jet throws up a stream of water to a considerable elevation. Near to this our attention was directed to an immense Spanish chestnut tree, its ample foliage covering a large extent of ground, and its mighty limbs extending over the greensward with the grace and majesty of a monarch of the forest ; the trunk is remarkably straight, and the height from the root to the lowest branch is estimated at fifty feet. A few yards further on we come to the Emperor Fountain, so named in honour of the visit of the late Czar Nicholas of Russia to Chatsworth, in 1844. This, one of the finest fountains in Europe, is situated immmediately opposite the south front of the mansion, and throws up a column of water to the height of 260 feet. When in full play it forms a striking feature, and the clear transparent element, rising in a silvery stream and overtopping the loftiest trees, may be seen for miles around.

Following our guide we descend by a flight of steps to the terrace which runs along the west front of the house. On one side is a handsome balustrade, adorned with sculptured figures and urns, and on the other is planted a number of cedars of Lebanon. Close to the walk are several trees, interesting from their historical associations. One, a young and vigorous oak, was planted by Her Majesty (then Princess Victoria) in commemoration of her visit in 1832. Near it is an American chestnut (*Castanea Americana*), planted at the same time by her mother, the Duchess of Kent, and also a sycamore, planted by his late Royal Highness Prince Albert, on the occasion of his visit with Her Majesty in 1843. Within a short distance of these is a Spanish chestnut, and a variegated sycamore (*Acer Pseudo-Plantanus variegatum*), planted, the one in 1816 by the late Emperor of Russia, and the other two years afterwards by his brother the Grand Duke Michael.

The terrace is connected with the lower garden by a broad flight of steps, beneath which we pass, and enter the Italian garden, one of the favourite places of resort of the late duke. This garden is planted with cedars of Lebanon, acacia, and other trees. The ground is laid out in ornamental flower beds, hedged with privet, an addition which at the first glance gives them a somewhat stiff and formal appearance. These parterres constitute the principal feature of this garden, and the sparkling and brilliant colours of the flowers, all harmoniously combined, produce a beautiful effect, presenting the appearance of mosaic work set within borders of the most vigorous green. In this delightful retreat the glowing productions of nature are skilfully blended with the elegancies and refinements of art. The centre is ornamented with a *jet d'eau*, and surrounding it an elegant balustrade, panelled and adorned with sculptured urns, vases, &c. Some of the panelled recesses contain groups of statuary in white marble, two of which are especially deserving of notice ; one, " The Dog and Pups," and the other, " The Goat and Kid," both by Beheme.

Continuing our route along the terrace walk, and by the west front of the hall, we reach the northern extremity, which is terminated by the lower archway of the entrance lodge, through which we pass, and again enter the park, where we are left to wander at will.

There are other attractions at Chatsworth, of which space will not permit us to give more than a passing notice. Not the least interesting of these are the fruit and vegetable gardens, situated about midway between the hall and the Baslow lodge. The visitor is first conducted through the New Holland House, containing a variety of plants and shrubs, the product of our Australian colonies. He is next ushered into the Amherstia House, built expressly for that most beautiful of trees the *Amherstia Nobilis*, of which it is said there are only two other specimens in Europe. The Victoria House is the next in succession ; this building was erected for the cultivation of the *Victoria Regia* or Royal Lily, the gem of the South American waters, and assuredly the finest of all aquatic plants. This plant was first introduced to this country in 1847, by seeds collected on the river Berbice in British Guiana, and it first revealed its magnificent bloom at Chatsworth, in November, 1849 ; the flower was presented to Her Majesty, in honour of whom the genus was named. It is grown in a large tank, thirty-four feet in diameter, the water being maintained at a proper temperature, and, to give it the character of a running stream, kept constantly in motion by means of a miniature revolving water-wheel fixed to one side. The leaves of the plant are of a circular form, five or six feet in diameter, and slightly turned up at the edge. The blossoms are of a brilliant rose colour, and measure twelve or fourteen inches across. In addition to the *Victoria Regia* a number of other aquatic plants, some specimens of the *Achimenes Longiflora*, a native of Mexico, and a plant called the *Nelumbium Speciosum*, or sacred bean of the Egyptians, are found in this conservatory. The Orchidaceous

House, containing a fine selection of the curious orchid tribe, completes the circuit of the kitchen gardens.

One of the most prominent objects in the park, being seen from almost every part of it, is the old hunting-tower,

THE OLD HUNTING-TOWER.

standing near the summit of a thickly-wooded hill, on the north-east side of the house, and approached by a path winding through the tall ancestral trees. It is a square building, flanked at each angle by a circular projection, rising above the roof in the form of turrets, and was originally designed as a place whence ladies might enjoy the sport of the chase without danger or fatigue. From the summit a splendid panoramic view is obtained of the house and grounds, with a wide extent of country beyond.

MARY QUEEN OF SCOTS' BOWER.

On the rising ground, midway between the house and the hunting-tower, are the stables, an extensive range of building erected by the fifth Duke of Devonshire, at a cost, it is said, of £40,000.

On leaving the entrance lodge we proceed by the northern end of the Italian garden, and along a carriage road leading to the bridge, just before reaching which, on the right hand side, is the bower of Mary Queen of Scots, almost the only memorial of the unfortunate Queen's fourteen years' imprisonment here. It is a low square tower, surrounded by a moat, and approached by a flight of steps. The top has been laid out for a garden, but is now overgrown with shrubs and trees, apparently of considerable antiquity. In this secluded spot, it is said, the unhappy princess spent many hours of her long captivity. Crossing the bridge a few minutes' walk brings us to the Edensor lodge, the southern boundary of the park.

It is with feelings of mingled pleasure and regret that we bade adieu to Chatsworth, with its palatial splendour, its pictures, its statuary, and magnificent furniture; its gardens and conservatories, its lakes, its fountains, its cascades, and all the varied combination of objects which art and ingenuity and taste have brought together. We could have loitered for hours with unceasing delight in its rich domain, threading the shady avenues, or reclining upon the sunny glades, where every scene is full of sylvan beauty, enriched with all the adventitious aids which the taste of man can bestow.

# CHAPTER IX.

EDENSOR at once bespeaks itself a model village, a kind of
sanitary Eden, where everything is new, and stiff, and stately,
nothing antiquated, free, or naturally beautiful, or that looks
as if it ever would become so.    The houses are all arranged
with mathematical order and regularity, and even the little
patches of garden seem as if they had been laid out with the
aid of a rule and compass.    The inhabitants are chiefly
persons employed upon the Chatsworth estate, and their
dwellings, which were erected at the cost of the late duke,
are all built in the ornamental villa fashion, the Anglo-Italian,
Swiss, and Gothic being the prevailing styles.    Each house
has a small garden attached, planted with shrubs and evergreens, and adorned with roses, hollyhocks, and other flowers.
The place has certainly a pretty appearance, but it lacks that
charm and interest which some of our less pretending, but
more homely and antiquated country villages possess.    We
love to see the old-fashioned black-and-white timber-houses,
recalling the days of our forefathers, with their high-peaked
gables and quaintly-ornamented bargeboards, their thatched
roofs and clustering chimneys peeping out from amid their
screen of leaves, their walls draped with ivy, and overhung
with roses and honeysuckles and sweetbriars, looking so cosy
and snug and comfortable, and speaking so unmistakably of
the happiness and contentment that reigns within.

The *Chatsworth Inn*, near the Swiss Lodge, is a large
establishment, where superior accommodation can be obtained,
and being contiguous to the park gates it is very convenient
for parties visiting the hall.    The church and the parsonage

are the only buildings that boast of any considerable antiquity. The former is a venerable structure, standing at the further end of the village, and occupies an elevated plot of ground environed by a belt of wide-spreading trees. The old church was taken down a few years ago, and the present structure,

EDENSOR CHURCH AND VILLAGE.

which was completed in 1870 from the designs of Sir Gilbert Scott, was erected on its site. It is an elegant Gothic building, comprising a nave, with side aisles, chancel, and monumental chapel, with a lofty tower and spire flanking the western end. The interior contains several memorials of the Cavendish family. In the chancel is a large alabaster monument, adorned with sculptured figures, life-size, to the memory of William, first Earl of Devonshire, who died in 1625. Near it is a brass, containing a long Latin inscription, to the memory of John Beton, a confidential servant of Mary Queen of Scots, who died in 1570, the year in which the unfortunate queen paid her first visit to Chatsworth ; and in the churchyard is the tomb over the remains of the late Duke of Devonshire, to which allusion has already been made.

Visitors proceeding to Bakewell from Edensor generally pass through the village, taking the route that leads by Pilsley, Handley Bank, and Birchill. The pedestrian who is not averse to an uphill walk we should recommend to take the path that runs over the summit of Ball Cross. This road is a more toilsome one, but the labour is amply compensated for by the splendid views of country which it affords.

Selecting the latter route, we cross the highway opposite the church, and, passing a few cottages on the left, begin the ascent by a steep and uneven road, along which green strips of grass here and there alternate with the deep cart ruts. The lane is narrow, and for some distance the prospect is shut out by tall, thick, tangled hedges and moss-grown trees, which fling out their spreading branches to meet those on the opposite side of the road ; but the shade is inviting, and we are glad to enjoy the delicious coolness, and escape the scorching rays of the sun. The wayfarers are few—a solitary keeper, sauntering leisurely along with his gun under his arm, and a couple of lads belabouring a passive-looking donkey, are all we meet upon the road. As we ascend the foliage becomes less dense, and through occasional openings in the hawthorn bushes we obtain glimpses of emerald-hued slopes, with groups of cattle pasturing, some quietly grazing, and others meditatively chewing their cud, and now and then whisking their tails to drive away the troublesome flies.

Still the road ascends, and as we advance the horizon spreads wider and wider. At length we reach the summit, and a glorious prospect breaks upon the sight. Selecting a mossy bank we sit down awhile to rest and leisurely to gaze upon the wide expanse of beauty that lies around us; and what pedestrian is there that knows not what an enjoyment it is when, having scaled some lofty eminence, you at length reach the top, and perhaps, overcome with heat and fatigue from the ascent, you are enabled, in undisturbed seclusion, to recline upon the soft green turf, communing with your own ideas as you gaze with raptured eye upon the beauty of the wide-spread landscape?

It is a lovely day. The sunbeams are dappling with playful shadows the rich greensward, and nature seems as if arrayed in her gayest attire. The air resounds with the hum of insects, the grasshoppers are " chittering" in the tall grass, and the birds are carolling joyously as they soar aloft into the bright blue sky. Before us spreads a beautiful valley, broken and undulating, backed by woods and gentle eminences, beyond which a range of pastoral hills, crowding one upon another, sweep around in an irregular circle, headland following headland, and ridge succeeding ridge, until their distant summits seem to mingle with the sky. Below, where the smoke comes curling through the trees, is the little village of Edensor, with its church peeping through the thick umbrage; beyond, that silvery line of light, twining and twisting, marks the course of the Derwent as it meanders through the fertile vale, its surface calm and unruffled, reflecting as from a mirror the branches of the trees which here and there adorn its sloping sides. On the rising ground on the opposite bank of the river stands the gem of all this gorgeous setting—the " Palace of the Peak," with its terraces and gardens, its glistening fountains and foaming cascades—a terrestrial paradise spread out before us like a panorama. When we saw it the sun was at the meridian, and threw a noontide glory over the scene, where all was flashing and glittering beneath a flood of light. It was impossible to witness such a prospect without a feeling of strong emotion; inspiration breathed around, and every object awakened enthusiasm.

We loitered for some time upon the top of the hill, the eye roving again and again over the boundless prospect until it seemed that the landscape had become familiar to us. At length we rose to depart, intending to descend by the opposite side of the hill into Bakewell. The road is alike rough and steep, and brings us rapidly down to a plantation with a variety of trees, among which the mountain ash, with its scarlet berries, makes a gay appearance. By-and-by the road turns, and we have trees on both sides, ash, oak, and larch, with thick bracken and underwood growing beneath ; another turn, and we come in sight of the old town of Bakewell, situate in the bosom of a valley replete with diversified scenery, through which the silvery Wye winds its sinuous course ; again we descend, rapidly winding round the base of the Castle Hill, and as we proceed the view expands, and we see the sweet vale of Haddon, with its undulating slopes and wooded hills.

At the foot of the hill we come upon the highroad and enter the town, which is approached from this side by a handsome stone bridge, with battlements and bold projecting piers. We wanted rest and refreshment, and found both at the *Castle*, a clean and comfortable inn, immediately opposite the post-office, and the first house on the right after crossing the bridge.

Bakewell may fairly be considered as the metropolis of the High Peak. It is the principal market town of North Derbyshire, and a polling-place for the county. Its history may be traced from a very remote period, the first mention we have dating so far back as the year 924, when Edward the Elder erected an intrenched fortress, and established a military station here, in order to overawe the disaffected Mercians. The remains of these fortifications may be traced even at the present day, and the names of some of the adjoining fields, as the "Warden-field," the "Castle-field," and the "Court-yard," seem in some degree to confirm the tradition. On the summit of the Castle Hill is a square plot with a tumulus on it, hollow at the top. This is believed to have been a portion of the rampart, which would appear to have been of considerable extent from the foundations that have been occasionally discovered. The Saxon name of the place was *Baderanwylla,* or *Badde cum Wel,* signifying the bathing well. In Domesday survey it is written *Badequelle,* or *Baquewell,* of which its modern appellation is clearly a corruption.

The situation of Bakewell is very pleasant, the houses being built in a deep valley, and up the sloping side of a steep limestone ridge that rises from the western bank of the Wye. The town has a quiet, staid, respectable appearance about it, and some of the buildings show unmistakable signs of antiquity. Under the direction of the Duke of Rutland, the lord of the manor, it has within the last few years been greatly improved, many of the older houses have been rebuilt, and the streets have been lighted with gas and paved and drained, and altogether it now presents a clean and comfortable aspect.

The Bakewell waters have been held in high repute from a period anterior to the Conquest. They are recommended as a tonic, and are said to be beneficial in affections of chronic rheumatism. The temperature is about 60° Fahrenheit. These waters were analysed by the late C. Sylvester, and ten quarts were found to contain crystallised sulphate of lime, 75 grains; super-carbonate of lime, 20 grains; crystallised sulphate of magnesia, 22 grains; muriate of magnesia, 1·6 grains; super-carbonate of iron, 3·1 grains. The baths are situated near the centre of the town; the principal one is 30 feet in length by 16 feet in width, and of proportionate depth; it is kept constantly supplied with fresh water, which on its influx emits a considerable quantity of carbonic acid gas; there are also shower and private warm baths attached. Adjoining the bath-room is the Bakewell and High Peak Institute, containing a library, reading-room, and museum, which are open to visitors under certain restrictions. Contiguous to this institution are the Bath Gardens, which afford an agreeable promenade.

Bakewell forms a desirable place of residence during the summer months. The climate is healthy, and the air being constantly agitated by the currents of wind which sweep through the valley, an agreeable freshness always prevails, whilst the lofty hills on each side shelter it from the cold blasts. It is also admirably adapted as a centre from whence

agreeable excursions may be made to the different places of
interest which surround it.   The principal hotel, the *Rutland
Arms*, is a large and well-conducted establishment ; and being
situated on the line of the great thoroughfare between London
and Manchester, was in the old coaching days a house of
considerable note.   It is now chiefly resorted to by persons
who come to see the attractions of the neighbourhood, or to

BAKEWELL CHURCH.

enjoy the sport of angling in the Wye, visitors to the house having the privilege of fishing in the river.

The church occupies a commanding position on the slope of a hill, and from its elevated situation forms a striking object, and may be seen from almost every part of the town. It is a fine old-fashioned structure, venerable in appearance, and rich in architectural beauty. Like most of our old English churches the style is varied—Saxon in one place and Norman in another, with examples of later periods in other parts of the fabric. The plan is cruciform, including a nave with side aisles, chancel, and north and south transepts. From the intersection of the cross rises an elegant octagon tower, resting upon a square base, and surmounted by a lofty spire. The old spire, having become dangerous from the weakness of the pillars which supported it, was removed in 1826, and in 1841 the tower, with the whole of the north and south transepts, and the Vernon chapel, were taken down and rebuilt, the original style being carefully adhered to in their restoration. New seats were added, the pulpit, reading-desk, and organ were rearranged, and four stained-glass windows were placed at the south end—the expense incurred in these alterations being estimated at £8,600.

In excavating the foundations a number of Saxon remains were discovered, including several incised gravestones or coffin lids, with crosses and other ornamental devices carved thereon, and fragments of stone on which were engraved Runic circles and curiously interlaced knots, resembling those upon the old cross in the churchyard—a style of ornamentation peculiar to the northern nations, by whom such circles were believed to be imbued with a sort of magical power. Many of these ancient remains are arranged in the porch, and some others, including several headstones, have been removed, and are now preserved in the museum at Lomberdale Park.

On reaching the churchyard we found the building locked, but a laughing, blue-eyed girl, in a gipsy hat, who came tripping past, kindly summoned to our aid the sexton, who lives close by. Presently the old man came hobbling along, jingling his huge keys, and we were admitted to the interior, passing through the south porch, in which is displayed the collection of sepulchral remains already referred to. The nave is separated from the aisles on each side by semicircular arches resting upon massive stone piers, and is lighted by narrow-headed windows, in single lights; above the archways rises the clerestory, crowned externally by an embattled parapet. At the western end is a Saxon archway, ornamented with heads, and other rude designs, above which are the remains of a Norman arcade, formed by intersecting arches enriched with the zigzag moulding peculiar to the period. Near to the archway is an ancient stone font of octagon form, each face of which is ornamented with sculptured figures that have become much decayed with the lapse of years.

The church contains a number of monuments, effigies, and other sepulchral memorials. They are chiefly in alabaster, and some have been richly painted and gilded in accordance with the fashion of the times when they were erected. The most remarkable is an altar tomb near the east end of the church, on which is the recumbent effigy of a knight in plate armour, with mail-gorget and pointed helmet. On the latter is inscribed the words, "ICH NAZAREN." This monument is to the memory of Sir Thomas Wendesley of Wendesley, Knt., who received his death-wound whilst fighting on the side of the house of Lancaster at the battle of Shrewsbury, 4th Henry IV. (1403), and was buried here. On one side of the tomb is a panel containing a quatrefoil, in the centre of which is a shield bearing the arms of Wendesley—erm. on a bend three escallops or. At the south-east end is a monument containing two half-length figures beneath a crocketted canopy, representing Sir Godfrey Foljambe and his wife Avena, "lord and lady of the manors of Hassop, Okebroke, Elton, Stanton, Darley, Overhall, and Lokhawe," who founded the chantry in honour of the holy cross attached to the church of Bakewell, 39th Edward III. (1366) The knight is habited in plate armour, with a pointed helmet. Over his head is an escutcheon charged with the arms of Foljambe—sa. a bend between six escallops or. Above the lady is an escutcheon bearing the arms of Darley—gu. six fleurs-de-lis, argt. three, two, and one.

The Vernon Chapel, situated to the east of the transepts, was founded in 1360 upon the walls of a former chapel, and is built in the later decorated style. This chapel was for many generations the principal burial-place of the Vernons and Manners, successive owners of the neighbouring mansion of Haddon, and contains several monuments of members of those families. In the centre is a large altar-tomb or cenotaph to the memory of Sir George Vernon, the renowned "King of the Peak," who died in 1561, and his two wives Margaret and Maude. The tomb contains several shields of arms, and on it is an effigy of the knight clothed in plate armour, wearing the pointed beard so characteristic of the period, and with him are the full-length figures of his wives, habited in the costume of Elizabeth's reign. Near to this monument is that of Sir John Manners, who died in 1611, and his wife Dorothy, one of the daughters and co-heiresses of the before-named Sir George Vernon, who conveyed the Haddon estate to the Manners family. There are several other monuments in this chapel, for the most part executed in alabaster. A handsome stained-glass window, by Hardman and Co., of Birmingham, has in recent years been placed here in memory of the late Duke of Rutland. It is of three lights, and illustrates Christ's Resurrection. In the centre light is a delicately-draped figure of the Saviour, represented as just rising from the tomb, with the right hand uplifted, as if in the act of benediction, and surrounded by a halo of rich ruby colour, above which are depicted a number of cherubim. The lower compartments of the side lights contain the representation of Roman soldiers, and in the upper portions are the figures of angels. Beneath is a brass bearing the following inscription: "The above window was erected by subscription in memory of John Henry, Duke of Rutland, who died 20th January, 1857, aged 79 years."

In the churchyard, near the angle formed by the junction of the south transept and chancel, is an ancient stone cross, somewhat similar in design to that at Eyam, already described, but not so elaborate in its details. The ornaments are of a Scriptural character, illustrating the Nativity, Crucifixion, Resurrection, and Ascension of Christ; but the figures are so much worn and defaced that it is difficult to decipher them. The height of the cross, exclusive of the pedestal, is about eight feet, and its width two feet.

M

Many of the head-stones are inscribed with epitaphs, some of them being of a serious character, while others are written in a humorous strain. The following, which we copied from a tomb near the west end of the church, is worthy a corner in the collection of those who are curious in such matters. The inscription, which is much worn, records the interment here of John Dale, barber-surgeon of Bakewell, and his two wives, Elizabeth, daughter of Godfrey Foljambe, and Sarah Bloodworth. Beneath are the following lines :—

> "This thing in life might raise some jealousy—
> Here all three lie together lovingly ;
> But from embraces here no pleasure flows,
> Alike are here all human joys and woes.
> Here Sarah's chiding John no longer hears ;
> And old John's rambling Sarah no more fears.
> A period's come to all their toilsome lives,
> The good man's quiet—still are both his wives."

The ancient parish of Bakewell is very extensive, comprising nine parochial chapelries and fourteen parishes, including a part of the chapelry of Buxton. So early as the year 1086, according to the Domesday survey, a church existed here, to which were attached two priests. In the reign of King John the church was granted to the canons of Lichfield, in return for which one of the prebendaries of that cathedral was to say mass for the soul of the king and his ancestors, and the dean and chapter of the same cathedral have still the patronage of the living.

We left Bakewell about six o'clock, intending to visit Haddon and stay the night at Rowsley.

Passing through the town, we strike off suddenly to the left, near the *Rutland Arms*, and proceed along the turnpike road—a pretty rural highway—that leads to Matlock and Derby.

The evening is cool and pleasant, rendering our walk the more agreeable ; and the air is balmy with the fragrant odours of the clover in the standing grass ; the insects have come forth by thousands to enjoy their little hour of life ; the white butterflies and the purple moths are revelling in the warm sunbeams ; and myriads of midges, ascending from the earth like a column of vapour, are performing their mazy gyrations with unceasing activity; a low, still murmuring is heard around,

> " Nature's ceaseless hum,
> Voice of the desert, never dumb."

A gentle breeze rustles through the branches of the trees, and the sun, playing at bo-peep through the leaves, mottles the path with the waving shadows of their overhanging boughs. The hedges which border the road are literally bedecked with the delicate blossoms of the dog rose, and the coppices are overhung with ferns and fox-gloves, that half hide the modest daisy and the lovely forget-me-not from the sight.

As we journey onwards the country spreads wider and wider, and the prospect, which at first was limited to a narrow range of vision, becomes more and more interesting. The road is continued through a valley some three miles in length, replete with varied and picturesque scenery—a vale that charms more by its sylvan beauty and fertile loveliness than by any features of a bold or striking character. To the right a succession of gentle hills, of varied form and elevation, ascend gradually from the plain, their sloping sides adorned with picturesque groups of trees and plantations, from the openings between which are seen, here and there, a villa or *cottage ornée* peeping out from amid the shrouding foliage. To the left the country spreads out in broad and ample meadows, through which the Wye pursues its sinuous course, forming, as it winds irregularly from side to side, innumerable bays and creeks, crowded with a variety of water lilies, ranunculuses, and other aquatic plants; sometimes the current glides along, clear and musical, its placid surface chequered by the shadows of the overhanging willows, at others its sparkling waters are seen foaming and splashing over the fragments of moss-grown rock, or eddying in innumerable ripples round the little islets of sedge and rushes that occasionally intercept its course. From the opposite bank of the river rises a precipitous ridge of limestone rock, clothed to the summit with waving woods, the sombre aspect of which forms a striking contrast to the rich hue of the recently-shorn meadow land, or the still brighter green of the thriving cornfield.

For the space of a mile there is nothing but the generally pleasing character of the vale to notice. Having traversed that distance, the old mansion of Haddon comes gradually upon the sight. At first the towers and turrets are seen

HADDON HALL.

peeping through the deep umbrage, and, as we continue our walk, the bold projecting bays and quaintly-mullioned windows of the hall itself become discernible. Seen from the highway, this venerable mansion has a very imposing appearance, borrowing magnitude and importance from the position it occupies. It is built on the declivity of a steep, rocky bank, that rises abruptly from the river, its embattled parapets and ancient towers partially shrouded with ivy, rising majestically above the venerable woods in which it is embosomed, giving it the appearance of a formidable fortress.

The time of our visit was a favourable one for seeing it to advantage. The clouds were gathering in the glowing west, where the beauty of the day was concentrated ; and the sun, having nearly finished his course, threw the rich illumination of his farewell beams over a picture of wide extent and surpassing loveliness, lighting up with brilliant touches the highest peaks of the distant hills, and flinging broad masses of shadow across the intervening valleys, gilding the towers and turrets of the old baronial hall, and wrapping the woods and meadows around in a deep glow of purple, that gave to the whole scene an air of rich and imposing grandeur.

Nearly opposite the second milestone we turned off the highroad, passing through a gate on the left, and across a pasture field, until we came to an old-fashioned bridge of three arches spanning the river, beyond which, at the foot of the hill, is the picturesque cottage of Mrs. Bath, the custodian of the hall, a quaint-looking structure almost as antiquated in appearance as the mansion itself, with a trim garden in front, in which are two ancient yew trees, clipped to resemble a boar's head and peacock, the respective crests of the Vernon and Manners families.

# CHAPTER X.

THE Manor of Bakewell, of which Haddon—or as it was
anciently written, "*Haduna*"—was a dependent ville, was
bestowed by the Conqueror, together with extensive domains
in this and other counties, upon his natural son, William
Peverel. Subsequently the ville of Haddon was given by one
of the Peverels to a retainer of the name of Avenell, by whom
it was held on the tenure of knight's service. In the latter
half of the twelfth century, the honour of Peverel having
passed by forfeit to King Henry II., the Avenells became
tenants in chief of the Crown. Of this family comparatively
little is known. About the time of Richard I., William Avenell,
the last of the line, left two daughters, his co-heiresses, one
of whom, Avicia, conveyed a moiety of the manor of Haddon,
being her portion of the estate, by marriage, to Richard, son
of Warine de Vernon, Baron of Shipbroke, a descendant of
Richard de Vernon, who came over to England with William
the Conqueror, and who was himself a descendant of the
Vernons, Lords of Vernon, in Normandy. The other daughter,
Elizabeth, became the wife of Simon Bassett, of Sapcote ;
and about the reign of Henry VI. a covenant was entered
into by which the Bassett's moiety of the Haddon estates
became vested in the Vernons. For several generations from
this time Haddon continued the residence of the Vernon
family, during which period it was always regarded as the
seat of feudal splendour and the most liberal hospitality.

Sir George Vernon, the last of this illustrious race of
feudatory chieftains who inherited the family possessions,

was renowned for his munificence and sumptuous style of living. His wealth and influence were alike unbounded; and for his princely hospitality and open house he was styled the " King of the Peak." He was lord of thirty manors, and kept a retinue of fourscore servants. During his lifetime the festivities of Christmastide were observed right royally; in accordance with the custom of the period, open house was kept for twelve days, the boar's head and the huge baron of beef graced the board, and the wassail-cup was circulated in the true style of old English hospitality.

Sir George was twice married, but had no male issue. His first wife was Margaret, daughter of Sir Gilbert Talbois; after her death he espoused Maude, daughter of Sir Ralph Longford, knight. He died 31st August (4th Elizabeth), 1561, leaving two daughters his co-heiresses, Margaret and Dorothy, both married at the time of his decease. Margaret was the wife of Sir Thomas Stanley, second son of Edward, third Earl of Derby, a nobleman not less renowned for his magnificence and liberality than the " King of the Peak," and of whom Camben says "that with Edward Earl of Derby's death the glory of hospitality seemed to fall asleep." Dorothy, the second daughter, married Sir John Manners, knight, second son of Thomas, thirteenth Baron Ros, and first Earl of Rutland, from whom is descended the present illustrious owner of Haddon, the Duke of Rutland. The eldest of these co-heiresses obtained Harleston, Tong, and other estates in Staffordshire; and Dorothy received as her dower the Derbyshire estates, including Haddon Hall.

The alliance between Dorothy Vernon and Sir John Manners is believed to have been a clandestine one. Tradition says that Sir George Vernon, having promised the hand of his second daughter to a younger son of the powerful Earl of Derby, looked with disfavour upon a union with Sir John Manners. It is further stated that young Manners, the better to obtain his object, disguised himself in the habit of a forester, and wandered for some time about the woods of Haddon, and that, during the festivities of a masked ball, given by Sir George in honour of the marriage of his eldest daughter with Sir Thomas Stanley, the Lady Dorothy made her escape through the side door of the anteroom adjoining the grand banqueting gallery, and eloped with her lover. This doorway, which bears the name of Dorothy Vernon's, is still shown to visitors.

DOROTHY VERNON'S DOORWAY.

Sir John Manners served the office of high sheriff of Derbyshire in 1594, and died in 1611, being succeeded by his eldest son, Sir George Manners, who was knighted by King James I. at Belvoir Castle, April 23, 1603. Sir George married Grace, the eldest daughter of Sir Henry Pierpont, knight, and by her had issue three sons, the eldest of whom, John Manners, of Haddon, on the death of George, seventh Earl of Rutland, without issue, in 1641, succeeded to the honours and possessions of the illustrious family of Manners, and in this line the title and estates have descended in direct succession to the present Duke of Rutland.

The same generous hospitality was displayed at Haddon under the successive Earls and Dukes of Rutland as under their maternal ancestors the Vernons. John Manners, the ninth earl, who was created by Queen Anne, in 1703, Duke of Rutland, kept, it is said, a retinue of 150 servants. He loved Haddon, as well he might; and so great was his attachment to a country life that, when he married his son to Lord Russell's daughter, he stipulated "that she should lose part of her jointure if ever she lived in town without her husband's consent."

The mansion of Haddon continued the family residence until about the beginning of the last century, when it was gradually forsaken, and finally abandoned for the more stately castle of Belvoir. Though unoccupied, and shorn of its splendour, it still remains in a tolerable state of preservation, and is justly considered one of the most perfect examples we have of the old English baronial mansion, presenting a striking picture of the past, and conveying a very complete idea of the domestic arrangement and mode of living which prevailed among our forefathers in a feudal age, when rude abundance crowned the board, and the comforts, the luxuries, and the refinements of modern days were unknown.

Formerly the old baronial residence was shown by an aged dependent of the Duke of Rutland's, named William Hage, whose ancestors had been in the service of the Manners family for a period extending over more than three centuries, and who used to delight in sounding the praises of the former lords, relating with a good deal of humour many anecdotes respecting the revelries at Haddon in his younger days. The hall and gardens are now under the care of Mrs. Bath, at whose cottage at the foot of the hill we obtained a guide to accompany us through the various apartments and intricate passages of the old mansion.

On reaching the entrance tower at the north-west angle of the building, the attention is arrested by a number of sculptured shields, containing the armorial bearings of the Vernons, and some of their alliances, among which may be distinguished those of the Pipes. The flagstone in front of this entrance is worn into a deep hollow by the frequent stepping in and out of the portal.

Passing through a little doorway in the ponderous gates, behind which is suspended an immense hoop some eight or ten feet in diameter, that formerly encircled the brewing tub, we ascend a flight of angular steps leading to the lower courtyard, a quadrangular area, around which are disposed some of the principal apartments. On reaching this court we are at once struck with the desolate and cheerless character of the place. A peculiar death-like stillness prevails, broken only by the sharp echoes of our footsteps ringing upon the broken pavement, and reverberating through the long corridors and labyrinthine passages of the old hall.

Proceeding along the lower or western side of the quadrangle, we reach first the Chaplain's Room, a gloomy apartment, which seems to have been made the depository for useless lumber. Here are shown a number of large pewter plates, an oaken cradle, in which the infant scions of the house of Manners were rocked in bygone ages, a pair of huge jack-boots, with antique spurs, a leather doublet, a hunting horn, an old rusty matchlock, and some other articles of an equally unecclesiastical character.

Leaving this room we pass beneath a low archway, and enter the vestibule communicating with the Domestic Chapel, one of the oldest and most interesting portions of the mansion. This chapel, which has evidently been erected at two distinct periods, comprises a chancel and nave, with side aisles. The south aisle, and the circular columns which separate it from the nave, exhibit the characteristics of the late Norman period, whilst the remaining portion is in that style of architecture known as the perpendicular Gothic, and which may be said to have prevailed about the beginning of the fifteenth century. The nave is furnished with long oaken benches, intended for the domestics and retainers when attending divine service, and against the side walls of the chancel are two high-backed pews, surmounted with ornamental railings, designed for the use of the family and guests of the lords of Haddon. The mouldings of these pews, as also those of the pulpit and reading-desk, were originally ornamented with burnished gilding, the traces of which are yet visible. In the south aisle is an ancient oak chest, on which is carved a fret, the arms of the Vernons, and near it is placed a circular stone font, attached by the plinth to one of the pillars, and apparently coeval with the original structure. Against the wall of the north aisle is a music gallery of the Elizabethan period, approached by a flight of steps, which the guide incorrectly describes as a confessional. Over the altar is a large traceried window of five lights, formerly ornamented with stained glass, the greater portion of which was stolen many years ago. The centre light contains a representation of the Crucifixion, in a tolerably perfect state, and beneath is the following inscription in black letter characters :—

𝔒rate pro animabus 𝔯icarbi 𝔙ernon et 𝔅enebicite uxors ejus qui fecerunt, 𝔄no 𝔇ni 𝔐ilessimo ccccxxbii.

The roof is of open timber work, in construction plain and simple, even to rudeness. From the date carved upon one of the beams it would appear to have been repaired in 1624. In the entrance porch is an ancient stoup of octagon form, embattled upon the edge, and in the sill of one of the windows is a piscina and sedilia.

Returning from the chapel we cross the court-yard, and are admitted into the porch of the Great Hall. This porch, with the tower above it, is advanced slightly forward from the line of the main structure, and is entered by an arched doorway, above which are two shields, one bearing the arms of Vernon (arg. a fret sable), and the other those of Pembrugge (barry of six, or and az). Within the portal is a Roman altar, found in the grounds some centuries ago. The inscription, which is now almost illegible, has been variously rendered. The following is the reading of Mr. Llewellyn Jewitt, F.S.A. :—

DEO
MARTI
BRACIACÆ
OS(IT)TIVS
CÆCILIANVS
PRÆFCOH
I AQVITANO
Y S

Beyond this porch is a passage leading to the upper court-
yard. On the left side of the passage is that most important
place in every old mansion—the buttery, with its large oaken
door, in the middle of which is a small wicket, just large
enough to hand out a trencher, and where such persons as
required it were supplied with refreshment. Adjoining the
buttery is a vaulted apartment, that would seem to have
been originally used as an ale cellar.

Following our guide we are next conducted along a dark
sloping passage leading to the great kitchen, contiguous to
which are the pantries, bakehouse, and larders. In the
kitchen are two immense fireplaces, with irons for a multitude
of spits, and other culinary requisites. Near the centre of
the floor is a huge chopping-block; and arranged against the
walls are a range of dressers, and a wooden table, the top of
which is scooped out in hollows to answer the purpose of
kneading troughs. This room has a peculiarly sombre and
cheerless appearance, strangely contrasting with that which
it must have presented in former days; and, as if to render
its desolateness more apparent, a couple of swallows had, at
the time of our visit, built their nest over one of the fireplaces,
and the birds, disturbed by our presence, were flitting about
in the deepening twilight.

Returning from the kitchen we are ushered into the Great
Hall, which is separated from the vestibule by an oaken
screen. In the earlier days of the Vernons, and before the
erection of the grand banqueting gallery, this was the principal entertaining room; and many a scene of jovial mirth and
roystering revelry, unrestrained by the laws which modern
etiquette imposes, has been witnessed within its walls. Opposite the entrance is a platform or daïs, raised a few inches
above the general level of the floor, on which stands the high
table, where in former times sat the lord of the soil, surrounded by his family and guests, carefully placed according
to their rank above the salt, whilst his vassals occupied the
long tables flanking the walls.

A gallery, where the "musicyons" played during dinner,
occupies two sides of the hall, the front of which, as well as
of the screen, is ornamented with oak panelling, enriched
with Gothic tracery, and liberally adorned with the trophies

of the chase. Two or three old-fashioned pictures, much decayed by age, are suspended against the walls—one of them being the portrait of John Ward, the maternal ancestor of William Hage, to whom we have already made allusion, and who, in 1527, was deerkeeper to the lord of Haddon, and another, that of Martin Middleton, of Hazelbadge, a former tenant of the estate. A singularly interesting relic, and one very suggestive of the domestic customs of a bygone age, is still preserved—a strong iron ring, resembling a handcuff, attached to the screen, in which it is said the wrist of any recreant who refused to quaff the orthodox quantity of liquor expected of him was confined, in an upright position,

THE GREAT HALL—HADDON.

above his head, while his companions poured the contents of the goblet which he had rejected down the sleeve of his doublet.

At the upper end of the hall is a doorway leading to a passage communicating with the garden, on one side of which is the entrance to the Dining-room. This apartment is of much smaller dimensions than the great hall, and being insufficiently lighted and wanting in elevation, it presents a sombre and gloomy appearance.  The walls are covered with richly-ornamented wainscot panelling, surmounted by an elegant cornice of carved woodwork, and the upper range of panels are adorned with shields of arms, representing the different alliances of the former owners of Haddon, alternating with boars' heads, the crest of the Vernons.  Over the fire-

DINING-ROOM PASSAGE—HADDON.

place is a panel on which is carved the royal arms, with the motto underneath—

𝕯𝖗𝖊𝖉𝖊 𝕲𝖔𝖉 𝖆𝖓𝖉 𝖍𝖔𝖓𝖔𝖗 𝖙𝖍𝖊 𝕶𝖞𝖓𝖌.

Near to this are displayed the initials of Sir George Vernon (the King of the Peak), and his lady, in cypher, with an heraldic shield, bearing the arms of their respective families quartered, and above the date 1545, probably the year in which this part of the mansion was completed.  The ceiling is divided into bays by deeply-moulded tranverse beams that appear to have been originally ornamented with painting and gilding, the traces of which are still discernible.  Near the entrance is a recess, with an oriel window looking towards the garden. The walls of this recess, like those of the hall itself, are covered with ornamental panelling, though of a slightly different design. Two of the panels contain portraits of Henry VII. (whose son, Prince Arthur, the elder brother of Henry VIII., occasionally resided here, under the guardianship of Sir Henry Vernon) and his queen, Elizabeth of York ; and near them is carved a grotesque head, with cap and bells, supposed to represent Will Somers, the celebrated Court jester.

ORIEL WINDOW—HADDON.

Returning to the Great Hall, we are next conducted by a rude staircase to a corridor leading to the Musicians' Gallery, in the Great Hall, and communicating with the upper range of apartments occupying the south side of the building. In this corridor are two paintings, one representing Abraham offering up his son Isaac, and the other Christ reproving Peter.

The first chamber we enter is the State Drawing-room, situate immediately over the Dining-room just described. The walls are covered with panelling, and hung with loose arras now much faded and decayed—the latter a convenience rendered necessary to conceal the rude workmanship, and to protect the inmates from the draughts caused by the ill-fitting doorways. Around the edge of the ceiling is an ornamented cornice executed in stucco. Near the entrance is a wainscoted recess, lighted by an oriel window of three lights, the ceiling of which is embellished with stucco-work of a geometrical pattern, enriched with roses and other ornaments. In this recess is still preserved an ancient state chair.

Near the upper end of the State Drawing-room, on the left hand side, is a doorway leading to the earl's dressing-room and bedchamber, both of which are fitted up in a similar style, and hung with old-fashioned tapestry, the subjects being of a varied character, consisting of Scriptural and sporting scenes. Adjoining the bedchamber is a small apartment denominated the valet's room, but which Mr. King, in his "Observations on Ancient Castles" (p. 176), believes, from the neatness and ornamental character of its decorations, to have been "My Lady's Chamber." This room, like the others, is hung with tapestry, behind which, on one side, is a doorway leading to a narrow flight of steps communicating with the lower court-yard.

Retracing our steps until we again reach the corridor, we notice, immediately opposite the drawing-room doorway, four or five steps formed of solid oak, ascending which we enter the Grand Gallery, or ball-room, the most splendid apartment of the series. This gallery is 109 feet 9 inches in length, with a width of 16 feet 10 inches, exclusive of the bays, and occupies the greater part of the south front of the mansion. The timber which forms the flooring is said to have been cut from a single tree that grew in the park, the steps at the entrance having been formed out of the root. The walls are covered with wainscoting, relieved with Corinthian pilasters, from the capitals of which spring a series of enriched semicircular archways, the spandrils between being embellished with carved escutcheons, shields of arms, and other heraldic insignia. Surmounting the whole is an elaborately decorated frieze and cornice, the former ornamented with roses and thistles alternating with boar's heads and peacocks, the respective crests of the Vernon and Manners families. The ceiling is slightly coved and most elaborately ornamented with lozenges, quatrefoils, shields of arms, &c.,

executed in stucco-work. It was originally adorned with painting and gilding, but the whole is now covered with whitewash. The extreme narrowness of this gallery is in part relieved by three deep recesses, the centre one of which measures 15 feet by 12 feet. The windows lighting these bays contain some tolerably well executed specimens of stained glass. In the first window appears the arms of

N

Manners impaling those of Vernon with their quarterings, the whole encircled by a garter; in the centre window is displayed the royal arms of England, surmounted by a crown; and the third window contains the arms of Shrewsbury and Manners. Over the fire-place is an old painting, representing Tomyris the Scythian queen, receiving the head of Cyrus; and at the further end of the room is a glass case, in which is preserved a cast of the face of Lady Grace Manners, taken immediately after her death, when she had attained the advanced age of ninety years. It is said that upwards of two hundred couples danced in this noble apartment on the celebration of the signing of the Treaty of Amiens, in 1802. In 1836 the hall was thrown open to the tenantry, when a grand ball was given in honour of the coming of age of the present Duke of Rutland, then Marquis of Granby; and in the month of August 1860, a bazaar and fancy fair was held here in aid of the funds for restoring the old church of St. Peter, at Derby.

A more favourable time could not have been selected for visiting this interesting relic of a bygone age. As we passed through the room the warm rays of the setting sun came streaming through the mullioned windows, shedding a soft and mellow light upon the quaint carvings and oaken panelling, and the clear note of a robin within the hall rang out its last requiem to the departing day.

At the further end of the gallery, on the north side, is a doorway, approached by a few steps, through which we are admitted to the ante-room, containing a number of old paintings of little value, among which are portraits of England's "Virgin Queen," the unfortunate Charles the First, with an exceedingly melancholy-looking countenance, and his nephews, the fiery Rupert and Prince Eugene—the two latter after Vandyck. Here is also a picture, said to be by Schnyder, representing swans and other domestic and wild fowl; and a boar hunt, believed to be the work of the same artist.

From the ante-room we pass to the State Bedroom—one of the most interesting apartments in the building. It is a handsome room, lofty, and well lighted, having a large bay window on the west side, overlooking the upper court-yard. The frieze and cornice are of stucco-work, similar in design to those of the ante-room adjoining—the boar's head and peacock repeatedly occurring. The walls are hung with tapestry from the manufactory of the Gobelins, at Paris, the subjects being taken from Æsop's Fables. Over the fireplace is a large bas-relief, in plaster, representing "Orpheus Charming the Beasts," most wretchedly executed. The State bed, a valuable relic, is still preserved, though in a very dilapidated condition. It is hung with a dark-coloured velvet, lined with white satin, embroidered, the design of which may still be traced. It is said to have been worked in the reign of Henry VI. by Eleanor, wife of Sir Robert Manners, and co-heiress of Lord Ros. The bed was once removed to Belvoir Castle, where George IV. is said to have slept in it. It is now surrounded by a light wooden railing to protect it from the careless handling of visitors. The floor of the oriel is raised a couple of steps, and in it is placed an old-fashioned dressing-table, resting against which is a large mirror, in an ornamental frame. Behind the tapestry is a door, by which we are admitted to a gloomy apartment, designated the State-room. This is believed to be one of the oldest rooms in Haddon, and is remarkable as exhibiting an almost total absence of ornamentation. The floors are formed of plaster, much worn by the constant tramping of feet; the windows are narrow, and the doorways and other details are of the most rude and primitive style of workmanship; the walls are, for the most part, hung with tapestry, the subjects illustrating passages from the life of Moses.

From this room a short passage conducts to the Eagle, or (as it is sometimes denominated) Peverel's Tower, occupying the north-east angle of the building, in which is a circular flight of rugged and uneven steps leading to the roof. The battlements of the tower are crenellated, and at the north-west corner is a square watch tower, or exploratory turret, where, in olden times, was stationed the sentinel, whose duty it was to keep watch against the approach of marauding neighbours. The top of this turret is reached by steps on the outside, somewhat difficult of access, and up which we climbed, the better to obtain a view of the delightful country that spreads around.

This elevation commands a fine prospect of the exterior of

the mansion, with its spacious courts and embattled parapets, its terraced gardens and balustered walls, and the majestic woods that encompass it. Beyond, the view takes in the valley of the Wye, and the charming dale through which winds the babbling Lathkill. Looking in a northerly direction the eye passes over the town of Bakewell, ranging along a lovely vale that extends in the direction of Ashford, Monsal Dale, and Cressbrook. Turning towards the south the views are more boldly featured. In the foreground is a succession of woods, pastures, meadows, and cornfields, beyond which a long range of lofty hills extends upon the horizon as far as the eye can reach, the dark aspect of the distant moorlands serving but to heighten the beauty of the nearer landscape. In front is Stanton Hall, for generations the seat of the old family of the Thornhills, nearly hidden by the groves of pine trees, and Stanton Moor, interesting from the numerous early British remains, and other relics of the far-off past which still exist upon its summit. To the extreme left is seen the pretty little village of Rowsley, beyond which the wide opening between the hills marks the course of the Derwent as it flows through the picturesque vale of Darley to Matlock.

We lingered for some time upon the summit of the old tower, watching the sun as he descended lower and lower in the gloomy west, until he finally disappeared behind a bank of ruby-coloured clouds. The lights which yet lingered upon the summits of the distant hills were gradually giving way to the deepening shadows, and ere long thick mists overspread the valleys, and ascended in broken wreaths along the slope of the mountains; the hills on the opposite side of the valley, faintly indicated through the dun medium which enshrouded them, began to assume a ghostly obscurity, and seemed as if invested with additional grandeur; then the last ray of the radiant orb, which glimmered with a dying faintness upon the mountain's brow, vanished from the sight, and every object became blended in undistinguishable gloom. The coolness of the air on this high point was most refreshing, but the profound silence that seemed to enwrap the world had become so intense as to be almost painful—

"All things were hush'd as nature's self lay dead."

A calm tranquillity spread around, not a sound disturbing the solemn stillness save the rippling of the stream through the meadows below, and which now and then came in fitful murmurs upon the ear; the gentle breezes seemed to have lulled themselves to sleep, and scarcely a leaf rustled upon the branches of the trees.

We have often travelled over this romantic country, and been charmed with the excellent variety of its scenery—we have scaled some of its lofty eminences, and explored some of its most lovely valleys—we have seen it in the vernal springtide, when the buds have been expanding into leaf, and the snowdrops and wild hyacinths have bedecked the emerald meads—we have seen it in the burning heat of summer, when flowers in rich abundance have sprung up wherever we happened to tread, and the woods which clothed the mountain slopes have presented one impenetrable mass of waving green—we have seen it in the pleasant autumn time, when the hills have been purple with heather, when the fields have been rich with the golden harvest, and the luxurious foliage has been gay with the most varied and gorgeous tints and colourings—and we have seen it in the stern winter, when all nature has been enveloped in a mantle of snow, and every brook and rivulet has been congealed, when the ice gems have decked the branches of the trees, and the hoar-frost has glittered on every plant and shrub— but never do we remember to have been so impressed with the beauty of its scenery, or to have felt the effect so impressive as on this occasion. The scene was one which, from its shadowy indistinctness, seemed to breathe of poetic imagery and spiritual aspirations, and cold indeed must be the heart of him who could contemplate it without experiencing a feeling of the profoundest gratitude to that divine Being who has spread before his creature man such a prospect of earthly beauty.

The deepening twilight reminded us that it was time to depart, and slowly descending from our eyrie, we retraced our steps, passing through the state-room and state bedroom, to the ante-room adjoining the grand gallery, on the east side of which there is a doorway with double doors, known as Dorothy Vernon's through which we passed and descended by a few steps to the terrace garden, planted with holly and yew trees. At one end of this garden a flight of steps, fifteen in number, leads to an avenue, screened on each side by lofty wide-spreading lime and cedar trees, which, from their

THE TERRACE—HADDON.

venerable appearance, must have been planted in the days of the Vernons. In the deep twilight a dreamy indistinctness spread around, and the dark green of the surrounding woods, mingling with the broad shadows of the over-arching trees, gave to the place quite a sombre and ghostly appearance.

This avenue has obtained the appellation of Dorothy Vernon's walk, from the popular tradition that it was a favourite retreat of that famous lady. On the north side of the terrace is an open balustrade, in the centre of which is a broad flight of steps communicating with the middle or principal garden—a square plot occupying the greater part of the south side of the mansion. The sides are laid out in parterres, bordered with edges of box and yew, and in the centre are two grass-plots, separated by a narrow gravelled walk.

Leaving the gardens we again enter the mansion by a doorway communicating with the great hall, through which we pass to the porch, and then cross the lower court-yard to the entrance tower and gateway by which we were first admitted.

There is nothing perhaps that can more forcibly illustrate the vast change that has taken place in the habits and customs of the English people, and the great advance that has been made in luxury and refinement, than a visit to the two mansions of Chatsworth and Haddon. In the one we have a building exhibiting throughout an entire unity of design, and a studied regard for personal comfort and convenience, combined with the most costly and luxurious elegance and splendour. The other presents us with a true type of the old English baronial hall, carrying the mind back into the dim antiquity of the Henrys and the Edwards, when the manor-house was but one remove from the castle, and, in fact, still retained many of the features and characteristics of those fortified buildings which it superseded, when the old feudal chief kept up a miniature regal establishment, and maintained a little army of roystering followers dependent on his will.

The old ancestral residence of Haddon has evidently been erected at different and remote periods, additions having been made from time to time, as the fashion of the age or the convenience of successive owners might require. Some writers are of opinion that it had its origin anterior to the Conquest, though, so far as our own observations went, there

is nothing in the present appearance of the structure that
would confirm such a supposition.    The Domesday survey,
which was completed some twenty years after the Conquest,
mentions the ville of Haddon, or Haduna, but is altogether
silent as to the existence of any building there.    The main
structure partakes more of the character of a baronial mansion than a fortified stronghold, though, as we have already
stated, it unites in itself some of the features of both, having
been erected at a time when the power of the feudal chieftain
was on the decline, when peace and good order having, to
some extent, been established, the castle or domestic citadel,
once so necessary for the defence of the chief and his retainers
from the attacks of marauding foes, had become no longer
requisite.    The south aisle of the chapel appears to be the
oldest portion of the building, evidently dating so far back
as the beginning of the twelfth century, at which time the
Peverels were lords of Haddon.    This may have been part of
a more ancient mansion existing here before the erection of
the present structure.    The north side, with the Eagle and
Entrance Towers, are of a later date than the chapel, and
were probably erected either during the occupancy of the
Avenells or their immediate successors.    Over the entrance
porch are two shields, one bearing the arms of Vernon, and
the other those of Pembrugge, and we may reasonably suppose
that this part of the mansion, with the great hall adjoining,
was built during the lifetime of Sir Richard Vernon, who was
entitled to quarter the arms of Pembrugge in right of his
mother, Juliana, the heiress of Sir Fulk de Pembrugge, and
which would fix the date about the middle of the fifteenth
century.    In the earliest periods of our history the hall was
the only large apartment in the entire edifice, and was
designed to accommodate the owner and his numerous
followers and servants.    It was essentially feudal in its
origin and purpose, and continued to be the chief feature of
every mansion until the decay of that social system in which
it had its origin.    The dining-room, as appears by the initials
and date, was completed in the latter part of the reign of
Henry VIII., and the drawing-room above was, no doubt,
erected contemporaneously with it, or very shortly afterwards.
The most modern part of the mansion is the south or terrace

front, extending along the greater part of the south side of the hall, the upper story of which is occupied by the long gallery. This, Lysons says, was built in the reign of Elizabeth, though the appearance and general characteristics of the exterior lead us to believe that it is of a somewhat earlier date. The decorations and fittings-up of the interior are indicative of a later period, and illustrate the great change which took place in the domestic architecture of this country about the middle of the sixteenth century, when the pure Gothic was gradually but decidedly superseded by an irregular and incongruous style, in the details of which the Italian features more or less predominate. The probability is that the building of this gallery was commenced in the lifetime of Sir George Vernon—the progress of refinement, and the change which society underwent at that era, having rendered such an apartment necessary for the exercise of the unbounded hospitality for which Haddon was celebrated during its occupancy by the " King of the Peak ; " and that it was completed after the estate had passed by marriage to the family of Manners, a supposition that is strengthened by the appearance of the peacock, the crest of the Manners, in the decorations.

From this period no further additions have been made. Though now quite deserted the fabric is carefully guarded from dilapidation, and presents, externally at least, much the same appearance that it did in the heyday of its glory ; though it could hardly have been so beautiful then as at the present time, the peculiar tinge and richness of colouring which age has given to it having been wanted in its earlier days.

It is impossible to contemplate this relic of antiquity in its now abject state without a feeling more akin to melancholy than pleasure, so utterly desolate is it in appearance, and so forcibly does it convey to the mind the idea of strength subdued and the mutability of earthly greatness. How many a page of eventful history, of heroic deeds, and great and illustrious actions can we not read in gazing momentarily upon these old time-stained remains ! As we cross the threshold the memory seems to be carried back into the far-off past, and the heart to dwell with those who once tenanted the structure, until we almost long for the return of those good old times when its walls echoed with the shouts of merry laughter, and mirth and minstrelsy, light-hearted gaiety and cheerfulness, prevailed within its deserted halls :—

> " Haddon, within thy silent halls,
>     Deserted courts and turrets high,
>   How mournfully on memory falls
>     Past scenes of antique pageantry.
>
> " A holy spell pervades the gloom,
>     A silent charm breathes all around,
>   And the dread stillness of the tomb
>     Reigns o'er thy hollow'd, haunted ground.
>
> " King of the Peak ! thy hearth is lone !
>     No sword-girt vassals gather there,
>   No minstrel's harp pours forth its tone
>     In praise of Maud or Margaret fair.
>
> " Where are the high and stately dames
>     Of princely Vernon's banner'd hall ?
>   And where the knights, and what their names,
>     Who led them forth to festival ?
>
> " They slumber low, and in the dust,
>     Prostrate and fall'n, the warrior lies—
>   His falchion's blade is dim with rust,
>     And quench'd the ray of beauty's eyes."

On leaving Haddon we crossed the Wye, at the base of the hill, by a little old-fashioned footbridge, so narrow as only to admit of one person passing at a time, and then struck across the meadows, at the further side of which we came upon the highroad, at Fillyford Bridge, at which point the Wye receives the waters of the Lathkill and the Bradford. Here the road, following the course of the stream, curves towards the left, and we continued our walk through a country well wooded and pleasingly diversified, the features of which, as we approached towards Darley Dale, assumed a more bold and striking character. At the distance of about a mile from the bridge we entered the village of Rowsley, a pleasant little rural hamlet, occupying the tongue of land formed by the confluence of the rivers Derwent and Wye.

One of the first buildings that meets the eye on entering is the far-famed *Peacock*, a comfortable roadside inn—the *beau-ideal* of an old English country hostelry, reminding one of the *Tabard*, or the *Bear and Ragged Staff*, of Queen Elizabeth's days—now the favourite resort of the disciples

THE " PEACOCK," ROWSLEY.

of good old Izaak Walton, if we may judge from the numerous piscatorial implements suspended in the porch.

The house is evidently of considerable antiquity, and with
its many-gabled roofs, its clustering chimneys, and quaintly-
mullioned windows, presents an appearance quite in keeping
with the neighbouring mansion of Haddon.   In the centre is
a projecting porch, nearly overgrown with ivy, in the upper
portion of which is a porch-chamber, surmounted externally
by an embattled parapet.   Over the doorway is the figure of
a peacock, with its tail outspread—or, to speak heraldically,
in pride—the crest of the Manners family, boldly carved in
stone, and beneath is the name—

JOHNSTE

VENSON,

with the date, 1652.   The name is probably that of some
former " Boniface," who presided here at the time when
Haddon was in its glory.

Here, within the snug and comfortable old parlour, we
spent a pleasant evening in the society of cheerful friends,
talking over the scenes and actions and vicissitudes of the
past, until it seemed that the present times had almost faded
from our view.   It was late—or, must we confess it? early
morning—ere we retired to our chamber, where, though much
fatigued, it was long before we could sink to slumber, so
busily was the mind occupied in thinking of the pomps and
pageantries and the gorgeous chivalric displays of the olden
time.   At last our fancies were fairly wearied out, and we
slept, to dream only of mailed warriors, and a long array of
knights and nobles, until, in imagination, we lived in the
midst of those glorious ancient days.

# CHAPTER XI.

THE morning following our arrival at Rowsley, we were up betimes, for we had a long walk before us. The day dawned with a thick and hazy appearance, giving promise that, when further advanced, it would be intensely hot. As we looked forth from our chamber window the misty exhalations of the night were rapidly breaking up and circling in fantastic wreaths along the mountain slopes, revealing here and there little patches of greensward, with now and then a whitened cottage that gleamed brightly in the morning sunlight. A few vapoury clouds hung about the pine-clad summits of Stanton, but the warmer rays that tinged with roseate hue the upland woods betokened their speedy dispersion. The country looked fresh and green and cheering, and everything appeared calm and tranquil, bespeaking the peace and quietude of country life, so different from the busy hum which greets the ear in a crowded city. The air was cool and bracing, and a delicious fragrance was wafted through the open casement from the purple clover and the new-mown hay. The dew bells trembled unbroken on the glossy leaves, and hung like strings of pearls from the twisting stems of the ivy that twined around the window. The heavens were vocal with the melodies of the feathered warblers, the thrush poured forth his sweetest lay, and the cry of the corn-crake and the soft voice of the cuckoo were heard mingling with the songs of the blackbird and the bullfinch, whilst the poet lark, as he soared aloft in the deep blue heavens, showered a rain of rapturous harmony—

" Joyous, and clear, and fresh, that music did surpass."

The rooks cawed loudly to each other out of the neighbouring woods, as if discussing the question of breakfast, and
the swallows meanwhile kept up a constant twittering from
their nests beneath the overhanging eaves. The little village
as yet seemed hardly awake, and, with the exception of a
solitary angler already on his way to ply the gentle art, there
was not an individual afoot to humanise or disturb the
slumbering scene ; even the cattle reclined drowsily under
the hedges, chewing their cud with a dreamy, imperturbable
gravity.

Breakfast was soon despatched, satchels were buckled on,
and the note-book having been referred to, and the ordnance
map once more consulted, we passed through the ivy-shrouded
portal of the *Peacock*, and were again " upon the road."

There is something wonderfully inspiriting in an early
morning work, the delightful coolness of the atmosphere gives
such a buoyancy and elasticity to the spirits, that it would
seem as if the earlier hours were specially intended for the
contemplation of nature and the enjoyment of rural scenery.
We were in high spirits as we quitted the *Peacock*, and the
beauty of the morning added to our hilarity, a gentle breeze
played through the branches of the trees, the old hills echoed
the " thousand melodies of morn," and the woods rang again
with the gush of harmony that issued from their foliaged
interiors.

Leaving the high road, we took the path which commences
directly opposite the inn, passing on the left a wheelwright's
shop and the Rowsley Schools—the latter a modest Gothic
building, with the date of erection (1840) carved conspicuously over the door ; then, after crossing a stone bridge
overhung with willows, that spans the Wye within a few
yards of its junction with the Derwent, we turned to the
right and kept the side of the river for about a quarter of a
mile, when the road turns again, and we had to ascend by a
steep and rugged path that winds round the slope of the hill,
stone walls broken into picturesque inequalities here and there
alternating with patches of thorn, bordering the way.

To the right rises a rocky mound, bearing the name of
Peak Tor, crowned with a plantation of firs and belted with
young sycamores and beech trees, whose straggling roots

protrude in places through the thin stratum of soil. We climbed to the top of this eminence in the hope that, from its summit, we might be able to command a view of the vale through which we had travelled the previous evening. In this we were not disappointed, but the trees were too thick to admit of an uninterrupted prospect being obtained, though the scenery was of the most varied and pleasing character, embracing almost every object that could enrich or diversify the landscape.

Looking across the country from this point, a lovely valley spreads out, through which the Wye, as it serpentines through the rich meadows, can be distinctly traced. Eastwards a range of swelling hills marks the entrance to Darley Dale. Beeley, with its noble woods and green slopes of pasture-land, chequered with lines and squares of hedge-rows, next comes in view, presenting an appearance which at once charms the eye. Further on are seen the plantations surrounding Chatsworth, with the old hunting-tower rising above the edge of the darkening foliage; and beyond can just be discerned the rocky ridge and barren slopes of Froggatt Edge, and the hills bordering the Derwent in the vicinity of Hathersage. Looking towards the north, the view is shut in by a bold ridge of limestone rock, clothed to the summit with waving woods, on the side of which the towers and turrets of Haddon are seen peeping through the thick umbrage. Westwards, the view is made up of level meadow-breadths, with woods and farms and villages backed by low undulations, beyond which rises a range of hills that extend in an irregular line towards the south.

Descending from Peak Tor, we struck across the meadows on the opposite side, and came again upon the road about half a mile from the point at which we had quitted it.

Still the road ascends, but becomes less steep as we approach Stanton. Presently we pass a few straggling cottages, with little patches of garden in front, rich in roses and carnations, that add their sweetness to the various odours of the trees. Then we come to a stone quarry, beyond which, on the left, is Sheepwalk Wood—a plantation of larch and fir. On the opposite side the road is bounded by a low stone fence, from the front of which there opens all

round the horizon a charming prospect. The scene viewed
from this point is most interesting; and we threw ourselves
upon the opposite bank, beneath the shade of a friendly tree,
to contemplate its beauties at leisure.

The woods which before partially intercepted our view
have now disappeared, and we can see across the country for
miles and miles. Whichever way we look a succession of
fertile vales, with prosperous gardens and orchards, green
meadows and pleasant pasture lands, crowd upon the eye,
with little villages and cottages scattered over the valleys,
and clustering on the hill sides. At the foot of the broad
green slope, the little river Bradford—ever an object of
beauty—is seen winding through the green meads, and
saluting the morning sun with its twinkling ripples; sometimes hidden beneath the overhanging boughs, then coming
forth again where least expected, now rushing rejoicingly
over its shallow bed, and anon subsiding into a smooth, full
current, until finally it becomes lost in the Wye at Fillyford
Bridge. On the extreme right are seen the hills bordering
the eastern side of Derwent Dale, and the picturesque village
of Rowsley, behind which rises Rowsley Moor and Manners
Wood—the latter sloping down to the very brink of the
river. Then we have the baronial residence of Haddon
shadowed by fine old ancestral elms and beeches. Further
northward, where the smoke hangs over the circling woods, is
Bakewell, the tapering spire of its church rising conspicuously
above the mountain slope. Burton-Closes comes prettily
in the view, and from the foot of the eminence on which it
stands, we can trace the Wye, like a gleam of silvery light,
pursuing its sinuous course through the meadows. Beyond
Bakewell the prospect takes in a wide range of hills, including
Longstone Edge, the Great Finn, and the barren moors
beyond Taddington. Looking westwards we see Pickering
Wood and Bowers Hall—the latter nearly hidden in the thick
umbrage—and beyond the embattled tower of Youlgreave
Church just overtopping the neighbouring hill. Carrying
the eye further towards the left, the country becomes more
open—a rich undulating vale spreading before us, watered
by numberless tributary streams, and exhibiting a pleasing
combination of picturesque scenery, embracing woods and

plantations, verdant meadows and pastures, and fields of waving grain, that give promise of a bounteous harvest; quiet little villages and ancient manors, old shady lanes, and quaint grey gables, with flag-covered roofs peering out from amid their screen of leaves, league upon league of hedgerows, and acres of cultivated verdure. The softer beauties of the foreground are agreeably contrasted with the abrupt acclivities in the middle distance, through the openings of which are seen a chain of hills, whose lofty summits seem to penetrate the clouds and give a character of grandeur to the scene. Nor are there wanting those exquisite contrasts of light and shade that are only to be seen in full perfection in the cool and fragrant hours of the opening day, when the dew is heavy on the grass, and surrounding objects seem as if deriving increased beauty from the misty veil through which they are surveyed.

As we lingered gazing upon the lovely landscape, the sun, which had now ascended above the horizon, shed its chastened radiance upon it, and his streaming rays, as they played through the branches of the overhanging trees, dappled the road with brilliant touches of light. A few gauzy clouds yet lingered in the heavens, and as the breeze swept across the plain their shadows drifted slowly by. Some places, however, were yet hidden in deep shadow, and others were only half revealed, lying too low to catch the early beams.

Journeying onwards we keep the road that skirts the edge of Sheepwalk Plantation, and as we advance a succession of pleasing views unfold themselves; trees border the roadside—tall elms and limes that spread their branches across the path until they meet and form a canopy overhead. By and by we come to Stanton-in-the-Peak, a pretty village pleasantly situated on the declivity of the hill. The church, a neat modern building in the Gothic style, with a tower and spire, lies below us on the right, and immediately in front is Stanton Hall, partially hidden from view by a high wall that bounds the park.

The mansion, which was built from designs by Linley of Doncaster, is pleasantly situated on the slope of a hill, with an extensive prospect across the country towards the west, and is sheltered from the cold and inclement winds of

o

the north and east by the high grounds and plantations behind.

The present owner of Stanton is William Pole Thornhill, Esq., a descendant of the ancient family of Thornhill, of Thornhill and Wharnebrook, in the parish of Hope. Mr. Thornhill succeeded to the estate on the death of his grandfather, Bache Thornhill, Esq., in 1830. In 1836 he served the office of High Sheriff of Derbyshire, and in 1853 he was elected a member of Parliament for the northern division of the same county, which until recently he continued to represent.*

Stanton is a picturesque little hamlet—village it can hardly be called, for it is too insignificant in size—consisting of a few rustic cottages scattered promiscuously over the hillside, or built in tiers, one above another, with their gables abutting upon the way. The dwellings, though small, have a cleanly appearance outside, and here and there through the open doors you may see that there are not wanting signs of homely comfort and contentment within.

An invitation to "sit down out of the hot sun and have a drink of milk," was the reply to our request for a cup of water from one of the cottagers. We felt loth to refuse such hospitality, but the heat was oppressive, and water seemed the more refreshing beverage of the two. The house was a model of neatness and order, and the furniture, though humble, was scrupulously clean. A case-clock stood in one corner, and in another was fixed an old-fashioned oaken cupboard, black with age, and bright with the rubbings of successive generations, and on the mantel-shelf a few china figures and some other simple ornaments were displayed— pleasurable tokens denoting the owner's thrift and tidiness. The good woman seemed quite cheerful and contented with her lot. She chatted about her domestic affairs, and told us that her husband was out working in the fields ; they had six children, she added, but the eldest lad was just beginning to bring in a little, so that, on the whole, they were doing very comfortably. They had plenty to eat, and wanted for nothing, and they had therefore no reason to complain. In addition to the burden of her household cares, we noticed that she

* Mr. Thornhill died at Brighton, February, 1875, in the 70th year of his age.

was suffering from a malady common in the mountain districts of the Peak, though confined almost exclusively to females—a goitre or endemic protuberance in the throat, generally known by the name of a Derbyshire neck, and which is supposed to be occasioned by some ingredient or peculiar property in the water.

From Stanton we continued our walk to Stanton Moor, a ridge of unbroken rock more than a mile in width, and which extends southwards to Birchover and Bradley rocks, a distance of nearly two miles. Formerly this was nothing but a wild uncultivated waste, but about fifty years ago the greater portion was enclosed and covered with plantations of fir, larch, and Spanish Chestnut. On the summit are numerous remains of antiquity, stone circles, rocking stones, barrows, &c., many of them of undoubtedly early British origin.

As it leaves Stanton the road ascends somewhat abruptly, houses border the way on one side, and on the other we have a long line of stone wall with tall trees overtopping it. As we sauntered leisurely along in the direction of the moor we overtook a farmer's labourer on his way to the hay-field—a hardy son of the soil, with the ruddy glow of health upon his cheek, and whose outward appearance denoted a greater affection for the mastication of bread and cheese than the study of archæology—to our inquiry as to the whereabouts of the Druids' stones, he replied, with an incredulous shake of the head, he had "never heerd of any on'y t' boundry stone in a field closy by, as shewed weere Stanton ended and Birchover began;" then, as if suddenly recollecting himself, he exclaimed, " Happen yo meon t' Cat Stone ; it's at t'other side o'th plantation." His directions were not of the most intelligible character, so we had no alternative but to trust to the ordnance map and the help of our pocket compass.

For some distance the road continues to ascend, when, after passing a stone quarry, the prospect is hidden by plantations on each side. On emerging from these the road declines towards the valley of the Derwent, and some very pleasing views are obtained of the country around Darley Dale. At this point we quitted the beaten path, and a short

walk across some fields brought us to the edge of the plantation before alluded to.

Now we had to scramble through the brushwood, picking
our way between the trees, here striding through heath and
fern, and there sinking nearly ankle deep in the soft spongy
soil.    Anon we came to little patches of green turf, and then
again we were sinking in moss and among masses of withered
and decayed vegetation the accumulation of years.    At first
the trees seemed but thinly planted, but as we advanced the
gloom became more apparent, and the branches of the pines,
meeting overhead, intermingled their leaves in a network of
exceeding beauty, through which we now and then got
glimpses of the blue arch of heaven, and the sun's rays as
they penetrated streaked the red-brown stems of the firs
with golden touches, producing a constant flickering of light
and shade.    The walk through the cool shade was quite
refreshing after our previous sultry march.    We listened with
delight to the whispering leaves and the soughing of the
wind as it played through the upper branches of the trees;
and we could hear the lowing of the herd in the distant
meadows, the cawing of the rooks, the impassioned song of
the nightingale, and the soft whispering " coo " of the wood-
pigeon—" Grey Bessey," as we used to call her in our childhood's days—a mingled harmony of which the ear never
tires.

As we passed along troops of squirrels sprang up the trees
from the ground, where they had been feeding on the young
acorns and pine cones, and herds of rabbits started from the
long heather and waving fern and scampered off through the
open glades, as the rustling sound of our footsteps betrayed
the presence of intruders.    Further on the solitude deepened
and all around seemed enveloped in one broad shadow, whilst
above nothing could be seen but the intermingling of the
foliage, which seemed to form a never-ending roof of sombre
green.    With the increasing gloom the sounds gradually died
away, and a death-like stillness followed—a stillness that was
*felt* rather than *heard*.

After wandering about for some time we came upon a
narrow foot track, and, following this for a short distance, we
reached the further side of the wood, which is terminated

by a precipitous ridge of rock commanding a charming view across the valley of the Derwent. The prospect which thus suddenly opened upon us was an agreeable surprise after our previous walk through the sombre shade.

Standing upon the verge of a crag which juts boldly out into the vale, and looking across the country, the eye passed over a pleasing combination of hills and dales, rocks and thickly-wooded dingles, diversified with fields and plantations, farms, villages, and rich pastures, that looked greener by contrast with the dark breadths of moorland beyond. The foreground was hidden from view by the thickly-foliaged trees at our feet; but the middle distance and the opposite hills appeared in all the fulness of their summer beauty. Everything seemed to rejoice in the gladdening light as the sun showered down a flood of intense brilliance upon the glowing landscape; and the river, as it meandered onwards with gleaming ripples far below, added a grace and charm to the whole.

This part of Stanton Moor is especially interesting to antiquaries, from the numerous remains of bygone ages that still exist. Of these not the least remarkable are three large upright stones standing upon the eastern edge of the moor, at distances of about a quarter of a mile apart from each other. The first is a huge monolithic block, called the Heart Stone, measuring eighty-three feet in circumference. Further on is a similar block, which, at the first glance, resembles the ruined tower of a church. This is denominated the Gorse Stone, a name that modern Eisteddfods has made us familiar with, and which antiquaries say is derived from the Celtic *gorsed dau*, or setting aloft. It is alleged to have been one of those sacred erections of the Druids from the summit of which they gave their laws, and made their solemn orations to the people.

Dr. Borlace, in his "Antiquities of Cornwall," says the Druids had places of elevation "called *gorsed dau;* in some places they were made of earth, and sometimes were upon the high rock from whence they used to pronounce their decrees."

The third of these singular blocks is situated a short distance south of the Gorse Stone, and bears the appellation of Cat Stone. It stands on the edge of the precipice, and is approached by a path that appears to have been formed through the surface of loose stones and rock.

Having spent some time in the examination of these interesting remains, we again penetrated the depths of the wood, and after wandering awhile among the intricacies of the trees, we came upon a Druidical circle, known popularly by the name of Nine Ladies, consisting of nine upright stones standing in a circle, about thirty-five feet in diameter, with another, called the King Stone, standing at a distance of about thirty-four yards to the west. There is no uniformity in the size or shape of these stones, the height ranging from two and a half to three feet, with a width varying from eighteen to twenty-four inches.

It was long supposed, though without much show of reason, that such circles had been intended by the Druids for places of assembly or courts of justice, but more careful investigation, combined with extensive excavations, has demonstrated that, in many cases at least, they had been erected to enclose sepulchral mounds, and in all probability Nine Ladies has been raised for a like purpose.

Near to this circle are several cairns or barrows, most of which have been opened, when various relics of an ancient population have been discovered. In one of them were found portions of a human skeleton, with a number of large blue glass beads, with orifices not larger than a tobacco pipe. These latter, from the description given of them, we should imagine to be of Roman rather than Celtic origin.

Andle Stone was the next object that claimed our attention. This relic lies at the western or opposite side of the wood. There was no track to guide us to it, and look which way we would, we could see nothing but a bewildering maze of trees, that stretched away in one dense twilight. Taking the bearings, as near as we could guess, with a pocket compass, we pushed forward in a direction nearly due west, and were soon again in the deep shade of the plantation, struggling among the thick brushwood and rank weeds, wading through heath and fern, sometimes stumbling over fragments of broken rock and the protruding roots of trees, and then striding over little patches of scrubby glade, where the dry mast and the fir-cones crackled beneath our feet. Further on the ground declined, and our progress was impeded by treacherous hollows, where the soil had been washed away by successive rains. Still we struggled on; then, as we approached the further side of the wood, the green gloom of the leafage gradually brightened, and in a few minutes more we emerged again into open daylight.

On this side the plantation is bounded by a cart road, after crossing which we climbed the bank on the opposite side, and found that our calculation had not misled us, for directly in front appeared Andle Stone, standing within a couple of hundred yards of the road. Scaling a stone wall we crossed a sloping meadow, and soon found ourselves at the foot.

This pile of grey unchiselled rock, which has withstood the blasts and storms of ages without any apparent diminution in its bulk, stands within a walled enclosure in the middle of a sloping meadow. It is about fifteen feet in height, and in some places the outline assumes such a regular form that we may almost imagine it to have been the work of art. On the south side a few iron rings have been attached, and holes cut in the face, so that the top may be reached without difficulty. We climbed to the summit, from whence a glorious prospect is obtained of the surrounding country, bounded by the soft blue hills that stretch away in the far distance. Near the edge we noticed a singular orifice, not unlike, in appearance, one of those saucer-like depressions that some antiquaries have denominated rock basins, that has been formed, in all probability, by the atmosphere acting upon the more friable parts of the stone through successive ages. On the north side is the following inscription, which appears to have been only recently cut :—

| Field Marshall | Lieut.-Colonel |
| Duke of Wellington, | William Thornhill,* |
| Died 14 Septr. 1852 ; | 7. Hussars, |
| Aged 82 years. | Died Decr. 1851 ; |
| | Aged 71 Years. |

Assaye, 1803—Waterloo, 1815.

* Colonel Thornhill was the second son of Bache Thornhill, of Stanton, and the uncle of Wm. Pole Thornhill.

Certainly a more durable monument could not have been found whereon to perpetuate the name of the hero of a hundred fights and his gallant companion in arms.

What was the origin or purpose of Andle Stone it would be difficult, if not impossible, now to determine. Major Rooke, who has described it with other antiquities in the locality, without assigning any reason for the conclusion, assumes it to have been a rock idol, and it may possibly have been one of those monuments to which the prohibition to worship stones, so frequently occurring in the earlier Christian ecclesiastical laws and ordinances, relate; but to what period or people it belongs is doubtful. Many such like blocks have been ascribed to the Britons of the ante-Roman period, without any reason other than that they carry with them no evidence of date. That this locality was once a favourite resort of the early Britons there can hardly be a doubt: the many vestiges which still exist, the remarkable circle called Nine Ladies, already described, the remains of a similar circle in Nine Stones close on Hartle Moor, and that magnificent monument of the past, The Arbelows, about three miles distant, are all so many attesting evidences of their presence.

# CHAPTER XII.

From Andlestone our way lay across the fields and through a patch of plantation, at the farther side of which a little rindle trickles through the tall grass on its way to a shallow pool, whose sides are fringed with grass and ferns and spreading bushes that reflect their varied forms upon its placid surface. Here and there a group of haymakers were reclining upon the grassy slopes in the quiet enjoyment of their mid-day meal, and more than one invitation did we get to stay and share their homely fare. Presently we struck into a meadow-path, and a few minutes brought us to a gate through which we passed, and soon afterwards entered the humble village of Birchover, a little straggling hamlet through which a rough and stony road winds irregularly as it descends towards the bottom of the valley, and where the houses present the appearance of having been built by instalments, and with little regard to regularity, some facing the road, others standing at right angles with it, and others again in the most inhospitable fashion turning their backs towards the wayfarer. On one of these humble dwellings is an inscription we thought worth transcribing. It is as follows :

> Many a day in La
> bour and Sorrow I
> Have Spent But now
> I find no rest is Li
> ke content
>                       S.P.A.
>         1751

The walk from Rowsley had tended greatly to sharpen the appetite, so we began to look about for a resting-place, where we could also obtain refreshment. Near the centre of the village we found a little roadside public-house, bearing the name of the *Red Lion*, though unaccompanied by the usual highly-coloured portrait of that imaginary animal; here we turned in, and soon found ourselves at home on the comfortable "settle" in the chimney neukin. The capabilities of the larder were but limited; hunger, however, is a capital sauce, and we enjoyed our simple fare none the less on that account. As we sat the hostess, a cheerful, motherly-looking dame, with a spice of quiet humour about her, chatted and talked upon the state of the crops, the prospect of the coming harvest, and all the varied topics that form the stock subject of conversation in a rural district. Her husband, she told us, worked hard, and tended his bit of ground when he came home at night from his day's work, and their customers, she added, were chiefly labourers and men employed in the neighbouring lead mines, some of whom were quiet and civil enough, but others were at times rough and noisy, though she always strove to prevent them from quarrelling. The house, we noticed, was sadly out of repair, and close by the doorway an uncovered sink or drain was gradually forming itself into a stagnant pool; to our remark thereon, she said, "It had been so for many a year; they had asked the owner often enough, but he wouldn't do nothing." To our reply that he was bound to keep his house in a habitable condition, she answered, "Why, yes, but folks don't always do what's right; you see he is a miserly sort of a man, and thinks more about his rent than poor folks' comfort, and he says he cannot see o' what use it would be;" and then she added, with a smile, "happen he knows no better, for you see he is *only* an old bachelor;" laying an emphasis on the *only*, which plainly indicated that in her opinion a man who was not a Benedict must, as natural consequence, be only half-civilised.

Leaving the *Red Lion*, we walked through the village, at the lower end of which, on the right side of the road, are the celebrated Rowtor Rocks—an assemblage of gritstone blocks, of every conceivable shape and size, piled one above another in the most confused manner—some standing upright, some lying horizontally, whilst others again lean in every degree of obliquity, and sometimes so slightly connected that you imagine every moment they may become detached from the parent heap and topple down, bringing the whole superincumbent pile, like an avalanche, with them. The several openings in this rocky promontory are covered with turf and overgrown with heath and ling, whilst every crevice presents to the eye quite a forest of ferns, the whole displaying a curious and picturesque combination of form and colour.

At the foot of the rocks is a little public-house bearing the appropriate name of the *Druid*, where resides the guide who usually accompanies visitors over the pile. We tapped at the door, but nobody answered, nor, on looking through the window, could we see anyone about the house, so that we had no alternative but to trust to our own guidance.

Passing through the pretty flower garden at the end of the house, we came to an ascending path leading to a narrow tunnel-like passage that winds between broken rocks, along which we had to walk in a stooping posture until we reached an open platform on the north side, covered over with green herbage; here we found a succession of gritstone blocks, of the most wild and grotesque forms, that extend from east to west, along the middle of the hill. In some of the rocks chambers or caves have been excavated, apparently within a recent period; the largest of them, which is about sixteen feet in length, has received the appelation of the "Echo," from the singular reverberation of sound that is heard within. Picking our way through the narrow intricacies—not without a feeling akin to terror, it must be confessed, for we could hardly believe that stones so carelessly put together could be very secure—we came next to an opening where a few steps have been formed, by which we ascended to a second platform. Here another range of rocks raise their unwieldly forms to a considerable elevation; resting on the top of them again are several blocks of irregular shape and somewhat less magnitude, and in the centre of this last group a stone pillar has been set up, from the top of which rises an iron rod, that formerly supported a weather-cock, now destroyed.

Near the eastern end is a large block twelve feet in height and about thirty feet in circumference, and supposed to weigh about fifty tons, which Pilkington describes as being so equally poised upon one end that a child might easily give it a vibratory motion. The stone is now immovable, having been forced from its equilibrium by the mischievous efforts of a number of young men who assembled for the purpose on Whit-Sunday, 1799. There are several other stones which it is said still retain their power of motion, though, in the absence of the guide, we were unable to discover the place where to touch.

On the north side, and near the western end of the upper pile, are three rudely-fashioned chairs that have been cut out of the solid rock; these were made about a century ago under the direction of Mr. Thomas Eyre, who then resided at Rowtor Hall, near the foot of the rocks.

The grey colour of this romantic pile agreeably harmonises with the mosses and lichens which chequer the steep and rugged sides, and fringe the ledges of the projecting rocks, blending their unobtrusive hues with the deeper colouring of the oak, the ash, and other hardy trees, that grow in luxurious profusion around.

The name Rowtor, or Roo-tor, the more correct designation, is derived from the words *roo*, to move, or rock backward and forwards, and *tor*, which signifies a hill or rock—an expression of frequent occurrence in this part of the kingdom. Some writers have affirmed that the place was a resort of the Druids, and that these immense blocks were raised to their present position by their exertions—the several rocking-stones having been objects of idolatrous worship. That some of the blocks have been added to the original mass is not improbable, but that the entire pile is the work of human ingenuity is hardly credible; the general appearance leads to the supposition that it is the work of nature, and has been occasioned by the subsiding of the surrounding strata; whilst, as regards the rocking-stones, which have been so often classed among Druidical remains, it is now pretty generally admitted by geologists and antiquaries, that many of the so-called Logan or Rocking-stones are not works of art, but the result of natural causes; in other words, that the constant action of the weather through countless ages has worn away the softer part of the sandstone, leaving the more solid portions in their present form. Rocking-stones, it may be remarked, with the rock-basins which frequently accompany them, are almost invariably found in the sandstone formations, a material which, from its soft and inadhesive quality, being purely a mechanical deposit, is peculiarly liable to be frittered away by the action of the elements, so that at times it is difficult, if not impossible, to determine what is of natural and what of artificial formation.

Nearly opposite the Rowtor Rocks we noticed an old Gothic stone building, with high-peaked gables, which in earlier days must have been a residence of some pretensions, though now exhibiting only a discordant mass of materials overgrown with grass and weeds. The roofs have been removed, the stone mullions of the windows broken, the chimneys destroyed, and docks, nettles, and briars flourish abundantly among the heaps of rubbish that encumber the floors of the ruined and deserted tenement.

From Birchover, a few minutes' walk across the fields brought us to the foot of Bradley Rocks, a ridge of gritstone that rises abruptly from the plain to a considerable altitude. On the top is one of those singular monuments believed to be

" The work of Druid hands of old—"

a rocking-stone, which, from its appearance, has much stronger claims to be considered a work of art than those already noticed as existing at Rowtor. It is a vast block of sandstone, of irregular shape, about thirty feet in diameter, and supposed to weigh fifty or sixty tons ; the under side is somewhat convex in form, and rests upon the edge of two horizontal blocks. In appearance it bears a striking resemblance to that singular insulated pile of rock near Constantine, in Cornwall, known as the Tolmên, and which Dr. Borlace, in his " Antiquities," conjectures to have been a rock-idol.

As the day wore on the heat became more oppressive, whilst the refreshing breeze seemed to have almost died away. Wearied with our walk, we look round for a resting-place, and selecting a cool retreat beneath the shadow of a clump of trees, we lay down upon a soft cushion of grass and fern to while away a half hour in the enjoyment of solitude and repose.

The view that met the gaze was one of charming and romantic beauty—rocks, hills, and valleys, with woods, meadows, and broad smiling fields combining to fill the mind with admiration and delight.   Before us spread a wide and open valley, agreeably diversified with woods, pastures, and signs of fruitful culture, that extended northwards until it became united with the lovely vale of Haddon, the further distance being bounded by a long chain of hills that rose one above another until their shadowy forms seemed to melt away upon the horizon.   Eastwards, the view was limited by a high ridge of limestone, clothed with plantations of larch and fir, that stretched away in the direction of Stanton and Rowsley, and against which the dark and gloomy pile of Birchover stood out in bold relief.   Bradley rocks were within a few yards of us, and as we looked across the valley the eye took in that singular heap of stones denominated Graned Tor, or Robin Hood's stride—the merry outlaw has left many memories behind him in these parts—with Durwood Tor and Cratliff rocks contiguous thereto, the three forming a group of rock scenery which for interest and singularity of aspect can hardly be equalled within the same limits in the kingdom.

On resuming our walk we quitted the beaten track, and struck across the sloping fields.   On nearing the bottom of the valley we came to the turnpike road that leads from Bakewell to Winster.   Crossing this, we descended to a brook that runs within a few feet of the roadway, but which is nearly hidden from view by the profusion of brambles and brushwood that grow along its brink.   To jump over seemed an easy matter, and, selecting a place that appeared favourable to our purpose, and where a little patch of verdant sward gave indication of dry ground, we sprang across, but to our surprise, sank ankle deep in a soft and pulpy moss of bog. Further on we found the ground to be equally treacherous and spongy, but as we ascended the slope the soil became more firm.

The scenery here is of the wildest character, the entire slope of the hill being strewn with enormous blocks of grit-stone, that lie scattered about in the most confused manner.

The general barrenness is in some degree relieved by a few dwarf oaks, with here and there a stunted birch or ash that has taken root, and contrived to obtain sustenance from the rocky soil. Altogether the scene, from its rugged, almost savage aspect, is one in which Salvator Rosa would have delighted in.

Picking our way between the shattered and weather-beaten masses, sometimes up to the knees in gorse, heath, and fern, we came at length to the foot of Cratliff Tor, a mass of rock, that rears its bold and naked front almost perpendicularly to a prodigious height, towering above the valley in awe and majesty. In some places the face of the rock presents a singular appearance, from the regular way in which the surface has been furrowed by the corroding hand of Time. At the foot a rude archway admits to a cave or recess, which is said to have been excavated by some anchorite, who made it his abode. On the right hand as you enter is a crucifix, about four feet in height, sculptured in relief, on which is a figure of the Saviour. The features of the effigy are defaced and the legs are broken off below the knees, but in other respects it is but little injured. By the side is a niche, intended probably to receive a lamp, and near to it is a seat which has been hewn out of the rock. The entrance is protected by a low stone wall, with a yew tree flanking each side.

Of the origin or purpose of this lonely cell nothing is known, nor is there any tradition extant to throw the halo of romance around it, though it is generally believed to have been the abode of a hermit or a place of pilgrimage. Perhaps some gloomy recluse, with mistaken zeal, may have made it his retreat, or perhaps some good and holy man, following the example of the pious St. Kevin, has sought its wild and rocky seclusion to escape the wiles and bewitching glances of his fair Kathleen.

Almost within a stone's-throw of Cratliff Tor is a curious heap of rocks, tumbled confusedly together by the hand of Nature in one mighty pile. The name of these rocks is Graned Tor, but they are popularly known by the designation of Robin Hood's Stride. Seen from the vale this pile has a very singular aspect; at each extremity are huge stones standing upright, eighteen feet high, and about sixty six feet asunder in a direct line. These stones, in the distance, resemble towers or chimneys, from which circumstance it is sometimes called Mock-Beggars' Hall. The base of the rocks is strewn with detached masses that appear at some time or other to have fallen from above. In one of them is a hollow cavity of oval form, four feet in length and two feet two inches wide, which Major Rooke represents as having been a rock-basin. Small trees and ivy grow from the fissures overhead, and dwarf oaks and hazel bushes on the ledges, whilst the space between the dislocated fragments is covered with short thick herbage, on which a few sheep are fed and fattened.

Contiguous to Robin Hood's Stride is Durwood Tor, another rocky ridge forming a part of the same group as Graned Tor and Cratliff Rock, on the top of which Major Rooke says there are three rock-basins, artificially formed, and an impending crag or rock canopy which overhangs what has been termed an "augurial seat," a statement we were content to take on trust, feeling little inclination after our previous ascents to clamber to the top to verify its truth.

In Gough's additions to the "Britannia" mention is made of the discovery here some years ago, on the removal of a large stone, of an urn half-full of burnt bones, and near it two ancient querns or hand-mill stones, flat at the top, and somewhat convex on the under side, about four and a half inches thick, and nearly a foot in diameter. The upper stone was so much less than the under one, that being placed on it, it could be turned round within its rim.

From Durwood Tor we descended into the valley, and came again upon the high road, at a point where the townships of Elton and Birchover join. Here the road begins to ascend, and some pretty views are afforded. On the right a bold acclivity rises abruptly from the way, clothed to the summit with soft green turf, and above the edge of which we now and then got a peep of the little square tower of Elton Church. To the left the eye ranged over an open valley, through which runs Hartle Brook, and where are seen the several rocky heights and the village of Birchover, already described.

Presently we came to a place where four roads meet, and, turning to the left, passed along a shady lane between tall hedgerows overrun with brambles and thorns, with pretty ferns shooting out here and there, intermingled with daisies and blue bells and other wild flowers; and thickly sprinkled with tall trees that spread their thickly foliaged boughs across the path. Now and then we got a glimpse of the surrounding scenery, and were enabled to note the various cliffs and crags which break out like scars upon the hill slopes; then, as we approached Winster, the views became more contracted, being shut in on one side by Wildminster Tor, a rugged crag that crowns a steep eminence, and on the other, limited to a few meadow breadths that slope down towards the foot of Stanton Moor.

Winster is one of those small rustic-looking market towns one expects to meet with in the heart of the country, where the aspiring notions of modern progress have made but little inroad. It is built along the side of a sloping eminence, and comprises a long straggling street of stone cottages and quaint old-fashioned shops, with a few habitations scattered irregularly over the hill side. It still lays some pretentions to importance and respectability, as is manifest by the ancient market-hall and the few stylish houses, which here and there rise above the old weather-beaten stone and rough-cast dwellings. The inhabitants are chiefly employed in mining operations at the numerous lead workings that exist hereabouts, the country for some distance round being burrowed and honeycombed like an extensive rabbit warren.

On entering the town we soon became aware, from the unusual bustle that prevailed, and the knots of idlers that were gathered around and upon the churchyard wall, that something important was going on. It happened to be, as we learned, the club feast day, or Winster Feast, as it is generally designated, a festival invariably observed with much gaiety and rejoicing. The day was a most auspicious one, and everything seemed full of joy and gladness, from the unclouded sun that sent down his scorching beams with benign complacency and cheering impartiality, to the little rustic urchins who skipped about uttering their merry laughter, and who seemed quite jubilant on the occasion. Service was going on at the time in the church, and as we loitered about the churchyard we could hear the deep tones

P

of the minister's voice, followed by the simple pathos of the congregation, repeating the responses of our simple but beautiful and impressive liturgy.

These friendly societies or clubs, as they are called by the country people, are established in almost every town and village in the Peak ; their object is so well understood, and their usefulness so widely appreciated that it is unnecessary here to dilate upon them ; they are often the poor man's only resource and refuge in time of sickness and affliction, and they furnish the means for decently interring himself and his family when death visits his lowly cot. Once in every year the members meet and hold a feast of fellowship and mutual congratulation, on which occasion labour is generally suspended, and the day observed as a holiday. The morning is usually ushered in by the ringing of a joyous peal ; then the members, arrayed in their holiday attire, each carrying their wand of office, and preceded by a band of musicians, with a banner in front, emblazoned with some appropriate device, and gaily decorated with ribbons, issue from the club room at the village inn, and perambulate the principal thoroughfares of the village, after which they proceed to the church, where a sermon is preached, and then the more important part of the drama, the "feast" begins, and mirth and humour, light-hearted gaiety and cheerfulness continue for the remainder of the day.

These rustic *fêtes* resemble in some respects the wakes of the northern counties, and seem to have superseded some of those lingering customs and usages that are gradually disappearing before the spread of refinement and the changed spirit of the times. They have this advantage, that whilst they foster habits of providence and forethought, they at the same time engender feelings of unity and good fellowship among the people, and are certainly a vast improvement upon the rude sports and pastimes that prevailed among our forefathers.

The church, the first object that engaged our attention, occupies a slightly elevated site on the right of the road as we enter the town. It is a small and unpretending structure, without any great antiquity or architectural beauty to boast of ; the tower, which appears to be the oldest part, reminds one of Gray's "ivy-mantled tower" at Stoke Pogis, the upper portion being so completely invested with ivy that scarcely a fragment of the masonry remains unobscured. On the western face is the following inscription: "Christopher Bagshaw and Roger Walker. Ch. W. 1711," the date being probably that of the year in which it was erected. In 1842 the body of the church was rebuilt, and the north aisle added, by which means 294 additional (free) sittings were obtained. The cost of these improvements was £1,600, raised by subscriptions aided by a grant of £150 from the Diocesan Society, and a like sum from the Society for Promoting the Englargement, Building, and Repairing of Churches. In the interior we noticed an ancient-looking circular stone font, adorned with rude carvings, which would appear to have belonged to an older church—the only object that seemed to merit particular attention. There are several monumental tablets arranged against the walls, though none of special interest, with the exception of one on the south side of the nave, which has been erected to perpetuate the memory of one who "lived and died a Christian"—Thomas Wall, an old veteran and a native of Winster, who died February 11th, 1853, aged 67. The inscription records that he was engaged in most of the actions of the Peninsular War, was colour-sergeant of the 95th Rifle Brigade, and highly esteemed by his officers and comrades, and was awarded a medal with the following clasps: Toulouse, Nive, St. Sebastian, Vittoria, Badajoz, Orthes, Nivelle, Pyrenees, Salamanca, Barrosa, and Cuidad Rodrigo.

The churchyard is a retired spot, nearly encircled by sombre lines that fling their broad shadows upon the upheaved turf, where "the rude forefathers of the hamlet sleep." Within are several fine old yews that have flourished through many ages, and now spread abroad a mournful gloom quite in character with the place itself.

Yew trees are found in many churchyards in Derbyshire and other parts of the kingdom, and their frequent occurrence naturally leads to the inquiry, "Why or for what purpose they were originally planted in these sacred depositories of the dead?" The generally received opinion is, that as the churchyard was a place least likely to be violated,

they were in ancient times there cultivated, in order to
secure their protection, and so obtain a supply of wood for
those famous *yew* bows which made our old English archers
so formidable in battle. The custom, however, is one whose
origin may be traced to a still more remote period. Before
the introduction of Christianity the yew, with certain other
trees, was supposed to be invested with a peculiar sanctity,
and was then not unfrequently planted near the graves of
departed relatives and friends, its perpetual verdure at the
same time rendering it strikingly emblematical of the eternal
youth and undying vigour of the soul. Allusion is made to
this custom in "Ossian," when, says the bard, speaking of
two lovers, "Here rests their dust, Cathullin ! These lonely
yews sprang from the tomb, and shade them from the storm."

On quitting the churchyard, we proceeded through the
town, passing on our way the old market-house, a quaint-
looking structure that carries the mind back to the days of
the earlier Georges ; near to it is the Hall, the residence of
the eminent antiquary and archæologist, Llewellynn Jewitt,
Esq., F.S.A., a somewhat imposing-looking building, surmounted by an ornamental balustrade ; in front is an inclosed
area or court, approached by an ample gateway, flanked by
tall stone gate-posts with ball terminations, which impart an
air of stately dignity that strongly contrasts with the rustic
aspect of the cobbler's shop close by, and the still more
primitive-looking smithy, against the door of which, as we
passed, the brawny-looking blacksmith, arrayed in his Sunday
gear, was quietly enjoying his pipe—he, like his neighbours,
having taken to himself a holiday in honour of Winster
Feast.

# CHAPTER XIII.

From Winster a pleasant rural highway leads to Wensley.
Merrily, and at a gipsy pace, we saunter along, now and
then stopping to gather some pretty wild flower, or to pick
up a bit of curious spar or glistening ore from the road.
The day is bright and clear, and the thick hedgerows that
border the way afford an agreeable shelter from the burning
rays of the July sun ; here and there a gnarled and twisted
oak, or a spreading sycamore, breaks the monotonous outline
of the bushes, and now and then a miner's cottage, with its
grey moss-grown gable, juts out upon the road ; then more
oaks and sycamores, and a thick undergrowth of brambles
and brushwood, with docks and nettles in luxurious profusion.

By-and-by we get charming views across the valley
towards the north, with gleamy vistas opening, through
which are admitted glimpses of Darley Dale, and the pale-
blue hills beyond, with yet more charms of verdure and
foliage.  Then we have green slopes and patches of meadow
land, intermingled with innumerable little dells that open
one into another, refreshing the eye with a rich picture of
beauty, fertility, and variety ; every ridge and hollow and
undulation is covered with a dense foliage of bracken and
underwood, while at the bottom of the valley a little babbling
stream sparkles in the joyous sunlight, and makes sweet
music as it breaks over the stony ledges in its shallow
channel.  Above, the sloping hill is covered with a dense

forest of gloomy-looking pines that extend for more than a
mile along the top ; a little further on the view is shut out
by an intervening eminence, and then another prospect opens
on the right, more broken and varied, but not so rich in
foliage as the one we have just quitted ; this is Wensley
Dale—a deep glen or dingle hemmed in with rocks, whose
sides are covered with thin mossy verdure, through which
the limestone crops out in great weather-beaten crags, the
bold and fantastic forms and cold grey colouring of which
agreeably harmonise with the surrounding landscape.    In
some places the ground is broken in picturesque hollows
overgrown with copse and briars, where the rocky fragments,
covered with clinging lichens, and half hidden by the thick
brushwood, produce a romantic beauty that is heightened by
the bold and hilly character of the surrounding country.

Wensley is a little rustic-looking hamlet, built on the edge
of a hill which overlooks the valley just named ; it contains
a few scattered dwellings, inhabited chiefly by miners, and a
solitary public-house—the *Red Lion,* as humble in appearance as its namesake at Birchover.

Here we stopped to dine off oatcake and cheese, the only
fare obtainable.    The landlord sat quietly smoking on a long
settle by the fireside, while his daughter, a buxom lass of
eighteen, was bustling about, attending to the wants of two
or three hardy-looking rustics, who were discussing the affairs
of the country over a social glass with the host.

The arrival of strangers was evidently an unusual occurrence, and our presence was therefore greeted with a kindly
welcome, the more so, we believe, that they were glad to see
fresh faces, and to hear how the world was jogging on elsewhere.    They immediately became communicative, and we
talked and chatted as if we had been old acquaintances ; the
conversation, though simple and unrefined, was characterised
by shrewdness and strong common-sense, and public men and
measures were talked of with a freedom of expression which
evidenced that in this out-of-the-way place there were men
who possessed sound judgment and independence of thought,
with a clear perception of what was due to others as well as
to themselves.

Contrasting the present with the past, an honest hearted

miller from Darley, who sat next to us, said: "They might talk of the good old times as they would, but in his opinion the poor were never so well off as now; more thought was taken for their wants, and there wasn't so wide a gap between them and th' big folk as there used to be. Schools and book larning had done a great deal, but he thought that example had done more, and for that they were indebted to that good-hearted motherly little woman as sat upo' th' throne o' England—Queen Victoria, God bless her;" and to give more force to his expression of loyalty he brought down his heavy palm upon the table with an energy that made the glasses ring again. Speaking of education, he said: "Larning was a fine thing, a very fine thing, and cheap books and cheap schools had done a great deal for the towns, but in country places folk hadn't the same chance, and he always thought it hard to see childer wantin' a bit a larnin' and not able to get it—'twasn't right, and England had a deal to answer for."

We could not but acknowledge the truth of our friend's remarks, for, with all our boasted civilisation, it is a well-known fact that a lamentable amount of ignorance still prevails, not only in the agricultural districts but among the masses of the population in our large towns, and those whom happier circumstances have endowed with light and know-ledge, must feel more and more the constraining obligation to diffuse that light among the less fortunate of those around them. The evil is no doubt attributable in some degree to the low social condition of the parents, and the indifference, or perhaps, to speak more correctly, the difficulty experienced by them in comprehending that which is so essential to the welfare of their offspring. When such a state of things exists it is manifestly necessary that the legislature should not only provide the means of education, but also make that education compulsory, for we hold that when parental responsibility is neglected or forgotten it becomes the duty of the State, as the guardian of our national virtue, to require the attendance of those helpless ones at some public school, where not only rudimentary instruction may be received, but the broad principles of Christian duty inculcated. It is to be hoped that at no distant day every child within these

realms may be able to claim education, not only as a privilege,
but as a right.*    Earnestly do we long for the coming of

> " That glorious time
> When, prizing knowledge as her noblest wealth
> And best protection, this imperial realm,
> Whilst she exacts allegiance, shall admit
> An obligation on her part to teach
> Them who are born to serve her and obey ;
> Binding herself by statute to secure
> For all the children whom her soil maintains
> The rudiments of letters."

Education, however, properly so called, must begin at
home, and as a means to attain that end we must attend
more to the subject of female training.   Men may indeed
constitute the rougher material and resisting portion of
which the fabric of society is built, but women are the finer
cement that unites and gives form and consistency to the
entire structure, and the influence which they exercise upon
the general well-being can hardly be over-estimated.   We
should endeavour then so to mould and instruct the rising
generation of the female community that they may be better
fitted to fulfil the duties of wives and mothers, that they may
be enabled to impart to the opening minds of their children
a desire for intellectual attainments, and to direct them to
virtuous and patriotic deeds.

Our earliest impressions are the most lasting, and the
habits formed in childhood, whether for good or for evil, are
those which are seldom or never eradicated.   The influence
of correct associations upon the tender mind is evidenced by
the charms of domestic ties, the possession of a healthy moral
tone of character, and generous and ennobling sentiments;
whilst children who are brought up in those desolate homes,
where intemperance, disorder, and degradation prevail, or
where evil passion, bickering, and strife are ever in the
ascendant, can only be expected to follow the vicious
examples set before them, and to tread in the beaten paths of
wickedness and vice.   Instruction may do much to humanise
and refine the mind, but there is that in the formation of

---

* The desire expressed nearly twenty years ago has now been realised by the
passing of the Education Act of 1870.

character which parents themselves can alone accomplish, for their natural position, and their love and tenderness, when rightly exercised, renders their influence paramount and permanent. There is in the unwritten code of the fireside a mystical power which transcends all rules and systems, and which is at once irresistible, omnipotent, and never-ending. In the education, therefore, of our rising youth, attention should first of all be directed to "home influences," and the cultivation of those happy associations which are ever cherished in the mind by the remembrance of—

> "Those first affections,
> Those shadowy recollections,
>     Which, be they what they may,
>     Are yet the fountain-light of all our day,
> Are yet a master-light of all our seeing,
>     Uphold us, cherish, and have power to make
> Our noisy years seem moments in the being
>     Of the eternal silence : truths that wake,
> To perish never ;
> Which neither listlessness, nor mad endeavour,
>     Nor man, nor boy,
> Nor all that is at enmity with joy,
> Can utterly abolish or destroy !"

When we rose to depart, our friend the miller volunteered to accompany us a little on the way, for, as he said, he knew the country well, and might be able to point out something that would be interesting to those who wished to explore the neighbourhood, and which perhaps otherwise might be passed by unnoticed. We could only regard this offer as a manifestation of kindly feeling, and therefore gladly availed ourselves of it.

Following the road that leads through the village, we descend rapidly towards the open valley. Approaching Wensley tollgate some pretty cottages are seen—relics of the olden time, with grey thatched roofs and stone gables overhung with ivy and climbing creepers. About half-way down the hill, and within a couple of hundred yards of Darley Bridge, three roads meet, and a guide-post indicates to the wayfarer the several places to which they lead. Here we parted with our companion in sight of the picturesque village of Darley, to which he was going, and, following his advice, directed our steps towards Oker Hill.

Turning to the right we proceeded along a level road that leads between cultivated fields and pastures, and in a few minutes reached the foot of the hill—a singular insulated eminence that rises abruptly from the plain, looking as if it had been heaved up by volcanic force. The steep sloping sides are broken into picturesque inequalities, but the absence of foliage gives a cold and cheerless aspect to the whole ; the soil near the base appears fertile, and towards the summit the ground is being gradually brought under cultivation, producing crops chiefly of oats and potatoes.

This mound is said to be the site of an intrenched fort or station, erected by the Roman legions to overawe the disaffected Britons, whom they had driven from the neighbouring lead mines ; and certainly a place better adapted by nature, either as a place of defence or as a harbour for assailants, cannot well be conceived. Some indications of these intrenchments may still be traced on the top of the hill. To this fortress or station the Romans gave the appellation of *Occursus*, or the hill of conflict, of which the present name of Oker is merely a corruption.

Passing through the first gate that affords us access, we cross a rough pasture at the foot of the slope, and then begin the ascent. Onwards we go in right good earnest ; for awhile we get over the ground pretty rapidly, but with increasing altitude the path becomes more toilsome, the short slippery grass rendering it almost impossible to obtain a firm foothold. Now we have left all shelter behind, and there is not a friendly shrub or bush to protect us from the scorching beams, or even a breath of wind to cool the parched and overheated atmosphere ; never mind, the day is gloriously fine, and the sun overhead pours down a flood of intense brilliance that enhances the beauty of the surrounding landscape. Onward and upward we toil, now winding round a deep hollow or gully, where the loose soil and earth have been washed away by successive rains ; then we go on, lengthening the way by frequent zigzagging from side to side. Occasionally we meet with little patches of turf, where the footing is easier, then we have to wade nearly knee-deep through forests of heather and bilberry. Still higher mounts the way, and the higher we go the more distant seems the top. Here the side of the hill is broken in gentle undulations, then another ascent and we reach the summit, when a delightful prospect opens to the view.

Looking round, the view ranges over a complete maze of hills—league after league of woods and fertile plains with acres of waving grain—rich meadow lands dotted with farms and villages, traversed with whitened roads and chequered with hedgerows that show where the hollow lanes intersect each other; deep groves, flashing waters, and little cots nestling among the trees, looking so snug and pretty with their gardens and orchards—in one direction; in another—gentle eminences clothed with plantations, and variegated with rock and herbage, and brown heathy wastes backed by a succession of blue hills that extend in far perspective until their pale summits seem to mingle with the few fleecy clouds that gauze the cerulean sky above. And through the midst of this charming scene the beauteous Derwent sweeps along with gleaming curves, now washing the foot of some projecting rock, now winding round some sylvan bank, where copse and honeysuckle and wild roses delightfully intermingle, and then hiding itself beneath the dark masses of foliage that hang pendent over its rippling bosom.

Westward the view is bounded by the hills about Wensley and Winster, and the thickly wooded heights of Stanton. Looking up the valley of the Derwent, by Darley Dale, we can trace the course of the river for miles as it serpentines through the soft and fertile vale, winding among mountains and rocks, and fields and fruitful meadows, sometimes loitering playfully behind the bends as if reluctant to leave so lovely a scene, and then again revealing its cheerful current as it sweeps along with many a graceful curve, until it becomes hidden beneath the overhanging woods that clothe the rocky portals of Matlock Dale. On the right, a succession of undulating eminences extend in the direction of Rowsley and Chatsworth, hill following hill, and ridge succeeding ridge, until their distant summits become blended with the azure above, brown or grey in colour, and of every variety of shape and form; in some places dark and rugged where the soil has been laid bare by successive torrents, and in others scarred and seamed and broken into little ravines that have been washed and widened by the rains and storms of centuries. The lower slopes, as they dip down towards the river, are hung with woods that become thicker and closer in texture as they approach the margin of the stream; and above, every projection and undulation, every hollow and ridge, is covered with rich green turf, broken only where the naked rock protrudes in rugged crags and desolated cliffs, or where the purple heather and flowering gorse grow in thick profusion.

The play of light and shade is admirable, and the few fleecy clouds that float across the valley are reflected upon the mountain slopes, and every knoll and projection looks more brilliant by contrast with the dark shadows thrown in rear.

Directly in front is seen the little village of Darley, pleasantly situated on the sylvan banks of the river, its venerable church nearly hidden by the sombre foliage of its ancient and wide-spreading yew—one of the finest in the kingdom. On the opposite side of the river, near the extremity of a little dell that opens into the vale, is Sydnope House, the seat of Sir Francis Darwin; and further on, below where a huge stone quarry reflects the brilliant rays of the sun, is a projecting knoll, adorned with plantations of larch and fir, on the slope of which stands Stancliff Hall, the residence of one who has earned for himself a world-wide reputation as the inventor of the rifled ordnance which bears his name, Sir Joseph Whitworth, of Manchester.

The top of Oker Hill forms a sloping plateau of some extent; near the southern verge are two sycamore trees, which are said to have been planted by two brothers, who, separating here, resolved that they would part for ever. The tradition states that such was the case, for each taking a different direction, they never met again. The circumstance has been related by Wordsworth in the following lines :—

> " 'Tis said that to the brow of yon fair hill
>   Two brothers clomb ; and turning face from face
>   Nor one look more exchanging, grief to still,
>   Or feed, each planted on that lofty place

A chosen tree.   Then eager to fulfil
Their courses, like two new-born rivers, they
In opposite directions urged their way
Down from the far-seen mount.   No blast might kill
Or blight that fond memorial.   The trees grew,
And now entwine their arms ; but ne'er again
Embraced those brothers upon earth's wide plain,
Nor aught of mutual joy or sorrow knew
Until their spirits mingled in the sea
That to itself takes all—Eternity !"

We loitered about the summit for some time, reluctant to
quit a scene where the wide expanse and the exquisite variety
of objects, embellished with every beauty and adornment
which the hand of nature could bestow, combined to create
in the mind feelings of gratification and delight.

The sun, now circling towards the west, reminds us that
it is time to depart ; descending rapidly by the opposite side
of the hill, we come to a farm-house, and then follow a footpath across the fields, which brings us to the brink of the
Derwent, here a wide and impetuous current that pursues its
busy way between sloping meadows and pastures, oftentimes
hidden from view by the overhanging oaks and alders which
grow upon its banks.   Presently the river inclines towards
the east, and we make a short cut across a pasture field and
meet it again at a point nearly opposite the Moot Hall Mine,
an old working which is said to be more productive of iron
pyrites or sulphate of iron than lead ore.

Keeping the right bank of the river we proceed along a
pleasant path where the trees border the way, and in some
places meet overhead.   Now and then we get pretty bits of
rugged scenery, where the rocks rise up on one side, grey
and lichened, and overgrown with brambles and wild roses ;
then we pass beneath the railway, which here crosses the
river by a flat and ugly-looking girder bridge ; beyond which
the road is continued for some distance between the river and
the railway.   By-and-by we come to the May Dale Mine,
where an opportunity is afforded us of seeing the process of
sorting, washing, and grinding the ore preparatory to its
being sent to the smelting furnace ; heaps of refuse are lying
about, among which may be found specimens of calcareous
and crystallised spar, some purely white, and others veined

in different colours, chiefly yellow and pea-green. The road still continues along the side of the river, and in a few minutes we come upon the highway at Matlock Bridge, a fine structure of four arches spanning the Derwent.

Here the scenery becomes more varied and interesting, and the beauties of Matlock Dale first begin to unfold themselves. In front is seen Matlock, or Matlock Town, as the people call it, to distinguish it from Matlock Bath, pleasantly situated on the lower slope of a hill, the foot of which is washed by the river. Like most towns in Derbyshire, the houses are built of stone, and present a cleanly and well-to-do appearance. They are surrounded by hills, except towards the north, whence a beautiful view opens along a wide and highly-cultivated valley that extends to Darley Dale and Rowsley.

The church, an ancient structure, erected at different periods, and restored in recent years, has a fine effect from the charming situation it occupies on the edge of a bold precipitous rock. The singular appearance of this rock cannot fail to arrest the attention of the tourist, from the peculiar dip or inclination of the strata which it exhibits ; the crest is covered with trees and brushwood, but the lower face is bare, and the several strata of which it is composed can be distinctly traced, presenting the appearance of a number of lines extending in a regular undulating or waved curvature for a distance of a couple of hundred yards, when they become lost by dipping under the shale near the town. The singular effect has been produced by one of those occurrences which geologists term "faults," and which are owing to the upheaving of the strata by volcanic force.

To the left of the spectator, and within a short distance of Matlock, is Matlock Bank, a little hamlet consisting of a few cottages scattered irregularly over the hillside, prominent in the midst of which is the hydropathic establishment erected by the late Mr. Smedley.

Matlock Bridge is rapidly rising into eminence, and promises soon to become a dangerous rival to Matlock Bath. A few years ago a company was formed for the erection of a market hall and hotel—the former, a neat structure in the pointed Gothic style, has been built, and the latter, when

VIEW FROM MATLOCK BANK.

completed, will be one of the handsomest buildings in the neighbourhood.

Leaving Matlock Bridge we proceed along the road, the scenery at every step increasing in beauty and assuming a more bold and striking character. As we advance the dale becomes more contracted, and near the *Boathouse*, a small public-house on the road side, we obtain the first view of Masson and the Heights of Abraham, a part of the great chain of hills that forms the eastern boundary of the Derwent. Approaching the toll-bar, the road, following the course of the river, makes a sudden curve towards the left, after passing which Matlock Dale, with the stupendous High Tor and the long line of lofty wooded rocks bordering the river, bursts upon the astonished beholder in all its glory and magnificence. No pencil can portray or pen describe the glorious scene, and language is impotent to convey an idea of the beauty of it. There are indeed few spots in England or elsewhere more romantically grand, or where such a varied and striking assemblage of rock and river scenery can be met with as is here presented to the view.

Matlock Dale is a deep and narrow winding valley that extends from Matlock Town to Cromford, a distance of nearly three miles, everywhere wildly romantic and rich in picturesque combinations. It is bounded on one side by lofty hills finely wooded and dotted over with little Swiss-like cottages and villas of every variety and form, embosomed in trees of richest foliage; some picturesquely built on the verge of craggy precipices and in out-of-the-way places that would seem to preclude the possibility of approach, whilst others are hidden to view by the thick umbrage, their presence being only indicated by the thin blue smoke that ascends and hangs in hazy wreaths about the tops of the uppermost trees. At the bottom of the valley the majestic Derwent sweeps majestically along, its placid surface rich with the reflected hues of the varied foliage that overhangs its devious course. On the opposite side of the river is seen a long range of limestone precipices curiously stratified, that rise abruptly from its banks and tower aloft to a prodigious height, finely diversified by a regular alternation of rock and wood, here mantled with light and elegant foliage, and there displaying broad masses of whitened surface, relieved by creeping lichens and variegated by the different colourings of the ferns and mosses that adorn their channelled fronts.

The first object that arrests the attention on entering the dale from the north is the High Tor, the boast and the glory of

HIGH TOR, MATLOCK.

Matlock, and one of the most striking examples of rock scenery in Derbyshire—a vast and imposing mass of limestone, with a bold convex front that lifts its precipitous form to a height of upwards of 350 feet, casting a perpetual gloom upon the vale below, and producing in the mind of the spectator feelings of mingled awe and admiration. The sloping base is covered for a considerable way upwards with a

Q

dense tangle of underwood—hazels, honeysuckles, wild roses, and brambles—from the midst of which rises a profusion of trees of different kinds, the elegant mountain ash, the pale drooping willow, the gnarled and knotted oak, and the delicate pensile birch, mingling their leafy branches in a density of luxurious verdance, beneath which the graceful Derwent glides along, frequently hidden by the overhanging trees that fling their broad leafy boles over its glittering waters, subduing the dazzling brilliance with their sombre shade; at times it becomes impetuous and even turbulent, as, wasting its strength in whitened foam, it dashes over the rocky fragments that impede its course, then again it subsides into a rippling current, and carols merrily, like a talkative companion by the side of the wayfarer. The upper portion of the Tor, for more than 150 feet, presents one vast mass of naked perpendicular rock, indented with rents and fissures, from the crevices behind which peep out tufts of grass and shrubs and flowers, with here and there a few stunted trees that seem to have sprung spontaneously from the opening, and which afford an inaccessible retreat to hundreds of noisy rooks and daws.

Within the last few years the grounds on the High Tor have been enclosed and laid out in ornamental walks that wind in and out among the shrubs and trees with which the whole hillside is covered, every turning bringing fresh beauties before the eye. Near the summit the walk has been continued over a narrow ledge of rock that extends round the very verge of the Tor, and from this giddy height an uninterrupted view is obtained of Matlock Bath, with its villas, its shops and cottages, the beauteous Derwent and the charming country surrounding it. A pathway has also been formed along the bottom of a deep perpendicular gorge or fissure caused by the shrinkage of the limestone, to which the name of the Fern Cave has been given, from the profusion of these and other wild plants and flowers that grow out from the interstices, and peep from every rent and crevice of the rock.

We lingered sometime in the contemplation of this impressive scene; evening was creeping on, and a calmer light spread around; one side of the vale was enveloped in shadow, and on the other the declining orb threw the rich radiance of his farewell beams, gilding with brilliant touches of light the highest peaks of the majestic Tor, and sparkling through the fringe of foliage that crests its lofty summit. The thrush, the goldfinch, and the yellow-hammer were sporting merrily about, and through the umbrageous trees we could discern the gaily plumaged kingfisher flitting beneath the pendant branches, and the swallows chasing the flies as they skimmed the surface of the stream; and the ear listened the while with delight to the gentle harmony of the dancing leaves, the busy hum of insects, and the song of birds, mingled with the echoes of the brawling and angry current that foamed and eddied along its rocky channel.

To the geologist the High Tor is especially interesting, from the fine section of the strata which it exhibits; near the base a stratum of toadstone intervenes, separating the first and second limestones, and on the opposite side of the dale these different strata are answerable to each other, affording strong presumptive evidence that the two sides were formerly united in one solid mass, which has been rent asunder by volcanic force at some remote period of the world's history. Farey, in his "Agricultural Survey of Derbyshire," has included the High Tor in his section of the three lowest assemblages of strata known in Derbyshire, commencing at Riber Top, and extending to the highest point of Masson.

Opposite the High Tor the river is spanned by a little wooden bridge that leads to the Crystallised Cavern, close to which is a mill for grinding barytes. This mineral, provincially termed "cawke," is found in considerable quantities in the limestone districts of the Peak; it is generally associated with calcareous spar, and frequently forms the matrix of the richest lead veins; it is of a dingy white or dull yellow tint, and after being washed and ground is manufactured into a pigment of a fine white colour, known among painters as Dutch lead.

Leaving the barytes mill we crossed a narrow channel that has been cut from the weir to a lead mine close by, and on the opposite side of which, at the foot of the rock, is the High Tor Grotto, or Crystallised Cavern. This, though less extensive than the other caverns at Matlock, will, from the splen-

dour of its mineral decorations, and the beauty and perfection
of its crystallisations, be inspected by the mineralogist with
great interest and satisfaction.

The High Tor Grotto is very easy of access, and may be
explored without difficulty.    Passing through the little
stone shealing erected at the entrance, and taking each a
lighted candle, we followed the guide along a level path that
penetrates into the heart of the Tor.    The roof and sides
of this natural excavation are everywhere encrusted with a
profusion of crystallisations of calcareous spar, chiefly of the
scalon-dodecahedron and double pyramid or dog-tooth shape;
many of the crystals are of perfect form, and some are of
very large size, measuring ten or twelve inches in length.
On entering the cavern the attention is arrested by an
immense layer of spar, presenting a vast aggregation of
dog-tooth crystals, intermingled with fluor spar and lead ore,
and here and there exhibiting traces of carbonate of copper,
iron pyrites, and other mineral substances.    Further on, on
the left, is a thin stratum of clay separating the trap or
toad-stone from the upper limestone measures; about midway
a rude kind of chandelier, garnished with candles, is suspended from the roof, and when this is lighted the effect is
brilliant in the extreme, the myriads of crystals, gleaming
with the reflected light, glitter and sparkle with a gem-like
lustre.   Near the further extremity the path gently descends,
the roof becomes lower, and presently a lake of clear water
is reached, some sixty feet across, beyond which the rocks
close in, when all further progress is precluded.

Whilst exploring the cavern we were startled by a loud
reverberation resembling the rumbling of distant thunder,
caused by the passage of a train through the tunnel over
our heads.

On regaining the entrance we found exposed for sale a
good collection of crystallisations, fluor spars, fossils, and
other natural productions of the neighbourhood, including
some fine specimens of dog-tooth spar, the crystals being
nearly a foot in length, and of a pale-green colour.    In the
collection we noticed a curious example of the barytes family,
found in the dunstone, near Middleton by Youlgreave.    The
transverse section of this substance, when polished, is of a

rich vandyke or reddish-brown colour, and its configurations bear some resemblance to the variegated tortoiseshell, though without the transparency, being curiously radiated in a series of concentric circles that have evidently been formed by successive depositions.

Continuing our walk towards Matlock Bath the buildings become more numerous, cottages and lodging-houses line the western side of the road, and rise in tiers along the slope of Masson; some are castellated, and others exhibit a curious blending of the Gothic and Italian features; many have little plots of garden in front, and their appearance is improved by the clustering ivy and the gorgeous blossoms of the golden laburnum with which their walls are bedecked.

Near the parsonage is an extensive quarry, from which the limestone is obtained, and as we passed by the men were busy at work upon the large blocks that had been brought down by a recent "blast," breaking them into smaller pieces preparatory to their removal to the furnace. The side of the quarry where the rock is exposed has a very singular appearance; the strata dips at an angle of about 45°, and every layer may be distinctly traced, seeming to the eye as though at the first formation of the earth they had been carefully laid on in successive courses.

Beyond this quarry the scenery loses somewhat of its wild and rocky character and assumes a more sylvan appearance. Presently we come to a place where a road branches off on the left, and, crossing the river, leads up to the railway station—a neat Swiss-like structure—whence it is continued through the little hamlet of Starkholmes and on to Matlock town, where it again joins the main road at a point near Matlock Bridge.

Nearly opposite the railway station the river sweeps towards the right, and following the curve we enter the thriving town of Matlock Bath.

# CHAPTER XIV.

THE history of Matlock Bath may be said to date only from
the close of the seventeenth century, when the mineral springs
first began to be applied to medicinal purposes, previous to
which it was nothing more than a wild uncultivated ravine,
having no road through, and without the sign of any human
habitation save a few wretched-looking miners' huts here and
there dotting the ledges and recesses of its craggy steeps.

About the year 1698 the tepid waters began to attract
attention, and in that year the first bath—a humble structure
of wood, lined with lead—was erected; this was afterwards
removed and its place supplied by a more substantial building
of stone, and a lodging and boarding house was at the same
time erected near the spring.

In process of time other springs were discovered, improvements were made, and additional baths and lodging-houses
built for the accommodation of the increasing number of
visitants. In 1815 Scarthin Rock was cut through, and a
new road made at considerable labour and expense, running
along the side of the Derwent, and extending the entire
length of the dale. The opening of a line of railway from
Ambergate to Rowsley has, perhaps more than anything else,
contributed to the advancement and extension of Matlock
Bath. Since then considerable improvements have been
made—the streets have been lighted with gas, many new
buildings have been erected, and altogether the place presents
the appearance of a busy and thriving little town; and since
the railway extension to Manchester has been completed, and
a direct line of communication with the North of England
opened up, there has been a still further accession of

visitors, and quiet sojourners are now startled by crowds of excursionists who hurry about and manifest an unabashed determination to see everything that is to be seen.  Indeed this is the weakness of Matlock.  It has laid itself out for this class of visitors, and, as a consequence, is becoming less and less like that Matlock of which, nearly a century ago, old Gough, the antiquary, described as being " much frequented by the neighbouring gentry for health and amusement, without the infection of southern manners."

The inhabitants are employed chiefly in the manufacture of gypsum and spar ornaments, and in the inlaying, engraving, and etching of marble—a branch of trade that has arrived at great perfection, and is now carried on to a considerable extent.  On the Parade there are several spar shops, or " museums," as they are generally designated, the windows of which are crowded with articles, natural and manufactured. These repositories form a pleasant lounge for visitors, and in the inspection of the different objects which they contain an agreeable half-hour may be spent.  The Centre Museum, to which we paid a visit, is the principal establishment.  In the showroom we found a choice assortment of vases, statuettes, figures, and ornaments, in spar and Derbyshire marble, with others exquisitely sculptured in Cararra and Italian alabaster. Among the chief attractions we noticed some tables executed in Ashford black marble, inlaid with wreaths of flowers worked in different coloured stones ; some good specimens of minerals—native and foreign ; fossils, shells, and petrifac-tions—or rather preparations of calcareous matter—may also be enumerated as among the objects of interest in this exhibition.

Petrifaction working, as it is called, has become an important, and certainly not the least lucrative, branch of the " curiosity " business at Matlock, there being several wells in the tufa where this curious and interesting operation of nature is carried on.  The process of incrustation is a very simple one.  The articles to be operated on (embracing almost every conceivable object, but chiefly birds' nests, baskets of fruit, moss, and the leaves and branches of trees) are placed on stands, and the water that filtrates through the tufa allowed to drip gently upon them.  The moisture, in percolating through the concrete mass, becomes strongly impregnated with lime, and on reaching the open air rapidly evaporates, when a calcareous deposit is formed that in time completely incrusts the object on which it falls, and gives to it the appearance and hardness of stone.

Of the constituent ingredients of those thermal springs, that have raised Matlock to the position of an inland Spa, but little can be said, no regular quantitive analysis of their chemical contents having as yet been made. According to Sir Charles Scudamore's account, published in "Turner's Elements of Chemistry," they contain but a very small quantity of solid ingredients, consisting chiefly of the muriates and sulphates of magnesia, lime, and soda, with free carbonic acid. They are but slightly tepid, the temperature averaging 68° Fahrenheit, or about 14° lower than those of Buxton, a circumstance which is attributed to the escape of caloric on their becoming diluted with land springs before emergence into light. Attempts have repeatedly been made to obviate this by boring higher up the hill, but hitherto without success, the source being, it is said, nearly two thousand feet within the mountain.

The Matlock waters are said to resemble very much those of Clifton, with this difference, that the latter contain a less proportion of the sulphate and carbonate of lime. They are considered efficacious in cases of chronic rheumatism, gout, consumption, pulmonary and nervous disorders; and when drank freely as a common beverage, are highly beneficial in dyspeptic and nephritic affections.

The bathing establishments are three in number; the first in point of order is, or rather was, the *Old Bath*, which some years ago was purchased by a joint-stock company, when a large and handsome building was commenced on the site of the old hotel, intended as a first-class hydropathic establishment, but the works have been deserted for a considerable period, the company not having had sufficient funds to carry out its plans. The hotel which preceded it was, with one exception, the oldest building in the town, and occupied the site of the first spring discovered here; the second is at the *New Bath Hotel*, nearly opposite the Lover's Leap; and the third in seniority, unlike the Old and New Baths, is unconnected with any hotel, being situated in the Fountain Gardens, at the north end of the Museum Parade.

There are few places in England or elsewhere that can compete with Matlock for grand and magnificent scenery— the roads are excellent, and the walks and drives in the immediate vicinity present an almost unlimited variety of aspect. Nature having done so much in this respect, the inhabitants, who are specially interested in the prosperity of the place, seem disposed to rely too exclusively upon its scenic advantages, as forming the attraction for visitors ; for, with the exception of the libraries, and the re-unions at the principal hotels, the place possesses but few resources for indoor recreation and amusement. There is no promenade, concert room, or place of public assembly, consequently the visitors remain isolated in their apartments, with little social intercourse existing among them. Under these circumstances it need excite no surprise that many who, though at first charmed with the scenery, feel, after a few days' residence, a difficulty in resisting the encroaches of *ennui*. Were the inhabitants a little more public-spirited, Matlock would become one of the most agreeable places in the kingdom, not less as a permanent residence than as a place of temporary sojourn for the invalid and pleasure-seeker. The climate is mild and healthy, and the atmosphere free from redundant humidity, whilst the lofty hill of Masson and the Heights of Abraham afford a welcome shelter from the cold and searching winds of the north and east.

Matlock derives additional interest from the fact that here Byron and the beautiful but ill-fated Mary Chaworth, the heiress of Annesley, and the last scion of an illustrious house, met and loved; an attachment, the deep and passionate feeling of which is evidenced in many of the writings of the great bard.

At this time Matlock was in the hey-day of its popularity, the *Old Bath* was usually crowded with a brilliant company of beauty and fashion, and the ball-room of the hotel was often the scene of much gaiety and display. Lord Byron was a frequent visitor, as was also Miss Chaworth ; and it was here an incident occurred, related by Moore in his life of Byron, which could not fail to have had its influence upon

such an acute and sensitive mind as that of the poet, and
may have helped to bring about the unhappy estrangement
of the two lovers, who were destined—

> " The one to end in madness, the other in despair."

The sun was declining when we entered Matlock Bath,
and our first care therefore was to secure quarters for the
night.   After tea we strolled forth into the town like other
new-comers, to gaze at the shop-windows and admire the
various objects, natural and manufactured, therein exposed
to view.   It was the height of Matlock "season," and the
footpaths were thronged with visitors who had turned out to
enjoy the coolness of the evening; equipages of every
description rattled along the pavement, and the Derwent
presented quite a gay and animated appearance from the
numerous pleasure parties afloat upon its surface, their oars,
as they dipped successively in the translucent stream, breaking
the water into myriads of ripples that gleamed and sparkled
in the golden light of the setting sun.

Starting from the further end of the dale we leave the
paper mill and the weir on the right, the road as it follows
the crescent-like sweep of the river ascending for some
distance.   After passing the toll-gate we come to the *New Bath
Hotel*, near to which is the post-office, and the original
petrifying well, where we see the process of petrifying or
incrustation going on in the manner already described.
Further on is the new church, a pretty cruciform structure
standing upon a slightly elevated plot of ground on the
left of the road, and a conspicuous object from almost every
part of the dale.

Before its erection the nearest churches were the parish
church at Matlock Town and the one at Cromford, the
former two miles and the latter one mile distant from the
Bath.   To supply the want of accommodation experienced by
visitors a subscription was commenced; in 1841 the first
stone of the present structure was laid by Archdeacon,
afterwards Bishop Shirley, and the building was completed
in October of the following year.

Continuing our walk along the side of the tufa bank of
the Old Bath Terrace we pass on the left the deserted

structure already referred to and the Royal Petrifying Well, so called in honour of the visit of Her Majesty, when Princess Victoria, in 1832. Here the road declines and we have a succession of pleasing views across the river, including the Lovers' Walk and the precipitous mural cliffs bounding the eastern side of the dale, their lofty peaks here and there starting through the thick woods which mantle their sides, presenting a constant alternation of naked rock and thick luxuriant foliage. Nearly opposite the obelisk at the end of the terrace a road leads down to the ferry, and close to this are the stables, the head-quarters and general rendezvous of the ostlers, stable-helpers, donkey drivers, guides, and gentlemen of varied yet undefined occupations, of which latter class Matlock seems to have rather an over-abundance. Here we find a knot of idlers engaged in friendly chat; there two or three guides are talking over the gains of the day, and making calculations upon the successes of to-morrow; near to the duck-pond a gentleman in a sleeved jacket and tight-fitting pantaloons is grooming down a horse, accompanying the operation with a continual hissing, the precise meaning or purpose of which it would be difficult to determine; close by is a picturesque group of singularly impassive-looking donkeys accompanied by some youthful members of the inhumane society, who are amusing themselves by constantly poking the sharp ends of their sticks between the ribs of the unfortunate animals, all the while keeping up a running commentary on the personal appearance of the passers by.

Leaving this spot with its motley assemblage we come next to the Museum Parade, the principal thoroughfare of Matlock and certainly not the least attractive if we may judge from the number of visitors loitering about the pavement. The side of the street here is lined with hotels, lodging-houses, museums, chemists, stationers, and confectioners' shops, and establishments for the sale of the thousand-and-one little knick-knacks that are only to be met with at a watering-place or pleasure resort.

Having walked the length of the Parade we retraced our steps, turning up the steep ascent at the end of *Hodgkinson's Hotel,* then passing the *Temple Hotel* and along the Temple

Walk until we came again to the Terrace in front of the Old Bath, from which, unquestionably, the best view of the town is obtained.

This terrace, which is elevated considerably above the road, is laid out in neat parterres; it originally formed part of the natural bank of the river and is composed almost entirely of tufa or stalagmitic concretions left by the tepid spring.

From the north side the view, though less extensive than some others in the locality, is almost unequalled for varied and romantic beauty, embracing nearly every object of interest and attraction in the neighbourhood—rock, wood, and water, with bold hills, verdant slopes, and picturesque cottages, being happily combined. Immediately in front is seen the Museum Parade, with its long row of shops and hotels, their delicate white and cream-coloured fronts agreeably harmonising with the varied greenery behind. On the slope of the hill, above the Parade, are the *Temple Hotel*, Gilderoy, Belle Vue, and a number of other showy houses and fantastically-built villas, perched on wooded hillocks, and peering out from amid thick plantations of oak, ash, and maple, and picturesque groups of mountain trees that display every variety of tint and foliage. Behind these are seen the zigzag walks and the Heights of Abraham, the latter rising majestically from the road, and seeming to bar up the further end of the dale; the bold acclivities, clothed with sombre masses of foliage, and crowned by a lofty prospect tower; and beyond, the view takes in the summit of proud Masson, which towers aloft to a height of nearly 800 feet. Through the opening on the right we catch a glimpse of the naked front of the magnificent High Tor, its proud head rising with infinite majesty over the surrounding landscape. Looking towards the east the view is still more beautiful. Far below, through occasional breaks in the trees, we can see the graceful Derwent sweeping noiselessly round the wooded hill in front of the Parade, its placid surface reflecting the sombre shadows of the overhanging branches which seem to interlace and cross each other in a network of impressive beauty. Bounding the eastern bank of the river are the Lovers' Walks and a lofty rampart of rock broken in perpendicular cliffs, partially clothed with a rich profusion of ferns, harts-tongue, and clinging ivy, and a variety of wild flowers that display their delicate colourings in all their natural beauty and loveliness.

The day was drawing to a close, and the unclouded sun, as he descended behind the western hills, shed a rich but subdued radiance over the landscape, producing a scene such as is only witnessed in those countries where nature exhibits her boldest features. A soft aerial tint spread over the hills, softening the outline of distant objects, and rendering them less obtrusive to the eye. As we lingered, gazing upon the glorious prospect, the valley before us became wrapped in a deep shadow that curtained in its embraces the lower slopes of the rocks and hills, while all above was gleaming with the beams of light that played about the summits, producing a constant variation of tint. Gradually, as the shadows of night crept higher and higher up the broad steeps, these vivid touches of brilliance died away, and in the deepening twilight the distant rocks seemed to melt away in dreamy indistinctness. Slowly the advancing night wrapped her mantle of darkness around every object, when earth and sky, mountain and valley, passed from the sight, and became lost in undistinguishable gloom.

As we looked across the dale, lights began to glimmer in the inns and dwelling-houses and far-off cots, then a gentle breeze sprang up that rustled plaintively through the branches of the trees, and now and then the deep baying of some distant watch-dog could be heard mingling with the soft murmuring of the river and the subdued hum of the few people who yet lingered about the Parade. One after another the starry host came forth, gemming the blue expanse of heaven with their twinkling fires; and then the moon—

"Resplendent orb of night,"

slowly arose from behind the darkened hills, and shed her soft and mellowed light upon the scene, faintly illuminating the precipitous rocks with her silvery lustre, and bathing with mild radiance the woods and undulating hills. Delightful was it to watch the pale beams struggling through the overhanging branches of the trees, and dancing and playing upon the rippling waters, here quivering on a thick fringe of foliage, and there casting a broad, deep, aud mysterious-looking shadow from some overhanging crag or pinnacle.

How different was now the scene from what we witnessed from this spot on the occasion of a former visit to Matlock. Then, after a day of sultry and oppressive heat, as evening approached, the northern heavens became overcast, and the darkening atmosphere threw a lurid sickly glare upon every object; a heavy dun-coloured cloud, which every moment increased in density, enveloped and hung around the head of Masson—a few drops splashed upon the pavement with a dull and leaden sound, and the distant muttering betokened the coming of a storm. A calm and almost preternatural stillness reigned around, which became painful in its intensity—the playful breeze, which just before frolicked through the trees, had died away—not a leaf stirred, and even the birds were mute, as if with fear at the approaching conflict of the elements. Suddenly a vivid, blinding flash, shot athwart the murky sky, and lit up with momentary brilliance the deep recesses of the dale, followed by one long deafening peal of thunder that reverberated from side to side with fearful intonation, seeming to shake the earth to its very centre. Now the winds blew with all their rage, and the rain poured down in sweeping torrents, flooding every path and alley, and adding to the din by their ceaseless aggravated roar; the overcharged mountain-currents poured down their rocky channels in foaming cascades, stream meeting stream, and lashing each other with fury, then surging and struggling onwards with impetuous rage, until they became swallowed up in the Derwent's angry flood. Flash after flash burst from the pitchy mantle above, darting round the hills, and licking every projecting crag and pinnacle with their forked and fiery tongues, until the whole hemisphere seemed wrapped in blue sulphurous flame. The rattling peals of thunder followed each other in almost uninterrupted succession, resounding from rock to rock in fearful and horrible confusion, and echoing along the valley, then bursting forth anew, and pealing hoarsely through the glens and fastnesses, now loudly, now indistinctly, mingling and commingling, until the imagination was wrought into a state of absolute terror with the idea that Chaos had come again. It was a scene to which, with slight variation, we might apply the noble poet's description :—

> "The sky was changed ! and such a change ! Oh, night,
> And storm, and darkness, ye are wondrous strong,
> Yet lovely in your strength, as is the light
> Of a dark eye in woman ! Far along
> From peak to peak, the rattling crags among,
> Leaps the live thunder ! Not from one lone cloud,
> But every mountain now hath found a tongue,
> And Masson answers through his misty shroud
> Back to the joyous Tor, who calls to him aloud."

The storm was but of brief duration : soon the rain ceased, and the misty vapours began to roll up the mountain sides ; the heavy watery clouds gradually passed away, the sky became clear, and the sun again shone forth in all his former brilliancy, illuminating the woods, the hills, the rocks, and the valleys, and producing almost magical effect as he shed the full radiance of his farewell beams upon the refreshed and invigorated landscape.

Descending from the terrace, we returned along the dale to our inn; a few visitors yet loitered about, and as we passed along the road we could occasionally hear the sounds of vocal harmony and the sweet strains of the flageolet proceeding from some boating party yet out upon the water.

# CHAPTER XV.

A BRIGHT and sunny morning succeeded to the moonlight
splendour of the previous night ; at an early hour we were
awoke from our slumber by the loud clanging of a factory
bell and the noisy clatter of the operatives proceeding to
their daily labour, sounds that savoured too much of our own
city of Cottonopolis to accord with the poetic features of the
surrounding scenery.

We had a pleasant stroll before breakfast along the side
of the river to Scarthin Rock, and through a portion of the
Willersley grounds to Cromford Bridge, passing on the way
the neat little chapel built by the Arkwrights. It was a
delightful morning, and everything seemed to rejoice in the
fascinating beauty of the opening day. Brightly shone the
sun upon the Derwent, and as it dashed over the foaming
weir its dancing waters quivered with a thousand sparkling
ripples, then the angry tumult subsiding it swept along,
soothing the ear with its cheerful music, and reflecting from
its mirrored surface the various and ever-changing forms of
beauty that adorn its banks. Brightly shone the sun upon
the face of nature—the wooded heights, the grassy slopes,
the broken and impending rocks gleamed in the early light,
and the groves rang with the melodies of their feathered
occupants ; a pure invigorating breeze that swept through
the dale gave buoyancy to the spirits, and every circumstance
which could cheer or enliven was present to add to our
enjoyment.

The first object that meets the eye at the bend of the road

is Glenorchy Chapel, a small brick building, with the name and date of erection (1777) painted over the entrance, and adjoining which is the minister's residence. The place was built by Sir Richard Arkwright, from whom it was purchased by Lady Glenorchy, and by her endowed as a chapel for the use of the Independents who worship here. On leaving the chapel, Willersley Castle, the seat of Peter Arkwright, Esq.,

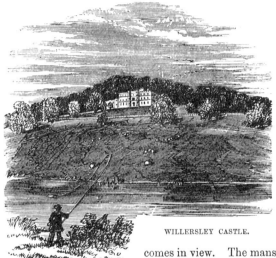

WILLERSLEY CASTLE.

comes in view. The mansion was erected in 1788, from the designs of Mr. William Thomas ; it is a quadrangular building in the castellated style, with embattled parapets and a tower gateway in the centre, flanked at each side by circular turrets which rise considerably above the roof. It occupies an elevated position near the top of a steep lawn, which slopes down towards the river, and commands some fine scenic views along the valley of the Derwent in the direction of Belper and Derby, including the lofty hills of Crich and Stonnis, with many minor eminences rich with wood and intervening verdure. On the north rises a succession of lofty heights clothed with thick waving woods,

R

the dark green of which forms an agreeable contrast to the delicate yellow colour of the mansion itself.

Willersley is not shown to strangers, but the gardens are thrown open to the public on Mondays and Thursdays, and are then much frequented, few visitors failing to avail themselves of the opportunity afforded of rambling through the park and the pleasure grounds.

Passing through an opening in Scarthin Rock, which leads to the entrance lodge, we proceed along a path called the Chapel Walk, that runs between the river and a magnificent pile of almost perpendicular rock, that rises on the right to a height of 150 feet, its rugged front split and rent in innumerable fissures, and adorned with shrubs and trees and richly-coloured lichens and mosses. On the opposite side of the river is seen Riber Hill, Wild Cat Tor, and the well-wooded cliffs rising beyond Willersley, and extending eastwards towards Lea Mills and Holloway. In the nearer foreground the view is of a more sylvan but not less beautiful character; and in front is the lawn rising gently from the water's edge, clothed with the richest turf, and dotted over with picturesque clumps of trees.

Continuing our walk, and passing close by the mills which are seen through the openings in the trees, we come next to Cromford Church, or chapel, as it is more generally designated, a small and unpretending structure, built in 1797, at the expense of Sir Richard Arkwright. Our visit was too early to enable us to get admission to the interior, in which there is a monument by Chantry, to the memory of Mrs. Arkwright and her children.

From the chapel to Cromford Bridge the distance is only a few yards. At this point three roads branch off, the one on the left, re-entering the grounds by a neat Gothic lodge, continues through sloping meadows to the house, and leads thence to Wild Cat Tor, a rugged and isolated mass of rock, from the summit of which is obtained one of the best views in the neighbourhood of Matlock, including within its limits the High Tor, Masson, the Heights of Abraham, Harp Edge, and Stonnis, with the narrow winding dale through which the Derwent pursues its busy course. On the right the road keeps along the northern bank of the river for a couple of miles, when it turns to the left and ascends by the edge of the plantation at Lea Hurst, and through Holloway to the lead mines and limestone quarries at Crich. The road in front is continued along the side of Riber Hill, and thence through Starkholmes to Matlock town. Before the opening of the road through Matlock Dale this was the only line of communication between Wirksworth, Cromford, and Darley. At that time the bridge was a narrow unpretending structure, what in this part of the country is termed a pack-saddle bridge, and many accidents are said to have happened by horses leaping the battlements. On the side of the bridge is an inscription recording one of these occurrences—a horse running away with his rider, bounded over the parapet into the stream, a depth of twenty or thirty feet, but fortunately both escaped unhurt. The bridge was widened when the new road was made, though but little attention was given to preserve a uniformity of appearance, for in the older portion the arch is of pointed Gothic character, whilst in the more recent addition it is of a semicircular form. The same incongruity is noticeable in the bridges at Matlock town and Darley, which were widened about the same time.

From this point we extended our ramble to Lea Hurst, the home of one of England's noblest daughters—Florence Nightingale—a name known and loved and honoured in every English home. Keeping to the right we continued along a shady lane, that leads beneath the railway and along the side of the river. Hedgerows studded here and there with copse of thorn and holly flank the way on the left, now and then alternating with patches of stone wall, grey and jagged and overgrown with mosses and lichens. Every turn of the road reveals some fresh picture, each seeming more beautiful than the one that preceded it, and the beauty of the river, which keeps us in pleasant companionship, is increased by the ever-changing character of the currents. Yonder by the bridge the water gleams and sparkles as it circles in playful eddies round the gray moss-grown stones, and leaps up now and then to kiss the mallows and yellow buttercups that fringe its reedy banks; here it flows swiftly and silently along, calm, deep, and placid, its tranquil bosom reflecting, as from a mirror, the varied forms of loveliness above and around—the mazy outline of the trees and waving bushes, the water-flags, the broad-leaved batter-docks, the overarching sky with a few white clouds sailing therein, and

> "The shadow of a lark
> Hung in the shadow of a heaven."

Though every object is given back with the most distinct vividness, we lose the ever-changing effect of the colours, deep and rich, and soft and delicate; still there is much to charm and delight the eye in these reflected pictures, and the effect is heightened by the gentle murmuring of sunny music which falls upon the ear—unconscious life, as it were, rioting in the full enjoyment of its own existence. As the eye roves across the country new beauties continually unfold themselves—little winding dales with clefts and dingles, through which trickle innumerable rills, varying the character and appearance of the valley, while they give additionally-pleasing features to the landscape. In the distance are seen the woods of Alderwasley, mantling the ridge of the rock that extends from Ambergate to Stonnis, and beyond the moors of Middleton and Cromford, with a multitude of hills of varied form and elevation that stretch away as far as the eye can reach.

About two miles from Cromford the road leaves the open valley and we ascend between steep acclivities that rise abruptly on each side, shaded by umbrageous trees—Bough Wood on the one hand, and the plantations of Lea on the other. A few minutes' walking brings us to a little cluster of houses—hamlet it can hardly be called, the dwellings are so few. Here the road divides, forming a kind of triangle, one path leading to Lea and Dethick, and the other passing through Upper Holloway and Crich to Wingfield. A few yards above the junction are the gates forming the lower entrance to Lea Hurst, and adjoining them is the Lodge, a pretty little Gothic building, with a still prettier garden attached.

The walk through the grounds from the lower gate is very pleasing. The road, which is well kept, though without any attempt at cultivation—the grass and flowers being allowed to grow and flourish as they will, so long as they do not encroach upon the gravelled path—leads through a thick plantation of birch and beech trees, interspersed with oak and ash, and an occasional sprinkling of fir and larch. Here and there a gleamy vista opens through which we obtain glimpses of the valley below, with its park-like meadows, its dark-hued plantations, its swelling and folding hills, its tangled hollows and shady dells, and the fertilising river, glowing with beauty and fraught with a thousand rural delights, winding its way through the yellow fields and sunny glades that stretch away in seemingly interminable succession. About half-way up the hill the road turns and at the angle a delightful prospect is obtained. Looking across the valley, the eye ranges over a wide expanse of country, green and undulating, and backed by a range of swelling hills that stretch away in far perspective—over leagues of waving wood and fields of ripening grain that give promise of an abundant harvest—over rich meadow-lands plentifully sprinkled with trees and chequered with hedgerows, showing where the quiet rural lanes intersect each other—and over hamlets, villages, and gray church towers, and little whitened farm-steads that gleam brightly in the summer sunshine. Riber Hill lifts its dusky brow in front; further on is seen Cromford Moor, the Hag Rocks, and the dark-hued heights of Alderwasley, with many a minor eminence, crowned with wood and clothed with intervening verdure. Wakebridge twinkles behind a thin white veil of smoke, and, beyond, Crich Cliff and Stand appear looming against the blue of heaven.

Onwards the road continues to ascend, the wood thickens, and the view becomes limited by the dense umbrage that spreads above and around : the lofty firs, the drooping branches of the birch trees and the pendant boughs of the oaks and beeches that almost sweep the ground, shutting us within a delightful solitude. From the edge of the plantation the road is continued over a gentle ascent flanked on one side by a grove of birch trees. On reaching the plateau we pass through a gate, and thence along a carriage drive that leads up to the principal entrance to the mansion, in front of which is a circular grass-plot or lawn with a sundial in the centre.

The house is a comparatively modern erection, built in the late Tudor or Elizabethan style, with quaint mullioned windows, clustering chimneys, and high-peaked gables terminating in orbicular hip-knobs; an oriel, crowned by an open balustrade, projects from the south end, and two bays extend beyond the line of the main structure on the west side, giving a diversity of outline in keeping with the general characteristics of the style. The flower gardens and shrubberies, which partially surround it, are fenced in by a dwarf wall, through which admission is gained by a

LEA HURST.

substantial-looking gateway on the south side, approached by a broad flight of steps. The hall itself is shrouded in trees, and half hidden by an exuberant mantle of ivy—the latter an addition that adds to the picturesqueness of its appearance. A better position for a gentleman's residence than that which it occupies can hardly be conceived. It stands upon an elevated plateau of some extent, and on the north side is sheltered from the cold winds by the woods of Lea and Holloway and the mountainous ridge that extends on to Crich; whilst on the south it commands a magnificent and uninterrupted view along the valley of the Derwent, in the direction of Ambergate and Belper, including within its limits some of the best-cultivated land and most beautiful and exquisitely-diversified scenery in Derbyshire.

The manor of Lea, which includes the neighbouring hamlets of Holloway and Dethick, boasts considerable antiquity, and possesses, in addition to the charm which more recent associations have thrown around it, much that is historically interesting. The manor was held so far back as the reign of King John by the De Alveleys, who erected a chapel here in the early part of the thirteenth century; from them a moiety of it was conveyed in marriage by an heiress to the great feudal house of the Ferrers, which moiety subsequently passed into the possession of the Dethicks, and from them to the Babingtons—both families of considerable note, numbering among their members several who attained to eminence and distinction, and not the least notable of whom was that Anthony Babington who was executed for treason against Queen Elizabeth, in conspiring with others to liberate the Queen of Scots from her unhappy captivity. The other portion of the manor passed successively through the families of De la Lea, Frecheville, Rollestone, Pershall, and Spateman, and ultimately to that of Nightingale—William Edward Shore Nightingale, Esq., the present proprietor, and father of Miss Nightingale, whose name has imparted so much interest to Lea Hurst, having inherited the estate through the female line—his father, William Shore, Esq., who assumed the arms and surname of Nightingale, having married the niece and sole heiress of Peter Nightingale, Esq., of Lea.

On leaving we passed along the drive to the upper gate, where we came again upon the high road at Holloway, a picturesque little mountain hamlet, comprising a few straggling groups of old-fashioned cottages that cluster irregularly along the steep side of the hill.

Shaping our course homewards we turned to the left, descending by a steep road that winds round the edge of a thick wood, and soon reached the open valley.

Varying the route a little we returned from Cromford Bridge to our inn by the turnpike road, passing on the way the extensive cotton mills of the Arkwrights, a large pile of building standing on the right of the road—the nursing place, as it has been styled, of the factory opulence and power of Great Britain.

On leaving Cromford Mills we passed through Scarthin Nick, a deep and narrow opening that has been cut through the limestone, presenting the appearance of huge walls of lifeless-looking rock rising abruptly on each side, their naked fronts contrasting with the brilliant verdure of the trees and shrubs which fringe their summits, though relieved in places by the plants and trailing flowers that depend from the rents and crevices in the strata.

At the end of Scarthin Nick the road again comes close upon the river, and following the sweep of the stream we come in sight of Matlock. After resting awhile we walked down to the Parade, the general starting-point for excursions, intending to visit some of the numerous caverns for which Matlock is celebrated.

As already observed in a former part of this work the limestone measures which extend over a large portion of the Peak of Derbyshire are deeply penetrated by rents and cavernous chambers, that have for the most part been formed either by the disruption or the shrinking of the strata. The whole country about Matlock seems penetrated with these openings, many of which have been turned to profitable account, there being those in the world, as Sir George Head humorously observes, "who, were an old woman to stand sentry over a jay's nest, would pay a shilling to be allowed to climb a tree and see it."

Among the owners of these caverns there exists a large amount of jealous rivalry, each proprietor loudly vaunting his own to be superior to any other. Some of these subterraneous cavities are very interesting, but none of them will compare either for extent or splendour of mineral decoration with those of Castleton.

The High Tor Grotto we have already described, and the Rutland, the Cumberland, and the Devonshire Caverns we purpose noticing in the course of our excursion.

The Cumberland Cavern was the first of the series we visited, the approach to which is by the zigzag walks leading up to the Heights of Abraham.

Leaving the Parade we ascend by a steep path at the end

of Hodgkinson's Hotel, then, turning to the right, pass Mr. Smedley's Phusitechnicon—whatever that may be—a spar shop, we imagine—and continue along what is called the Cork-screw Walk until we reach the lower or octagon lodge, when the attention is arrested by a board bearing the characteristic inscription, " Heights of Abraham, 6d. each."

No visitor can remain many hours in Matlock without becoming aware of the fact that the inhabitants are a money-getting race. Nature has dealt bountifully with them and they eagerly avail themselves of every opportunity of turning these advantages to account. In this respect Matlock contrasts unfavourably with the liberal spirit displayed at Buxton, and were it possible to transport the Corbar Woods, the Park, the Cliff, even the covered walk beneath the Crescent, from the latter place to Matlock, we verily believe they would be seized upon and converted into so many sources of revenue. If, after having wandered some time among the gloomy avenues of the cavern, you feel inclined to enjoy the pure air and invigorating breeze from the top of Abraham's Heights, a toll of sixpence is demanded; should curiosity prompt you to see where the Dungeon Tors have slipped from the parent rock you are met by a similar charge; or if at all amorously inclined, and you desire to seek the shady retirement of the Lovers' Walks, the same sum is claimed every time you enter, though this last charge is professedly for ferrying you across the river when a simple rustic bridge might be made which would answer the purpose infinitely better; and in this way the receivers of these several tolls realise a pretty considerable sum-total of sixpences during the season. We make these remarks in no unfriendly spirit; but we feel persuaded that were the inhabitants of Matlock to manifest a little more liberality in this respect their interests would not suffer thereby.

Having paid the entrance-fee, a shilling, which includes admission to the Rutland Cavern, we are permitted to ascend the " Heights" and to wander at will among the labyrinth of walks that have been formed over the steep front of the hill.

The Heights of Abraham, a name given to the lower slopes of Masson, from their supposed resemblance to those of

Quebec, is a favourite place of resort with visitors, few, however brief their stay, failing to make the ascent, and assuredly a more charming and delightful spot even Matlock itself cannot boast. When the noonday sun pours down a flood of intense brilliance upon the landscape, and every object seems to glow with radiant heat, delightful is it to wander in the cool retirement of these shady walks, or to recline upon one of the numerous seats embowered by trees and bushes, watching the sparkling sunbeams as they dart through the intricate canopy of leaves, dappling the moss-grown rock and verdant sward with their flickering touches of light, or gazing through the occasional breaks in the umbrage upon the varied assemblage of objects spread around.

Nearly the whole front of the hill is covered with a profusion of trees—larch and fir, intermingled with dwarf oak, ash, and birch, beneath whose shade the laburnum, lilac, wild bramble, and numerous other shrubs display their varied hues, while the ground is covered with beautiful ferns and a rich variety of wild flowers, whose brilliant colourings, agreeably harmonising with the deep green of the spreading foliage, give a character of sylvan loveliness to the scene. As we ascend, the road at first winds from side to side, and then diverges in various directions among the trees, the sides everywhere exhibiting a jungle of weeds and flowers — the harebell, the wild geranium, and the sweet lily of the valley blending their delicate tints with the more vivid colourings of the blooming gorse, the foxglove, and the ragwort or yellow-top, as it is sometimes called. Here and there the gray rock protrudes, and then we come to hollows and glens fringed with a profusion of drooping ferns, and exquisitely festooned with creeping ivy and brambles, and an interweaving of the long leaves of the harts-tongue and the delicate maiden-hair. With increasing height, the openings in the trees become more frequent, and we have at every turn a succession of ever-varying yet ever-pleasing glimpses of scenery. A little more than half way up the Heights is the Cavern Terrace, a broad path that has been formed of the loose refuse brought out of the adjoining cavern. Here a few rustic seats have been placed offering an invitation to rest. Surrounded by woods and sheltered by the thickly foliaged branches of the trees we found it difficult to refuse the mute invitation, and so sat down awhile leisurely to gaze upon the beauteous scene spread below. The morning was delightful, and the sun now high in the heavens shone out with unusual brilliance, filling the Orient with his golden splendour, and imparting a charm to the surrounding landscape, until every object seemed to share in the universal gladness. Where his bright rays had failed to penetrate the dew still lay upon the grass, and the pearly drops sparkled upon the countless spider webs that stretched from bough to bough; a thin filmy veil, which had hitherto hung over the dale, was fast melting away and disappearing in white fleecy clouds that floated round the adjacent hills; the Parade, with its busy throng was partially hidden from view by the lower part of the hill, but the Temple, the Old Bath, the Church, and the shops bordering the road as far as the weir, could be distinctly seen; and these, with the few Swiss-like cottages crowning the cliffs and peering out from the thick woods— their pale blue smoke slowly curling up into the pure morning air—gave life and interest and added to the picturesqueness of the scene. Across the dale the Derwent could be traced winding round the base of the impending crags, now sparkling in the bright sunlight, and now hiding from view beneath the overhanging trees. The further side of the valley was enveloped in deep shadow but all besides was gleaming with light, and the slant rays, as they played through the branches of the trees, lighting up the edge of the woods and streaking with golden touches the bold front of the rocks, gave an indescribable charm that filled the mind with admiration and delight.

The entrance to the Rutland Cavern is on this terrace, but the examination of its subterranean wonders we must reserve until our return from the Prospect Tower on the top of the Heights. Quitting our resting-place we again ascend by a still more steep and intricate path, overshadowed by the thick umbrage. Here art has evidently been summoned to the aid of nature, and as a result we have a happy blending of tall young trees with wide-spreading elms, maples, and a variety of shrubs, while from between the ramifications of the straggling roots spring up long waving ferns, rank grasses, and gigantic weeds, that grow in wild luxuriance and thicken into underwood, deriving sustenance from the little rills that trickle down the mountain side.

And so we go on, winding round precipitous slopes of rock and sward, and now and then stopping to peep through the breaks in the foliage at the long range of beetling cliffs opposite—gaunt masses of gray and naked rock that tower aloft to a prodigious height, grim and savage enough at times, but now revealing many a charm, as the slanting beams of the morning sun illume their rugged crests, revealing every cleft and cavity, and chequering their broad sides with a succession of varying shadows.

By-and-by we come to an alcove, in which it is said Montgomery, the poet, penned his famous impromptu on Matlock scenery :—

> " Here in wild pomp magnificently bleak,
> Stupendous Matlock towers amid the Peak,
> Here rocks on rocks, on forests forests rise,
> Spurn the low earth and mingle with the skies.
> Great Nature, slumbering by fair Derwent's stream,
> Conceiv'd these giant mountains in a dream."

The last couplet, with some slight alteration, he afterwards adopted in his poem, " The West Indies."

Still the path goes higher, and as we mount upwards new beauties reveal themselves at every step. Now the ascent becomes more abrupt, and the grandeur of the scene below proportionately increases ; at length the summit is gained, and amply are we rewarded for our toil by the glorious prospect that meets the gaze.

On the platform stands the Victoria Tower, a neat stone erection, from the summit of which is obtained one of the finest and most extensive panoramic views which nature anywhere presents, including it is said within its limits the larger portion of five counties.

The atmosphere was now perfectly clear, and the vast prospect lay before us, unobscured by cloud or vapour, so that the eye was enabled to range over an expanse limited only by the pale blue range of circling hills that stretched away upon the horizon until their summits, softened and blended by the mellowing tints of distance, could hardly be distinguished from the few light vapours that gauzed the azure dome above. All within this limit was one continuity of swelling eminences, that rose and fell like the heaving waves of the rolling ocean; whichever way we looked nothing but an infinity of mountain tops could be seen, relieved with wood, and rock, and herbage, and broken up into endless varieties of form and colour.

Glorious was the prospect from these lofty heights; and the pleasant breeze, the sunshine, and the exquisite variety of scene, combined to exercise an inspiriting influence upon the mind. Refreshing was the view over the green and beautiful expanse, which, as it lay rejoicing in the summer sheen, seemed to look up with benignant smile at the cloudless sky above. What pen can tell of the beams of light that played around the summits of those hills as the gorgeous sun poured down his fervent rays, steeping the entire landscape in brilliance, and bathing every object in radiant beauty?

After contemplating for awhile this glorious prospect the mind is enabled to occupy itself with the details, and to note the various physiognomy of the country. The openings in the hills show where the dales wander, and enable us to trace the entrance to every lovely vale that breaks the lofty ridges. Following the long rocky chain that extends from north to south, the eye passes over the beautiful and picturesque valley that bosoms the graceful Derwent—

> " Exulting and abounding river !
> Making its waves a blessing as they flow,
> Through banks whose beauty would endure for ever,
> Could man but leave its bright creation so."

From this elevated situation the High Tor loses much of its grandeur and sublimity, and sinks into comparative insignificance when contrasted with the majestic Masson, which rears its gigantic head considerably above us. At our feet is a dense mass of waving wood, through which we now and then catch a glimpse of a cottage or villa happily disposed upon some jutting promontory; far below this again is the deep valley watered by the Derwent, on the banks of which cluster the neat and cleanly white buildings that constitute the town of Matlock Bath. Bounding the eastern side of the river is a long range of mural precipices, prominent among which is Riber Hill,

> " Whose dusky brow
> Wears, like a regal diadem, the round
> Of ancient battlements and ramparts high,
> And frowns upon the vales."

In front is Matlock Town and Bridge, and on the slope of the hill the hydropathic establishment and the straggling cottages forming the village of Matlock Bank. Looking more towards the north the eye passes over acres of meadow land, and over many a sloping hill and smiling farmstead and gray village church, until it reaches the blue range of Yorkshire hills, which bar up the view, meeting the sky and forming an admirable perspective. Darley Dale appears in all its picturesque beauty—picturesque from whatever quarter beheld—and midway between is Oker Hill, the summit of which we scaled in our walk yesterday, rising abruptly from the plain, a mute but eloquent memorial that tells of days of dim antiquity, and carries the mind back to that period of our history when these peaceful valleys echoed the clang and fell shout of war, as the trained legionaries of imperial Rome fiercely contended in unholy strife with the brave and heroic Britons for the mineral treasures of their native soil, when the verdant slopes of Oker streamed with the life blood of a bold and ardent race, who, if they knew not how to fight, knew at least how brave men should die.

Looking towards the south, the eye, as it traverses the romantic valley of the Derwent, is arrested for a moment by the graceful spire of the church, a striking feature in the landscape. Then, following the course of the stream, it takes in on one side the steep sides of Masson, dotted over with habitations, some near and others far apart; the moors of Middleton and Bonsall, the graceful curve of Harp Edge, the Hag Rocks, and Cromford Moor ; and, beyond, Black Rocks, or Stonnis, with its pine-crowned head towering above the landscape in infinite majesty, and rivalling in altitude the lofty eminence on which we stand. On the other side of the valley is seen the Lover's Leap, Wild-Cat Tor, the range of battlemented cliffs, and the masses of intermingled rock and foliage that extend to Willersley Castle. Further on are the woods of Willersley, Lea, and Holloway, Tansley Moor and Crish Chase Cliff, the latter with its lofty tower standing in relief against the blue of heaven; whilst between an opening in the rocks the eye looks over a wide and fertile vale through sloping meadows crowned with luxuriant woods, unbroken save where the craggy rocks jut out like massive buttresses to the hills in rear. In middle distance is seen the broad outline of Barrel Edge, the wooded heights of Alderwasley, and many a minor eminence crested with wood and clothed with verdant sward; whilst far beyond a multitude of undulating hills crowd upon the horizon, summit after summit crossing and recrossing each other in seemingly endless succession, until their dim outlines become lost in the shadowy distance. Woods and hollows, rocks, hills, and mountains, with new-shorn meadows and fields of ripening grain, dotted with trees and bordered with hedgerows that look more green and beautiful by contrast with the brown and heathery slopes around; the quiet villages and farmsteads scattered over the hillsides, the little towns rejoicing in the bright sunshine; the rugged perpendicular rocks, all purple and gray, crowned and flanked with hanging woods; the deep valley, and the river sweeping along with shining curves, shooting round projecting crags and promontories, leaping from ledge to ledge, and throwing up the bright glistening foam bubbles as it goes: all these rich varieties of nature combine to produce a scene which thrills the heart with delight, and which for grandeur and extent is hardly equalled in the Peak.

As we loitered about the summit we were told of this hill and that mountain and of such a cliff and such a tor, and we gazed again and again upon the glorious prospect until our eyes became wearied with the effort to distinguish the one from the other.

# CHAPTER XVI.

FROM the Prospect Tower which crowns the Heights of Abraham we descend by a circuitous pathway that winds hither and thither through a plantation of fir, oak, and ash, with a teeming undergrowth of brambles and briars. The trees meet overhead, and as the breeze plays sportively through their branches we catch glimpses of the sunshine and the blue sky above and the sparkling river gurgling and splashing in the depths below. As we descend lower the gloom increases, and the subdued light seems to impart a tinge of greenness to the crags and precipices that gives to the place quite an aspect of sombre impressiveness. The rocks are covered in places with ferns and mosses, and every inch of ground, every crevice, is hidden by a dense tangle of climbers and creeping plants.

Pursuing the devious path

" With mazy error under pendant shades "

we come again to the terrace on which is the entrance to the Rutland Cavern.

This cavern, originally known as the Old Nestor Mine—a name by which it is still held under the Duchy of Lancaster—claims pre-eminence over the other subterranean curiosities of Matlock, both for the extent of its excavations and the abundance and variety of its fossil productions and mineral incrustations. It has been worked as a lead mine for ages, so far back it is said as the time when the Romans were occupiers of the soil; and it is recorded that, during the reigns of the earlier Henrys and the Edwards, convicts were sent and condemned to labour in it. In some parts of the mine they show the manner in which, in those distant ages, the ore was obtained when the use of gunpowder was unknown.

Having obtained the services of a guide we enter by a small doorway in the side of the rock, and, receiving each a lighted candle, set forward to explore the inner recesses. A few paces take us beyond the last gleam of day, and the light, as it gradually fades away, is succeeded by a deepening and almost impenetrable gloom. Having proceeded for some distance along a narrow passage, that has been blasted out of the rock, the pathway ascends and discloses a number of natural archways and lofty openings, which, diverging by degrees, lead to several clefts and cavities that radiate and extend into the innermost parts of the mountain. The dimensions of some of these openings are of considerable magnitude, and their appearance is at once grand and imposing. To the geologist and the lover of science they afford an unfailing source of interest from the several examples and combinations of lead, zinc, and other metallic ores, iron and copper pyrites and calamite, as well as the infinite variety of brilliant crystallisations of the carbonate and fluate of lime which they exhibit.

Then we continue along undulating passages—now on gravel and crushed spar, and now on the bare rock, between natural barriers that slope gently upwards until they meet and form a roof overhead. In some places steps have been cut out of the limestone for the convenience of explorers, and in others we meet with pools of water so limpid that, in the treacherous and uncertain light, we are in danger of setting our feet in them in mistake for the solid floor. Now and then our attention is called to the vast cracks and rents in the roof, caused by the shrinking of the strata ; and the guide clambers up on to the great bulging masses of rock and shows us the effect of the reflected light upon their grotesque and uncouth forms ; and as we stand in the gloom and note the interesting and brilliant variety of spars that gleam and sparkle on their sides and on every projection in the roof, strange feelings come over us, and the imagination becomes excited with admiration and surprise as we gaze upon the immense cavities and singular formations which nature here reveals.

Following the guide along the labyrinth of passages that lead through these recesses, we come to an opening of seemingly immeasurable extent, where all above is space and darkness, creating an idea of almost unlimited vastness and profundity. Whilst we are vainly endeavouring to penetrate the deep gloom the attendant applies a light to a chemical

RUTLAND CAVERN, MATLOCK.

preparation he carries with him, and in an instant, as if by a stroke of a magician's wand, the whole place is illuminated, a sickly lurid glare resting upon every projecting and impending rock, penetrating the deepest recesses, and lighting up the shadowy forms that lie scattered around, rendering the vastness a thousand-fold greater and raising a feeling of the profoundest awe and wonder. The display is but of brief duration, for before we have time to take an adequate survey the sickly flame expires and we are again left in all but perfect darkness. This chamber and the stone on which the light is placed have received the fanciful names of the Roman Gallery and the Druid's Altar, a style of nomenclature too much in vogue at Matlock, and which, instead of adding to the interest, only tends to throw an air of ridicule over what is really beautiful and attractive in itself.

Having penetrated to the furthest recesses of the mine shown to visitors, we return by devious windings and vaulted passages that lead to numerous openings and cavities, and as we move slowly through the gloom each projecting and over-hanging point of rock displays itself in a succession of flitting gleams and shadows that render the scene singularly striking and impressive.

As we approach the entrance the bright rays of the midday sun come streaming through the doorway, lighting up the sides of the rocks and filling the mouth of the cavern with a radiance that seems more brilliant by contrast with the darkness and gloom from which we have just emerged.

Leaving the Cavern Terrace, we descend by a tortuous path embowered by woods, where the lavish foliage of the beech and chestnut trees is backed by the tall stiff pines, and where the jagged and broken rocks, which here and there thrust their gray heads through the turf, are nearly hidden again by the clustering ivy and the trailing plants and flowers which, sheltered from the scorching heat, here thrive in luxuriant profusion. As we saunter through the pleasant shade the sunshine breaks through the verdant canopy in fitful gleams, streaking the pathway with bright golden touches, the leaves rustle overhead, and the birds chirrup merrily as they flit to and fro among the waving branches; and we can hear the hum of insects busy among the tall grass and the waving ferns, the rushing of the river in the valley below, and the low still murmuring of sunny music—sounds of which the ear never tires.

Quitting the romantic Heights by the lower lodge we passed along the lower slope of the hill and thence on to the Parade, where we spent an agreeable half-hour in examining the vases, statuettes, and other objects of art manufactured and exhibited in Mr. Walker's Museum.

In the afternoon we had a pleasant stroll to the Dungeon Tors, or Romantic Rocks, as they are more generally called, and the Cumberland Cavern—two favourite places of resort, situate within a short distance of each other on the side of Masson.

On reaching the foot of the Old Bath Terrace we placed ourselves under the care of one of the numerous guides who are always to be met with in that locality, on the look-out for visitors.

Starting from the *Old Bath* a few yards bring us to a little cottage in front of which are exposed for sale a variety of spar ornaments, fossils, guide-books, and cheap engravings of Derbyshire scenery. Here a toll of sixpence is demanded for the privilege of seeing the Tors—if a visit to the cavern is included, a shilling is the stipulated charge. Having paid the old lady her fee we are conducted along a well-gravelled path that winds around rocky acclivities partly screened by trees and mantled with green ivy and flowering plants, the varied tints agreeably contrasting with the cold gray colouring of the limestone cliff. Like the Heights of Abraham, of which the slope may be said to be a continuation, the ground everywhere exhibits a profusion of shrubs, mosses, and wild flowers; great crags overhang the way, and delicate lichens peep out from every niche and crevice. Anon the vegetation thickens, the brambles and underwood become more dense, and the lovely blue sky tempers its soft light as it peeps through the network of branches which meet overhead, crossing and recrossing each other until they impart a green tinge to everything around.

A great portion of the walk is carried over a stratum of toadstone forty feet in thickness, part of a bed which extends for a considerable distance, attesting the presence of that volcanic agency whose paroxysmal action formed the continents and lifted the hills and mountains to their present elevation.

Proceeding southwards a few minutes' walking brings us to the Tors, a singular group of isolated rocks—huge monolithic blocks—that have been riven from the parent mass by that mighty catastrophe which shook the earth to its foundation. The smaller fragments are scattered about in the most picturesque disorder, but the vast obelisk-shaped stones or "tors" stand boldly out and still maintain their upright position. Some of them attain a height of forty feet and exhibit a sharp and clearly-defined outline, with angles so exactly corresponding with those on the parent cliff that, were it possible to remove them, they might again be fitted to the mass from which they have been torn.

The whole assemblage is embosomed in wood—oak, ash, elm, and sycamore, with hazels and brambles in thick profusion ; the "tall patrician trees blending with the plebeian underwood," and their leafy branches meeting in a rich canopy overhead, whose deep shadow creates a sombre and mysterious gloom in perfect harmony with the loveliness of the scene. The huge beetling rampart of rock which bounds one side of the path is covered with lichens and mosses, whilst every inch of ground, every fragment, and every stone is hidden by rank weeds and grass, and trailing plants, among which the hartstongue sways its long and drooping clusters of graceful fronds, and the white convolvulus, the gaudy foxglove, the purple periwinkle, and the golden-hued furze exhibit their varied blossoms in a world of floral beauty. Clusters of delicate bluebells gem the path and tinge the mossy banks with their azure hue, the white cestus and the woody nightshade are here ; the delicate lily of the valley peeps forth from the overlapping verdure, swaying its drooping blossoms to and fro as it perfumes the air with its fragrant incense, and the tall Canterbury-bell lifts up its elegant chalice to catch the moisture that trickles down the indented fissures of the crags. The giant tors are fringed with the lighter foliage of the woodbine and briar, the wild gooseberry and bramble, and hung and festooned with the graceful tendrils of the ivy, which droop in long streamers or creep over the surface of the rock, mingling their glossy leaves with the mosses and lichens and wild strawberries that grow on every ledge and jutting fragment. A cold sepulchral gloom pervades the place, rendered more imposing by the deep and solemn stillness that prevails, a stillness broken only occasionally by the drops of moisture that trickle in intervals from the rocky ledges, plashing from leaf to leaf, then falling to the earth with a heavy leaden sound, that startles you by its sullen reverberations.

Though occupying an area comparatively small, there is no place, we conceive, even at Matlock, where nature presents so many attractions, a more picturesque or charming retreat than this secluded spot. Shut in by rock and wood, you seem completely isolated from the outer world, and the mind becomes impressed with these scenes of savage and romantic beauty, and estranged as it were from earthly objects. It is just the place for a day dream : a chill perpetual shade, and a stillness almost painful in its intensity hangs over all—everything, in fact, bespeaks solitude and seclusion, with nothing to break or mar the quietude of repose.

Contiguous to the Romantic Rocks is the Fluor Cavern, an old lead-mine, formerly shown to visitors, but now abandoned. It is only of limited extent, though interesting, the sides of the passages in many places being formed of the cubic fluor spar.

Still keeping the elevated ground, a path that leads through the thickly-planted scrub conducts us to the Cumberland Cavern, situated on the upper slope of Masson. This cavern has been long, and is still occasionally, worked as a lead-mine.

To those who take an interest in such exhibitions, the Cumberland Cavern will convey a very good idea of underground scenery ; it contains more natural excavations, and, with the exception of the Rutland, its ramifications extend over a larger area than those of any of the other caverns at Matlock. In a geological point of view it is also interesting, exhibiting so many interruptions and dislocations of the strata, with a numerous variety of spar and stalactitic incrustations.

There is nothing about the entrance at all indicative of the wonders displayed within—a small opening in the face of the rock being the only evidence of its existence. The guide unlocked the door, and we walked in a few yards whilst he got his lights in readiness. The first part of the journey is made along a gallery or level, which has been blasted out of the rock by the miners in their search for ore ; whilst passing through this the attention is directed to the first and second clay measures which separate the limestone beds. In this level a dubious twilight prevails, which gradually deepens into gloom as we advance ; nearer the further end a flight of rugged and uneven steps conducts to the lower recesses of the mine, and as we descend these, a long narrow tunnel-like passage is pointed out that diverges in the direction of the river, and which is believed to have been an old working. Still descending we wind between rugged walls of gray rock, dotted over with stalactitic formations, and dripping with moisture, which seems to ooze through the sides, whilst from the roof the water drops in constant plashes, forming small saucer-like depressions in the floor. On reaching the lowest step the roof slopes down, and we have to proceed for some distance in a stooping posture to avoid being caught against the sharp and jagged projections overhead. By-and-by we come to a huge unbroken block of limestone, bearing the name of the Harpsichord, from its supposed resemblance to that instrument, and which appears to have fallen from the superincumbent mass. Passing this the path becomes more toilsome and difficult, leading over a surface broken and uneven, and strewn with stones and fragments of rock, winding round chasms and long narrow passages that look more gloomy from the absence of ornament, then through rude cavernous openings hung with stalactites, and abounding with delicate incrustations of calcareous spar. In some places vast rents reveal themselves in the roof, caused by the cooling of the great limestone bubble in a primeval age; the rocks yawn, and multitudes of detached blocks lie scattered about in horrible confusion; and the further we penetrate the wilder becomes the scene.

We had some difficulty in keeping pace with the guide, who tripped lightly on before us, striding over the rocky fragments with the utmost confidence, as if darkness and gloom were familiar to him.

We now appear to be within the very heart of the mountain, and from this point the path begins to ascend, short slopes alternating with rude steps that have been formed out of the rock, and as we wend our way through the mighty fissures and undulating passages we meet with several varieties of spar and stalactite, among the most remarkable of which is that beautiful substance denominated snow-fossil; fluate of lime also occurs in abundance, generally crystallised in cubes, and possessing great beauty and diversity of colour. Further on we come to a vast natural vestibule or gallery, running in a north-westerly direction, 300 feet in length, the roof extending the entire distance in one flat horizontal surface. At the further extremity of this gallery is the Great or Roman Hall, an immense opening which has remained

through countless ages untouched by the hand of man ; here
the scene that presents itself is of the wildest character,
immense masses of rock meet the eye, some standing singly
and others grouped together or piled upon each other in the
most picturesque and fanciful shapes, as if they had fallen
from the roof by some violent convulsion of the earth, their
huge shadowy forms looming through the deep gloom like
spectral giants. From this point we have a good retrospective view of the gallery through which we have just passed—
the guide having placed a few lighted candles at intervals
upon the sides, the entire length is revealed, and we are
enabled fully to comprehend the magnitude and regularity
of form of this great work of nature. In this cavern a
stratum of clay intervenes between the upper lime and the
dunstone or magnesian beds.

From the Roman Hall we descend by a flight of steps,
when the scene becomes still more chaotic ; the strata is
riven and dislocated and tossed up into every form of superposition ; immense fragments which have fallen from above
bestrew the ground, and huge beetling crags jut out overhead, apparently so insecure as to threaten every moment to
topple down and crush you beneath the weight of their
misshapen forms. In one place we noticed an immense
block of solid limestone, said to be forty tons in weight,
which has become detached, and is so exactly poised that it
seems to rest only on two points of the adjoining rock.

After a while the eye becomes more familiarised with the
gloom, and objects that at first appeared only in shadowy
indistinctness begin to assume more clearly defined forms.
Plodding on through the mazy intricacies, now scrambling
and picking our way over the slippery and unsteady fragments, and now stopping to examine the curious spars and
veins of ore, we come to a still lower cavity dignified by
the name of the Queen's Palace. This, like the others, contains an assemblage of rocky fragments tumbled confusedly
together by the hand of nature. Here the roof suddenly
descends, seeming to bar up all further advance, and for
some distance we have to creep in a stooping posture through
narrow openings until we come to another subterranean
chamber, the top of which, like the ceiling of a house, is

supported by perpendicular walls of rock, and presents a surface flat and perfectly level, abounding with marine shells, entrochi, coralloids, and other organic remains. This would appear to have been a place of special interest to a class of visitors, who have gratified their mischievous propensities by scratching their names and initials upon almost every accessible spot, conveying to posterity the interesting information that Brown, Jones, and Robinson have, on the dates recorded, explored these subterranean recesses.

Passing beneath a natural archway, regularly formed and incrusted with spar and stalactitic formations, we come to another cavern distinguished by the name of the Sailor's Hall. The roof of this apartment is less elevated than some of the others, and is covered with letters and hieroglyphics, visitors who have not been sufficiently industrious to carve their names and initials having satisfied themselves with tracing them in smoke on the top by the aid of their candles. Crossing this chamber we ascend by a narrow passage that leads through two recesses, from the further one of which branches off a tunnel-like opening that extends for a considerable distance, and is terminated by a deep pool of water.

Having completed the exploration of the natural caverns we proceed along the old workings of the mine until we reach the shaft employed in drawing up the lead ore to the surface. Here again the water trickles down and the walls are slimy with the constant drip. While we linger to admire the delicate stalactitic incrustations that are continually accumulating on the walls, the guide holds up his candle to show us the effect of the reflected light upon their polished surfaces, and as we stand in the gloom the picturesque groups gleam and sparkle with the most brilliant effect.

Near to this shaft the attention is directed to two veins of lead ore which further on become united. Associated with the ore is found the sulphate of barytes, denominated by the miners "cawke"—a substance which, under the name of Dutch lead, is used in the adulteration of paint.

We are now more than four hundred yards from the entrance, and three hundred feet below the surface of the mountain. From this part we descend and proceed by a long narrow passage formed between continually dripping quartz walls, hung with stalactites that have been formed by the constant dripping of the water through the fissures of the limestone overhead ; some are but mere nipples an inch or two in length, others depend in long spiral icicles from the roof, or hang in festoons from the ledges of the rock ; in some places the incrustation spreads over the entire surface, and as the crystallisations accumulate they assume various uncouth shapes and forms, over which the moisture trickles in tiny streams as it falls to the ground with ceaseless patter, and as the dim candlelight flickers upon the great white masses they glitter and sparkle with a brilliant gem-like lustre. And so on we go, ascending and descending through natural openings and passages that have been widened and levelled, now on the smooth gravel, now on the naked limestone, now scrambling over great stony fragments, and now stooping as the rocks seem to close in upon us, until we again reach the point from which we started.

Not the least attractive feature in connection with the Cumberland Cavern is the magnificent prospect which bursts upon the view on regaining the entrance ; from this point the eye takes in nearly the whole of the picturesque scenery along the dale with the hills adjacent—the High Tor, Masson, the winding river, and the vast limestone crags opposite, backed by the lofty hill of Riber, with Scarthin Rock, Crich Cliff, and Stonnis in the further distance. The view embraces every feature of landscape scenery—hill and dale, wood and village, rock and river, with the minor accessories of culti-vated fields, pleasant mansions, and smiling cottages.

When we came forth into the open air, after a sojourn of more than an hour in the bowels of the mountain, the sun, which had long passed the meridian, shed a rich but softened radiance over the scene, illuminating the rocks and hills, lighting up the vales, and dancing and playing upon the rippling waters with a marvellously beautiful effect.

There is yet another of those natural openings on the side of Masson—the Devonshire Cavern—smaller than those we have already described, but possessing much to engage the attention of those who are interested in these curious formations. The interior presents the appearance of a wide and expanding opening fashioned in the inner recesses of the earth, and still exhibiting the same rough and chaotic state that nature left it in. Vast piles of rock of every conceivable shape and size lie strewn about, some apparently so slightly connected that you wonder how they have so long retained their position, and as the feeble light of your candle falls upon their huge shadowy forms the imagination becomes excited, and you liken them to things the most unearthly. You hear the trickling and see the flickering of the water as it oozes through the limestone, falling with sullen and monotonous patter as it has fallen for unnumbered centuries. The roof of the cavern has the appearance of an immense layer of solid rock, extending for a distance of wellnigh 200 feet, and supported on either side by perpendicular walls of limestone; the surface is entirely free from inequalities, and slopes rapidly—the angle of dip being about 45°—and as you gaze upon it you realise something of the mighty force by which only these mountain masses could have been upheaved.

Near the south end of Masson the road separates—one path leading through the upper wood to the picturesque village of Bonsall, the other continuing for some distance along the side of the hill, and then descending to the bottom of the dale.

Following the lower way we came upon the highroad at a point close to the tollgate, immediately opposite the weir, from which a few minutes' walking brought us to our quarters. Exercise and mountain air are excellent sharpeners of the appetite, and we sat down to our evening repast with all the relish and enjoyment of Sancho Panza at Camacho's wedding.

# CHAPTER XVII.

IN perfect contrast to that of the preceding day, the morning
broke with a gloomy and threatening aspect, the sky was
lowering and the mists hung heavy around the mountain tops,
and soon the clouds, which had been gathering in murky
masses overhead, began to descend in thick and driving
showers of drizzling rain. A dense vapour filled the dale, and
the chilly atmosphere spoke more of dreary November than
bright July. Patter, patter, patter, unceasingly, until it
became a perfect downpour. The bushes were dripping with
moisture, and the trees seemed to bend beneath the weight
of water. Every hollow was filled by a pool, and every path
and wheel-track by a stream, in which the children loitered to
slop and splash as they passed along on their way to school.
The cattle stood in groups, vainly endeavouring to find shelter
under the trees, and the sheep upon the mountain slopes
looked utterly bedraggled and wretched. Everything looked
damp and cheerless, and the entire landscape presented a
drenched and half-drowned appearance ; pedestrians were few,
and visitors seemed to have disappeared altogether. The
postman, as he hurried by, gathered his cape more closely
round him, and looked the picture of misery and despair;
Chanticleer, who yesterday strutted about with dignified mien,
crowing defiance to his brethren, now strode along with
drooping crest and tail draggled and trailing in the mud; and
Jack—poor shaggy-coated Jack—who so lately capered about
and wagged his tail with glee, seemed to share in the general
depression, and crept into the parlour all wet and shivering,
where he stowed himself beneath the sofa, and, burying his

nose between his paws, endeavoured to dream the gloomy hours away.

The time passed wearily as we sat watching the heavy rain-clouds and counting the number of rain-drops that hung from the window frames, and chased each other in little streams down the glass. Whilst gazing upon the moist and gloomy scene, wondering if there was any chance of the clouds breaking, our host, who, like us, had been watching the weather, looked in to tell us it was about to clear up, for Masson had thrown off his night-cap, and the glass had gone up a tenth. Happily, he was correct in his prediction, for about ten o'clock the rain ceased, a gentle breeze sprang up, and soon the thick black clouds began to separate and pass off in heavy masses over the mountain tops, their place being taken by a misty haze that hung like a halo over the landscape. Suddenly the sun broke through, and the face of nature again began to wear a cheerful aspect, smiling through her tears like " hope upon a mourner's cheek." The effect of this sudden burst of sunshine was almost magical: rocks, hills, and valleys, which before were wrapped in sombre gloom, were now brilliantly illuminated, and the woods and meadows, refreshed by the heavy showers, appeared in all their varied hues, exhibiting a hundred tints of light and glory.

With a hearty shake of the hand we bade good-bye to our host, and set forward again on our journey. The atmosphere was chill, and the roads were heavy in mire, but we were cheered by the rays of the sun which now shone forth in great beauty, and so kept briskly on until we passed through Scarthin Nick, when, turning suddenly to the right, we entered Cromford, a little market town, which owes its prosperity to the Arkwrights, whose extensive cotton mills are close by.

Previous to the erection of the first spinning factory by Sir Richard Arkwright in 1771, Cromford was only an inconsiderable village, though boasting of some antiquity. At the time of the Domesday survey, the manor, then called Crunforde, was held by the king, subsequently it became the property of the Meynells, from whom it passed to the Leches and other families. In 1776 it was conveyed by purchase to the Nightingales of Lea Hurst, and thirteen years afterwards it was sold to Sir Richard Arkwright, whose descendant, Peter Arkwright, Esq., of Willersley, is the present lord of the manor. Cotton-spinning is the chief source of employment ; but mining is also carried on to a considerable extent, the hills round being rich in mineral deposits, for which the Cromford Canal and the High Peak Railway afford a ready means of transit to the different parts of the country ; there is also a station here on the Midland Railway. The town is pleasantly situated in the midst of a valley surrounded by hills and limestone rocks, and well supplied with water—two streams passing through it—Bonsall Brook, which descends through the Via Gellia, and Cromford Moor Sough, as it is called, which first reveals itself in a large reservoir or dam opposite the *Greyhound Inn*, in the Market Place.

On passing through the town we leave the Wirksworth Road, near the upper end, and, taking a westerly course, proceed along a path that leads past the paint works, where Dutch lead or barytes, mineral black, yellow, and a variety of other substances that are found in abundance in the neighbouring mines, are worked into pigments. Near the tollgate we turn to the left, and enter Bonsall Hollow—a deep and narrow dell, whose rocky sides are clothed with verdure, and nearly hidden with elm and ash trees and a thick underwood, among which a few jutting crags are occasionally seen. A small but busy stream runs along the side of the road, receiving as it proceeds many tributary rills and springs that issue from the mountain sides ; frequently it spreads itself out into reservoirs or sheets of water, which have been formed for the preservation of fish, then breaking over the stony barriers it falls in beautiful cascades, foaming and splashing and wreathing itself in frequent windings as it continues on its course. About half-way through the hollow a lofty rock juts boldly out into the dale, its naked front covered with loose stones and "screes," which are continually falling down the side on to the path that sweeps round its base. A little farther on a road branches off on the right to Bonsall—as quaintly picturesque and interesting a village as any in Derbyshire, with an ancient church that stands upon a rock keeping maternal watch over the place, and a lofty market cross that springs from a basement formed by an ascent of a dozen steps or more. Taking the opposite turn we pass a small public-house, called the *Pig of Lead*, and enter Via Gellia, a romantic and picturesque dale, which has been so named in compliment to the late Mr. Philip Gell, of Hopton, at whose expense the road that leads through was formed. Near the entrance is an establishment for the manufacturing of red lead, and also the cupola furnace of Mr. Alsop, where the ore is smelted and converted into pigs of lead.

The Via Gellia is a pretty secluded valley, about half-a-mile in length, formed by an opening in the rocks, which rise to a considerable altitude on each side; their huge forms, broken into a variety of shapes, now and then jutting out in rugged crags, and frequently presenting a regular serrated crest of rock fringed with shrubs and grass. The character of the scenery is softened and rendered more beautiful by the variety of foliage with which the steep acclivities are clothed. Here we have a bold cliff covered with waving birch and mountain ash; there a patch of greensward plentifully besprinkled with dwarf oaks and hazels; further on are alders, chestnuts, and willows, that wave their branches above the lighter foliage of the woodbine, the wild briar, and the bramble. For the most part the lower slopes are overgrown with shrubs and brushwood, whilst above the ample foliage of the larger trees is backed by the tall spines of the firs, whose dark-green tints contrast with the gray colouring of the rocks, which here and there shoot up in fantastic pinnacles. "Screes" and broken fragments of limestone intermingle their varied forms, and give an air of grandeur that is heightened in effect by the sombre shadows of the clouds which at times hang about the loftiest peaks and overspread the precipitous sides of the hills. About the entrance to the dale the vegetation has a dwarfed and blighted appearance, caused by the vapours from the neighbouring lead works, but further on it attains to a more vigorous and luxuriant growth, and a little babbling brook that meanders along the side of the road adds its charms to the scene, imparting to it a sprightliness and vivacity that cannot fail to delight the eye. The course of this stream is constantly interrupted by the green holmes and rushy islets that grow up out of its lucid waters; occasionally it is impeded in its progress by fragments of rock, over which it rushes, making innumerable falls, its surface as it hurries on broken into a thousand dimples, and bedecked with long trains of glistening foam which gather in little fairy-like rings round the mossy eyots, and the tufts of grass met with on the way ; all along its margin is fringed with reeds and flowers, and an infinite variety of aquatic plants, that wave their slender stems among the circling eddies, and play and sport with every ripple as it flutters by, while the trees which overhang the brink cross and recross each other in an intricate network, and now and then dip their drooping branches in the glistening stream.

As we passed along the sky became clear, and the sun shone forth with great brilliancy, dispelling the cloud patches that hung like a misty veil about the tops of the highest rocks ; and the rays, as they streamed through the clefts and openings, lit up the woods, and played among the branches of the trees, revealing many a touch of beauty, while the great white clouds that rolled overhead, driven by the brisk wind, flecked the hillsides with their dark moving shadows. The little stream danced merrily past, singing as it went, the sunshine glistening on its placid waters, and gleaming on the pebbles beneath. As we advanced the seclusion deepened, the leaves rustled overhead, and the birds twittered in the branches with an expression richer and fuller as it seemed than in more frequented places; and as we sauntered leisurely along we now and then paused to listen to the soft farewell notes of the cuckoo, and the thrilling and impassioned songs of the blackbird and the thrush mingling with the sweet melodies of the numerous feathered warblers hidden in the leafy solitudes above.

About half-way up the valley we passed a little cottage, the first habitation we had met with ; its clean whitewashed front was nearly obscured by laburnums and climbing roses, and the diminutive but ornamental plot of garden in front, gorgeous with the gay colourings of the many-tinted flowers, looked like an oasis in the midst of a wilderness of rock and wood, and conveyed to the mind a poetical idea of peace and quietude undescribable.  A little further on is a charming cascade that issues from Dunsley Spring ; breaking the crest of wood it rushes down the precipitous cliff in a narrow line of foam, leaping and dashing from crag to crag, then plunging and swirling in a hollow below, from which it escapes by a channel beneath the footpath into the neighbouring stream ; the dancing spray gives a prodigious vigour to the green ferns and the wild vegetation that flourishes along its side, and you look with pleasure upon the luxuriant patches of moss and weeds that grow in every dripping nook and cranny. The water, like many of the springs in the neighbourhood, is strongly impregnated with lime, and the constant dripping has in some places completely incrusted the moss and leaves with a calcareous deposit, and thus formed a natural bed of tufa. A few paces beyond another waterfall is formed by two rills, which unite themselves in a single stream after a descent of about 150 feet down the almost perpendicular front of the rock. Near the foot of this cataract a Gothic cottage has been erected, a little rustic-looking structure built of curiously-channeled and weather-beaten fragments of limestone, so arranged as to give it a studiously romantic and fanciful appearance that hardly accords with the natural beauty of the surrounding scene.

Near the western termination of the valley the hills close in, their sides become more steep and rugged, here and there "screes" and loose stones take the place of wood and sward, and gradually the prospect assumes a wilder and more dreary character. In front a huge eminence lifts its unwieldy form to a vast altitude, threatening opposition to all further progress, its steep front clothed with scant herbage, and sprinkled with a few dwarfed and blighted-looking trees and bushes. Near the foot the road curves gently towards the right, when the valley again expands, hills and dales appear in the distance, seeming to intersect each other, the foliage becomes thicker, and the country generally more picturesque and beautiful. From this point the road gently ascends, and a walk of half-a-mile brings us to the tollgate, where the paths separate, one leading to Hopton and Carsington, and the other by Grange Mill to Winster and Bakewell.

Following the latter we proceed along Griff Dale, a narrow mountain glen threaded by a winding stream, whose banks, diverging back from each other, present a pleasing diversity

T

of scene—rock and wood, precipice and slope, succeeding in agreeable alternation.

For some distance the road ascends, and as we advance we see many pretty effects of rushing water, as the noisy brook struggles along its freakish channel—here circling in playful eddies round great hummocks and rushy eyots, there fretting and chafing as it breaks over the rocky fragments and moss-grown boulders, and anon subsiding into a clear full current wherein are deep basins, gullies, and shallow pools ; in some places its course is dammed up by drift-wood that has been brought down by its swollen floods, and over these it dashes in foaming cataracts, then boils and eddies along with noisy tumult. For a distance of a mile the sides are adorned with luxuriant foliage—dwarf oak and ash, with thorns, wild gooseberries, and a thick undergrowth, covering the slopes down to the very brink of the stream. Further on the views are more wild and romantic, and present a greater variety of picturesque combinations. The rocks here become more boldly featured, often presenting a naked and precipitous front, crested with jutting crags and weather-beaten cliffs ; in some places covered with ivy, and chequered with moss and trailing plants, whilst high up the dark foliage of the yew and the light verdure of the ash is occasionally seen shooting out from the rocky clefts. A shady path branches off on the left, and ascends by an opening in the hills to Griff Wood ; then we come to a little bridge spanning the stream, on the opposite side of which a steep and rutty road leads up to the hamlet of Ible. Now the character of the scenery changes, the hills fall back, and in place of crags and rocky steeps we have a succession of undulating eminences clothed with greensward, but cheerless and uninviting in their aspect from the absence of wood ; a solitary bush or tree only now and then appearing by the wayside, too few and far between to adorn the landscape, and serving only to remind us of their general absence. Valley Mill is soon passed, and in a few minutes more we reach Grange Mill, where we quit the Winster road and pass through the tollbar on the left.

For a distance of about a mile and a half beyond the country, though not absolutely barren, is as dreary and uninteresting as can well be imagined ; poor ill-cultivated meadows, not long since reclaimed from the moorland wastes, stretch away on each side of the road, their cold and cheerless slopes chequered with stone walls, and dotted here and there with patches of plantation. Approaching the edge of Brassington Moor, we meet with some rock scenery, but only on a diminutive scale ; then we pass a solitary farmhouse, after which the road sweeps to the right, and the same cheerless landscape continues until Long Cliff Wharf is reached, where the Cromford and High Peak Railway (an undertaking of little public utility) crosses the way.

On passing beneath the railway arch the character of the scenery changes, and the sudden contrast has an almost magical effect. We seem now to have left the region of bleak moors and stone fences behind, and in front, as far as the eye can reach, spreads out a magnificent prospect, broken and undulating, and presenting an almost endless diversity of form and feature—rocks, mountains, and valleys, with woods, meadows, and pasture lands contributing to form a picture of no ordinary beauty. Among the hills are glens and ravines, in which rugged rocks and verdant acclivities intermingle their varied forms and colourings, and give a touch of savage grandeur to the scene, which is heightened in effect by the dark shadows of the floating clouds. Here and there a limestone bluff shoots up crowned with larch and fir, and fringed with ash trees and underwood, and now and then a savage-looking crag, all bleached and weather-beaten, juts out from the soft greensward, its wild and uncouth form presenting a striking contrast to the fertile loveliness and beauty spread around. In middle distance is seen a succession of gentle eminences, everywhere exhibiting signs of fertility and cultivation, and beyond the view is bounded by the blue range of hills that border the valley of the Dove and extend in an irregular line along the horizon until their pale summits become lost in the infinity of space.

For some little distance the road is carried under the rocky and turretted acclivities of Long Cliff, when it curves towards the right and descends rapidly into the bottom of the valley. On the opposite side of the narrow dingle is Rhe Tor, a pretty knoll clothed with wood, from the edge of which juts out a singular isolated crag completely mantled with ivy, looking like the ruined tower of some ancient village church. Near to this, on the side of Ballidon Moor, is a small farmstead delightfully situated on the rising slope, sheltered by the ample foliage behind, and surrounded by a natural amphitheatre of rocky pinnacles and crags.

As we descend the views become confined; crags and cliffs still break out on the hillsides, the summits of which are split and rent in a variety of fantastic shapes, and present a singular and curious effect. Hoe Cliff and Brassington Rocks, standing boldly out on the left, start through the thick herbage which mantles their sides in lofty-pointed crags; and on the opposite side is a rocky ridge, called White Edge.

At the bottom of the valley, where a road branches off to Brassington village, is Hipley tollbar. The gatekeeper, who was seated on a bench near the door reading a newspaper, looked up as we approached, and wishing to verify our course, we inquired, after apologising for interrupting him, the way from Bradbourn to Tissington, and the road thence to Ashbourn—he rose from his seat and proffered all the information he possessed, regretting that he could not leave the "gate," or he would have accompanied us a little way further to the turn of the road, whence he could have pointed out the path over the hills. When we started forward again he came running after and called to us, "Will you have a drink o' beer, it's rather close (sultry), and it 'll help you on your way." Hot weather and a dusty road justified the acceptance of the proffered hospitality, and when we again resumed our walk we thought of the

> "Honest offered courtesy,
> Which oft is sooner found in lowly sheds,
> With smoky rafters, than in tap'stry halls
> And courts of princes, where it first was named,
> And yet is most pretended."

A few paces beyond the tollgate Hipley Rock appears in front, lifting its huge form to a great elevation—its sides covered with thick plantations of larch and fir; for some little distance further the road is peculiarly romantic and beautiful, being hemmed in on each side by precipitous cliffs indented with numerous cracks and fissures, whose effect is heightened by the trees and trailing plants that grow out of the gaping cliffs, screening and softening the gaunt aspect of their cold gray naked fronts.

Onwards the country becomes more rural and cultivated, and though lacking in those bolder features which gave an interest to the region through which we had just passed, it yet possesses many attractions to delight the eye, and is replete with varied and picturesque scenery. Tall hedges embower the road sides, their banks full of wild beauty, and rife with the buds and flowers of the delightful summer time; fine lofty trees shadow the way, rugged pollards and spreading sycamores, with now and then a silvery birch that waves its maze of pendant branches in the passing breeze, their roots hidden among grass and weeds and ferns, among which the wild geranium and the modest pansy are here and there seen peeping from between the prickly branches of the rambling bramble; then we have a blending of wild strawberries and maidenhair, with a wealth of floral beauty, the varied tints of which no pen could possibly describe. Broad rolling meads spread out right and left, through which the

> " Cold springs run
> To warm their chilliest bubbles in the grass,"

and as we passed along the sun threw his cheerful glances through the screen of leaves; all nature seemed alive and stirring, and everywhere the haymakers were at work, making the welkin ring again with their merry songs and cheerful laughter; the heavens were vocal with the melodies of the sweet swinging birds, and the atmosphere was loaded with the rich perfume of the early harvest time. The distant slopes were seen rising above the nearer foliage, and now and then the whitened walls of some quiet homestead gleamed brightly in the mid-day sun. Tissington pastures stretched away in wide sweeps upon the right, and on the left the broad square battlemented tower of Bradbourn Church could be seen peeping above a grove of trees on the top of a verdant knoll, reminding one of Goldsmith's " Sweet Auburn," with its village church "that tops the neighbouring hill."

" Seemingly a healthy country this," we remarked to an

aged labourer who was repairing a gate-post, and whom we
complimented upon his ruddy looks. "Yea, mestur," he
replied, "we be'en pretty contented hereabouts, and niver
nowt ails us, bout it be a bit o' rheumatiz like in our owd
days." "But an indifferent prospect, then," we added, "for
a doctor to settle amongst you." "No," he rejoined, "he'd
find but a poorish sort o' pasture here, for we get'n our
physic from th' shippon, and our pills we fetch 'n mostly
from th' baker's shop." Happy country! happy people! Of
you it may be said with some degree of truth, that "your
wealth consists not in the abundance of your riches but in
the fewness of your wants."

Near the further extremity of the vale the road inclines
towards the south, and the Schoo, a rivulet that descends
from the hills, ripples alongside in pleasant companionship,
babbling and fretting as it pursues its mazy course, half-hidden
and half-revealed, among the hanging bushes.

About a couple of hundred yards beyond the tollbar is
Bradbourn Mill, as pretty a rustic "bit" as ever delighted
the eye of an artist—the mill with its overshot wheel, the
quaint old house adjoining with its Elizabethan gables and
clustering chimneys, backed by a plantation of larch and
spruce firs, the habitation of a colony of loquacious rooks,
and the sparkling stream, spanned by a primitive-looking
bridge, combine to form a picture worthy of the best efforts
of a Creswick or a Birket Foster.

Opposite the mill we leave the Ashbourn Road, passing
through a gate on the right, and over a little foot-bridge,
when we have to ascend by a field path that leads by the side
of a steep bank, covered from base to summit with rich greensward. The walk is toilsome, but never mind, there is a
pleasant breeze, the sun shines, and the eye is enabled to
range uninterruptedly over a landscape green and umbrageous,
and pleasing from its varied and undulating aspect.

As we mount higher the prospect widens, and we linger to
gaze upon the lovely scene. In front spreads out a beautiful
and fertile valley, adorned with meadows, fields, and pastures,
in which cattle are grazing, and the haymakers are busy at
work. The pretty village of Bradbourn, clustering round its
venerable church, is seen crowning an eminence on the left,

Hipley Rock, White Edge, and Brassington Rocks appear in mid-distance, and beyond them a succession of hills rise one above another, until their rounded summits mingle with the mountainous heights in the vicinity of Matlock. On the right we can trace the sparkling Schoo as it wanders with gleaming curves through the secluded and romantic dale, ever in close company with the white and winding road. Eastwards the horizon is bounded by a vast expanse of heathy moors and trackless wastes that stretch away to the farthest point of distance. Some places are half concealed by the straying mists, whilst others are resplendent with the brilliance of the gleaming sunshine, and, in all, the charm is heightened by the undulating and ever-varying character of the surface.

Continuing along the top of the hill, the country at every step assumes a more cultivated character, the roads are good, the hedges are well trimmed, and the fields and plantations indicate the vicinity of a stately mansion. Near to a farmhouse, called the Bent, we pass through a gate, and thence along a shady lane, bordered with tall umbrageous trees, whose spreading branches meet overhead, excluding the sun's rays, and creating a perpetual gloom. Through the openings we get a glimpse of Wibben Hill, a little conical knoll that rises on the right, with a few fir trees planted within a walled enclosure on the top, then the road gently descends. Darfield Barn, another farmhouse, is passed, and in few minutes more we enter the pretty little village of Tissington.

Tissington is one of the most romantic villages in Derbyshire. It is nearly hidden by thick woods and plantations that environ it on almost every side, and the air of comfort and respectability which prevails cannot fail to impress the mind of the visitor with favourable anticipations. The houses, though few in number, have a neat and cleanly appearance, every lintel and door-sill being clustered with jasmines and roses, and every dwelling having its plot of garden in front, bright with flowers, among which the tall proud lilies and stately hollyhocks are seen blending with the dark green shrubs, and luxuriant evergreens. Tissington is truly a model village, and there is a touching simplicity and calm repose about its rustic and peace-breathing abodes

that inspires you with a poetical idea of the contentment and
purity of life that reigns within; so soothing in comparison
with the turmoil and bustle and immorality of a crowded
town.

The church is a small but picturesque structure, with
an air of venerable antiquity about it that well accords
with the primitive character of the locality—its low broad
massive tower, its quaint old porch, its heavy oaken doors,
its antique arches, its grim grotesque-looking corbels, and its
rude and ancient pillars, were all raised in times gone by,
probably by the hands of some who are now sleeping beneath
the shadow of its venerable walls. It stands upon an elevated
plot of ground by the roadside, surrounded by spreading
beeches, and is approached by a path leading through an
avenue of aged yews, that look as ancient as the building
itself, and whose sombre gloom gives a solemn repose and
shaded sanctity that well accords with the natural charms of
the place.

We walked through the quiet graveyard, striding through
the tall waving grass, as we picked our way among the
sinking and half-worn stones—

> "Where many a holy text around is strewn,
> To teach the rustic moralist to die."

Among the various works of human creation which adorn
the land there are none that awaken in the mind so many
holy and solemn, yet soothing and pleasing, recollections, or
which so powerfully impress the heart and the imagination
with a deep feeling and attachment for our native country,
as an ancient village church; however unpretending the
structure may be, the idea of orderly conduct and moral
feeling is ever associated with it, and importance and respectability is given to the habitations which, like humble
vassals, gather round. How pleasing is it on that perpetually
recurring day—that brightest gift of God to man—when the
grasp of earthly tyranny is loosed, when the noise and whirl
and the turmoil of busy life is hushed, when man rests from
his labours, and everything rests with him—to hear the bells
ringing out from the old gray towers; to watch the rustic
groups issuing from nooks and corners and streaming through

the quiet rural lanes, all bent upon offering up, as with one heart and with one voice, in the same language and in the same words, their supplications to the throne of God for grace, and peace, and forgiveness.

Blessings and ten thousand blessings be on those gray and hallowed fanes that stand on many a wooded hill and on many a verdant plain, within the length and breadth of this our dear and native land. We should never look upon them but with feelings of the devoutest gratitude and veneration, and it should be our delight to watch over them with jealous care, and to cherish them as the most precious gifts that the munificence of former days has bequeathed to us.

Opposite to the church is Tissington Hall, the ancient family residence of the Fitzherberts, an old Gothic mansion, nearly hidden in wood, which was garrisoned by the Royalists during the troublesome times of Charles the First. A short distance from the hall stands a modern brick structure, built in the Elizabethan style, with an open arcade in front, and an octagon projection at one end, over the entrance to which is a lozenge-shaped shield charged with the armorial bearings of the Fitzherberts—gules, three lions rampant, or, inscribed with the initials F.F., and the date 1837. One portion of this building is occupied as a school, and the other is appropriated to the use of the village post-office.

Tissington derives considerable interest from the circumstance of its being the annual scene of one of those lingering customs that bear the impress of past times and generations, and whose origin has been so far back as to have become lost in the dim antiquity of ages, but which is believed to owe its existence to an incident recorded in the book of Numbers (xxi., 16-18), when the Israelites in their journey through the wilderness digged a well at Beer, and with joy and gratitude for the gift of water, sang the song, "Spring up, O well; sing ye unto it."

The festival of well-dressing, or well-flowering, as it is sometimes called, formerly prevailed in different parts of the country, but appears now to be almost exclusively confined to this particular village; though an attempt has of late years been made to revive the custom at Buxton and some other places in Derbyshire.

Ascension Day is that annually set apart for the observance of this custom, which is made a time of mutual feasting and rejoicing, and the pleasant exchange of hospitalities. On the occasion the five wells or springs, which are situated in dif-- ferent parts of the hamlet, are decorated with arches and niches, adorned with mosaics and arabesques, formed of dif- ferent coloured flowers and evergreens, and inscribed with appropriate Scripture texts. The business of the day is usually commenced by a service at the church, after which the clergyman in his surplice, attended by the village choir, and followed by the entire congregation, walk in procession to the nearest well, when all form in a circle round, a psalm is read, and afterwards a hymn of thanksgiving sung; and the same thing is repeated at each well in succession. After- wards the bailiff of Sir Henry Fitzherbert announces that the hall is open for all who are willing to partake of the baronet's hospitality, and the remainder of the day is spent in feasting, dancing, and merry-making.

# CHAPTER XVIII.

On leaving the village of Tissington we entered the grounds of Sir Henry Fitzherbert, and proceeded along an avenue shaded by magnificent limes, whose spreading branches, meeting overhead, admitted only now and then glimpses of the blue sky above. A rustic told us that Sir Henry did not like folks making a common highroad through his park, but as nobody stopped or turned us back, we quietly kept on our way. The avenue is about half-a-mile in length, and is terminated by a triple gateway, close to which is the gate-keeper's lodge, a neat little Gothic building corresponding in style with the mansion itself.

On passing through the gates we come upon the highway from Buxton by Newhaven to Ashbourn. Directly opposite the lodge a by-way branches off, passing through Thorp to Ilam and Dovedale, the entrance to which latter is, as the guide-post informed us, only two miles distant. Ashbourn, however, claims our attention, and we must lengthen our journey considerably before we begin to explore the romantic windings of the Dove.

Turning to the left we proceeded along the Ashbourn road, and in a few minutes reached the *Blue Bell*, a little roadside hostelry, the first house of entertainment we had seen since leaving Grange Mill, some six or seven miles distant ; for, be it known to travellers, Tissington possesses neither inn, tavern, or other place where the tired wayfarer can claim rest and refreshment. The *Blue Bell* was very quiet, and it appeared that we were the only guests; the host, an old man, with the snows of seventy winters upon his brow, sat, or rather reclined, upon a settle in the corner, whilst a fair-haired boy—apparently a grandchild—who was seated by his side read to him from one of those venerable folios which ancient divines have written for man's instruction, telling him of God's doings with His faithful people. As we entered he looked over his spectacles with a scrutinising glance, wished us a kindly good day, and then turned his attention again to the little reader. Our inquiry for dinner was met by an invitation from the good woman of the house to sit down. She had not much choice, she said, to offer, but she would do her best for us, and of course we could expect no more. Our walk of eleven miles from Matlock proved a capital stimulant to the appetite, and we sat down with a determination to do justice to our simple repast, and from which we rose with the conviction that we had no reason to feel dissatisfied with the entertainment the *Blue Bell* affords.

A quarter of a mile from the public-house the road begins to decline, and continues to descend for some distance. We are now in a part of Derbyshire where every step affords increasing signs of fertility and cultivation, and instead of barren moors and stone walls we have a rich agricultural district which, at the time we passed through, was covered with heavy and abundant crops. The excellence of the soil is everywhere manifest in the increasing depth of verdure and in the flourishing aspect of the hedgerows and trees. The pastures are flowery and dotted over with well-formed cattle, the fields are heavy with the ripening grain, and the tall grass waves upon the hilly slopes. The bright green contrasts beautifully with the soft blue and purple distance, and the charms of the country are heightened by a babbling stream that flows with many a mazy curve through the bottom of the valley.

We are now journeying towards Ashbourn, a pleasant three miles' walk along one of those old-fashioned country roads whose quiet pastoral beauty reminds one of a Surrey lane, being nearly embowered with tall thick hedges rich with luxuriant foliage and sweet with the blossoms of the dog-rose and the wild honeysuckle. At every few yards we get peeps into the fields, where the haymakers are busy at work spreading out the newly-mown grass, and now and then we obtain a glimpse of smiling uplands and distant hills adorned with hanging woods.

A mile from Tissington Lodge is Bentley, or Fenny Bentley, as it is sometimes called, to distinguish it from Hungry Bentley, a village beyond Ashbourn—a little rural hamlet consisting of a few stone and red brick cottages built irregularly about the bottom of the valley. The church, a pretty Gothic structure, occupying the site of a more ancient building, stands upon a gentle slope on the right, and the school stands upon the opposite side of the way.

After crossing the little river Schoo the ground rises, the road, as it ascends, continuing between fat fields and pleasant pastures, and on reaching the high land the tall tapering spire of Ashbourn Church comes in view, rising above the distant woods in front. Now the road becomes a level, and for half-a-mile or more is carried along the upper slope of the hill ; gradually the prospect widens, and on the right many a pleasing view is obtained of the opposite hill slopes, chequered over with clumps of trees and patches of plantation. A little rivulet winds with many a rippling curve along the bottom of the valley, between bright green meadow breadths and fields of waving grain, and everywhere the landscape is dotted with little farmsteads and cottages. Sandybrook Hall, a modern residence, with its gardens and pleasure-grounds, appears on the left, and opposite the road is skirted by a row of curiously gnarled and knotted oaks. Then we come to the tollhouse, a pretty Gothic building with pointed over-hanging roofs, ornamented with barge-boards and hip-knobs. Beyond the tollgate the road falls rapidly, and a few minutes' walking brings us to the old town of Ashbourn, pleasantly situated in the bottom of a picturesque and fertile valley, sheltered by lofty hills on the north, and on the south commanding an extensive prospect over a richly-cultivated country, along which the Dove meanders through some of the finest scenery in the county.

Ashbourn is one of the most agreeable country towns in the kingdom—there is such an air of staid, old-fashioned comfort and respectability about it; at the first glance you would imagine it to be an old ecclesiastical city, and this idea is strengthened on beholding its magnificent Gothic church, which is almost cathedral-like in its proportions; the buildings, too, have a venerable and stately appearance that well accords with the dignity of such a place, and ever and anon, as you pass along, your eye is caught by some quaintly-mullioned window, or old projecting gable; there is, too, an absence of that din and bustle observable in the large manufacturing towns, which the spirit of modern activity has thronged with a population of restless, keen, and money-getting people. That it is a place of some pretension is evident from the number of substantial residences that are seen mingling their bright red brick fronts with the more primitive-looking dwellings of weather-beaten stone and thatch; but, notwithstanding its antiquated features, a searching eye will discover signs of modern progress and improvement in the numerous incongruities caused by the attempts to make plate-glass and fancy gilding harmonise with the simpler but more substantial structures of a former age. Among the more noticeable evidences of advancement, we may mention the fact of its having become a railway town, the North Staffordshire Company having constructed a branch from their main line near Rocester. The railway, however, only approaches the outskirts of the town, and terminates in such a peaceful and unostentatious manner that you can hardly object to its presence; in fact, it seems as if almost ashamed of disturbing the peace and quietude of the place.

The town consists of one main street half-a-mile in length, with several lesser streets branching off at right angles on each side. The Grammar School, a large substantial stone building founded in the reign of Queen Elizabeth, stands on one side of the principal thoroughfare, and nearly opposite are the Alms-houses, founded by Christopher Pegg, in 1669, for the accommodation of six poor widows or widowers of the town of Ashbourn, on one of the walls of which is a shield charged with the arms of the generous benefactor—arg. a chevron between three wedges, sable. Within a short distance of the Alms-houses is the house formerly the residence of

Dr. John Taylor, the intimate friend and associate of Dr. Johnson, the great lexicographer.

Ashbourn Hall, a square stuccoed erection, stands on a slope overlooking the little river Henmore. The mansion itself possesses few architectural excellences, but the gardens and pleasure-grounds are laid out with considerable taste ; and the river, as it winds through the park, spreading itself out in a series of lakes and pools which are separated from each other by miniature waterfalls and cascades, adds to their sylvan beauty.

The hall was from a very early period the seat of the Cockaynes, one of the most famous Derbyshire families, which numbered among its members many eminent statesmen and warriors. Sir Aston Cockayne, the last male representative of this branch of the family, joined with his son in the sale of Ashbourn Hall, and other estates, to Sir William Boothby, Bart., and from that time until within a recent period Ashbourn Hall continued the residence of the Boothby's, a family distinguished for their high intellectual attainments.

We refreshed at the *Green Man Hotel*, an old-established house, and afterwards strolled through the town to the bridge, from whence a good view of the hall is obtained ; thence we proceeded along Church Street to the church, the glory and the boast of Ashbourn.

It stands at the western end of the town, on the road to Hanging Bridge, and is surrounded by a spacious graveyard partially environed by trees. It is a large and handsome structure of great antiquity, built in the form of a cross, and includes a nave, chancel, and north and south transepts, with a square tower rising from the intersection, surmounted by a lofty and elegantly ornamented octagon spire, pierced with five rows of spire lights, and enriched at the angles with ball-flower ornaments. This spire attains a height of 212 feet, and from its remarkable lightness and beauty has been named "The Pride of the Peak."

On entering the churchyard we passed along a narrow avenue of closely-clipped limes, at the further extremity of which the edifice itself appeared, revealing all the elegance and beauty of its vast proportions. The time of our visit was a most favourable one, and we saw it to great advantage.

The sky was clear, and the sun, which had long passed the meridian, shed a warm and mellow light upon the sacred pile, touching the traceried windows, the graceful arches, and delicate carvings, with exquisite beauty, increased by the broad shadows which brought out the more prominent parts in bold relief. The building exhibits the characteristics of the different periods, from the severe early English of the thirteenth century to the florid perpendicular which immediately preceded the Reformation, when English ecclesiastical architecture may be said to have attained its full development. At the first general view the beholder is struck with the apparent order and unity of design manifest; but upon a more close examination, the building is found to be made up of parts belonging to totally distinct styles, yet so arranged as to harmonise and blend together without producing in the mind of the spectator any strong impressions of contrast. In some places there is a certain massiveness noticeable, which at times borders on heaviness, but the effect of the whole is noble and imposing.

The church is believed to occupy the site of a more ancient foundation, which is known to have existed at a period anterior to the Conquest. The present building was dedicated by Hugh de Patishul, Bishop of Coventry, in honour of St. Oswald, as appears by the following inscription on an ancient brass plate found when repairing the church some years ago, and now affixed to a marble tablet against one of the piers :
" *Anno ab incarnacione D'ni* M.CC.XLI. viii. *kl. Maii dedicata est hec Eccia. et hoc Altare consecratum in honore Sci. Oswaldi Regis et Martiris a venerabili Patre Domino Hugone de Patishul Coventrensi Episcopo.*" A fac-simile of this plate, which is about eight inches by four, is given in the *Gentleman's Magazine* for September, 1772, p. 416. The sides of the nave and choir appear to be the oldest portions of the building, and exhibit the usual heavy buttresses and long lancet windows of the time of Henry III., whilst the north and south transepts, and the east end of the choir, give evidence of a later period in the lighter and more ornamental workmanship they display.

The interior is particularly light and spacious, and exhibits some good examples of architectural carving. The roof of the nave is supported by a series of pointed arches, springing on each side from massive clustered columns, with moulded and ornamental capitals. The author of " Peak Scenery," in describing this church, says these pillars have in several places been strangely defaced and cut away in order that some unmeaning monumental tablets might be more conveniently put against them. " It is a pity," he adds, "that the churchwardens who allowed such a mutilation were not made to do penance for such an instance of bad taste." Happily the reproach no longer applies, for among the improvements and restorations effected some years ago, under the direction of Mr. Cottingham, these unsightly tablets were removed to places more suited for their reception. At the same time a large monument, which partially blocked up a beautiful lancet window, was transferred to another part of the church, and placed against a blank wall, so as not to interfere with the architectural features of the building.

The north and south sides of the chancel appear to have been built about the same time as the nave, but the east end is of a much later date, and is lighted by a magnificent perpendicular window of seven lights, transomed, the upper portion being divided into small panel-like compartments by smaller mullions, which spring from the principal lights, and are carried vertically up through the head. The principal as well as the subordinate lights of this window are deeply cusped and foliated. The windows of the north transept are in the decorated style, and those in the south are of the later florid or perpendicular period.

The church contains many ancient and curious monuments, tablets, and other sepulchral memorials, some of them of an elaborate and costly character. In the south transept is a fine altar-tomb of alabaster, on which are the recumbent figures of Sir Humphrey Bradbourne, Knight, of Lea, and his wife, Elizabeth, daughter of Sir William Turvill, of New-hall, Warwickshire. The knight is habited in plate armour, with a collar of s.s. and a short sword by his side ; his wife is robed in a close-fitting gown and kirtle, with a ruff and head-dress of the time of Elizabeth ; on each side of the tomb are sculptured figures, one side representing the sons and the other the daughters of Sir Humphrey, each holding an

U

escutcheon charged with the arms of the Bradbournes, impaled with those of their respective alliances. At the west end is a shield encircled by a garter, bearing the arms of the several families with whom the Bradbournes claim to quarter, and two other smaller shields, one charged with the arms of Bradbourne and the other with those of Turvill. There is a second altar-tomb and some other memorials of the Bradbournes in this transept.

The north transept appears to have been appropriated as a mortuary chapel for the Cockayne and Boothby families, whose memories are perpetuated in numerous monumental effigies and altar-tombs. One, a large embattled altar-tomb, is enriched with quatrefoils and Gothic tracery; on the top are two effigies sculptured in alabaster, representing a knight in plate armour with pointed helmet, and by his side the figure of a man habited as a Palmer, with a purse and dagger attached to his girdle. On the breast of the knight are displayed three cocks, the arms of the Cockayne family. There is no inscription on the tomb, but it is believed to be that of John Cockayne, who died in 1373. Near to this is a marble tombstone, bearing the following inscription :—

> " Here lyeth Sir Thomas Cockaine,
> Made knight at Turney and Turwyne ;
> Who builded here fayre houses twayne,
> With many profittes that remayne :
> And three fayre parks impaled he,
> For his successors here to be ;
> And did his house and name restore,
> Which others had decayed before ;
> And was a knight so worshipfull,
> So virtuous, wyse, and pitifull ;
> His dedes deserve that his good name
> Lyve here in everlasting fame."

There are several monumental tablets of the Boothbys, the epitaphs of which are from the pen of the late Sir Brooke Boothby, Bart., a gentleman whose classic taste has been made known to the world through the publication of a volume of poems, entitled, " Sorrows Sacred to Penelope," a work written in memory of his only child, who died in 1791, at the age of six years. Her monument, which stands near the middle of the transept, cannot fail to arrest the attention and call forth the admiration of every beholder. It is executed in a white statuary marble, and represents the deceased, in a sleeping attitude, reclining upon a mattress; the arms are drawn up, and rest upon the pillow, and the feet are thrown negligently one over the other; the sereneness of feature and attitude, and the idea of repose which marks the expression of the countenance, are well conveyed, and the general contour is at once natural and graceful, the drapery being so arranged as to fall in numerous flowing lines, by which delicacy and power are at the same time preserved. The whole is a happy embodiment of those lines in which Byron describes the first hours of death —

> " Before decay's effacing fingers
> Have swept the lines where beauty lingers."

On the pedestal supporting the figure is the following inscription :—

> "To Penelope,
> Only child of Sir Brooke Boothby and Dame Susannah Boothby,
> Born April 11th, 1785 ; Died March 13th, 1791.
>
> She was in form and intellect most exquisite.
> The unfortunate parents ventured their all on this frail bark, and the wreck was total."

---

" Omnia tecum una perierunt gaudia nostra. Tu vero felix et beata Penelope mea. Quæ tot tautisque miseriis una morte perfuncta es."

---

> " Lei che'l ciel ne mostra terra n'asconde.
> Le crespe chiome d'or puro lucente.
> E'l lampoggiar del Angellico riso,
> Che soleau far in terra un Paradiso,
> Poca polvere son che nulla sente."

---

" Beauté, c'est donc ici ton dernier azyle. Son cercueil ne la contient pas toute entière. Il attend le reste de sa proie ; Il ne l'attendra pas longtemps."

The following line, inscribed upon a tablet, is indicative of the feelings of the youthful sufferer :—

> " I was not in safety, neither had I rest, and trouble came."

This work of art, which is believed to have furnished the idea for Chantry's celebrated group, the "Sleeping Children," in Lichfield Cathedral, is from the chisel of Banks, and is

generally considered to be his master-piece.  As of Chantry's
" Sleeping Children," so may it be said of this, " a man must
be made of unnaturally stern stuff who can contemplate it
unmoved."

Within a few feet of this monument a plain flagstone
records the death of the frisky Dean Langton, of Clogher,
who was killed by falling with his horse over a precipice in
Dovedale, 28th July, 1761.  It is somewhat singular that
no Christian name is given, and what is perhaps more
remarkable, there is, as we were told, no entry of the burial
recorded in the parish register.

There are some other monuments in the church, and on
the walls are disposed several tablets, the more lowly memorials of members of different local families, who, though not
so eminent, were perhaps not less virtuous than those whose
tombs we have already described—*Requiescat in pace.*

At Mayfield Cottage, a small and unostentatious country
residence, about two miles from Ashbourn, Tom Moore,
Ireland's genial bard, lived for a considerable period ; many
of his letters to Byron, since published in Earl Russell's
" Life of Moore," were dated from it ; here he composed the
greater part of " Lalla Rookh ;" and the beautiful lines,
" Those Evening Bells," were inspired by the sweet music of
Ashbourn church bells—

> "Those evening bells ! those evening bells !
> How many a tale their music tells,
> Of youth, and home, and that sweet time,
> When last I heard their soothing chime.
>
> Those joyous hours are passed away !
> And many a heart, that then was gay,
> Within the tomb now darkly dwells,
> And hears no more those evening bells.
>
> And so 'twill be when I am gone ;
> That tuneful peal will still ring on,
> While other bards shall walk these dells,
> And sing your praise, sweet evening bells ! "

We left Ashbourn in the afternoon, intending to spend a
half-hour at Ilam, and then proceed through Dovedale to
Hartington, where we had arranged to take up our quarters
for the night.

On leaving the town the road diverges to the left, and descends somewhat abruptly until it reaches the Schoo, which is spanned by an old-fashioned stone bridge. Having crossed the stream, we continued along an unfrequented path that winds irregularly among pleasant rural scenery, and soon reached the open valley, where the prospect, though less striking and romantic than in some other parts of Derbyshire, includes within its ample sweep many charming combinations of sylvan and meadow scenery, among which the tourist, as he journeys through, loiters with sensations of delight. The valley is of considerable extent, fertile, and well cultivated, spreading out in broad level pastures that alternate with rich harvest fields, plentifully sprinkled with trees, and shaded by woods, among which lie snug little farms and homesteads, half hidden in the abundant foliage. Apart from the expanse, there is a charm in the varieties of colour, and the eye is delighted with the constant alternations of light and shade, caused by the diversied character of the more distant landscape, which rises and falls in a succession of undulating eminences, that stretch away until they mingle with the far-off hills of Staffordshire. The Dove adds its beauties to the scene, and spreads its wavy crystals as it serpentines through the luxuriant meads, gambolling playfully beneath the spreading branches of the trees which overhang its banks. There is no lack of clean and homely-looking cottages, and here and there is seen a straggling village or rural hamlet, partly shaded with trees, and partly raised above the groves by which it is surrounded, whilst in the distance a few green swells rising above the circling woods mark the summit of the Staffordshire Downs.

Approaching Mappleton the bold forms of Bunster Hill and Thorp Cloud are seen towering proudly above the intervening foliage. Okeover Hall, a plain but substantial brick mansion, the seat of Haughton Charles Okeover, Esq., whose ancestors have been lords of the manor of Okeover from the time of the Conquest, stands a little distance off on the Staffordshire side of the Dove. It occupies a pleasant position on a gentle rise of land that swells gradually from the river ; the grounds are laid out in lawns, gardens, and groves, and an amphitheatre of lofty woods closes in the scene behind. Okeover Church, a neat Gothic structure with a square tower, stands within a few yards of the hall, and together they form a pleasing group in the prospect.

Mappleton is a quiet rural village, pleasantly situated on the foot of a sloping eminence that commands a fine view across the valley of the Dove to the Staffordshire hills beyond ; the houses are mostly old red brick structures, which stand bordering on the highway in an irregular line ; the bald and cheerless aspect of the brickwork, so lifeless-looking in comparison with the warm gray colouring of the native stone, is in some degree relieved by the trees and gardens which prettily intermingle with the houses, and divest them of that cold and uninviting character they would otherwise assume. The church, an unpretending edifice, stands a little way back from the road ; like the dwellings, it is built of brick, of an oblong form, with a tower, the top of which is of a domi-circular shape, and crowned by a small metal urn.

Leaving Mappleton, we have some pleasant sylvan scenery on the left where the green meadows slope down to the river, and the tall firs and spreading elms that border the road intermingle their hues and diffuse a perpetual gloom. On the right the view is shut out by a plantation, on reaching the further end of which the road begins to rise, and continues on the ascent until we reach Spend Lane, from whence a fine retrospective view is obtained of the valley of the Dove, with its broad-rolling fields, its orchards and gardens, its rich pastures and dark-hued plantations, its undulating hills and wood-crowned eminences, its wide expanse of hill and dale, and the river, ever an object of beauty, glinting through the trees, and gleaming fitfully at every bend as it pursues its mazy course through the yellow fields and sunny glades that extend in seemingly interminable succession.

Keeping on along Spend Lane the road becomes more level, but the views are partially excluded by the thick copse. Never mind, there is much to delight the eye among the wealth of flowering brambles and the beautiful variety of wild plants. It is just the place for a summer saunter, quiet and secluded, with but few wayfarers, so that you may shape your ideas and fancies without much fear of interruption. The tall trees spring from the thick undergrowth and form a verdant archway overhead, and the sunlight flecks the path where it comes glinting through the whispering leaves; gleamy vistas open here and there, and you feel the exhilarating influence of the uninterrupted breeze as you stop to look over the surrounding country.

Two miles from Mappleton we leave the highroad and pass through a gate on the left, which admits to a by-path that leads across the fields, and brings us to the edge of a hilly ridge, from which we descend by a rough and narrow cart road, where we have to look to our footing, so full is it of deep wheel-ruts and hollows and gullies, where the stones and loose soil have been washed away by successive rains. It is steep withal, so much so, that anything short of a double-quick step is out of the question; high banks rise on each side, crowned with dwarf oaks, hollies, and hazels, and bedecked and fringed with ferns, harebells, and gaudy foxgloves, that struggle for space with the brambles, dog-roses, and wild gooseberries that flourish in wild and untrimmed prodigality.

Arrived at the bottom we find two or three poorish-looking cottages with patches of garden sheltered by tall trees; passing these we have next to struggle up a loose stony lane nearly as rough and uneven as that we have just descended, and as we scramble up we are reminded of the frightful descriptions given by travellers of the Derbyshire roads a century ago. Near the top is Thorp, a picturesque hamlet consisting of a few weather-beaten cottages built irregularly over the slope of the hill, with an old-world look about them that carries the mind back to the rude simplicity of former days. The church, a quaint little structure, stands near the verge of a precipice overlooking a picturesque dell; it exhibits the heavy architectural features of the Norman period, and has a plain squat square tower at the western end nearly grown over with ivy. The parsonage stands close by, and is almost as quaint-looking as the church itself; in front is a flower garden, with a few fantastically-clipped yews, and several gnarled and knotted oak-tree stumps, which detract somewhat from the effect by giving it too much the appearance of affected rusticity.

Onwards the road keeps the high ground, running in an

irregular line along the hillside; on the right appears the head of Thorp Cloud rising like a mighty cone, its steep sides bare of wood, but carpeted with the richest turf, guarding the eastern entrance to Dovedale, opposite to which, on the left of the road, is a little public-house, bearing the ambitious title of the *Dovedale Hotel*, a house frequented by picnic parties, and the class of visitors who come to view the natural attractions of the locality.

The entrance to Dovedale is only a few minutes' walk from the hotel by a field path across the flank of the hill. We had determined, however, before entering the dale, to walk over to Ilam, a place which, though (being on the Staffordshire side of the river) not coming strictly within the limits of a Peak ramble, is nevertheless resorted to by all who visit this part of Derbyshire, and followed a beaten track that leads down to the bridge.

As we descend the grassy acclivities at the foot of Thorp Cloud a fine view of Ilam Hall is obtained. The village itself is screened by an intervening grove of trees, but the mansion, with its lofty flag-tower, and embattled parapets, its lawns and gardens and conservatories, appears before us in all the fulness of its magnificence, environed by majestic woods, whose sombre foliage is delightfully relieved and contrasted by the delicate colouring of the masonry; the whole presenting a combination of architectural grandeur and sylvan loveliness rarely equalled. The nearer foreground is well stored with picturesque objects, and happily harmonises with the surrounding landscape, the beauty being enhanced by the glowing beams of the declining sun, which diffuse a warm roseate tint over the ripening fields and new-mown meadows; lengthening the shadow of the hedgerow fences, and softening and blending the outlines of the more distant eminences. The Manifold enlivens the scene, twinkling in the golden light as it hurries on to join the Dove, and seeming to rejoice in having once more gained the light of day after its subterraneous journey through the dark recesses of the earth.

As we have already stated in our notice of Ashbourn, Dr. Johnson frequently visited this part of the country, and it is believed that when he wrote " Rasselas," the scenery around Ilam furnished him with the idea of his happy valley.

Near the bottom of the valley we pass Thorp Mill, and then take across the bridge and along the road, which for some distance runs parallel with the Manifold. On the right is seen the entrance to Dovedale, and the lofty eminence of Bunster Hill, and on the left we catch glimpses of the surrounding country; the views, however, are limited to a narrow range of vision by the intervening woods, but the river keeps us pleasant companionship coursing merrily onwards, and now and then revealing its glistening surface as it sweeps along between the double row of spreading limes and sycamores that bound its course.

Ilam, though insignificant in size, and scant in population, has all the appearance and characteristics of a model village; it consists of a few groups of cottages built chiefly of stone and party-coloured tiles, with curious spiral chimneys and quaint overhanging gables; the houses, though humble in appearance, are scrupulously neat and clean, and the honeysuckled porches and little gardens in front, nearly smothered in roses, and hollyhocks, and lilies, give you an idea of rural happiness quite cheering to behold.

The first object that arrests the attention on entering the village is a beautiful decorated Gothic cross, erected some few years ago by Mr. Watts Russell in memory of his wife. It stands near the foot of the bridge, and is a beautiful specimen of ornamental carving. The form is hexagonal, and on each face of the lower stage is a trefoiled opening surmounted by a richly-crocketted canopy, the panel of the one on the west side—that fronting the hall—bearing the following inscription in old English characters :—

> " This Cross and Fountain,
> erected by her Husband,
> perpetuate the memory of
> One who lives in the hearts
> of many in this Village and
> Neighbourhood,
> MARY WATTS RUSSELL,
> MDCCCXL.

> Free as for all these crystal waters flow,
> Her gentle eyes would weep for others' woe ;
> Dried is that fount ; but long may this endure
> To be a Well of Comfort to the Poor."

Above the openings are six canopied niches, each containing an emblematic figure sculptured in stone, and the whole is crowned by a crocketted spire-like erection, terminating in a small ornamental cross. As will be seen by the inscription above quoted, it is designed as a well and drinking-fountain for the use of the villagers.

The hall is romantically situated on a gentle eminence, which slopes gradually towards the river. It is a comparatively modern erection, built in the castellated style of the late Tudor period, with an embattled tower in the centre, a long array of square mullioned windows in front, and a covered arcade on the ground floor.

We passed through the lodge gate into the park, and thence along a gravelled path to the church, which stands in front of the hall, being separated from the lawn only by a wire fence and a border of dwarf shrubs and flowers. It is a picturesque though unpretending structure of early English foundation, with additions of a later period, but bearing evidence of having been recently restored—happily without entirely destroying the effect of its ancient features. Some idea of what the original building was may be gathered from the description given of it by the author of " Peak Scenery :" " The tower," he says, "appears to be a structure of foliage, for the stonework is so invested with ivy as to be almost obscured with its verdant covering, and the dial of the clock is half buried amongst thickly-entwined leaves. Ash, alder, and wild roses, of the most luxuriant growth and colour, flourish close around the walls of the church, and the adjoining burial ground is covered with the richest verdure, amongst which a gray stone occasionally appears inscribed to the memory of those who sleep beneath." The building has a low square tower at the western end, surmounted by a wedge-shaped roof, which reminds one of the small continental churches. There is an entrance porch near the south-west end, and a chapel on the same side, over the doorway of which are the letters $\begin{smallmatrix} & R\,M \\ R\,P & N\,H \end{smallmatrix}$ and the date 1618. The chancel is lighted by a triplet window, filled with stained glass, illustrating the Sufferings and Death of Christ. On the north side of the chancel is the family vault of the Russells, over which has been erected an octagon mortuary chapel. The door was locked, consequently we had not an opportunity of viewing the beautiful monument within—one of Chantry's best works—which it contains. The following description of it is given by Rhodes, the intimate friend of the great sculptor : " In this fine monument the venerable Pike Watts is represented on his bed of death, from which he has half raised himself by a final effort of expiring nature, to perform the last solemn act of a long and virtuous life. His only daughter and her children—all that were dearest to him in life—surround his couch and bend at his side as they receive from his lips the blessings and benedictions of a dying parent. Nothing can be more affecting than this family group. The figures have the semblance of beings l:ke ourselves, with passions, feelings, and affections similar to our own ; we can therefore sympathise in their affliction and mingle our tears with theirs. Fame, justice, wisdom, fortitude, charity, faith, religion, are all represented by certain understood modifications of the human form, and they may be bodied forth in the marble with great skill and felicity of execution. But, in comparison with the work now referred to, how cold and feeble are the effects they produce ! As specimens of beautiful workmanship they may excite admiration, but they cannot reach the heart, nor call its finer and more touching sympathies into action."

In the churchyard are a few stunted yews, and the remains of an ancient Runic cross, liberally adorned with a succession of interlaced knots and figures sculptured in relief on the sides, but so much defaced by age as to have become nearly obliterated.

As we turned to depart we were saluted with the sound of youthful voices, and on looking round beheld a group of three or four rosy-faced, chubby-cheeked children, seated behind a tomb in a retired part of the graveyard, one of whom thus early evinced an ambitious fondness for despotic power by acting the part of schoolmistress, teaching her younger playmates their letters from an imaginary alphabet formed of plaited rushes and dock leaves. Each wore a scarlet cloak and a little bonnet with a blue ribbon across, and the bright colouring of their attire contrasting with the surrounding greenery gave them quite a picturesque appearance. When we approached they gazed at us for a moment with an air of childish wonder, and then scampered off, tripping lightly over the turf like so many fairies. As we passed through the village on our return, we met with several children all habited in the same gay costume, and on inquiry learned that they belonged to the village school, which is supported by the liberality of Mrs. Jesse Watts Russell.

Leaving the park by the lodge we retraced our steps, making right good speed, the more so that the lengthening shadows reminded us of the near approach of night.

# CHAPTER XIX.

FROM Ilam there is a short cut to the entrance to Dovedale,
by a path that branches off the road near the village, and
leads over the side of Bunster Hill.

Evening comes on calm and golden, and as we mount the
steep slopes the slanting beams of the declining sun come
streaming upon us with dazzling, almost blinding effect; the
bold acclivities of the hill are covered with short thick grass,
among which narrow foot-tracks run in and out, and everywhere sheep are seen grazing upon the verdant knolls, or
crouching in their sunny lairs; and the silly creatures,
startled at the appearance of intruders, take to flight, and
give themselves a world of unnecessary trouble, bleating
timidly, and running away whenever we pass near.

A few minutes' brisk walking brings us to the *Izaak
Walton*, an inn well known to tourists, and a favourite resort
of the disciples of the honest and cheerful-hearted old
angler whose name it bears. Passing by the rear of the
house we cross a meadow bounded by a stone fence, and
then strike into a footpath which soon brings us to the brink
of the Dove, whence a narrow foot-bridge affords access to
the opposite or Derbyshire side, the only one by which the
intricate windings of the dale can with safety be explored.

The entrance to Dovedale is an introduction quite in
character with the marvels beyond, and the spectator becomes
almost startled by the wild and savage grandeur of the prospect to which a few steps have so suddenly introduced him—
so striking in contrast with the calm and placid beauty of

the lovely valley through which it is approached. The green pastures, the sunny glades, the fair and fertile meadows, the rising slopes mantled with waving woods, the gentle flowing river, and the warm rich landscape, have hardly faded from the sight ere he finds himself in the midst of a scene where Nature exhibits some of her most striking and majestic features, and where, instead of the sweet melodies of the birds, the bleating of flocks, and the gladsome hum of sunny music, he has to listen to the angry brawling of the tortuous stream, as it frets and chafes round the little islets, or dashes with impetuosity over the rocky barriers that here and there impede its course.

Bunster Hill on the one side, and Thorp Cloud on the other, two abrupt and lofty eminences, the former 1,200 feet in height, and the latter attaining to an almost equal elevation, stand, like mighty sentinels, guarding the approach to this narrow and gloomy ravine. Passing between these rocky portals we are admitted into a secluded valley or glen, through which flows a clear and rapid stream, with green banks and shelving slopes, hemmed in by bold and lofty hills, mantled with thick scrub and brushwood, through which frequently protrude gray weather-beaten crags and walls of naked limestone rock. Half-a-mile from the entrance we come to a sudden bend, when the dale expands, and, pausing to look around, we find ourselves in a vast amphitheatre of rock and foliage, where crag and " screes," and wood and water, blend together in varied and picturesque combinations. On the opposite side of the dale rises a mountain ridge, clothed with a dense forest of larch and pine, which sweeps down almost to the brink of the river. The near side, though not so well wooded, presents a greater diversity of form, and being less bold and precipitous there is a happier commingling of lines. Pacing slowly on the rugged path leads up and down, over little knolls and across patches of sward. Now it narrows into a mere track, anon it winds through rank grass and trailing weeds, and among beds of nettles and broad-leaved batter docks ; and the river, as it ripples merrily on, delights the ear with the sound of its babbling waters, revealing fresh beauties at every curve and sinuosity—here it glides smoothly and tranquilly along, there it dashes tumultuously over the rocky fragments and moss-begrown stones that lie across its channel, and now and then it spreads out into lakes and shallow pools, some of which, from the long drought, have become little else than marshy ponds, overgrown with sedge and rushes, and the rich greenery of aquatic vegetation.

By-and-by the scenery becomes more boldly featured and assumes a wilder and more savage character. Beyond, the view is shut out by a lofty beetling cliff that protrudes its unwieldy form far out into the stream, threatening a barrier to all further progress. Here the road quits the margin of the river and mounts up to the top of the precipice, from the verge of which the unfortunate Dean of Clogher, Mr. Langton, lost his life a century ago, when attempting to ascend on horseback.

From the summit of this eminence the views are very fine, and the combination of scenery included within the limits is at once strikingly impressive, and rich and beautifully varied, On the Staffordshire side of the river the rocks rise in abrupt and imposing masses, their bleached and hoary fronts seamed and channeled in innumerable rents and fissures—here riven, jagged, and shattered, there roughened with furze and green with moss and trailing ivy. The lower acclivities are overgrown with hawthorn, wildbriar, and brushwood, and above, the evergreen holly, the mournful yew, and the drooping birch, mingle their foliage and cast a verdurous shade on all below. The nearer foreground is broken into picturesque inequalities, and the rocky nature of the soil is strangely and fantastically displayed. Here and there huge isolated cliffs and columnar crags, of the most uncouth forms, standing singly and in groups, thrust themselves out through the turf and spreading thicket, some pinnacled and castellated, others grim and spectral like, springing up abruptly like the spire of a church; others again, broken, rugged, and shelving, bedecked and fringed with moss and ferns, and adorned with graceful foliage which hangs like wreaths from every ledge and cleft. Each particular rock has been named by the neighbouring peasantry or guides, and one group, more striking than the others, has received the appellation of Tissington Spires or the Twelve Apostles.

Descending again to the bottom of the dale we come

presently to a singular insulated pile of limestone which rises
with massive grandeur from the opposite bank of the river.
The lower portion is compact, but above the rock is perforated
and indented with numerous cavities and fissures, and crested
with riven and serrated crags and pinnacles which, from
their supposed resemblance to the battlemented parapets of
an ecclesiastical building, have acquired for it the name of
Dovedale Church.   Edwards, in his poem, "The Tour of the
Dove," makes allusion to this spot in the following lines :—

> "Thou venerable fane ! thy walls were reared,
>     Thy ivied arches springing roofed the void,
> Thy fretted spires above the trees appeared,
>     Ere science one fair order had employed—
>     One metal, gold or silver unalloyed,
> To shape and ornament her piles with grace ;
>     And yet the high emotions here enjoyed,
> The humbling thoughts that human pride abase,
> Might well befit the service of a holier place.

> "I glance around the dale from right to left—
>     It seems as paradise were passing by,
> And I behold it from this sacred cleft,
>     Flowers yield their fragrance ; trees, luxuriant, high,
>     Climb the rude rocks ; and in the orient sky,
> O'er yonder peak, the sun reveals his fires ;
>     The sparkling stream of Dove has caught his eye ;
> His glory lightens all the cliffs and spires ;
> I see, I feel, my spirit glows with rapt desires.

> "O hither bring the harp from Judah's palms,
>     With psaltery, sackbut, dulcimer and lute ;
> The music tuned of old to golden psalms
>     This crag-built church, these rocky aisles will suit :
>     They come—the wilderness no more is mute ;
> The winds have brought the harpings of the sky ;
>     Dove breathes her dulcet tones, the lark his flute ;
> The psaltery, trees, the sackbut, caves supply,
> And one harmonious voice of praise ascends on high."

A few paces higher up the dale, on the Derbyshire side,
is Reynard's Hall—a cavernous chamber or opening formed
by the shrinking of the strata during the cooling of the
great limestone bubble.   The ascent to this is by a steep
and rugged path strewn with loose stones and crumbling
rock, where you have to tread with caution for fear of being

precipitated over the slippery crags into the stream below. A broad mass of naked perpendicular rock shoots boldly up from the mountain side until it attains an elevation of 200 or 300 feet. Near the top it is perforated by a naturally-formed archway, 40 feet high and about 20 feet wide, giving admission to an open space or court, and thence by an opening in the parent rock to an inner chamber or recess called "the hall." There is a smaller opening a little lower dow which bears the name of Reynard's Kitchen.

Reynard's Hall is a favourite resort of the numerous pleasure-seekers and picnic parties who visit Dovedale during the summer months; and the broken glass, orange peel, and other fragmentary remains we find scattered about, tell the story of frolic, feast, and fun. Cotton alludes to this cavern in the following stanza of his poem, "Retirement:"—

> " Oh, my beloved caves! from Dogstar's heat,
>   And all anxieties, my safe retreat;
>   What safety, privacy, what true delight,
>   In th' artificial night,
>   Your gloomy entrails make,
>   Have I taken, do I take!
>   How oft when grief has made me fly
>   To hide me from society,
>   Ev'n of my dearest friends, have I
>   In your recesses' friendly shade
>   All my sorrows open laid,
>   And my most secret woes entrusted to your privacy!"

We are now in the wildest part of the dale, and the scene viewed from these heights is one of striking and almost unique grandeur. In whichever direction we gaze the eye takes in a multitudinous assemblage of cliffs and promontories—some gray, some purple, and some, as the stream of sunlight falls upon them, having a rich golden hue that reminds us of the soft aerial haze with which Turner delighted to envelope his gorgeous productions. High rocks overhang the valley, and lofty hills look down upon them again, and the wonderful combination of crag and woodland gives to all a charm which almost fascinates by its magnificence and beauty. All within the limits is chaos and confusion, huge fragments that have been rent from the neighbouring bluffs and headlands bestrew the slopes and

x

lie scattered about in the most picturesque disorder—some naked, channelled, and weather-worn, and others partially hidden in wild ivy and brushwood, with occasionally a stunted yew or verdant holly peering out from crevices so high up that we can hardly distinguish one from the other, and through the midst, the river rushes on with headlong force, twisting and eddying, and swirling and splashing from side to side, leaping from ledge to ledge, or precipitating itself over the rocky heaps in masses of whitened foam that look whiter by contrast with the blackness of the shattered crags, or the deep greenery of the turfy slopes.

A scene of more utter loneliness or stern magnificence it would be difficult to conceive ; it is

> "A solitude where nought of life is seen,
> A silence that forbids all earthly sound ;"

and even the birds seem to shun a seclusion so mysterious and profound. Shut out from the world, the sense of isolation begets a feeling of admiration for these scenes of savage beauty ; and as we gaze upon the weird and uncouth forms we become impressed with an idea of the irresistible force of that mighty power which, in the convulsive throes of a primeval world, could disrupt and rend asunder these mountain masses and scatter the giant fragments about in the confused manner we now see, and, to quote the words of Cuvier, "we begin to comprehend the full extent and grandeur of those ancient events which have preceded the existence of our species." As we speculate upon the mighty changes that have been wrought we mentally compare the present time with that of ages so immeasurably remote that no man can tell their number or duration, and we think of the awful and mysterious silence and the grim solitude that prevailed through that long period—a solitude broken only by the conflict of elements or the rude shock of earthquakes rending and tearing up the solid pavements of the globe, when

> "Earth was from her centre heaved."

We sat down upon a ledge of rock, enjoying the prospect, and listening to the cool splash and sullen echoing of the water as it forced its way over the intrusive masses lying at the bottom and in the bed of the stream. The highest peaks of the nearer cliffs were bathed in a flood of golden sunshine that disclosed every seam and furrow which the erosive hand of time has ploughed down their naked fronts, making them seem almost luminous, and barely distinguishable from the ruby clouds above. The Staffordshire side of the dale was enveloped in deepest gloom, and as the dark shadows of the gathering mists floated slowly over their shelving sides they presented a striking contrast to the bright emerald green of the velvety sward and the brilliant-hued foliage of the mantling woods upon the opposite slopes.

Loth to quit a scene so full of marvellous and romantic beauty, we lingered until the sun changed the clouds in the glowing west into purple and gold, and the long level rays that streamed through the openings in the hills fringed the wavy outline of the rocks with roseate hue and warned us of the near approach of night.

Descending by a treacherous path we reach once more the margin of the stream, and follow its mazy windings until it makes a sudden bend, when we double the curve and meet it again at the opposite side. Now the dale contracts, the rocks close in, and the river, pent up within a narrow gorge, rushes down with angry force, foaming, roaring, and splashing on its way. Still the glen narrows until it becomes little more than a mere sluice, when the beetling cliffs, almost meeting overhead, shut out the light and create a gloom even at mid-day. The passage now becomes more difficult, and we have to pick our way with circumspection, striding from ledge to ledge, and from one rocky lump to another, wherever a foothold can be obtained, pausing now and then to admire the effect of the rushing water as it breaks over the barriers in multitudinous cascades and eddies on with never-ceasing tumult; and as we listen to the gurgling splash the eye rests with pleasure on the luxuriant grasses and ferns, and the delicate aquatic plants and flowers that grow in every hollow and in every dripping nook and cranny.

Further on the path becomes so narrow as hardly to afford footing for a goat, and we have to creep cautiously round walls of perpendicular rock, nearly hidden with climbers and trailing weeds, and overhung with trees, which almost shut out the stream as they dip their drooping boughs into the turbid waters. A little further on, and the trees no longer screen the view; then, as we approach the northern end of the gorge, Pickering Tor, an immense obelisk-shaped pillar of rock, that has been riven from the neighbouring mass, and now juts out into the bed of the stream, is seen guarding the outlet on one side; and the Steeples, two detached columnar pinnacles that rise perpendicularly from the craggy slopes, stand sentinel-like on the other.

Emerging from the narrow defile the dale expands, and again the character of the scenery changes; the rocks recede, and give place to grassy slopes and banks clothed with heather and brushwood, and plentifully sprinkled with trees; and the stream, less turbulent, bubbles cheerfully along, loitering in quiet bends, where it stays to kiss the mossy-coated stones and drifted boulders. Occasionally a rugged cliff appears, round which it glides, forming little hollows and pools, where, beneath the shadow of the spreading foliage, the angler may be sure of meeting with the speckled trout or dainty grayling.

Onwards we go, past wood and rock and "scree" and sward, through brake and thicket, over patches of soft spongy turf and around cliffs and promontories, where gray and rugged crags thrust themselves up like rude rock towers, from clumps of hazel and thorn, or peer out from amid the matted foliage of oak and ash. Every turn reveals a change of scene, each equally beautiful, though different in character; then we come to Dove Holes, two cavernous openings, within a singularly-formed archway, high up in the face of the rock. Did time permit we might scramble up to examine the curious recesses and enjoy the prospect from above, but the increasing gloom warns us to advance.

We have now reached the termination of that portion of Dovedale usually visited by tourists, the upper division being but rarely traversed. The scenery beyond, though not so boldly featured, possesses a character peculiarly its own, and is scarcely less beautiful and romantic than that which we have already endeavoured to describe. Apart from its natural charms, this portion of the dale derives an especial interest from its being so intimately associated with the name of that genial-hearted angler, Izaak Walton, and his "dear son," Charles Cotton—associations which have rendered it dear to every lover of the "gentle art." In this stream those well-known lessons on the art of fly-fishing and angling for trout and grayling were obtained, and, under the inspiration of the surrounding scenery, those thoughts and maxims, which Cotton has embodied in such quaint and simple phraseology, were called forth.

After passing Dove Holes the changing aspect of the scenery at once becomes manifest. We now enter an open valley where the footpath curves in and out between narrow tracts of meadow land, and coarse swampy patches, in which grow tufts of sedge and rushes. On one side the river is bounded by a lofty ridge of moorland hill; on the other the outline is more broken and varied—here and there the limestone crops out through the turf, and occasionally a hoary crag appears, its base buried in underwood, and its weatherbeaten front bedecked with ferns and ivy. Generally the wild features predominate, but there is not that happy blending of the component parts noticeable in other places, and the lack of verdure gives an air of dreary barrenness to the scene.

But we must hasten on, for night comes on apace, the last gleams of golden light, that hung like a halo on the rocky cliffs, flickering as if loth to depart, have faded away, leaving behind a thin filmy veil, so tender and transparent that we can see the azure beyond, and a solitary star twinkling therein. The great undulating summits of the opposite hills stand out in clear and bold relief against the western sky, where an amber radiance yet lingers, whilst the lower slopes are involved in a shadow which no eye can penetrate, and surrounding objects, seen through the dubious and indistinct atmosphere, assume the most vague and shadowy shapes. The tranquil water gives back the mountain forms in all their stern and rugged massiveness, and the few fleecy clouds that float above gradually change their hue from a brilliant orange to a gorgeous crimson, and then the crimson deepens into purple, and as the sun sinks below the horizon the purple becomes colourless and dark, and all appears involved in sombre gloom. A solemn stillness reigns around, with not a sound to disturb the slumbering scene, save the rippling of the stream over the stony shallows, or the soughing of the wind through the gaps and rifts of the mountains.

Approaching Mill Dale the valley loses much of its cheerless aspect, the trees become more numerous, and vegetation more abundant; there are signs of cultivation, too, though "few and far between," sufficient, however, to show that even in this wild and desolate region the hand of industry may be profitably employed. As we follow the sweep of the river we see wreaths of cottage smoke curling up from between an opening in the hills, and a solitary light glimmers through the screen of leaves. Then we come to a road which crosses the stream by a little rustic bridge, and leads thence through a narrow ravine, and by a steep and rutty path up the hillside. With more daylight we might follow that road on to Alstonfield, where there is an ancient village church that well deserves inspection, "a very pretty church," as Viator bears witness to in the well-known colloquy with Piscator, when he facetiously inquires, "Have you churches in this country, sir?" to which Piscator replies, "You see we have : but had you seen none, why should you make that doubt, sir?" and Viator answers, "Why, if you will not be angry, I'll tell you : I thought myself a stage or two beyond Christendom."

Nestling in a hollow beneath the shadow of two lofty hills is seen the cluster of cottages which constitutes the hamlet of Mill Dale, all looking so cheerful and happy in their seclusion from the outer world that the peaceful quietude suggests the idea that the place must have been the abode of Wordsworth's Lucy, who

> "Dwelt among the untrodden ways,
> Beside the springs of Dove ;
> A Maid whom there was none to praise,
> And very few to love.
>
> " A violet by a mossy stone,
> Half hidden from the eye,
> Fair as a star, when only one
> Is shining in the sky.
>
> " She lived unknown, and few could know
> When Lucy ceased to be ;
> But she is in her grave, and, oh !
> The difference to me."

Mill Dale is a pretty little mountain village, stony and somewhat rough, it is true, but there are signs of fruitfulness in the well-stocked gardens, and the luxuriant hedgerows and the tall trees which wave their spreading branches in the evening breeze look more beautiful by contrast with the barrenness of the surrounding scenery, giving you the idea of an oasis in a wilderness of sterility. The villagers were mostly lounging about their doors, and here and there a group were seated upon a grassy bank, chatting quietly and enjoying the evening coolness. When we crossed the little bridge they gazed at us with an air of inquiry, and wondered at our temerity in coming through the dale so late without a guide; then they cautioned us not to proceed further, but to take the highroad to Hartington—"it was a little more round," they said, "but the river path was difficult, and lonesome, too." We did not object to the loneliness, and as to the difficulties, if our calculations did not mislead us, the moon would serve before another mile was traversed, so we thanked them for their advice, and then, recrossing the bridge, resumed our journey.

On the left, a little beyond the village, rises a lofty hill which casts a frowning shadow on all below. We have come across it on a former excursion, but we feel as little inclination to renew the acquaintance as Viator did when he took leave of it with the exclamation, "Why, farewell, Hanson Toot; I'll no more on thee; I'll go twenty mile about first. Puh! I sweat, that my shirt sticks to my back."

Onwards the twilight deepens, and the darkness becomes more dark; strange, uncouth, and shadowy forms meet the eye at every turn. On each side high hills and steep acclivities lift their giant heads one above another, masses of intermingled gray and brown, dark, wild and forbidding—their barrenness at times relieved by clumps of trees and patches of scrubby gorse, with now and then a wooded enclosure or plantation of hazel, birch, and alder running down almost to the water's edge. Here and there a solitary crag or blackened rock starts abruptly from out the sombre mass of foliage, grim and spectral-looking; the mis-shapen masses, viewed through the dun obscurity, seem invested with additional magnitude, and the imagination, full of strange fancies, likens them to

things the most unearthly. The silent river glides swiftly
by, its placid surface scarcely broken by a ripple, occasionally
widening into little bays and creeks, bedded with cress, and
fringed with willow-weed. Cliff follows cliff, and bend succeeds
to bend; here a fallen tree obstructs the path, there an abandoned and solitary-looking sheep-wash stands between us and
the stream; now the moon, rising behind the mountain ridge,
cheers us with his beams, every moment increasing in
brilliance; and then, as we round a rocky point, we come all
at once upon a scene of tranquil and almost supernatural
beauty. So sudden is the transition that the effect seems
magical, and the whole picture one delicious dreamy vision.
Before us stretches an open valley, whose undulating surface
lies sleeping beneath a flood of soft and mellow light, which
brings out with marvellous effect all the picturesque and
ever-varying combinations which river and mountain scenery
are capable of assuming. The dark woods and rugged hills
upon the right are wrapped in the deepest shadow, which
finely contrasts with the mild radiance mantling the opposite
slopes; the cold beams struggle through the overhanging
branches, and play sportively in every rocky gorge and
recess, and the river, as it sweeps along, calm and unruffled,
reflects, as from a mirror, the placid beams of the full-orbed
moon. It is a scene such as that described by Homer in the
famous simile, which Pope has so happily translated—

> " As when the moon, refulgent lamp of night,
> O'er heaven's clear azure spreads her sacred light,
> When not a breath disturbs the deep serene,
> And not a cloud o'ercasts the solemn scene,
> Around her throne the vivid planets roll,
> And stars unnumber'd gild the glowing pole;
> O'er the dark trees a yellower verdure shed,
> And tip with silver every mountain's head;
> There shine the vales, the rocks in prospect rise,
> A flood of glory bursts from all the skies.

Amid a scene of such solemn and impressive grandeur, it
is impossible to remain unmoved, the stilly calmness of the
night, and the soft and soothing influences around, combine
to excite the most pleasurable emotions; inspiration seems
to breathe in all, and the mind becomes impressed with
feelings of gratitude and adoration.

Following the devious course of the stream we come presently to Load Mill, and soon afterwards reach Cold-Eaton Bridge, where the river is crossed by a mountain path that leads up to Hope Dale. Still keeping the Derbyshire side, a few minutes more brings us to Narrow Dale, a deep and gloomy ravine that extends northwards for two or three miles. The country here loses much of its softness and beauty, and assumes at every step a more sombre and savage character; the hills draw closer together, and become more rugged and abrupt; the path too becomes more toilsome, running in and out, now close under a cliff or beneath an impending mass of rock, then winding among broom and gorse, and then again following the stony shore, where it becomes wilder and rougher, and more bestrewn with stones and boulders. Then we come to a bend where the cliffs almost meet overhead, and we creep round a ledge of rock, so narrow that no beast of burden could follow. So tortuous is the course of the stream, and so completely is it hemmed in, that it is scarcely possible to see the watery channel for more than a few yards ahead. Sometimes a jutting rock advances far across the path, and as we sweep round we come upon another seemingly still more impassable. The generally savage character of this part of the dale is at times relieved by spots of exquisite beauty, whose charms are heightened by the soft and silvery radiance which displays the wonderfully varied colourings of the woods and rocks, whilst the few clouds that sail across the heavens produce an exquisite and ever-changing combination of light and shade.

So we keep on, past rocks and cliffs and crags and stony slopes; past little eyots of rushes, and forests of nettles; past narrow glens, and dingles, where lurks a soft and mysterious beauty that almost tempts us to explore their farthest recesses; past scenes, ever changing, ever beautiful, until the mind becomes lost in a dream of delicious enjoyment, in which the impressions received are as fugitive and evanescent as the flitting shadows which chase each other along the mountain slopes.

Leaving Narrow Dale we come to a wild-looking gorge that runs up between an opening in the cliffs to Woscote or Wolfscote Hill; crossing this by a little bridge we enter a barren reach, and then pass to the Staffordshire side over stepping stones conveniently placed across the channel. Another bend or two and Pike Pool is reached—a romantic-looking spot, with a rock, as Cotton describes it, "in the fashion of a spire steeple, and almost as big," standing in the midst, which caused Viator to exclaim, "What have we got here? A rock springing up in the middle of the river! This is one of the oddest sights that ever I saw!" And Piscator answers, "Why, sir, from that Pike, that you see standing up there from the rock, that is called Pike Pool: and young Mr. Izaak Walton was so pleased with it as to draw it in landscape in black and white, in a blank book I have at home, as he has done several prospects of my house also, which I keep for a memorial of his favour."

Beyond Pike Pool the rocks rise for the most part in perpendicular cliffs, finely diversified by a regular alternation of wood and crag, and displaying here and there a broad front of limestone, relieved with trailing creepers and a variety of indigenous plants, with shrubs and trees, sometimes thickly grouped, among which the mountain ash with its scarlet berries makes quite a gay appearance when contrasted with the mournful shade of the pendent birch. Long shadows lie across the path and upon the wooded slopes, the moonlight streams through the matted branches of the trees and quivers upon the ashen sprays, and the mild radiance falling upon the naked rocks gives a finish of beauty, whilst it faintly and timidly lights up the inner recesses and half conceals the jagged projections and waving ferns behind. In the openings between the rocks lie deep hollows and shadowy pools, half-hidden by the hanging bushes, and as we go by we hear the bittern's plaintive voice

" Booming in the sedgy hollow,"

and now and then a solitary bird, scared by the sound of footsteps, darts suddenly from out the leafy thicket, and flits mysteriously across the dark and silent waters.

A few yards further and we come to a place rendered famous from its Waltonian associations—the "little fishing house," which Cotton erected as a memento of the elder Izaak's friendship, and dedicated, as the inscription still shows, to the brotherhood of the angle. It is a neat little stone structure, standing upon a narrow neck or tongue of land formed by a sudden bend of the river, and is nearly hidden by surrounding foliage. Its position and appearance have been well described by Viator: "I am the most pleased," he says, "with this little house of anything I ever saw. It stands in a kind of peninsula, too, with a delicate clear river about. I dare hardly go in, lest I should not like it so well within as without; but by your leave I'll try. Why, this is better and better; fine lights, finely wainscotted, and all exceedingly neat, with a marble table and all in the middle." Externally, at least, it presents much the same appearance now that it did two hundred years ago, when the two anglers sat and smoked their pipes, which Cotton tells us "was commonly their breakfast." In form it is square, with an overhanging pyramidal roof, surmounted at the apex by an ornamental pinnacle or hip-knob. Over the doorway is a square panel bearing the inscription—

PISCATORIBUS
SACRUM
1674:

and beneath this a stone forming the key of the arch on which is carved a monogram, displaying the initials I. W. and C. C., "the two first letters of my father Walton's name and mine twisted in cipher," which Walton saw "cut in the stone before it was set up."

Near to and within sight of the fishing-house is, or rather was, Beresford Hall, an ancient residence which originally belonged to the Beresfords. The family went to Ireland in the time of the first James, and the estate passed to the Stanhopes of Elvaston, whose heiress married "thriftless" Cotton, the father of Charles Cotton, the angler poet. The estate has since become by purchase the property of William Carr Beresford, Viscount and Baron Beresford, a distinguished Peninsular officer, who espoused, in 1832, Louisa, widow of Thomas Hope, Esq., and daughter of the Most Reverend William Beresford, Lord Decies, Archbishop of Tuam. His lordship pulled down the old hall on the site of which he has since erected a more commodious mansion.

We have now reached the end of the second great division of Dovedale; beyond, the valley is continued by the little town of Longnor and Glutton Dale to the foot of the Axe-Edge, near Buxton, whence the river takes its rise. Throughout the entire length the scenery is picturesque and pleasingly diversified, though it does not exhibit those bold and striking features which give so much interest to the lower divisions. The river narrows until it becomes a mere mountain rivulet, and generally the country assumes a milder and more pastoral character.

Dovedale has long ranked as a stronghold of romantic scenery, and to recapitulate its attractions is to say in brief that it exhibits grandeur of effect, with a gracefulness and beauty of detail rarely equalled within the same limits. The great charm consists in the diversity of form and outline, and the exquisite variety and wonderful colourings of the vegetation, displaying almost every shade from the brightest green to a russet brown or nearly sombre black. The interest is increased, too, by the constantly changing character of the scenery, every few yards presenting a picture entirely different in aspect, yet perfect and complete in itself, and distinguished by its own peculiar and characteristic beauties, oftentimes displaying a contrast singularly impressive and magnificent. Sometimes these distinct characteristics closely combine, when we have all the sternness and rugged grandeur of rock scenery united with the most luxuriant foliage and the richest vegetation.

From the time when Cotton sang the "Wonders of the Peak," and hymned the praises of his "beloved nymph fair Dove," the beauties of Dovedale have been often celebrated in verse, and as frequently described in prose ; whilst painters have found in them a never-failing source of inspiration ; but the pen of the writer and the pencil of the artist are alike powerless—no description however graphic, no picture however brilliant, can convey an adequate idea of the charms of this romantic dale. Its beauties, to be thoroughly appreciated, must be seen ; they may be witnessed, but assuredly they can never be told.

On leaving "Beresford's enchanting glen" and the little fishing house, we followed the margin of the river for a short distance, then, after crossing a narrow foot-bridge, we struck into a field-path which brought us out upon the highway about half-a-mile from Hartington. The lights gleaming from the windows of the *Sleigh Arms* were a welcome sight as we approached the town, and a few minutes later, tired with our wanderings, we reached the inn just as the inmates were preparing for bed.

Soundly did we sleep that night after our lengthened ramble, and the bright sunbeams were streaming through the windows, and the birds had been long twittering in the fresh cool leaves, ere we awoke from our refreshing slumbers.

# CHAPTER XX.

THE *Sleigh Arms* at Hartington is a quiet old-fashioned
country inn, where good entertainment and a cheerful but
unaffected welcome are sure to await you ; it is a house in
which good old Izaak Walton himself would have delighted
to take his ease, and, for aught we know, he may have done
so, humming the ballad of " The Milkmaid's Song" while he
superintended the dressing of his own trout. Breakfast in
such a place is not the least among the delights of home
travel, for the fresh-laid eggs, the equally fresh butter, and
the thick clotted cream, beget an appetite and a relish
unknown to those who dwell in towns.

Hartington, which gives the second title to the Dukes of
Devonshire, is an old-fashioned and somewhat important
country town ; it is thoroughly Derbyshire in appearance—
cold and stony-looking, but possessing, withal, much of the
ideal of a country village, with, however, but little of the beau-
ideal about it. The houses, which stand in an in-and-out,
irregular, haphazard sort of way, with a happy disregard of
taste and order, are built of native rock, with the outer walls
white-washed or rough-cast, and the roofs of gray flag, with now
and then a covering of primitive thatch by way of variety ;
but anyone with a quick eye and a ready pencil may find many
a picturesque " bit" worth carrying away, notwithstanding
the unpromising nature of the materials. The *Sleigh Arms*
stands on one side of an open area or square, and the wheelwright's shop, the blacksmith's forge, and a small public-

house or two on the other; higher up a few old-fashioned shops abut upon the tortuous thoroughfare, displaying in their windows a miscellaneous collection of wares—provisions, drapery, and everything besides; and beyond these is seen the tower of the parish church rising above the neighbouring buildings, giving by its presence an air of importance and respectability to the motley habitations scattered irregularly around it.

Hartington Hall was originally the property and residence of the Bateman family, lineally descended from William Bateman, of South Wingfield, living in the time of Richard II., who were settled here, as appears by an entry in the Herald's College, in the early part of the sixteenth century. The hall, which is now occupied as a farm-house, is the property of Richard Thomas Bateman, Esq., the present representative of the family.

From a younger branch of this family was descended the late Thomas Bateman, Esq., of Lomberdale House and Middleton Hall, Derbyshire, an earnest and diligent antiquary, well known for his knowledge and extensive researches in the ethnology and archæology of the Celtic and Anglo-Saxon periods, and also as a contributor to the Journal of the British Archæological Association, and the author of "Vestiges of the Antiquities of Derbyshire," a "Catalogue of Antiquities," and "Ten Years' Digging in the Celtic and Anglo-Saxon Grave Mounds"—works highly prized by those learned in antiquarian matters, and quoted as authorities by the most eminent writers on our earlier history and antiquities, and the last of which was issued only a few days before his decease, which took place August 28, 1861. At his residence, Lomberdale House, near Bakewell, Mr. Bateman succeeded in bringing together one of the largest and most important collections of Early British and Anglo-Saxon antiquities in the kingdom, including coins, glass, pottery, and a variety of implements of a military and domestic character, obtained chiefly during his unwearying investigations in the barrows and grave mounds of Derbyshire and other counties.

After breakfast we paid a visit to the church, which stands upon slightly elevated ground near the north side of the town. It is an ancient structure, apparently of the thirteenth century, with additions of a later date, and is built in the form of a cross, with a nave, chancel, north and south transepts, and a low square buttressed and battlemented tower at the western end. Within the last few years the church has undergone a complete renovation, fortunately without losing its ancient features, a very correct taste having been displayed in the carrying out of the restorations, which are all in perfect keeping with the original character of the edifice.

On entering the churchyard we stood for some moments in contemplation of the northern landscape, with its shadowy outline and rugged undulating bosom, dotted here and there with snow-white habitations that gleamed brightly in the morning sunlight, making the bleak pastures and uncultivated wastes look still more barren and desolate. The country hereabouts, even in its summer dress, has a dreary appearance; but in winter, when the ground is laid with snow, and the shrubs and trees have lost their verdant covering, the prospect must be wild and cheerless in the extreme.

We found the door of the church fastened, but whilst we stood peering through one of the windows, the sexton, who happened to be passing, volunteered to bring the keys and show us the interior. Notwithstanding its modernised appearance it still retains many of its original characteristics. In the chancel are some quaint carvings, an antique piscina, and some other objects deserving attention. There are also in different parts of the church several monumental tablets, which preserve the memory of some who now lie mouldering in the earth below. The roof of the nave is of open timber-work, supported on each side by pointed arches resting upon clustered columns, with ornamental capitals and base mouldings; the seats are all of pitch-pine, stained to imitate oak, and the floors are laid with tiles disposed in simple geometrical patterns. On one side of the centre aisle is the pulpit, a modern erection of hexagonal form, standing upon a pedestal of Caen stone; and on the opposite side of the same is the reading-desk of corresponding design. In the eastern end of the chancel is a memorial window in the decorated style, filled with stained glass. The five principal lights are illustrative of passages in the life of our Saviour, the Crucifixion occupying the centre compartment, and in the subordinate lights beneath are the *Agnus Dei*, and the emblems of the four Evangelists. At the foot of the window is the following inscription :—

𝔗o the glory of God, and in memory of John Sleigh, April 5th, 1858.

On the south side of the churchyard is an ancient stone coffin that has been dug up at some time or other, a few dwarfed but venerable-looking yewtrees, and, near the tower, the remains of an old Runic cross, ornamented with curiously interlaced knots, somewhat after the fashion of those carved upon the old cross in Bakewell churchyard.

Having completed our inspection of the church we bade adieu to Hartington and resumed our excursion, intending to follow the highway for a short distance, and then take across country in the direction of Arbelows—about three miles distant. For about a mile the road gradually ascends; on one side the views are limited to a succession of barren moors and dreary wastes, but on the other an extensive prospect is obtained up the valley of the Dove, in the direction of Longnor and Buxton, the eye passing over a range of undulating slopes which stretch away, woodland beyond woodland, and ridge beyond ridge, until their outlines become obscured by the vapoury haze, whilst far beyond the shadowy form of Axe Edge is seen hanging upon the horizon like a pale blue cloud, carrying the mind away into the infinity of space.

On reaching the high ground above Hartington we leave the beaten path and take a course as nearly direct as we can guess with the aid of a pocket compass, descend into the valley and then mount the opposite hill, on the way scaling several stone walls and crossing enclosures so poor that we wonder how the black-faced sheep we see browsing about manage to find pasture. With increasing elevation the land becomes more sterile, and here and there the lime is seen cropping out in gray and blackened masses—earth's stony crust protruding its bare-worn form through the thin covering of turf, making the scant herbage and stunted gorse look still more dreary and desolate. A solitary clump of trees crowns the

Y

hill, passing which we again descend, picking our way over moss-grown knolls and between rocky fragments of every size and shape, which lie scattered irregularly over the barren slopes.

A short run brings us to Parsley-Hay Wharf—a depôt of the Cromford and High Peak Railway Company—distant about a mile from Newhaven. The country hereabouts, though not absolutely barren, is as cheerless and uninviting as can well be imagined ; far as the eye can reach nothing is seen but a wild infinity of bleak hills and heathy moors which stretch away until they grow dim on the distant edge of the sky, stone walls abound, and here and there a plantation of firs is seen, the dwarfed appearance of the trees only serving to heighten the effects of the sterility by which they are surrounded. A few hundred yards beyond the railway we cross the line of the old Roman road from Buxton to Little Chester, and a quarter of a mile further turn off the Bakewell Road and follow a field path which leads to a homestead rejoicing in the name of Bunker's Hill Farm, close to which is the famous circle of stones called the Arbelows, or more correctly the Arbor Low, justly considered one of the most interesting monuments of antiquity in Derbyshire.

This curious memorial of an ancient population is situated on a piece of gently rising ground commanding an extensive prospect towards the north-east. It consists of a circular area one hundred and fifty feet in diameter, surrounded by a series of rough unhewn blocks of native limestone of various shapes and sizes, ranging from six to seven feet in length, and in width from three to four feet. The stones forming the circle, instead of standing in an upright position like the Nine Ladies on Stanton Moor, and other Druidical remains of the same class, lie horizontally upon the ground and incline towards the centre, where there are two or three larger stones, supposed to have been originally a cromlech. There are about thirty or thirty-five stones in the group, but the exact number cannot be determined, some of them having evidently been broken. The opinion long prevailed among the neighbouring peasantry—and the belief is not yet quite obsolete—that it was impossible for anyone to count these stones correctly, and also that treasure was buried beneath one of them; the first part of the tradition has doubtless arisen from the fact just named, their fragmentary character rendering it difficult to say which are and which are not those forming the original circle, whilst, as regards the treasure, it is hardly likely that anyone will take the trouble to disprove it, so that in all probability this curious relic of former times will be handed down to succeeding generations with the traditions and superstitions accompanying it alike untouched.

The area on which the circle stands is surrounded by a deep entrenchment about 18 feet across, and circumscribed by a vallum or embankment 20 feet in height. The earthworks remain in a very perfect state of preservation, and the entrances on the north and south sides of the enclosure can still be distinctly traced. Near the south entrance to the circle are the remains of a barrow or burial mound, which was opened in 1782 by Mr. Hayman Rooke, when the fragments of an urn, some half-burnt bones, and the horns of a stag were discovered.

It was long taken for granted that all such circles had been places of worship or courts of justice, and some antiquaries are of opinion that the circle at Arbor Low was the great Druidical Temple, or place of assembly in the Peak. With the scanty and uncertain materials we possess it is difficult to arrive at anything like a satisfactory conclusion on this subject, and therefore, in the absence of any positive information to the contrary, it would be rash to assert that such was not the purpose for which these rude and weather-beaten stones were reared; but, as we have already stated in a former part of this work, later experience and more complete investigation have shown that, in many cases at least, these so-called temples are nothing more than monuments, which the earlier possessors of the soil have raised to mark the last resting-places of the honoured dead, and the name of Arbor Low would seem to point to the sepulchral character of the one just described, the word *low*, which is still common in many parts of Derbyshire, being merely a corruption of the Anglo-Saxon *hlœw*, equivalent to *bearw* or barrow, a name used by archæologists for a sepulchral mound—both words having the same signification as the Latin *tumulus*.

From Arbor Low we had a wearisome walk of a mile or more over a dreary and uninteresting country, the monotonous character of which is only relieved by the intersecting lines of stone wall, where we fear we left behind some unpleasant mementoes of our excursion in the shape of damaged fences—sins of commission which it is to be hoped the cwners would look upon as venial, if only on account of the very frequency of their occurrence.

Keeping on, we come presently to One Ash Grange, a substantial farm-house, with an ample range of outbuilding contiguous thereto, delightfully situated within a hollow or natural basin, nearly environed by undulating ridges of meadow land. The farm, which includes about 800 acres of land, belongs to the Duke of Devonshire, from whom it is held by Mr. Henry Bowman, whose ancestors have resided here for nearly a couple of centuries. The manor of One Ash, or as it is written in the Domesday survey, Aneise, originally formed a part of the Haddon estate, and was held under the great feudal house of the Peverels by the Avenells, lords of Haddon, one of whom, William Avenell, gave the lands to Roche Abbey, in Yorkshire. At that time it is said to have been a kind of penal settlement, to which refractory monks were occasionally sent.

Beyond the Grange the country improves somewhat in character, the fields look more cheerful, trees become more numerous, and the herbage more fresh and abundant; the tower of Moneyash Church forms a pretty feature in the landscape, and in the distance is some picturesque rock scenery, backed by a range of swelling hills which sweep round in an irregular circle until they meet the rocky chain bounding the eastern side of the river Derwent.

Hitherto the morning had been dull and overcast, but as the day wore on the heavy dun-coloured clouds, which had hung like a pall over the earth, gradually disappeared, leaving behind a few fleecy reminiscences, which, as they sailed across the heavens, reflected their fantastic forms in clearly defined shadows, that chased each other in rapid succession over the broad brown heathy plains, whilst the sun showered down a blaze of light which illumined and brought out with magical effect all the projections and inequalities of the loftier hills, and diffused a brilliant radiance that happily contrasted with the intermixture of cool shadows which overspread the less-elevated portions of the landscape. A thin misty veil obscured the deeper valleys, and hung upon the adjacent hills, the playful wreaths crawling lazily upwards, one after another, as they slowly dissolved before the sun's increasing brilliance; here and there could be seen a line of pale blue smoke which, as it mounted up into the pure morning air, gave animation and interest to the scene; and a gentle health-inspiring breeze came across the moors, bearing with it the sweet fragrance of the new-mown hay, and the refreshing odours of a thousand shrubs and flowers. The cool invigorating breeze, and the enlivening beauty of the day, had a wonderfully inspiriting effect upon the mind, and gave a buoyancy to the feelings which added greatly to our enjoyment; even the birds seemed to experience the cheering influence, and warbled as they sported about in the warm sunshine with an expression richer and more melodious, their joyous notes welling up in voluptuous fulness as they chanted forth their merry madrigals.

Proceeding in a northerly direction we kept on until we came to the edge of Ricklow Dale, a wild secluded ravine, from whence the greater portion of the gray marble of Derbyshire is obtained. The scenery here is of an extremely gloomy and savage character; on each side of the dale stand out great grim lifeless walls of naked rock, with crags and headlands jutting up one after another, between which are narrow strips of verdure, speckled with oak scrubs and stunted hawthorns. The bottom of the dale and the lower acclivities are strewn with huge blocks and fragments that have been toppled down from the impending heights, some gray with clinging moss, others blackened and weather-stained, looking dark and cold in the shade, with scarcely a feature to redeem their generally barren and savage aspect; conveying to the mind the idea of the remains of old chaos left unorganised.

The descent was an undertaking difficult and dangerous withal, every few yards bringing us to the verge of some crag or precipice, beyond which a step would with certainty have precipitated us into the depths below. Nothing daunted, however, we began the task, creeping slowly round a ledge of rock, then struggling down the hillside through crag and brake, and over broad slippery heaps of shingle and loose stones, which swept down after us in loud rattling sheets, to the infinite terror and dismay of the few half-starved sheep who were quietly browsing among the clefts and hollows beneath. Manifold difficulties beset our path; sometimes we had to crawl between the roots of bushes, then to wade through heath and fern, and among copsewood and briars, which thickened in places until they became barriers to further progress, when we had to give up and seek out a fresh track. Still downwards, over shelving slopes and crumbling boulders that afforded but a treacherous footing, now and then plunging ankle deep in hollows, thick with decayed brown leaves, and concealed from view by the over-hanging vegetation; fresh brakes and thickets, more scrambling, battering, and scratches, another slope or two, and then the bottom of the dale was reached, when we had time to breathe and look around us.

Wearied with our exertions, we sat down on a cushion of moss, to rest and enjoy the solitude and seclusion, listening the while to the joyous hum of the gauze-winged insects, and watching the great white clouds as they floated slowly across the clear blue sky above.

Down in the valley we lose the cheering influence of the brilliant sunshine; but never mind, the cool shade looks more inviting after our toilsome descent, and the pleasant breeze that sweeps through the narrow opening is inexpressibly delightful. The solitude seems complete, the deep silence that prevails being only deepened by the solemn unvarying monotone of the soughing wind. Now and then we catch the dreamy voice of the stock dove, calling softly and sadly from the bosom of the distant woods, and occasionally a solitary curlew is seen hanging like a speck overhead, then wheeling round and round as it utters its peculiar plaintive cry; but the solemn stillness of the scene loses nothing of its force. Here and there we can discern a stray sheep standing upon a knoll or rocky point, gazing at us with a mingled expression of wonder and fear, but no other living creature can we see; all seems an untrodden solitude, and the subdued light, the stony slopes, and the rugged crags, streaked with ivy and roughened with shaggy scrub, give to the place an aspect the impressiveness of which every moment becomes more and more evident to the senses.

Thoroughly refreshed we started forward again, bending our steps down the dale in the direction of Over Haddon. The bottom of the glen for a distance of a hundred yards or so below the point at which we entered is rough and stony, but free from moisture, then it becomes damp and spongy, and a few paces further on a little rindle is seen issuing from an opening high up in the face of the rock, splashing from ledge to ledge as it descends, and trickling through the short thick grass like a line of liquid silver ; another and another succeeds, and then their waters unite in a rippling shallow which disports itself among tufts of grass and weeds, bubbling in limpid rills round mossy stones and shattered fragments of rock, and now and then spreading out in marshy pools, fringed with mallows and yellow loose-strife, and overgrown with cress and green aquatic plants. A few yards lower down a rustic foot-bridge has been thrown across, beyond this the beck widens until it becomes a tolerably rapid stream, forming the source of the Lathkill, a busy sparkling river which gives name to one of the most charming dales anywhere met with in the Peak of Derbyshire, abounding in picturesque scenery, and presenting an assemblage of parts exquisitely beautiful in their forms and combinations.

Crossing the little foot-bridge we took the left side of the river, proceeding along a narrow beaten track that has been formed close upon its brink. The northern side of the dale for some distance has a wild and desolate, almost savage, appearance, the narrow channel being closely hemmed in by a continuous range of precipitous cliffs and naked lifeless-looking steeps of greater or lesser elevation, whose shelving slopes are broken up into innumerable ridges and hollows, thinly sprinkled with copsewood and scrub, with here and there a patch of short, thin, slippery verdure, alternating with acres of screes and broad stony banks pitched as steep as the roof of a house, down which the loose boulders and loosely compacted crags have been shivering for countless ages before the crumbling influences of the winter's frost and

summer's thunderstorm. The higher acclivities are crested
with rugged weather-beaten pinnacles and spiral cliffs, round
which, as we gazed upwards into

> "The summer heaven's delicious blue."

the vapoury mists were coquetting in playful wreaths, whilst
the gleaming rays of the mid-day sun came streaming across,
gilding the rocky ridge with a brilliant radiance that agreeably harmonised with the dark opposing shadows of the
opposite cliffs; each reflecting upon the other a reciprocal
charm and forming a combination at once delightful and
impressive.

The opposite side of the river presents a perfect contrast,
a long chain of noble bluffs rising sheer from the water, and
sweeping round in a continuous and well-defined circle, their
steep sides clothed from base to summit with wood—oak,
elm, ash, and willow—their hoary stems and silver leaves
mingling their various hues with the tangled brakes covered
with maples, hazels, and alders, forming a regular amphitheatre of rock and foliage that extends in lengthened vista,
whilst its bold undulating summit-lines cut sharply against
the brilliant blue.

Pacing slowly onwards through the deep cool shade, where
the pebble stones rattle beneath our feet and the flinty
causeway looks as if it had been stolen from the watery
channel, we follow the devious windings of the river which
now, widened into an ample stream, dances merrily past,
babbling as it goes, and murmuring its admiration of the
scene in a never-ending song of joyousness, now and then
coming out of the shade and going into it again, gladdened
meanwhile by the long bright arrowy rays which shoot down
the ravine, and, stealing one after another through the
intricacy of leaves, be-gem its surface with a thousand sparkling ripples.     Then the current quickens and becomes noisy
in its mazy course ; a little further on and the rocks form a
dam across the channel, over which it precipitates itself in
glistening sheets, boiling and eddying and swirling and
splashing among the rocky fragments beneath, then hurrying
onwards with ungovernable impetuosity, making falls innumerable, and throwing up on its way a long train of snow-

white foam bubbles that gleam and flutter in the passing breeze. Cataract succeeds to cataract, and then follows a long straight reach where the eye ranges further and further into scenes of increasing beauty, until it becomes fascinated by the manifold and ever-varying combinations of rock and wood and water ; anon the angry waves subside, and the river glides onward in a smooth full current, here walled in by steep precipitous rocks, there embowered by trees and bushes, and fringed with ferns and shrubs and flowering plants, every leaf and twig of which are reflected in its limpid waters; now forming deep basins, darkened with the shrouding shadows of the overhanging trees, then spreading out in glistening pools and broad transparent shallows, dimpled over with the fleeting silver rings where the trout rise to catch the aquatic insects that float upon the surface.

Ever the solitude deepens, and the stillness becomes more intense, the birds are hushed in their foliaged homes and even the summer breeze holds its breath, as if afraid to disturb the prevailing quietude. A few sheep quietly browsing on the grassy slopes, and a solitary angler whipping the stream, are the only signs of animation we can see, and the verdant shade seems to become greener and gloomier at every step. Strong contrasts of colour occasionally enrich the effect, the glowing amber-coloured crags and tottering battlements which crown the giddy heights look more bright and golden where opposed to the cool gray rock shadows below, and here and there we have a blending together of red and green and purple in one rich monotone, with masses of rock dappled with every hue, from the warm brown tinge of the clinging lichens to the cold dun-colour of the flitting cloud shadows through which the horizontal lines of strata and the dark yews and glossy hollies look blacker and blacker.

Lower down the path curves freakishly in and out among docks and weeds and marsh plants, then we come to a bend where the river is dammed up and the bright sparkling waters tumble over the stony weir in foaming breadths, roaring and splashing in the descent with loud and angry intonation. It is a spot that would delight the eye of an artist, and many a charming sketch might he carry away with him. Sheltering in a rocky nook close by the margin of the stream is an old-fashioned corn mill, an object that detracts nothing from the sylvan beauty of the scenery; this, with the sedgy mill-race, and the old revolving wheel, dripping with water and nearly overgrown with damp green moss, forms a soft and quiet picture which naturally excites in the mind ideas of rural simplicity and peaceful retirement. On the opposite side of the river a narrow rift in the great wooded cliff gives us a glimpse of the dark shady glen between, and the tiny prattling rill that trickles down from its solitary home amid the hills.

The dale now expands, and the northern bank becoming less abrupt and craggy loses some of its more harsh and rugged features. On leaving the old mill we cross a little green paddock, and then follow an ascending path that leads through a plantation of fir, ash, and beech trees, whose trunks are nearly hidden by the profusion of wild roses and brambles which spread around and reach down almost to the water's edge. The spreading branches meet overhead, forming a canopy of tenderest green, whose umbrageous shade is relieved at intervals by broad masses of bleached and weather-beaten rock. Through the interlacings of the trees we get occasional peeps of the clear blue sky above, and the broad rapid river sweeping along in silent majesty beneath, with the steep precipices and wooded hills that bound the opposite shore.

And so we go on among rocks and trees, along the edge of meadows, over grassy mounds, and through narrow paths that bend hither and thither, under woods, past brakes and thickets and crags and rugged slopes; past scenes savage, romantic, picturesque, and beautiful, where sylvan loveliness and majestic grandeur have been lavished in rich and varied profusion. Then we enter a more open part of the dale, where the rounded hillocks of brown earthy refuse and glistening spar which border the wayside, and the spades and mattocks and other mining tools and implements scattered about, indicate the metalliferous nature of the strata, and attest the character of the operations here pursued.

The mine here was worked for a period of twenty years by Messrs. Alsop, Taylor, and Co., and was then the scene of active industry and profitable labour; it has unfortunately since been overflowed with water, and is now very nearly deserted, the yield of ore, where obtainable, being, it is said, hardly sufficient to repay the cost of working; the great wheel has been removed, and altogether the place presents the appearance of utter neglect and desolation. On the left a narrow opening in the face of the rock marks the entrance or " drift" of the mine, where the subterranean levels have been driven in search of ore; close by is a little hut or shealing in which such lead as can be obtained after it has been washed, pulverised, and separated from the quartz, spar, and other adventitious substances which adhere to it in its natural state, is stored ready for removal to the smelting furnace, and a few yards lower down a line of posts are seen standing in the bed of the stream, which formerly supported the wooden trough or trench that conveyed the water to the overshot wheel.

Gradually the prospect widens, the hills recede, and the impetuous current expands its glassy surface to the smooth turfy banks which separate it from the stony slopes. With increasing breadth, however, we lose the luxurious summer verdance which gave a charm to some of the more confined parts of the dale. The opposite cliffs are mantled with thick foliage, but on the nearer side of the river the cold and naked rock again appears, its gray surface at times relieved with straggling brambles and tufts of golden-blossomed furze, interwoven with foxgloves, and drooping hartstongue, and wreathed and festooned with the delicate stems and glossy leaves of the lovely blue-eyed campanula. Small shrubs and flowers grow out of the fissures high overhead, and trees and bushes hang from the lower ledges, and the bright rays, as they steal through the wind-shaken leaves, brighten the hoary weather-stained rock with streaks of flickering light.

Pleasant is it as with light elastic step we journey on, still keeping the margin of the river, and watching the while its bright clear waters as they flow merrily onwards in the warm sunshine. Every bend reveals a change of scene. Here the stream is rippling and fluttering among the flags and osiers, there it is plunged in shade by the overhanging trees, and anon it is meandering among the gray rocks and mossy stones, which nature's careless hand has strewn along its channel.

Half-a-mile brings us to Sough Mill, a low stone building with a pretty cottage adjoining, and a still prettier flower garden, wherein grow gaudy dahlias and tall tree fuchsias, with quite a wealth of roses, carnations, and verbenas. There are signs of homely comfort and prosperity within and sounds of rural life greet the ear without. Young ducks and poultry are gobbling and pecking about the pavement, and a flock of pigeons are blinking and croodling at us from the edge of the low-flagged roof, while, above the rumbling and din of the crushing "burrs," we can hear the miller's lusty voice singing some old and favourite ditty. A happy man is he, thought sits lightly on his brow, and he looks as jovial and contented as if care and sorrow were alike unknown.

Close by, a quaint and rudely-fashioned bridge happily unites with the natural features of the scene. A long row of square blocks or "lepping" stones, as they are provincially called, have been sunk in the bed of the river, and broad flags laid upon the top, so as to afford an easy communication with the opposite bank. Moss and ferns grow luxuriantly in the water-worn hollows and dripping crannies, and the impetuous Lathkill, interrupted in its progress, divides itself into numberless eddies, as it flows through the narrow openings, and then hurries down the vale fretting and chafing, as if impatient at the temporary obstruction.

From the further side of the bridge a zigzag pathway leads up through a plantation of larch, fir, and scrub, to Meadow Place, formerly a monastery, but now a farm-house. Some remains of the ancient chapel, which had been converted into a barn, existed until within a recent period, when they were pulled down to make room for a more convenient structure. A few of the old carvings were secured by the late Thomas Bateman, Esq., and are now preserved in the museum at Lomberdale House, about a mile distant.

Again the path becomes rough and broken, and, as it leaves the stony shore, it twists in and out over hazel banks, and among damp blocks of limestone and heaps of grass-grown rubbish; then it mounts up to the top of a rocky knoll, where we pause to look back upon the mazy scene through which we have passed, and glorious is the prospect that meets the gaze. Rocks and cliffs, of every shape and form, hem in the upper end of the dale. Here and there a bold headland appears fringed with foliage, whilst tall trees and shrubs and flowery thickets mantle the lower slopes; and now and then a gray old ivy-coated crag is seen rising from amid the thick umbrage. In mid-distance the old mill peeps through the shrouding foliage, gleaming like a great white patch in the warm sunshine. Dark glens and shady hollows break the hilly slopes; and, further on, the eye passes over a succession of rocky ridges that stretch away until they become lost in the distant haze; and through the midst of all the beauteous prospect the half-concealed river is seen winding hither and thither in many a gleaming curve, almost fascinating by the swift motion of its dancing waters as it tumbles from one rocky ledge to another, making falls innumerable, its murmuring song the while resounding through the dale in soft and gentle cadences.

High up, on the north side of the valley, rises a broad, grassy slope, and higher still is seen a cluster of cottages— the little hamlet of Over Haddon peeping above the trees. Pacing slowly onwards, between brushwood and thorns, where the road zigzags, with many a rise and fall among shrubs and crags and turfy hillocks, we come presently to an open valley where the river sweeps boldly towards the south, and the hills, as they fall back, become less elevated, and are succeeded by dark woods and fertile plains, between which the current glides swiftly and silently along, deepening and widening as it flows.

Before us Conksbury Bridge—a low stone structure of four arches, over which the old Ashbourn road is carried—bestrides the stream; a mile lower down its waters unite with those of the river Bradford, and about two miles further on, both become merged in the Wye, at a place called Fillyford Bridge, about midway between Rowsley and Haddon Hall.

At Conksbury Bridge we leave the valley of the Lathkill, and ascend the hillside by a steep and winding road, which is continued over a broad tract of tableland, where the view is limited to green fields and pastures. By-and-by we get glimpses of Rowsley Moor, and the range of hills bordering the course of the Derwent in the direction of Darley Dale, and then, one after another, the embattled towers and turrets of Haddon Hall are seen peering out from amid the dark waving woods. The graceful spire of Bakewell Church rises like a landmark in front; and on the right, Burton Closes, the whitened road, and the busy Wye, serpentining through the meadows below, severally add to the interest of the picture.

The road winds as it leaves the high ground, and, to save an unnecessary detour, we turn off to the right, into a beaten path that leads over two or three enclosed pastures, and across a narrow dingle; thence past the new cemetery, where two pretty Gothic chapels have been erected, and again enter the highway. A rapid descent along a broken and uneven road, shaded by tall trees, brings us to the bottom of the valley, and in a few minutes more we enter the pleasant old town of Bakewell, very nearly at the point whence we quitted it four days before.

# CHAPTER XXI.

OUR stay at Bakewell was necessarily brief, for the day had
got far advanced, and we had determined to explore the valley
of the Wye upwards, and, if possible, reach Buxton before
nightfall ; so after a hasty meal we turned our backs upon
the ancient *Badde cum Wel*, or bathing well of the Saxons,
and resumed our pleasant journeyings.

The atmosphere was glowing with vernal heat, and the
white glaring road became so painful to the eye that we were
glad to turn aside out of the burning rays of the sun and
seek the cool shade of the tall hedges and spreading trees,
where, as we trod the parched and dusty grass, we could look
through the twinkling leaves at the bright green meadows,
and along the lengthened verdure of the fields to the upland
pastures whence came the faint lowing of the kine and the
playful bleatings of the flocks.

The road, as it leaves the town, enters upon an open valley
where some pretty views occur ; the several parts which enter
into the composition being happily disposed. The path keeps
more or less close to the Wye, which winds freakishly in and
out along the vale, its surface mirrowed by a thousand forms
of beauty. On the opposite side Holme Wood mantles the
broad slope with the shadow of its rich summer foliage, half-
hiding the old embattled mansion in a density of luxurious
verdance ; and on the left the rocks rise in rugged crags,

whose beauty is enhanced by a scattered growth of hazels, thorns, and brambles, with ferns, harebells, and flaunting foxgloves in profusion. Here and there the trap or toadstone (Derbyshire basalt) bed reveals itself, its volcanic origin being evidenced by the blighted character of the scant herbage which clings to its charred and scoriated surface. Presently we come to Lumford Mill, a cotton factory that formerly belonged to the Arkwrights, with its two ponderous water wheels dashing the spray from their revolving buckets in glistening showers. Then the road quits the green level and ascends between tree-shaded banks and rudely-constructed stone walls, the limestone blocks of which exhibit everywhere a thick conglomerate of primeval shells, once the habitations of living races, which tell us of the earlier history of our globe, and indicate a time when these high lands were submerged in ocean. The river lies below, meandering pleasantly between thick woods and over moss-clad stones, and now and then spreading out in shallow green-tinged pools that look like sheets of liquid emerald. Every tree that overhangs the path is a bower of vernal beauty, in which the little songsters are chanting their gladsome lays, and the wandering breeze rustles through in sportive wantonness. Through an opening in the elevated ridge opposite we get a glimpse of Longstone Edge and the heathy moors that stretch away in long perspective to join the Yorkshire hills, and the patches of sunshine that gleam upon their purple sides reveal to the eye many a touch of beauty.

Now we lose sight of the valley as we descend between plantations where the tall poplars mingle with the dark firs and spreading ash trees. After passing through the tollgate the prospect again opens, when Ashford Hall, the seat of the Hon. G. H. Cavendish, one of the members for the county, with its green lawns and parterres and well-trimmed paths comes in sight. The hall is a square stone building in the Italian style, crowned with an open balustrade and delightfully situated on a gently-elevated slope, commanding some fine views along the valley of the Wye in the direction of Bakewell and Haddon. In front the ground declines towards the river, which here expands in artificial lakes and reedy shallows where numerous wild-fowl congregate; clumps of trees adorn the banks, and in the water are wooded islands round which as we passed swans were sailing in graceful majesty.

Nearly opposite the hall we cross the Wye by a handsome bridge of four arches, and in a few minutes more enter Ashford.

Ashford, or Ashford-in-the-Water as it is sometimes called, is a quiet old-fashioned country village, which is sure to win the admiration of a stranger, gladdening the eye by its simple rural beauty. There is a comfortable well-to-do appearance about the place, which is heightened by the cleanliness and thrift everywhere manifest; the little cottages have most of them trim flower beds and pebbled paths in front, with patches of yellow stone-crop or green house-leek adorning the roofs, while nearly every door-post and window is bordered with a colouring of brown umber, or enlivened by a coating of white-wash, outward indications that speak much in favour of the domestic virtues of the inhabitants. There is a good inn—the *Devonshire Arms*—in the village, two or three repositories for the sale of marble and spar ornaments, and a few shops, in one of which, where the window is open to admit the welcome breeze, the shoemaker is hammering leisurely away, lifting up his head to look out every time a wayfarer goes by.

The church stands a little way back from the road, near the further end of the village. It is a venerable structure, surrounded by a spacious graveyard planted with yewtrees of many a century's growth, whose fan-like boughs throw a perpetual gloom upon the narrow grass-grown mounds and nodding head-stones of those who are slumbering beneath. There is not much about the building to attract attention, though the crumbling buttresses and time-eaten mouldings are calculated to imbue the stranger with anticipations, and lead him to expect a treasury of interesting memorials within. On the south wall, near the entrance, is a semi-circular slab, on which is rudely sculptured the figure of a wild boar and another animal—a wolf apparently—crouching beneath a tree. This stone has evidently belonged to some more ancient building than that to which it is now affixed; beneath it is a small tablet, on which is inscribed the following text:

z

"The boar out of the wood doth waste it, and the wild beast of the field doth devour it."—Psalm lxxx., 13.

Leaving the village we pass on the left the Rookery, an old-fashioned residence, nearly overgrown with ivy, delightfully situated in a sheltered hollow overlooking the sparkling Wye, where trim lawns and flower beds and tastefully laid out pleasure grounds have taken the place of the wilder charms of untrimmed nature. The gardens are environed by noble timber trees, in which a colony of rooks have established their abode, and in front an ivy-shrouded bridge which spans the river gives access to the plumy woods that mantle the opposite slopes, and adds its charms to the romantic beauties of the scene.

A few yards farther on are the marble works belonging to Messrs. Twigg and Co., one of the oldest establishments of the kind in the kingdom. Here the different kinds of Derbyshire marble are sawn into slabs, polished, and worked into a variety of useful and ornamental articles.

Some of the finest marbles of the country are obtained in the immediate neighbourhood of Ashford; these include the entrochal, the corroloid, the bird-eye, the rosewood, and the black, the latter being procured from an excavated mine in the hill near to the works. Some of these marbles are considered by competent judges to be fully equal in lusture and colouring to those of foreign countries.

For a mile or more the road follows the indented course of the river, which keeps us in pleasant companionship as it winds to and fro among the verdant meadows on the left. Here the character of the scenery changes; steep grassy knolls rise on one side of the dale, gaunt and dreary looking, with scarcely a bush or tree to relieve their general barrenness; and the few black-faced sheep that browse their shelving slopes skip away as we pass by, bleating tremulously, and halting now and then as they turn round to gaze at us with an air of mingled curiosity and fear. On the opposite side the dark-hued woods of Shacklow clothe the broad face of the mountain with a dense umbrage, through which narrow foot-tracks run in and out in a kind of zigzag fashion. Then we come to the new bridge, where some pretty views occur; here the river passes under the road and then continues along its side, sparkling brilliantly as it courses its way beneath the drooping branches of the trees. On the left the rocks rise in rugged masses, their channeled and weather-worn fronts, patched with moss and short grass, and wellnigh hidden with a covering of rowan trees and the tangled bushes of the bramble and wild honeysuckle. In a grassy hollow by the wayside, sheltered by thorns and briar-roses, an old moss-grown trough, fed by a limpid rill that comes trickling down from the ferny heights above, affords a welcome sight to the thirsty wayfarer. Tufts of nettles and broad-leaved batter-docks border the path, and here and there long strips of grass alternate with the rutted wheel tracks; tall trees separate us from the rippling stream, ivy wraps their stems, and their spreading branches reaching overhead afford a welcome shelter from the arrowy rays of the scorching sun. Beneath the shadow of an impending crag a stone-breaker is indus-triously pursuing his monotonous vocation, who wipes the perspiration from his brow, and, looking up, wishes us a kindly good day as we pass on; a few yards further and we have to stand aside while a farmer's cart goes by bearing its fragrant load from a neighbouring hayfield. These, and a variety of objects, equally trivial in themselves, form a suc-cession of roadside pictures, the contemplation of which serves to beguile the time and add to the enjoyment of our excursion.

The country now becomes more boldly featured, and on rounding a sharp bend of the river, Brushfield, a lofty wooded eminence, appears in front, a pretty little farmhouse crowning its highest point. On the right Great Finn rears its giant form to an immense elevation, and through the opening between these two hills we get the first view of the entrance to Monsall Dale.

Here the road and the river diverge from each other, the former winding through a picturesque dale bounded by steep rocks and impending crags, freaked with ivy and richly-coloured lichens, and adorned with a variety of foliage, among which hazels and thorns, and wild roses and trailing honey-suckles, are scattered in thick profusion. The road gradually ascends for a couple of miles, when Taddington is reached—a cold, bleak, stony-looking village, with a fine old Gothic church standing in the midst of a field a short distance back from the way.   Beyond the village the road attains a still higher elevation, and commands a wide extent of country bounded by a vast chain of rugged hills and barren moorlands; thence it is continued along the edge and down the fearfully precipitous side of Topley Pike, on reaching the foot of which it rejoins the Wye and accompanies it three miles further to Buxton.

From Brushfield to Buxton the distance is eight miles.   It is not, however, by keeping to the highways that the natural beauties of the country can be best observed ; thoroughly to be appreciated they must be sought and wooed by earnest worshippers, the valleys and secluded glens must be explored, and the shady rills and mountain streams must be tracked through all their various and wayward meanderings.   Monsall Dale and Miller's Dale claim our attention, and we must therefore lengthen our journey considerably to follow the intricate windings of the charming river Wye.

Bounding over a low stone fence which skirts the road, a beaten track that leads across a green paddock brings us to a narrow rindle that comes tumbling and splashing along its rocky channel.   In a crevice close by a thread of water trickles down the scrubby hillside and falls from ledge to ledge of the mossy headed rocks on to a bed of tufa, which it has worn into quaint arches and fantastic shapes.   The petrifying quality of the water is here manifest in the accumulated mass which is daily receiving a fresh deposit of calcareous matter from the surcharged stream.   Further on we come to the margin of the river, which leaps over the impeding rocks in a succession of beautiful falls.   The upper part of the dell, viewed from this point, reveals many a touch of savage grandeur, whose effect is heightened by the dark shadow of the opposing hill.   At every turn a change of scene occurs, and we are constantly halting as some picture more beautiful than the last breaks upon the sight.

As we advance the path becomes more difficult and the aspect of nature more primitive.   Finn Cop heaves his huge form in majestic sullenness, and looks sternly down upon the mortal who ventures to intrude upon his seclusion ; and further on Hobb's House appears in view.   Dark-wooded slopes and barren crumbling rocks bound both sides of the rapid stream, which rushes below tumbling over the craggy ledges in silvery sheets, gurgling beneath the overarching trees, lurking in shady hollows by our side, and spreading out in silent pools that reflect darkly the rugged forms of the impending cliffs.

Onwards the path freaks in and out through brambles and heather, over miry patches and across rutty hollows worn by the rills that trickle down the mountain sides. Grim crags break through the grassy acclivities on the left, and here and there a few trees and patches of undergrowth impart a sense of shelter to the opposite slopes. Higher up the glen a picturesque cascade appears, where the river, dammed up, breaks over its stony barrier in sheets of glistening foam that look whiter by contrast with the blackness of the riven rocks. Then we reach the railway, which is here carried across the dale by a viaduct of five semicircular arches 70 feet above the river—an engineering work that has aroused the anger of Mr. Ruskin, who, in his "Fors Clavigera," pathetically laments the introduction of a railway into the valley of the Wye. "That valley," he says, "where you might expect to catch sight of Pan Apollo and the Muses is now desecrated in order that a Buxton fool may be able to find himself in Bakewell at the end of twelve minutes, and *vice versâ*," forgetting apparently that the Arcadian god and his associates must long before have been scared from these haunts by the rattle of the Derby coach and the tootling of the guard's bugle. Passing beneath we still keep the margin of the stream, which is crossed by a narrow foot-bridge resting on ledges of rock, and protected by a rude handrail ; here the Wye makes a sudden turn to the left, and the long reach of Monsall Dale appears in all the fulness of its beauty.

This dale, the Arcadia of the Peak, as it has been called, has been panegyrised by nearly every writer who has undertaken to describe the natural beauties of Derbyshire. As a vale view it is eminently picturesque and attractive, pleasing rather than imposing, conveying to the mind an idea more of tranquil loveliness than of rugged grandeur. The deep valley, the little farm, and the few cottages clustering near,

the river serpentining from side to side, the green hills
descending like headlands to the ocean, and the folded bluffs
stretching away to the brown heathy moors that bar up the
distance, have an exceedingly pretty effect, but there is not
that variety of form and outline, that intermingling of rock
and foliage, and that happy blending of parts and colourings
which give a charm to some other of the Derbyshire dales.
Matlock Dale viewed from the top of Stonnis, Darley Dale
from Oker, and Lathkill Dale seen from near Over Haddon
exhibit, we conceive, in a far higher degree those various
features and characteristics, and those exquisite ever-changing
and inexhaustible combinations, which are the true sources of
beauty in landscape scenery.

The best view of Monsall Dale is obtained from the edge of
the cliff near Longstone House, which may be easily reached
by a road that leads up from the farm at the foot, and seen
from this point the appearance is very striking, the effect
being rendered more imposing by the suddenness with which
it comes upon the sight after traversing the bleak summits of
Longstone Edge, a circumstance to which, perhaps more than
anything else, may be attributed that unqualified praise which
tourists have bestowed upon it.

It was from this spot that, now some years ago, we first
beheld the dale ; we had been spending a few days at Bakewell, when our host kindly offered to drive us over and show
us, as he said, "the nicest bit of scenery in all Derbyshire."
Turning off at Ashford we took the higher road, which soon
brought us to the *Bull's Head*, and on rounding the corner of
the house, the sweet vale, tranquilly reposing in the lap of
loveliness, appeared unexpectedly before us, "looking like a
fragment rent from heaven,"

> "A calm and beauteous spot,
> A glorious vale far down beneath the rocks,
> Where peace and bliss might, undisturbed, repose,
> And man forget the names of sin and hate."

Bold grassy acclivites clothed with brushwood and dwarf
foliage, among which a sombre yew now and then displays its
dark form in contrast to the varied greenery of the surrounding verdure, bound both sides of the deep secluded valley,

through which the river winds in many a gleaming curve between bright green meadow breadths, its glassy surface at times broken by stony barriers which divide it into numerous cascades of surpassing loveliness. Sheltering in a deep hollow at the foot of the cliff, where the river makes a sudden bend to the westward, an old-fashioned farm-house is seen, partially overgrown with ivy and screened by a few tall ash trees and spreading oaks; in front the little wooden bridge before alluded to happily unites with the natural features of the scene, and farther on two or three rustic cottages border the stream, close to which a row of " lepping " stones, round whose moss-grown sides the river frets and bubbles in lively eddies, gives access to the opposite bank. Higher up a deep opening in the steep acclivities on the right marks the entrance to Cressbrook Dale, and beyond, the pine-crowned heights overlooking Miller's Dale appear in view. On the left the hills rise and fall in a succession of undulating eminences, their sloping sides velveted with richest turf, and broken here and there with little hollows and coppice-clothed promontories, round which the green-tinged river steals in silent meanders, as if unwilling to disturb the sweet tranquillity which everywhere prevails. Beyond, Priest Cliff, Chelmerton Low, and the moors above Taddington loom darkly against the serene of the heavens ; and in the far distance the huge form of Axe Edge, backed by a multitude of hills that stretch away until you can hardly distinguish their pale summits from the few fleecy clouds that streak the azure above, fill up the horizon. Here and there a line of thin blue smoke ascends from some secluded dwelling, and hangs in lazy wreaths over the tops of the surrounding trees, now and then the willows and the drooping birches rustle plaintively in the wind, and the murmuring of the stream as it ripples over its craggy bed breaks in gentle cadences upon the ear, rendering the stillness still more impressive.

Everything breathes tranquillity and peace, conveying to the mind the idea of sweet repose ; solitary, however, the place is not, for though the dwellings are few and far between, the signs of life are everywhere apparent—in the air, in the water, on the green hillsides, and in every brake and thicket ; the hills echo with the bleatings of the flocks, and the cattle

luxuriating in the coolness of the rippling shallows, call to
each other in cheerful lowings ; the white moths and gaudy-
coloured butterflies flit to and fro in the warm sunshine, and
the river is dimpled over with silvery rings where the trout
rise to catch the incautious flies that sport over its surface ;
the voice of the moor-cock comes loud and clear from the
opposite hill, and the wailing of the white-breasted plover is
heard in the shady dingles, whilst from the bushes overhead
the throstle sends forth his lay in gushing songs of gladness.
The sunlight quivers upon the dancing waters and gleams
upon the mountain slopes, and the clouds, driven athwart
the sky by the passing breeze, map the verdant sward with a
succession of flitting lights and shadows, giving a character
and variety that adds to the manifold beauties of the scene.

The sun veering towards the westward reminded us that
daylight was beginning to decline when we started forward
again.

From the farm-house, a rural lane leads on between hedges
crowned with thorns and holly, interspersed with patches of
gray stone wall ; now and then the sparkling river, from which
the copse only separates us, glints through the openings as
we go by, the nodding trees meet overhead in a verdant
canopy, and the warm rays that steal through the twinkling
leaves look brighter for the medium of shade through which
they have to pass.   A barn and two or three stone cottages
stand with their backs to the road, which is raised a few feet
above the stream ; a quarter of a mile beyond these is Cressbrook Mill, where manufacturing industry has established
itself, and a tower-like factory chimney obtrudes its unpoetic
form upon the romantic beauties of uncultivated nature.

The mill, a plain rough-cast building belonging to Messrs.
M'Connel, who carry on the trade of cotton-spinning and
manufacturing, is most delightfully situated in a capacious
hollow or recess, formed by the natural curvature of the
stream, and sheltered in rear by a lofty eminence, the higher
acclivities of which are clothed with plantations of fir and
other hardy trees, whose sombre shade is relieved by a
number of pretty Swiss-like cottages, that have been built
by the owners of the mill for the use of their workpeople.

On the right a deep glen leads up between impending cliffs

and precipices to Wardlow Miers, through the gloomy solitude of which a noisy brook riots and disports itself, circling and eddying beneath the shadow of the frowning rocks, and now and then leaping up to kiss the straggling brambles that depend from their gray and weather-beaten sides. An abundance of water-cress is nurtured upon the margin and in the channel of the stream, round which the water bubbles in limpid rills, then rattles merrily on over the shining pebbles, murmuring its admiration of the surrounding beauty in a thousand songs of joyousness. Near its confluence with the Wye the stream precipitates itself through a narrow opening in the rocks over rude fragments of limestone, making a very pretty cascade as it descends. On the eastern side, Hay Cop, a lofty eminence which rises from the bottom of the valley, guards the entrance to the dell, the sides of which are mantled over with luxuriant foliage, save where now and then a shattered crag or a fantastic pinnacle overgrown with ivy thrusts out its unwieldy and misshapen form.

From Cressbrook to Litton Mill, a distance of more than a mile, the margin of the stream is but rarely traversed by human footsteps. It is only after a long dry season that this can be accomplished, and then the effort is attended with considerable risk and danger—a narrow shelving ledge of rock, on which the hand of art has never ventured to exercise itself, being the only footing afforded. Here the Wye sweeps along in an impetuous current between impending rocks and perpendicular cliffs, richly diversified with lichens and creeping plants, and adorned with a wonderful variety of trees and shrubs, through whose deep shade the naked surface of the rock occasionally appears.

At Cressbrook, unable to ford the river, we are compelled to leave the bottom of the valley, and follow a toilsome road that leads up the steep side of the hill, passing on the way the gardens and pleasure grounds attached to Mr. M'Connel's residence. At every step the road becomes more abrupt and laborious. With increasing height, however, the horizon expands, and the river, though hidden by the intervening woods, reminds us of its presence by the ceaseless murmur of its rapid waters. From the summit a fine retrospective view of Monsall Dale is obtained. The foreground is well broken up, and the several parts are grouped in a manner highly picturesque; whilst the river, spreading out its mirrored surface as it wreathes itself in frequent windings, carries the eye to remoter scenes of beauty, whose broken outline and undulating surface happily unite with the natural charms of the nearer landscape.

After passing the picturesque group of cottages at the top of the hill we leave the Tideswell road, and turn into a path that leads between plantations of fir and larch, through the openings of which, on the left, we now and then get a glint of the river meandering on far down in the depths of the rocky hollow. Presently we reach the open country again, when a rapid descent down the grassy acclivities of Slack Side brings us to that part of the valley of the Wye which forms the eastern entrance to Miller's Dale.

At the point where the road regains the margin of the river, a few clean-looking cottages are seen sheltering within a rocky hollow, and contiguous to them is Litton Mill, now belonging to Messrs. Moore and Sons, cotton spinners and doublers, but formerly a merino spinning and manufacturing establishment, owned by Mr. Henry Newton, a son of William Newton, the " Peak Minstrel," whose poetic effusions in early life attracted the attention of Anna Seward and the poet Hayley.

This self-taught bard appears to have had a warm admirer in Miss Seward, who inscribed to him a poem which appeared first in the *Gentleman's Magazine,* and was subsequently included in her collected works. In her published correspondence, edited by Sir Walter Scott, his name is also of frequent occurrence, and some of her letters are addressed to him.

Nearly opposite the mill a stone weir has been constructed, and the river, dammed up, expands its glassy surface in shaded mirrors that reflect every leaf and twig, and soften the rugged forms and hoary wrinkles of the ever-gazing cliffs, then sweeps over the stony barrier in one unbroken sheet of water, all fringed with whitened foam.

We have now entered upon the beauties of Miller's Dale, which, as we advance, presents us with a succession of pleasingly diversified scenes—rock and wood, and cliff and slope, occurring with almost endless repetition, everywhere enlivened by the playful meanderings of the charming river Wye.

For a considerable distance the road winds along the margin of the stream, and

> " In this tract,
> How long so e'er the wanderer roves, each step
> Shall wake fresh beauties, each short point present
> A different picture ; new, and yet the same."

The left side of the dale, looking up, displays a long breast of limestone broken into picturesque inequalities, with bold, weather-worn crags and beetling precipices, embellished with scattered and overhanging trees and shrubs, that partially clothe without concealing their broken and shattered ruggedness. The near side of the dale, though not so picturesque in appearance, has much to interest the geologist and the student of nature. The characteristics of the limestone formation are here strongly exemplified, and in the upheaved and riven masses we have an illustration of that powerful agency which has disrupted the inner strata of the globe, producing that diversity of form and aspect we now see, and bringing to light that hidden mineral wealth so essential to the health, the happiness, and the wellbeing, and so needful for the numerous wants of man. The rocks, though boldly featured and of considerable elevation, have hardly a tree or shrub to adorn their rugged sides, and relieve their generally cold and lifeless appearance. Here and there their barren fronts are tinged with brown and gray, and in some places the softer beds, exposed to the decaying action of the atmosphere, are crumbling away and undermining the superincumbent strata, fragments of which have become detached, and now lie strewn around the base in chaotic heaps, while occasionally a huge block hangs impending over the path, as if caught in the act of falling from above.

Near Litton Mill, a road branches off on the right which leads through an opening in the hills to Tideswell, an ancient market town a mile and a half distant, that derives its name from an ebbing and flowing well that is said to have formerly existed in the locality. The chief object of interest is the church, which, from its size and architectural beauty, has been styled the "Cathedral of the Peak." It is a handsome cruciform structure erected about the middle of the fourteenth century, with windows rich with the richest tracery

TIDESWELL CHURCH.

of the late decorated period of Gothic architecture. The plan includes a nave with side aisles, north and south transepts, chancel, and a lofty tower at the west end, surmounted by four embattled turrets, somewhat heavy in design, each terminating in an octagonal pinnacle, enriched with crocket-work. The building, which has been long neglected, has lately been restored at considerable cost, the windows have been filled with stained glass, and the chancel has been fitted with elaborately-carved oak stalls, the gift of a native of the town—the late Mr. John Harrop of Manchester. The interior, which is well deserving of attention, contains some ancient and interesting tombs and monumental brasses. Among them are the tombs of Lord Lytton's progenitors, the name being derived from the neighbouring village of Litton, with which Lord Lytton's more remote ancestors were connected. There is also one to the memory of John, son of Thomas Foljambe, who in 1358 was a liberal contributor to the foundation. In the chancel, which is lighted by nine richly-ornamented Gothic windows, there is a raised tomb commemorating the decease, in 1462, of Samson Meverell, who received the honour of knighthood from John Duke of Bedford, for military services in France ; the sides are open, and show the carved effigy of an embalmed corpse lying on a winding-sheet. There is also a monument to the memory of Robert Pursglove, Mary's Suffragan Bishop of Hull, who in the reign of Queen Elizabeth founded the Grammar School, which stands on the north side of the churchyard, and endowed the almshouse for twelve poor people. On a black marble slab there is an effigy of the reverend prelate in his pontifical robes, accompanied by a long and tedious inscription in verse.

At Tideswell was born William Bugshaw, more popularly known as "The Apostle of the Peak," and the author of "De Spiritualibus Pecci; or, Notes About God's Work in the High Peak," who on that unhappy St. Bartholomew's Day in 1662 withdrew from the vicarage of Glossop, and became minister of a congregation of Nonconformists at Great Hucklow, in Hope parish, where he died in 1702.

The town of Tideswell, which has a cold, cheerless, and uninviting aspect, is situated in a hollow surrounded by bleak and barren hills ; a clear rivulet flows along the principal thoroughfare, on each side of which are scattered promiscuously the poor, mean-looking dwellings of the inhabitants, who are employed chiefly in mining and hand-loom weaving.

Close by the church is the *George*, a good inn and posting house, and hard by is the vicarage, a remnant of former days.

At Wheston, a little hamlet adjoining the town, there is an ancient cross of rather elegant design, the lone memorial of days gone by, that merits inspection.

Retracing our steps we soon regain the banks of the Wye and continue our onward journey, for evening creeps on, and a long seven miles yet intervene between us and Buxton.

Near where the road to Tideswell leads off, a rudely-fashioned bridge, formed of the boles of a tree, with the branches laid across and grass sods upon the top, has been thrown from side to side of the river; and high up on the opposite steeps, where the lazy cloud-shadows are coquetting and playing upon the jutting crags, the railway again comes into sight. Steep embankments and great mounds of rubbish and broken rock cover acres and acres of the green hillside, spreading away into the woods and thickets, and bearing down in their descent the thorns and bushes that struggle for existence on the more exposed crags. On the right a huge beetling cliff thrusts its misshapen form far out into the pathway, dense masses of shells of endless variety and form are embedded in the marble rock—the work of myriads of marine creatures—presenting to the eye a whole history of birth, and growth, and propagation, and death.

Winding round the base of the cliff, Raven Tor, an immense limestone rock appears in front, naked except towards the top, where a few hazel bushes and dwarf trees shoot out from the clefts and fissures, adorning its precipitous sides with picturesque beauty. Here the dale expands, and in a deep hollow a curiously stratified rock occurs, at the foot of which yawns a gloomy cavern that nature has scooped out in one of her convulsive throes. At every step the signs of volcanic action are manifest in the superposition and conformation of the strata, and along the base of the limestone ridge the out-cropping toadstone exhibits its dark brown hue, attesting its igneous origin by its scoriaceous and lava-like appearance.

The country now improves in appearance, and every step leads us further and further into scenes of increasing beauty,

and the wonderful combinations of crag and woodland give
to all a charm which almost fascinates by its constantly varying character, while the background that fills in the far-off
vista, softened and blended by the mellowing effects of
atmosphere, shows how that in more senses than one " distance lends enchantment to the view." Priest Cliff rears its
giant back, looking black and cold in the sombre shade, but
the precipitous cliffs which wall in the near side of the dale
are bathed in a flood of golden sunshine, that discloses
every rent and crevice, and brings out with marvellous effect
the beautiful changes of tints and the variegated colourings
of the vegetation which clothes their rugged steeps. The
stillness that prevails is only deepened by the gentle rippling
of the stream which flashes and glitters in the leafy hollow,
lingering in quiet bends and spreading out in deep green
pools, and anon dancing merrily along the transparent shallows, where the rocky fragments and shining pebbles are
distorted by the changing refraction of the eddies. Higher
up the river divides itself into numerous rills, whose dimpled
waters give life and motion to an infinite variety of aquatic
plants and flowers, and as it flows on it now and then breaks
over the moss-grown crags that have been toppled down from
the wood-crowned heights. Onwards the path leads beneath
a thick shade of oak and ash and hazel, and under jutting
crags whose deformities are concealed by a luxuriant covering
of copse and brushwood; while to heighten the charm a
little rill comes trickling down the hillside, and passing
beneath the pathway adds its tribute to the pellucid waters
of the Wye. High up on the right a solitary cottage, which
nature has taken a fancy to adorn, looks down upon the
beauteous scene, and a few yards further on we come to a
little public-house, significantly named the *Anglers' Rest*,
where we refreshed on oatcake and cheese, the only fare the
humble larder could afford.

A short distance beyond the public-house is Tideswell
corn-mill, an old-fashioned whitewashed building, with two
or three cottages standing near, the whole forming an exceedingly picturesque grouping. Here the path is joined by a
road that comes down from the town of Tideswell, passing
through some interesting scenery, and close by is the station

for Miller's Dale, contiguous to which are some extensive
limestone quarries.

Near the entrance to Monk's Dale the railway is carried
across the river, and a few yards beyond the viaduct is the
tollgate, standing close to the bridge where the road turns to
the left, and leads up by Sandy Dale to Taddington, and
thence to Buxton. Peterson Pike shuts in one side of this
road, and Diamond Hill bounds the other, in which latter
the mineralogist will find something to interest him in the
quartz crystals, or Buxton diamonds, as they are locally
termed, that are found congregating in clusters among the
loose and perishing toadstone.

Bent upon still further exploring the freakish meanderings
of the Wye, we leave once more the beaten path and plunge
into the deep shade of a plantation that clothes the northern
bank of the river.

An old weather-worn notice board, affixed to the stump of
a tree, conveys a warning to trespassers ; sight-seeing, however, and not poaching, is our object ; and as, moreover, the
caution applies only to those who are caught in the act, we
pass the silent monitor by unheeded.

The river, here pent up within narrow bounds, is so completely hemmed in by woods that it is only when close upon
the brink that an intruder can be seen, and as no unfriendly
voice summons us to return, we keep on through the leafy
labyrinth, winding hither and thither through the green shade
between copse and brushwood, and in and out, with many a
rise and fall among rocks and trees. Manifold difficulties
beset our path, crag and scrub, bramble and thicket, alternate
in quick succession, and the spreading branches meet overhead
in a dense tangle, through which, now and then, a long spear-
like ray from the declining sun steals down into the vernal
shade, here throwing out a white willow stem like a gleam of
silver, and there brightening a hoary trunk with brilliant
touches, lighting up the while the rustling leaves until their
glowing golden green renders but more sombre looking the
dark masses that remain enveloped in shade. Onwards we
go, picking our way between rocky fragments and clumps of
brushwood, striding over moss and fern, and pushing through
the undergrowth, where the prickly briars thicken into

barriers. Now and then we come to level patches that afford us breathing time, and through the openings we can see the river surging onwards, its surface broken into a rich chequer-work of woodland shadows, that alternate with the snowy sheets of glistening foam. Now we are plunging into pits and hollows concealed by rank vegetation, and anon scrambling over the loose stony shingle ; then we come to a coarse swampy bottom where we have to step from one rushy clump to another, with the risk of leaping short and plunging ankle deep in the soft spongy turf.

As we passed through the plantation a rough brown-coloured lurcher dog crossed our path, and made direct for the cover above, snuffing the ground as he went, then threading in and out among the matted undergrowth : presently a low whistle was heard, and directly afterwards we came up with a suspicious-looking fellow, evidently bent upon some nefarious act ; on seeing us approach, he eyed us over with a scrutinising glance, and apprehensive perhaps that we might communicate our suspicions, he summoned the sagacious but dishonest brute to a seemingly more reputable occupation.

Emerging from the green shade of the wood we come upon a more open part of the dale, where the railway crosses by a viaduct of three arches, passing beneath which we continue along a narrow track that has been scooped out of the side of the rock, laying bare the dark and blighted-looking toadstone. The rocks above are deeply fissured, yet so adorned with roses and honeysuckles, and so festooned with ivy and ferns and creeping plants, that every deformity is softened or concealed from view.

Further on the defile widens and the hills fall back, leaving a margin of coltsfoot and dock leaves, and green meadow breadths that creep up towards the rocky heights. The grassy slopes on the right are covered with plantations of fir, and on the opposite side the precipitous steeps are crowned with hoary crags and pinnacles that rise starkly from the clumps of furze and peer out from the intertwining boughs of the oak and mountain ash. In the distance a massive ivy-coated turret, like the tower of a ruined castle, shoots above the mantling foliage, and on coming nearer, we find it to be an isolated limestone crag, from which the soft and perishable beds have fallen away, leaving it solitary and alone.

A few paces higher up a rude wooden bridge crosses the river, and passing this we come to a sunny glade, where the red short-horns are grazing or reclining upon the green turf, chewing their cud with the most staid and sober gravity. Here and there the naked rock crops out, and huge fragments that have rolled down from above bestrew the path. Then we come to a picturesque dell, which leads off on the right; had we time we might follow it on to Wormhill, a secluded village hard by, with an ancient church overshadowed by sombre yews, and a parsonage the very picture of quietude and repose. Tradition says the place was originally called Wolfhill, from the number of those animals that harboured in the surrounding woods; be that as it may, we know that in early times it was held by a family of the name of Wolfhunt, by the service of chasing and taking all the wolves that should come into the King's forest of the High Peak. Where the dell leads off a noisy brook rushes down from the hills with angry force, leaping over the rocky ledges and mossy stones, then spreading itself out into innumerable rills as it nears the Wye, where its waters are wellnigh hidden by the rich water-cresses, and the numberless aquatic plants that spread their slender stems upon its surface.

After crossing the stream the character of the scenery changes, and we have a transition from one species of beauty to another—romantic loveliness being succeeded by majestic grandeur. The dale suddenly contracts, vast limestone cliffs, rugged and uneven, tower up to a considerable height, and the river, pent up within its narrow bounds, rushes onwards with noisy tumult. Creeping round a jutting promontory, the first grand burst of the sequestered dell in which the sublime Chee Tor is situated is obtained—a scene far excelling in stupendous beauty anything that is met with along the entire course of the Wye, and for magnificence having scarcely its equal within the limits of the Peak.

Here the impending rocks refuse to yield

> "Along their rugged base,
> A flinty footpath's niggard space,"

and we have to leave the brink of the stream and clamber up the stony ledges of the long crescent-like cliffs, from near the top of which a steep and perilous path leads through the brushwood, and continues along the very edge of the precipice which overhangs the river. The path, or sheep track, for it is nothing more, is covered with a thin slippery verdure. Over this we must pass or give up, conscious the while that one false step must inevitably precipitate us headlong into the waters of the Wye three hundred feet beneath.

Viewed from this eminence the gulf below is truly magnificent, and the scene above is scarcely less impressive. A deep semicircular chasm yawns at our feet, at the bottom of which a foaming stream makes a circuitous bend, and, as it hurries along its stony channel, dashes with impetuous rage over the rocky fragments that have toppled down from the impending heights, while, in front, the mighty Tor is seen rising in solemn grandeur from the water's edge, and lifting its hoary head in awe and majesty to a height of upwards of three hundred feet, exhibiting all its huge breadth of outline and the magnificent curvature of its bold convex form. The perpendicular front of the Tor, from its base almost to its summit, is naked, presenting to the eye a great grim lifeless-looking surface of limestone rock, sparingly tinted with lichens and mosses, and adorned with a few ferns and hardy plants that have attached themselves to the clefts and ledges. Near the top the face is indented with numerous rents and fissures, and the summit is fringed with a variety of shrubs and trees, thickly tenanted by a loquacious fraternity of rooks and daws, who here build their nests and rear their young, inaccessible to the foot of plunder, and secure from the hand of violence.

It is impossible to contemplate this magnificent example of rock scenery, sublime as it is in every aspect, without feeling the force of Milton's well-known lines—

> "These are Thy glorious works, Parent of Good,
> Almighty ; Thine this universal frame,
> How wondrous thus."

---

> "Tor ! pale and huge, with breast that time has braved,
> With verdurous mantle crown'd and feet stream-laved,

> Thou standest in thy greatness, solemn stone !
> Kingly—not solitary, yet alone.
> At mortals and their periods thou dost mock—
> Oh for a history of thine own times, Rock !
> For thou art of a world that knew not man,
> Creation of a time, ere time began.
> I deem thou wast a denizen of that sea
> The Spirit moved on, in whose depth of gloom
> Thou grewest into marble."

The rock on which we stand makes a crescent-like sweep answerable to the semicircular front of the Tor, from which, by its corresponding form and stratification, it would seem to have been riven by some mighty effort of nature—

> " Amid the wreck of matter, and the crash of worlds."

It attains to pretty nearly the same elevation, but presents a greater diversity of aspect, the upper surface being divided by narrow horizontal ledges or terraces, where the softer strata has been worn away by the action of the weather. These ledges are clothed with a profuse vegetation, and fringed with mountain ash, wych-elm, and birch trees, which in many places bend their graceful foliage over the abyss, and reflect their closely-entwined branches in the water far beneath, producing a mass of shadow, deep, broad, and sombre.

The vale of rocks, with its high impending cliffs, its rocky rampart, its tottering battlements, and its various combinations of crag and foliage, presents a scene of wild magnificence and grandeur, the effect of which is increased by the dark water rushing with foaming impetuosity through the leafy chasm beneath. Yet, withal, there is an undefinable, an almost secret beauty, whose inexpressible charm haunts the visitor, who looks upon it for long, and fills him with sensations of wonder and delight ; as we gaze upon it we almost wish that the impression might be so indelibly fixed upon the mind's eye as that it would continue there for ever.

The stupendous beauty of Chee Dale was heightened in effect by the circumstances under which we viewed it. As we gazed upon the scene, evening was fast approaching, and a delicate haze, which brightened into a rich amber colour, overspread the empurpled hills and waving woods. The foreground where we stood, the deep valley and the solemn Tor, were veiled in sombre shadow, but all above was gleaming with light; and the declining sun, as he sank gradually in the western heavens, shed a soft radiance upon the landscape, and tipped with golden hue the higher cliffs and the fringe of foliage that hung upon their summits, displaying an illumination which no pencil or pen could imitate or describe.

The less venturesome tourist will find a path which leads from this point over the top of the hill, and thence past a farm-house into Great Rock's Dale, where he may regain the valley of the Wye at the lepping stones opposite Blackwell Mill, about a mile above Chee Tor. We preferred, however, following the more hazardous track which commands the picturesque windings of the river as it flows through Chee Dale, and, resuming our walk, crept cautiously along, not without some unpleasant misgivings, it must be confessed, through the thick underwood that clothes the narrow ledge of rock.

Half-a-mile brings us to the bend of the river, where the cliffs on both sides have been tunnelled for the railway, which here crosses the dale by a short but lofty viaduct. A little further on another turn occurs, where the line again emerges into open day and recrosses the river.

Scrambling down the flinty embankment we pass over a narrow foot-bridge to the opposite bank, then enter the long ravine called Blackwell Dale, where the vegetation thins off, and the country at every step assumes a more barren and open character. The defile gradually widens, and the hills, as they retire, swell up on both sides in lofty green slopes, crags shoot through the turf, and occasionally the grassy ridges are streaked with gorse and scrub, and relieved with patches of plantation. Many picturesque passages occur, but there is not that majestic grandeur in the scenery which gives so great a charm to the more confined recesses of Chee Dale. There is much, however, to delight the eye in the multitudinous variety of plants and flowers that are found growing by the river's brink and clustering about the craggy steeps—delights which, though unknown to the mere superficial observer, are yet fully comprehended by the true lover of nature; for in the long palm-like ferns, in the tremulous bright water-cresses, in the meadow crane's-bill with its azure flowers, in the lovely meadow-sweet, in the little campanula, in the tufts of rushes, in the intricate tangles of waving sedge, aye, even in the meanest plant that hides itself beneath the serried grasses, there is much that is beautiful, interesting, and suggestive of thought ; there are incalculable gradations of colour, beautiful and delicately-shaded as the rainbow, and forms varied and intricate, yet so harmonious and so perfect in their order as to seem by their unerring symmetry a miracle to our view. As we look upon these living things we see manifested the presence of the Creator in His works, and our dead hearts quicken and throb with the living power of His will.

Presently we come to Blackwell Mill, in front of which a long row of " leppings " forms a sort of causeway across the stream, communicating with a pathway that leads up through a wild and barren-looking mountain glen, called Great Rock's Dale, along the side of which the Midland Company have lately carried their extension line.

Hence the country becomes more pleasingly diversified, the hills that hem in the valley are boldly featured, and woods and plantations appear in greater profusion, while the sparkling river adds a beauty to the whole by its ever-varying character. On the left Topley Pike lifts its huge form to an immense elevation, its steep front clothed almost to the summit with dark firs and a matted undergrowth of brushwood and brambles.

Down the precipitous and seemingly inaccessible sides of this stupendous cliff the Buxton road has been carried. As we looked up a carriage passed on, but so diminutive did it appear that it was with difficulty the eye could follow it along the fearful and giddy heights.

From Blackwell Mill a footpath leads through a plantation that borders the side of the river, and leaves it again at the foot of Topley Pike, where it joins the highroad.

Darkness creeps upon us.

> "Now twilight slowly o'er the landscape steals,
> And solemn gloom each fading shape conceals."

The blue arch of heaven, from the zenith to the horizon, is cloudless, and the air is strangely clear, without a sign of rising mist or vapour. A gloomy shadow overspreads the dale, in which the various colourings of the woods and rocks blend in one deep monotone of sombre gray, and the grim cliffs and riven crags stand out blacker and blacker every moment against the western sky. A calm stillness prevails, which is broken only by the rippling river and the moaning of the night wind as it plays gently among the whispering leaves; a soothing influence is spread around, and pure and holy thoughts seem to descend with the falling dew.

From the foot of Topley Pike our route lies close by the side of the Wye, which, with the road and the railway, occupies the entire space between the rocky barriers that hem in both sides of the dale. Instead of cold bleak hills we have now steep, precipitous limestone cliffs, split and broken into romantic masses, the loftier crags, partly naked, channeled, and weatherworn; and partly embellished with a rich embroidery of lichens, moss, and ivy, and the lower acclivities clothed with tangled underwood, from which grow up spreading ashes, oaks, and withies, whose intermingling branches afford shelter for myriads of rooks and daws. Tall trees spread out their leafy boles, and half conceal the shallow stream, in the dark rippling waters of which their pendant branches at times actually droop. The steep and noble eminences swelling above the mantling woods, and the turreted crags rising starkly from out the straggling copse, seen through the dun obscurity, assume various shadowy and uncouth shapes, and the broken arches of the little ruined bridge that leads to Cowlow strangely accords with the weird-like character of the scene, the effect of which is in naught diminished by the rushing of the river over its rugged bed in the black profound beyond.

A narrow road leads up the steep side of the hill, on the left, to the pretty hamlet of King Sterndale, and a few paces beyond a bank of tufa is seen, an immense aggregation of vegetable matter that has been hardened into stone by the petrifying quality of the water which issues from an opening high up in the face of the rock, and precipitates itself down the steep slope, leaping and splashing from ledge to ledge like a beam of silvery light. Further on, on the right, Pig Tor, a savage looking headland, nearly isolated from the parent cliff, thrusts its misshapen form far out into the dale, and on rounding the sharp angle of the naked rock we enter upon the romantic beauties of Ashwood Dale. A light twinkles through the gloom, and on coming up we find it to issue from the casement of the pretty little ivy-shrouded tollhouse, which half hides itself beneath the impending heights at the point where the railway crosses the road by a lofty viaduct.

The rising moon, now slowly sailing into sight sheds a soft mild lustre upon the scene, through which can faintly be discerned the rugged steeps and the shadowy forms of the half-concealed cliffs. As she rides in the blue expanse her brilliance floods the landscape with a silvery radiance, beneath which the rocky precipices are softened into beauty, and everything seems to experience the chastening influence of her sweet enchanting smile. The nearer eminences upon the left are wrapped in darkness by the thick woods which root themselves down almost to the edge of the roadway, and across the dale the vast masses of rock rise in gloomy majesty, their dark recesses contrasting with the bright effulgence that rests upon their exalted summits. In all there is an inexpressible charm, an undefinable and almost secret beauty, amid which the mere sensation of existence seems a glorious luxury.

Dale End Mill is passed, and a little further on we come to a roadside public-house—the *Devonshire Arms*—where a group of labourers are lounging about the doorway, some engaged in friendly chat, while others are lying by the side of the way in a state of divided allegiance between Bacchus and Morpheus. Then the defile narrows, leaving barely sufficient room for the river and the road, and the rocky rampart that forms the boundary is nearly hidden by luxuriant masses of foliage that flourish along its base, above which a dark-leaved holly or a sombre yew is now and then seen peering out from the clefts in the topmost heights.

Presently we come to the Lover's Leap, a finely-formed rock that rises abruptly from the road, crested upon the summit with firs and other hardy trees. On the left a narrow rift in the limestone forms the entrance to Sherbrook Dell, a quiet secluded glen, whose romantic beauty lures you to explore its inner recesses. On entering the narrow gorge the pathway bends, and the spectator finds himself shut in by precipitous rocks, the harsh and rugged forms of which are softened by the profusion of rose-bushes and shrubs, and by the variety of plants and flowers that grow out from the interstices of the crags, and peep from every rent and crevice. Near the further end of the dell a rapid streamlet makes a fall of several feet, rebounding from a projecting ledge in masses of swirling foam, then plunging into a deep hollow, whence it escapes fretting and chafing over the rude fragments of shattered rock, and stealing through the broadleaved docks and water plants that grow in wild luxuriance by the side, and in every dripping nook and cranny.

In this secluded spot many rare and interesting plants and ferns are found growing in their wild state, and the zealous botanical tourist may find pleasing excitement and gratification in adding to his collection from the various mosses and lichens adhering to the moist and slippery rocks, and which always thrive and flourish most in places where dampness prevails and the sun but seldom or never penetrates.

A few paces beyond the Lover's Leap a road called the Duke's Drive ascends abruptly on the left, and leads along the summit of the rocks, whence it is continued by the edge of Stadon Moor to the old Ashbourn road, which it joins near Cote Heath, about half-a-mile from Upper Buxton. Further on the dale loses some of its more romantic features, then we come to a handsome stone bridge spanning the Wye, close to which a road branches off on the right, and leads up to the pleasant village of Fairfield. Crossing the river we turn to the left, and a few minutes later enter the town of Buxton to receive a cheering welcome from kind and hospitable friends who claim us for their own during our brief sojourn in the most fashionable of the northern Spas.

VIEW OF BUXTON.

# CHAPTER XXII.

BUXTON, which ranks as one of the pleasantest and most
fashionable of our English health resorts, also claims to be
one of the oldest Spas in the kingdom ; the thermal springs,
to which mainly it owes its prosperity, having been in repute
from a very remote period.

The lower part of the town—the most fashionable quarter—
occupies a sheltered position on the banks of the little river
Wye, near its source and at the extreme edge of the mountain-
limestone formation. The valley in which it is situated has
an elevation of one thousand feet above the level of the sea,
and is screened from the cold winds of the north, north-east,
and north-west, by an irregular circle of undulating eminences
clothed with wood and copse and moorland heath, which
rise occasionally in bold and swelling hills to an altitude of
upwards of two thousand feet.

That the medicinal property of its waters was, as some
have imagined, known to those wild Celtic tribes who first
inhabited these islands seems hardly likely, though it is
evident, from various concurrent testimony, that during the
period of Roman occupation, Buxton was a place of considerable note, and it is therefore more than probable that we owe
to the enterprising and more polished subjects of the Cæsars
the discovery of these tepid mineral springs.

After the departure of the Roman legions from Britain,

and during the periods of internal anarchy and discord, of Saxon conquest and Danish spoliation, the Baths of Buxton would appear to have fallen into neglect, if they were not entirely deserted. Though the monkish historians are silent upon the subject it is evident that during the Middle Ages their ancient fame had revived, and in the fifteenth and sixteenth centuries the reputation of their curative efficacy had again brought the waters into great repute; the Chapel of St. Ann, the tutelary saint, being at that time hung round with the crutches of those who had experienced the healing influence of the thermal springs.

The earnest zeal for the demolition of graven images, relics, and "other monuments of idolatry, superstition, and hypocrisy," which characterised the earlier period of the Reformation, caused these interesting memorials to be destroyed, and the baths themselves to be closed for a time.

The arbitrary decree was, however, soon annulled, and the fame of the Buxton waters extending, the Earl of Shrewsbury, early in the reign of Queen Elizabeth, erected a convenient house, called the Hall, for the reception of visitants, on the site of the present building of the same name; the accommodation of the place at that time being inadequate to the requirements of the numbers of people resorting thither for relief.

By the erection of this building the Earl may be said to have laid the foundation of Buxton's future prosperity, for notwithstanding the difficult and almost inaccessible nature of the roads, and the then wild, dreary, and uninviting aspect of the surrounding country, the increased accommodation caused the town to be much more resorted to than before, and shortly afterwards it was honoured with the presence of a succession of distinguished visitors.

In 1573 Mary Queen of Scots, who was then a prisoner in the charge of the Earl of Shrewsbury, and suffering from "chronic rheumatism, and neuralgic pain and indurated liver," repaired to Buxton for the benefit of the waters, accompanied by the Earl and his Countess, the celebrated "Bess of Hardwicke." The ill-fated Queen appears to have found great relief from her visit, which was repeated in 1576, in 1580, and again in 1582, the beneficial effects she experienced thereby being testified in the following passage quoted in Miss Sinclair's "Lives of the Queens of Scotland:" "It is incredible how it (the water) has relaxed the tension of the nerves and relieved my body of the dropsical humours with which, in consequence of my debility, it had been discharged." Buxton was the only place in England that made a favourable impression upon Mary, or to which she may be said to have become in any degree attached. On the occasion of her last visit she wrote upon a pane of glass in the window of her room the following kindly farewell, adopting, with slight variation, Cæsar's verses upon Feltria :—

> " Buxtona, quæ calidæ celebrabere nomine lymphæ,
> Forte mihi posthac non adeunda, vale !"

> " Buxton, whose fame thy milk-warm waters tell,
> Whom I, perhaps, no more shall see, farewell !"*

The relief afforded to Queen Mary enhanced the fame of the Buxton waters ; Lord Burleigh, Elizabeth's prime minister, resorted thither on several occasions between the years 1572 and 1580; the Earl of Sussex, Lord Chamberlain, was also a visitor about the same time, and in Lodge's " Illustrations " it is recorded that in 1596 Queen Elizabeth so ordered her progress that she might remain twenty-one days within sufficient distance of Buxton, for her favourite, the Earl of Leicester, to have water brought to him daily, the physicians having resolved that wheresoever the Earl of Leicester was, "he must drynke and use Buxton's water twenty days together."

To restrain the itinerant migrations of the poor, and for the more effectual suppression of vagrancy, a legislative enactment was passed in 39th Elizabeth (1597), which is interesting so far as it furnishes an illustration of the state of society at

---

* Quaint old Fuller gives a slightly different version of the " distick made and written by her own hand on a pane of glass at Buxton Well : —

> ' Buxtona, quæ calidæ celebraris nomine lymphæ,
> Forte mihi posthac non adeunda, vale !'

> Buxton, who dost with waters warm excel,
> By me, perchance, never more seen, farewell !"

" So it is," he says, " in the glass I had in my hand, though," he adds, " it be celebrabere in Camden's Britannia."

that time, and the estimation in which the Buxton waters were then held. By a clause in the Act it is provided "that none resorting to Bath or Buxton Wells should beg, but should have relief from their parishes, and a pass under the hands of two Justices of the Peace, fixing the time of their return, nor were they to beg there under pain of incurring the penalties of the Act."

The reign of Elizabeth forms the most interesting period in the annals of Buxton, and for nearly a century afterwards there is little or nothing of local history worth recording. During this time, however, the town progressively increased in importance, and in 1670 William, third Earl of Devonshire, who inherited the Buxton estates by descent from Elizabeth, Countess of Shrewsbury, pulled down the old hall and erected a larger and more commodious edifice upon its site. This building, which has been altered and enlarged from time to time as the number of visitors had increased, still exists; it now forms one of the principal houses of entertainment, and bears the name of the *Old Hall Hotel.*

Macaulay, in his "History of England," adverting to the rise of various watering-places in the kingdom, thus speaks of Buxton, quoting as his authority a "Tour in Derbyshire," by Thomas Browne, son of Sir Thomas : "England, however, was not, in the seventeenth century, destitute of watering-places. The gentry of Derbyshire and of the neighbouring counties repaired to Buxton, where they were crowded into low wooden sheds, and regaled with oatcake, and with a viand which the hosts call mutton, but which the guests strongly suspected to be dog." This description can hardly be accepted as a correct one, for, as we have already shown, Buxton possessed, long prior to this period, a house of entertainment capable of supplying its guests with every comfort and convenience that the age could command.

The country around Buxton was at this time, and for many years afterwards, in a condition anything but satisfactory or favourable to the progress of the place. The difficulties of the Derbyshire roads were proverbial, and those in the mountain districts of the Peak were wretched in the extreme, so that travelling from remote distances must have been hazardous as well as tedious, and we can therefore only look upon it as an additional proof of the efficacy of the waters in relieving and curing disease, that they were held in such high esteem, and so much resorted to, ere the well-paved roads, the pleasure grounds, and other accessories, which now add so much to the attraction of Buxton, had been called into existence.

As Buxton continued to increase, the means of accommodation became too small for the number of visitors who resorted thither, both for health and pleasure ; and in 1780 the fifth Duke of Devonshire commenced the erection of that magnificent pile of building—the Crescent—the pride and boast of the town.

This structure, which was erected from the designs and under the superintendence of Mr. John Carr, an architect of high reputation in his day, is, for elegance and simplicity of design, unsurpassed by any building of a similar character in the kingdom. The site chosen, however, is an unfortunate one for giving due effect to the architectural beauty and proportions of the building. Being situated in a hollow, with a sloping mound immediately in front, it can only be seen from the cliff, or from the circumscribed area in front. In the former case, "a bird's eye" view is obtained, which is seldom or never favourable for architectural display; and in the latter, the spectator is thrown so close upon the building that the lines assume a distorted appearance, and the parts seem out of proportion, consequently it fails to convey that idea of grandeur and magnificence it might have done if more favourably situated. This circumstance is the more to be regretted when it is remembered that, to make room for the building, the Wye had to be arched over for a considerable distance, and the fine avenue of trees that extended to the New Gardens ruthlessly cut down ; whilst had it been erected only a few yards further back, on the elevated slope near the church, a far more noble and imposing effect would have been the result.

The plan, as the name indicates, is in form that of the segment of a circle, with a wing flanking each extremity of the arc. The diameter of the inner line of radius is 200 feet clear, and the length of each wing 58 feet 3 inches, making the entire frontage 316 feet 6 inches. The basement is raised

2 feet 6 inches above the ground line, and on this is a covered
arcade of rusticated character 7 feet wide, in which are the
entrances to St. Ann's and the Crescent Hotels, the Assembly
Rooms, and some other establishments.    Immediately over
the arcade an ornamental balustrade is carried along the
front, and returned at each end of the fabric.    The spaces
between the windows of the two upper stories are occupied
by fluted Doric pilasters, 26 feet in height, which give support
to an elaborate architrave and cornice, the latter crowned by
an open balustrade extending the whole length of the façade,
in the centre of which, surrounded by military trophies, is a
sculptured shield charged with the arms of the Duke of
Devonshire.

In the rear of the Crescent is a plain substantial building,
of quadrangular form, called the Square, occupied chiefly by
boarding-houses and private dwellings.  This structure, which
is characterised by extreme simplicity of design, is connected
with the Crescent by a colonnade, that extends along three
sides of the pile, forming with that of the last-named building
a covered promenade 175 yards in length.

The next building of importance, and that which, after the
Crescent, forms the most striking feature in the general view
of Buxton, is the extensive and magnificent erection formerly
known as the Great Stables, but now in part appropriated to
the use of the Devonshire Hospital Charity.    This structure,
which occupies a commanding site on the high ground behind
the Crescent, is built in the form of an irregular octagon, or
perhaps, to speak more correctly, a square with the angles
cut off.   The elevations are neat and chaste, and the general
arrangement is well adapted for the purpose for which it was
originally intended.    The centre of each of the four façades,
which are of two stories, surmounted by a pediment, project
slightly from the main structure, and are occupied by archways giving access to the area within, which is arranged in
the form of a circle 138 feet in diameter, surrounded by a
covered ride 24 feet wide, where formerly visitors were in the
habit of taking exercise in bad weather.

These three buildings—the Crescent, the Square, and the
Stables—were completed in 1796 at a cost of £120,000, the
proceeds, it is said, of the Ecton Copper Mine, in Stafford-

shire, belonging to the Devonshire estate, but which is now exhausted.

Another of the architectural adornments which Buxton owes to the liberality of the Devonshire family, is the church of St. John, erected at the expense of the late Duke. The edifice, which is built in the Tuscan order, occupies a slightly elevated position on rising ground a little to the north of the Crescent, and near the Manchester road. A chaste but substantial tower surmounts the western end, and the east front is approached by a quadra-stile portico, supporting a massive pediment, on the tympanum of which is inscribed the date of erection, MDCCCXII.

It is a fact worthy of remark, as illustrating the treacherous and uncertain character of the soil, that this elegant structure, though placed on the side of a hill, is actually built on piles.

The Old Church—a plain unpretending structure of considerable antiquity—occupied a position in that part of the town designated Higher Buxton. It was formerly adorned with a statue of St. Ann, which, as we have already shown, was destroyed at the time of the Reformation, when, for the purpose of more completely eradicating the superstitious veneration which attached to the memory of the tutelary saint, the church was dedicated to St. John. The fabric— which was small and inconvenient—has been superseded by a new erection, for which the Duke of Devonshire gave the site and a donation of £1,000 towards the building fund. The new church—dedicated to St. James—is a pretty Gothic structure. It is built of limestone, and includes a nave, with side aisles and chancel, terminating in an octagonal apse, the whole being surmounted by an octagonal tower and spire, which springs from the intersection of the nave and choir.

Since the beginning of the present century the neighbourhood of Buxton has been greatly improved. The heathy wastes and barren moors which environ the town have gradually been brought under cultivation. Thorn hedges have to a great extent succeeded the cold and cheerless-looking stone walls; and on the adjacent hills some hundreds of acres have been covered with thriving plantations, which, whilst affording shelter from the cold winds, add to the

2B

beauty of the scenery by relieving it of that dreary, bleak, and inhospitable appearance it formerly assumed. Under the skilful direction of Sir Jeffry Wyatville the rocky eminence fronting the Crescent, called St. Ann's Cliff, has

WATERFALL, SERPENTINE WALKS.

been transformed from a heap of deformity into an ornamental promenade, forming an agreeable foreground to the classic structure of Carr. The ground westwards of the Crescent has been laid out in ornamental walks, which extend for a considerable distance, winding in and out among purling streams and through agreeably-diversified shrubberies and plantations, whose sylvan shade affords an agreeable retreat, and adds greatly to the picturesque appearance of the locality. The water has been dammed up in places and little fairy-like cascades formed; and here and there a pretty rustic bridge has been thrown across with the happiest effect. In the more open valley the small streams that constitute the source of the Wye have been spread out so as to form an artificial lake of considerable magnitude. These gardens have in recent years been transferred by the Duke of Devonshire to the Buxton Improvements Company, under whose direction they have been re-laid and the walks considerably extended. An elegant cast-iron bridge has been thrown across the Wye; and smaller bridges of the same material span its tributaries and communicate with the covered stand erected for the band, which plays at intervals daily during the season.

The Pavilion, which stands upon an elevated terrace on the north side of the new gardens, was erected a few years ago by the Buxton Improvements Company, from the designs of Mr. Edward Milner, of Norwood, the garden architect of the Crystal Palace. It is a building 400 feet in length, constructed of iron and glass, arranged in a series of enarchments, with ornamental cornices and trellis-work surrounding the whole. The building rises from a basement of stone, and contains a central hall for concerts and assemblies, with pedimental fronts advancing some distance from the line of the main structure, and flanked at each end with conservatories and waiting rooms. The terrace on which it stands overlooks the river Wye, the mimic waterfalls, the rustic bridges, and the winding walks, which extend a distance of two miles or more. The work was commenced in 1870, and completed on the 10th August, 1871, at a cost of £12,000. It forms a pleasant lounge for visitors, and will be found a great advantage to invalids and aged persons, who may now be induced to extend their sojourn to the autumn, and even through the winter months. Though only a few years have elapsed since the Pavilion was opened it has already proved too small for the increasing number of visitors. In December, 1875, the foundation-stone was laid of a new building connected by corridors with that already existing. The principal apartment is octagon in form, and with the corridors will give additional accommodation to upwards of 2,000 people. As a further attraction a skating rink has been prepared on

THE PAVILION, BUXTON.

the terrace contiguous to the Pavilion. The cost of these additions will, it is estimated, amount to £12,000.

By the erection of the Pavilion the Buxton Improvements Company have added largely to the attractions of the place. Hitherto Buxton has suffered to some extent as compared with the other English watering-places, there having been (with the exception of the ball-room in the Crescent) no enclosed promenade room or place of general assembly, the only approach to anything like a covered walk being the arcade extending along the front of the Crescent, which had the double disadvantage of being too narrow and too much exposed to wind and weather to be of any real service. Accommodation of this kind was very necessary in a place where so many invalids were brought together, and where the climate is so variable and uncertain. The want, which has long been felt, has now happily been supplied— a cheerful, light, and spacious promenade and concert-room being available that will serve for the band in cold or rainy seasons, and also as a central point for re-union in the evenings and in the long winter months when the weather is unfavourable for outdoor recreation, and which will thus tend largely to develop the social capabilities of the town.

To the north of the new gardens, and separated from them by the Macclesfield Road, is the Park, comprising about 120 acres of land. Here the Lee Wood Hotel and several handsome villa residences have been built, and others are in course of construction.

By the direction of the late Mr. Smithers, the agent of the estate, an old gritstone quarry on the side of Corbar Hill has been transformed from an unsightly mass of broken rock into an object of beauty and attraction, forming a valuable addition to the resources of the place. The steep slopes have been thickly planted with dwarf oaks, beech, horse-chestnut, larch, fir, and a variety of other trees, whose spreading branches meet overhead and cast a constant gloom and shadow over the scene, while the perpendicular walls of gritstone and the shelf-like hollows and rugged inequalities of the quarry have been faced with foliage and adorned with the most luxurious vegetation. Everywhere the turf is covered with shrubs and evergreens—the laurel, the rhododendron, and the glossy-leaved holly mingling their leaves with those of the sweetbriar, the lilac, and the golden laburnum. Through the woodland shade a labyrinth of gravelled walks have been formed, which ramify and extend in every direction—up and down and in and out, amid brambles, woodbine, and wildbriars, and round gaunt masses of rock, where every crack and crevice and every chink and cranny—all but the impenetrable surface of the stone—has been hung and festooned with long strings of ivy and climbers and trailing weeds, and adorned with an exquisite variety of ferns that thrive luxuriantly in all their native loveliness, spreading out their graceful fronds in an intricate network of beauty, which, heightened in effect by the over-arching trees, imparts a green mysterious hue to every object around.

In proportion as the fame of the healing waters has spread the inhabitants of Buxton have increased in number, the visitors have become more numerous, and a larger and larger amount of hotel and boarding-house accommodation has been provided to keep pace with the growing requirements of those resorting thither. Within the last few years building has been carried on to a considerable extent; new ranges of natural and hot baths have been erected, which for comfort and convenience are unsurpassed; and a spacious market-hall has been opened; a neat little Norman church has been erected at Burbage—a thriving hamlet in the immediate vicinity of the town; a Roman Catholic Chapel, Wesleyan and Primitive Methodist Chapels, and a place of worship for the use of the Independent denomination have been built, the latter a large Gothic structure, with a tower surmounted by a lofty octagon spire. The Palace Hotel, a large and handsome structure, has been erected by a joint-stock company on the high ground abutting upon the Manchester Road, and forms a prominent object among the architectural adornments of the place. Several well-built and tastefully-designed villa residences have been erected on what is now called Terrace Road, a thoroughfare leading from the lower part of the town, by the side of St. Ann's Cliff, to Higher Buxton; a range of substantial stone buildings have been completed, occupying a commanding site on the south side of Cavendish Terrace, or the Broad Walk, as it is more generally termed, a broad gravelled promenade extending from the Old Hall to the Tonic Bath, and overlooking the New Gardens; and many other additions and improvements have been effected or are still in progress.

Under the powers of the Local Government Act the town has been thoroughly drained, and its sanitary condition improved thereby, whilst the system of local government which the Act allows, has secured a greater attention to and supervision in the laying out and paving of the several roads and thoroughfares.

It is somewhat remarkable that a place of so much note should have remained so long without a line of railway. Until within recent years the nearest stations were those of Whaley Bridge and Rowsley, the former eight and the latter sixteen miles distant. In the old-fashioned coaching days the town had the advantage of being situated on the line of the great thoroughfare between London and the north, but the extension of the railway system gradually diverted the traffic into other channels, and rendered the place more difficult of access. Fortunately for the inhabitants, and indeed for the public generally, this want, which had been long and increasingly felt, has been supplied, the London and North-Western Company having continued their line from Whaley Bridge to Buxton, whilst the Midland Company have constructed an extension of their Ambergate, Matlock, and Rowsley branch, which, passing along the valley of the Wye, by Monsall Dale, Miller's Dale, and Chee Dale, connects itself with the former at a point near the Quadrant, on the north side of the town. From near the Miller's Dale station of this this line a branch has been continued to Marple, on the Manchester, Sheffield, and Lincolnshire Company's railway, thus giving additional communication with Manchester and all the great towns and manufacturing districts of the kingdom. What has been gained in time, however, by these increased facilities, has been more than lost in prospect, and visitors are now deprived of the pleasant stage-coach drive, with its never-failing accompaniment of chat and anecdote.

Thus, by degrees, as we have shown, Buxton, the military station of the Roman era, and the straggling hamlet of Queen Elizabeth's days, grew into a village, the village became a town, and the town has increased in importance until, with its Crescent and baths, its spacious hotels and boarding-houses, its promenades and ornamented pleasure-grounds, its dry soil and pure mountain air, its hills and rocks, its healthy locality and beautiful scenery, and the many and various attendant accessories which it offers for the comfort and recreation of those in search of renovated health, or who delight in change of scene, it has become one of the most fashionable and attractive of our English health resorts; indeed, there is scarcely another Spa in the kingdom which presents to the lover of nature so many sources of interest and amusement.

Surrounded by numerous places of agreeable and convenient resort, it offers to the health-seeker facilities and even inducements for bodily exercise which must tend to drive away that

> " Army of phantoms vast and wan"

that

> " Beleaguer the human soul."

To the admirer of rugged scenery Ashwood Dale and the valley of the Wye, with the secluded dells diverging therefrom, furnish abundant materials for the imitative pencil of the artist; whilst the geologist and mineralogist will find ample scope for their researches in the variety of the stratified rocks, and the order and superposition of the carboniferous beds. The botanist will find a not less interesting field of observation in the many varieties of the British flora to be obtained amongst the rocks and dells: the different degrees of altitude, and consequent variations of climate, with the diversified character of the undulating surface and attendant changes in the nature of the soil, accommodating the growth of a great variety of native wild-flowers—there being scarcely a plant, it is said, indigenous to Britain, which may not be found in the mountains or in the valleys in the neighbourhood. The numerous sites of historical and antiquarian interest, with the barrows, or lows as they are locally termed, and other remains of the Celtic and Roman periods, are a guarantee that the archæologist will here find an equally fruitful field of study; whilst for those who take less interest in such pursuits, or whose tastes and inclinations are more of a sportive turn, the sparkling Wye with its ample store of trout and grayling, and the extensive moors which environ the town, abounding with grouse, partridge, and a variety of other game, have each their own attractions.

The hotel accommodation at Buxton is of a superior order. The Palace Hotel we have already mentioned; this, with St. Ann's and the Old Hall, where the *crême de la société* mostly congregate, are admirably conducted and furnished with every luxury and convenience befitting the more wealthy and aristocratic class of visitors who frequent them; those who avail themselves of the extra advantages which they offer have to pay in purse pretty smartly; but the charges, though high, are by no means extravagant, considering the comfort and attendance provided. At the minor hotels living is much cheaper, and at most of them a *table d' hôte* is provided, at which the oldest inmate generally presides, and where you have the usual amount of social chit-chat, and small-talk and gossip, and may in a very short period learn all the doings and misdoings, and the petty scandal of the place.

The principal hotels are—

The PALACE, near the Manchester Road.

St. ANN's, at the western extremity of the Crescent.

The CRESCENT (formerly the Great Hotel), at the eastern extremity of the same building.

The OLD HALL, adjoining the natural Baths.

The LEE WOOD, in Devonshire Park.

The ROYAL, the SHAKSPERE, and the GROVE, in Spring Gardens.

The GEORGE, in the rear of the Crescent.

The MIDLAND (formerly Wye Bridge House), at the corner of the Bakewell and Fairfield Roads.

The BURLINGTON, at the foot of Hall Bank.

The EAGLE, on the Eagle Parade.

The KING'S HEAD, adjoining the Market House.

The CHESHIRE CHEESE, in Higher Buxton.

In addition to the Hotels named is the ROYAL HYDRO-PATHIC AND BOARDING ESTABLISHMENT (formerly the Royal Hotel), in Spring Gardens.

For those who visit Buxton *solus* the hotels are of course the most convenient, but families, and those who prefer living in a retired manner, will find the lodging-houses more agreeable and somewhat less expensive. The charges here, it may be remarked, vary considerably at different periods of the year, and are regulated to some extent by the longer or shorter term for which the apartments are taken.

The following description of life at Buxton is from an article which appeared in *Tait's Magazine*, some years ago : " There are, indeed, many splendid places, and there is much beautiful scenery within a moderate day's journey, which it is both delightful and salutary to visit ; such as Chatsworth, Haddon Hall, Bakewell, Matlock, and the wonders of the Peak. All these make Buxton a pleasant place to go away from of a morning. But to those who are obliged to confine themselves within its circling hills it is the heaviest and most uninteresting town that 1,500 strangers in search of health and hilarity were ever cooped up in. They hobble up that wearisome treadmill, the Hall Bank, and toddle down it again ; sit on the benches observing the new arrivals, and admiring the well-graduated courtesy with which mine host of St. Ann's, in his white waistcoat, pays his graceful *devoirs* to each handsome turn-out that turns in to his hospitable doors. They gaze at the vases, obelisks, and other pretty trinkets of spar and marble, with which the museum keepers try to inveigle the money out of their pockets. They drink the water, plunge into the water, talk, read, and dream of the water, and wonder how it does not relieve them of their spasms and aches all at once. They count all the coaches, and take note of the numerous passengers ; watch the arrival of the several mails, up the country and down the country, and bother the life out of the postmistress with asking for letters two or three times a day. They mount into the promenade room to read the newspapers and *Quarterly Review;* go about cheapening windfall apples and sour gooseberries ; consult the state of the weathercock on the top of the church tower, and ever and anon send inquiring glances towards the town clock to know how long it is to dinner time. Such is life *in* Buxton."

In the foregoing description the colouring is very highly toned, and altogether the picture is about as applicable to Buxton as it is to any other English watering-place; certainly, in our own experience, we have found Buxton to be anything but a heavy and uninteresting town. Exclusiveness, or, as Dr. Granville designates it, "shyness-cum-stiffness," a fault in respect of which the generality of English people are incorrigible, prevails here to some extent as elsewhere, but on the whole a good deal of social feeling is found to exist among the several classes of visitors.

It will be readily imagined that in a town containing so large a proportion of invalids and idlers, the circulating libraries, where fiction and cheap literature abound, form the chief centres and rendezvous of whatever there is of life or fashion in the place. The other sources of amusement, in addition to the libraries, are the Pavilion and the ornamental walks and gardens ; concerts are given frequently and a band plays twice a day in the grounds, lectures on various subjects of general interest are given from time to time, balls and assemblies frequently take place during the season in a showy and handsome room in the Crescent ; and if we might judge from the eagerness with which every festival, anniversary, or charitable object is availed of as an excuse for a bazaar, or fancy fair, we should imagine Buxton to be the opposite of a dull or monotonous place.

The climate of Buxton is of course affected in a great degree by the physical character of the locality, and like all other mountain districts, subject to sudden changes and variations of temperature. The fall of rain is greater than in places of less elevation, though below that of some other parts of the Peak district, the neighbouring hills often attracting the heavy clouds ere they reach the town, but the effect is less observable in consequence of the dry and absorbent nature of the soil on the limestone formation—the ground soon dries, and even after heavy rains the visitor may walk out almost immediately without inconvenience. Though the quantity of rain which falls is above the average, the number of dull drizzling days is by no means proportionately great ; periods of unsettled weather with partial showers are of frequent occurrence, and at times the rain comes down heavily, but is as often succeeded by brilliancy and sunshine. Cold winds prevail, especially during the latter part of the season, but their force is in some degree broken by the loftier elevations that surround the town, and being pure and invigorating in their quality, and free from redundant humidity, they do less harm than elsewhere.

The atmosphere is remarkably healthy and free from malarious influences, and the inhabitants enjoy a comparative immunity from epidemic and endemic diseases; and even when such do occur they are seldom malignant, unless imported from other towns—a circumstance which may be attributed partly to the altitude of the place, and partly to the freedom from fogs, and the comparatively small amount of the aqueous exhalations and other sources of miasmatous impurity.

It hardly comes within the scope of a work like this to give anything like an elaborate disquisition on the origin and chemical properties of thermal springs, else we might be tempted to indulge in some curious inquiries respecting that subterranean laboratory from whence emanate those health-giving waters which for countless ages have continued their unceasing flow. It is believed that all hot springs derive their source from one common origin—that the boiling Geysers of Iceland, the hot springs of Pfiffers and Carlsbad, and the thermal waters of Bath and Buxton, all owe their existence to volcanic action. Certain it is that such springs are more generally found in the neighbourhood of active or extinct volcanoes, or in localities where the riven rocks and broken and disrupted strata, and the frequent occurrence of trap, toadstone, and other substances of an igneous character, bear evidence of the same paroxysmal force, whilst water of a high degree of temperature is almost invariably associated with such eruptive outbreaks.

The active mineral principles of thermal waters are the sulphates of soda or magnesia, the hydrochlorates and the muriates of soda and lime, the chlorides of sodium and magnesium, the carbonates of soda, magnesia, and iron, and the sulphurets of sodium and calcium; and their gaseous constituents are most commonly nitrogen, oxygen, carbonic acid, and sulphuretted hydrogen : the ingredients being the same as those ejected from the bowels of the earth during volcanic eruptions.

Many ingenious speculations have been indulged in, and different theories from time to time propounded, to account for the formation of thermal springs, but the most probable cause which has yet been assigned is the supposition that water pressed down by its own superincumbent weight forces its way through the rents and fissures in the bed of the ocean, and percolates through the deeply-seated strata, until it comes in contact with the internal seas of boiling lava, when a volume of steam is generated, which, finding vent through the ruptured and dislocated rock, rushes upwards with immense force, gradually condensing until it reaches the surface, whence it issues at various degrees of heat, from gentle warmth to that of boiling water; the temperature depending upon the length, or rather the depth of its rocky channel, and the quantity of water from land springs which may happen to become mixed with it in its upward progress; and its chemical properties being acquired by the absorption of various mineral ingredients during its long and intricate passage through the earth's crust.

The Buxton waters as they issue from the earth maintain an uniform temperature of 82° Fahrenheit. The principal spring finds its way through several openings or fissures on the edge of the mountain limestone in the space between the Crescent and the *Old Hall Hotel*, which forms the site of the natural baths. In 1852 some interesting experiments were made, when it was ascertained that the quantity of water discharged was at the rate of 129½ gallons per minute; this flow is devoted exclusively to the supply of the natural baths, and is, in addition to the drinking well, and the spring called Bingham's Well, near the centre of the Crescent, which furnishes the supply for the hotel baths.

The water is transparent, sparkling, and inodorous, and possesses a slight tinge of bluish green, but the colouring is so faint as to be scarcely perceptible; it is almost tasteless, being in fact rather insipid as compared with waters of a lower degree of temperature, and when drank it has not unfrequently a stimulating effect, producing in invalids of full habit and sanguineous temperament a slight giddiness which is sometimes followed by flushing and headache, a circumstance which renders it necessary that care should be taken not to employ the water in improper cases. The peculiar brilliancy of the water is no doubt owing to the quantity of nitrogen present, and which, on exposure to the air, escapes in innumerable minute bubbles, causing a sparkling effervescence resembling that of artificially aërated water.

Many analyses of the water have been made from time to time, all differing slightly from each other, though agreeing in the leading features of their constituents.

About the time that the new baths were being erected a very careful analysis was made by Dr. Playfair, at the request of the late Duke of Devonshire, when, in order to make sure of every ingredient coming under observation, one hundred gallons of the water were evaporated down to about half-a-gallon. The following table shows the saline ingredients of an imperial gallon, and the relative proportion of the constituents as then determined :—

|  | | | | | | Grains. |
|---|---|---|---|---|---|---|
| Silica | - | - | - | - | - | 0·666 |
| Oxide of iron and alumina | | - | - | - | 0·240 |
| Carbonate of lime - | - | - | - | - | 7·773 |
| Sulphate of lime - | - | - | - | - | 2·323 |
| Carbonate of magnesia | - | - | - | - | 4·543 |
| Chloride of magnesium | - | - | - | - | 0·114 |
| Chloride of sodium | - | - | - | - | 2·420 |
| Chloride of potassium | - | - | - | - | 2·500 |
| Fluorine (as fluoride of calcium) | - | - | - | trace. |
| Phosphoric acid (as phosphate of lime) | - | - | trace. |
|  | | | | | | 20·579 |

|  | | | | I. | II. | Mean. |
|---|---|---|---|---|---|---|
| Carbonic acid | - | - | 1·169 | 1·164 | 1·167 |
| Nitrogen | - | - | - | 98·831 | 98·836 | 98·833 |
| Oxygen | - | - | - | trace. | trace. | trace. |
|  | | | | 100·000 | 100·000 | 100·000 |

From the analysis and proportion of the gases, Dr. Playfair assumes that, at the moment of issue, the water is charged with 206 cubic inches of nitrogen, and 15·66 cubic inches of carbonic acid, per gallon.

One remarkable feature in this analysis is the large proportion of nitrogen said to be contained. Dr. Playfair, in his report says : "I am inclined to ascribe the medicinal effects of the water almost entirely to its gaseous constituents. The water, deprived of its gases, has the composition of an ordinary spring water, with the exception of the fluorine and phosphoric acid, both of which are present in mere traces ; and it is therefore difficult to conceive that they can have any medicinal effect when the water is used for baths."

The value of nitrogen, as an effective element in mineral waters, is a subject upon which much difference of opinion exists ; in opposition to the opinion of Dr. Playfair, Professor Muspratt says, that " being an *insoluble gas*, it is not absorbed into the system, and even *supposing that it could be absorbed*, it could not exert any beneficial result." Dr. Lee, in his work on the "Watering-places of England," alluding to this subject, after expressing it as his belief that the properties of the Buxton water must remain unexplained, puts forward, as a suggestion, the following inquiry: "Can the oxidating process, which in all probability disengages the azote, have to do with the thermal heat ?"

Amid such a conflict of medical opinion it seems more than probable that the particular element which imparts such peculiar efficacy to these waters must, in the present state of scientific knowledge, remain a mystery. All that is left to us is the coincidence of a large quantity of nitrogen gas with the extraordinary medicinal properties of the water. To the invalid it is a matter of secondary importance, so long as a cure is effected, by what means that result is brought about ; and we have the broad fact before us that, for ages past, this power has been wonderfully manifested in relieving the most obstinate cases of gout and rheumatism, and repairing the ravages made upon the constitution by those diseases. The virtues of the water have been celebrated in the following lines, which are said to have been written upon the wall of one of the old baths by a physician visiting Buckstone :—

> " Corpore debilior Grani se proluit undis :
> Quærit aquas Aponi, quem febris atra necat :
> Ut penitus renem purget ; cur Psaulia tanti,
> Vel, quæ lucinæ gaudia, Calderiæ ?
> Sola mihi Buxtona placit : Buxtona Brittanis
> Undæ Grani, Aponus, Psaulia, Calderæ."

" In Grana's famed baths the feeble patient laves ;
  Whom dismal fevers seize, in Apon's waves
  At Psauli shall a purge so dear be bought ?
  For teeming throes Calderiæ far he sought,
  When here at Buxton (Britain's choice), appear
  Gran, Apon, Psauli, and Calderiæ* near."

The following are the solid ingredients and gaseous constituents of an imperial gallon of the water, as ascertained
by Dr. Muspratt in 1860 :—

|  |  |  |  |  | Grains. |
|---|---|---|---|---|---|
| Carbonate of lime | • | - | • | • | 8·541 |
| Carbonate of magnesia | - | • | - | - | 3·741 |
| Carbonate of protoxyde of iron | - | • | - | 0·082 |
| Sulphate of lime - | • | - | - | • | 0·330 |
| Chloride of calcium | - | • | - | • | 1·227 |
| Chloride of magnesium | - | • | • | - | 0·463 |
| Chloride of sodium | - | • | - | - | 2·405 |
| Chloride of potassium | - | - | - | - | 0·260 |
| Silica    - | • | - | • | - | 1·044 |
| Nitric acid | - | • | - | - | trace. |
| Organic matter    - | - | • | - | - | 0·341 |
| Fluoride of calcium | - | - | • | - | trace. |
| Phosphate of lime | • | - | • | - | trace. |
|  |  |  |  |  | 18·434 |
| Free carbonic acid | • | • | - | 3·5 cubic inches. |
| Nitrogen  - | - | • | • | - 504· | ,, |

It will be seen that this analysis differs in some respects
from that of Dr. Playfair, the quantity of silica given being
greater, whilst the proportion of sulphate of lime and chloride
of potassium is considerably less ; and the aggregate amount
of solid ingredients obtained is less by about two grains.   As,
however, Dr. Playfair's analysis was derived from the residue
of one hundred gallons of water, it may, as regards the saline
constituents, be considered as the more authoritative of the
two.

Dr. Robertson, who possesses a large practical knowledge
of the Buxton waters, and who holds the appointment of
senior physician to the Bath Charity and Devonshire Hospital,

* Places noted for the virtue of their waters.

in his work on the Buxton mineral waters, says : " The diseases for the relief of which the Buxton baths are found to be the most eminently useful, are rheumatism, gout, neuralgia, and certain forms of spinal, uterine, and dyspeptic affections. Many of the disordered conditions which are incidental to old age—much of the deranged health incidental to middle age in females—much of the uterine irregularity and disturbed condition incidental to females at various periods of life—much of the nervous weakness that is indicated by tic-doloreux in its various forms, sciatica, &c.—much of the functional derangement of the kidneys which is consequent upon exposure, intemperance, or advanced life—much of the disordered and painful conditions of the bladder, &c., dependent on old age, gout, &c.—much of the local loss of nervous, and thence of muscular power, dependent upon the poisonous effects of lead, mercury, &c., are usually remediable, and in an important degree, by the use of these mineral baths. The painful or crippling consequences which often follow such injuries as fractures, dislocations, sprains, bruises of tendons and ligaments, and the like, are commonly influenced and relieved by the use of these baths in the most satisfactory degree."

Dr. Granville, so well known by his works on the German and English Spas, compares the waters with those of Schlangenbad, which are of the same temperature. "Here," he says, "at Buxton, we have a water at nearly the same degree of heat, with fewer ingredients, still producing not only similar, but even more energetic effects. Those effects," he adds, "are seen even more strikingly produced by the application of a large quantity of water to the whole body, than when only a small portion is taken internally." And, in another part of his work he bears the following testimony to their curative powers : " In fine, I can conscientiously aver, from my extended experience of mineral waters throughout Germany, the Pyrenees, Italy, and England, that persons afflicted with any affection within the limited ranges of disease specified (general debility, partial paralysis, and that peculiar state of weakness which is the result of rheumatic affection and repeated attacks of gout, and also exhaustion brought on from imprudence, either in very early or in adult life, and

2c

affecting the spine), who require the aid of a suitable mineral water, will find that needful aid at Buxton, provided they abjure, on proceeding thither, the sad and interfering practice of constantly drugging their stomachs by way of *treatment*, and leave nature alone—namely, the mineral waters and the pure, elastic, and bracing mountain air of the Spa."

In addition to the more important thermal waters Buxton possesses an excellent tonic chalybeate, which has long enjoyed a well-deserved reputation. This spring rises from out of a narrow bed of shale lying between the limestone and gritstone formations on the north side of the Crescent. This water is of the ordinary temperature of the atmosphere, and when taken up in a glass tumbler appears colourless. It is perfectly inodorous, but possesses a decided taste of iron, which, from the small quantity present (little more than a grain to the imperial gallon), can only be apparent from the limited amount of saline ingredient accompanying it—the red precipitate on the side of the drinking fountain manifesting the existence of that substance as the predominating constituent. Being almost free from alum it is less astringent in its action than many of the other English chalybeates, and, therefore, with persons of weak digestive power, it is found more beneficial than other waters of the same class which possess greater strength.

When drank the water should always be taken at the spring-head; and when administered in this way its effect is very beneficial, producing a feeling of invigoration, with increase of appetite and digestion and muscular power, without inducing headache or feverishness; and in cases of nervous hypochondriasis and weakness arising from excess, anxiety, or a too sedentary occupation, it is of very great service. In fact, persons may visit Buxton with advantage who do not at all require the application of the thermal waters, but who may derive benefit from the use of its chalybeate, combined with the invigorating power of its pure and bracing mountain air.

The following table shows the amount of solid ingredients in an imperial gallon of the water, according to the analysis made by Dr. Lyon Playfair in 1852 :—

|  |  |  |  |  | Grains. |
|---|---|---|---|---|---|
| Proto-carbonate of iron | - | - | - | - | 1·044 |
| Silica | - | - | - | - | 1·160 |
| Alumina | - | - | - | - | trace. |
| Sulphate of lime | - | - | - | - | 2·483 |
| Sulphate of magnesia | - | - | - | - | 0·431 |
| Carbonate of magnesia | - | - | - | - | 0·303 |
| Sulphate of potash | - | - | - | - | 0·147 |
| Chloride of sodium | - | - | - | - | 1·054 |
| Chloride of potassium | - | - | - | - | 0·460 |
|  |  |  |  |  | 7·082 |

The ranges of building forming the Buxton Baths are situated at the two extreme ends of the Crescent. The present light and elegant structures were erected in 1852, and occupy pretty nearly the same sites as the dark, dingy, and cheerless bath-rooms which they superseded.

The natural or tepid baths are contained in the western range of building, and occupy the space between the Crescent and the Old Hall Hotel, with a frontage towards the south corresponding with the elegant architecture of the first-named building. The façade is divided into five compartments by rusticated pilasters that support the cornice and balustrade ; each compartment is panelled, the three centre ones being slightly advanced, and occupied with circular-headed recesses, fluted and fitted with jets from which a column of water may be made to play. The baths are nine in number, and consist of two piscinæ or public baths, and three private baths with convenient dressing rooms for gentlemen ; and one public and three private baths for ladies. They are all floored with white marble and lined with white enamelled tiles ; and the public baths are provided with pump douches, whereby a continuous jet or stream of water may be projected with considerable force upon any particular part without subjecting the rest of the body to its action, an arrangement very convenient in cases of spinal weakness and chronic localised ailments, or in sprains and local forms of paralysis. Douche closets, furnished with a shower-bath apparatus, are also attached to each of the private baths. The dressing-rooms are well warmed, lighted, and ventilated, and fitted with every comfort and convenience that modern art or science could suggest.

The baths are approached by two corridors leading from the west end of the Crescent Colonnade. On the south side of these corridors is a lofty and well-lighted pump-room for the use of the drinkers of the water, occupying the site of the original St. Ann's Well, and close to the spot where the tepid springs issue from the fissures of the limestone rock. On the north side of the corridors is a recently-erected pump-room, in which is an ornamental fountain for the supply of the chalybeate water.

The Hot Baths adjoin the eastern end of the Crescent, their principal elevations fronting St. Ann's Cliff and the Manchester Road. This building is constructed principally of glass and iron, with a basement of dressed stone, and, as will be gathered from the nature of the materials employed, it differs materially in design from the natural baths. The sides are divided by iron columns into a series of enarchments, supporting an ornamental trellis-work and cornice, from which dwarf pinnacles spring at intervals. A glass-roofed arcade on the south side affords communication with the colonnade of the Crescent, so that invalids may pass from one to the other without exposure to the weather. The range comprises two public hot baths for gentlemen, 25 feet by 16 feet, and one for ladies of the same dimensions, kept at a temperature of 92° to 93°, and fitted with dressing-rooms, hot douche apparatus, and all other necessary comforts and appliances; there are also several private hot baths for gentlemen and ladies, each lined throughout with marble. There is also a cold plunging bath, 25 feet 6 inches long by 15 feet 6 inches wide, lined with white enamelled tiles and floored with white marble, and furnished with separate dressing-rooms and other requisites; this is supplied with the pure water that percolates through the gritstone formation.

As an evidence of the rapid progress which Buxton has made of late, it may be mentioned that at the public baths the receipts have increased within the past decade from £500 a year to over £6,000.

Any description of the Buxton baths and mineral waters would be incomplete which did not include some notice of

that most valuable and efficient institution, the Buxton Bath
Charity and Devonshire Hospital, one of the most deserving
institutions of the class that benevolence ever established,
and which has been the means of providing pecuniary aid
and medical assistance to hundreds of poor disabled sufferers
who have come from almost all parts of the kingdom to cast
out their podagra in these waters of life, and to find in
them a healing virtue which they had sought for elsewhere
in vain.

There is reason to believe that from a very early period
the invalided poor were allowed the free use of the baths,
and that they were in the habit of receiving gratuitous aid
and advice from the medical men in attendance at the baths.
Dr. Jones, writing in 1572, alludes to the "Treasury of the
Bath" as being partly devoted "to the use of the poor that
only for help do come hither." And one of the most confirmatory evidences of the power of the Buxton waters in
relieving and curing disease is furnished by the fact that they
should from so early a period, and under such disadvantageous
circumstances, have been resorted to by so many of the
impotent poor, a circumstance that at one time was considered to be so serious an injury to the inhabitants of the
neighbouring village of Fairfield that, as set forth in a
petition addressed by them to Queen Elizabeth, they were
unable to maintain their minister, through "extreme
poverty" consequent upon "the frequent access of divers
poor, sick, and impotent persons repairing to the fountain of
Buxton," "for whose maintenance and relief the inhabitants
were daily charitably moved to apply their own goods."

There is no evidence to show how or at what date the
present Bath Charity was called into existence, but it is
believed to have originated in 1779, when a subscription
fund was commenced for the assistance of poor bathers, the
number of whom should not exceed "sixteen objects at one
time." From these small beginnings the institution has
continued to grow and prosper until it has reached its
present high state of usefulness and efficiency.

The distance from the bath at which many of the recipients
of the charity were compelled to reside, rendering it difficult
for the more infirm to avail themselves of the use of the

waters with that regularity necessary to secure their restoration to health, it was deemed advisable to establish a Bath Hospital, for the better lodgment and accommodation of the patients, and by this means increase the usefulness of this ancient charity among the needy classes who are enabled to avail themselves of it. By the liberality of the late Duke of Devonshire this design has been carried into effect; the extensive range of building known as the Great Stables has been transformed into a hospital, which, from the excellence of its internal arrangements, as well as from its dry and elevated position and its close proximity to the baths, is admirably adapted for the reception of patients.

The building, which is thoroughly warmed and ventilated, is arranged in wards, capable of receiving about twenty persons in each, and in separate chambers for separate patients in each division. There are spacious dormitories affording separate beds for 120 patients, in addition to the beds provided for cases of accident and those required by the servants of the establishment, and there is ample space for the number being increased to 200 when required. The hospital contains refectories, where those who are not incapacitated take their meals together, and there are, likewise, rooms for seeing out-patients in, and all the other appurtenances of a well-arranged building. The grounds in front have lately been made over to the charity, thus securing for the building a detached position as well as adding to the out-door advantages of the patients. Over the principal entrance to the hospital an inscription testifies to the benevolence of the late Duke of Devonshire in the following terms: "The last munificent charity of William Spencer, sixth Duke of Devonshire, who allowed these buildings to be converted to the use of the sick poor. January, A.D. 1858."

The Hospital was opened January 1st, 1859, and the number of in-patients admitted in the first twelve months was 622. The total under treatment in the year ending December 31st, 1875, was 1,567, of which 1,350 were discharged cured or relieved.

Those who have the means and the inclination may readily obtain the privilege of being able to confer upon the sick and needy the benefits of this admirably conducted institution.

In-patients are supplied with board and lodging, medical advice, and medicines, and have the use of the baths and waters. According to the rules, annual subscribers are entitled to recommend a patient for three weeks to the full benefit of the institution for every guinea subscribed. Life subscribers have the same privilege for every twenty guineas. Non-subscribers have the same privilege on the payment of thirty shillings. Four out-patients may be recommended instead of one in-patient. Out-patients receive medical advice, medicines, and the use of the baths and waters.

# CHAPTER XXIII.

OUR first morning at Buxton dawned with the promise of a continuance of fine weather. When we awoke and looked through the window of our chamber, the first faint flickering streaks of golden light were breaking in upon the shadowy eastern sky, and thin gray mists, which spread over the valleys, and hung like a veil around the head of Corbar Hill, and upon the mountain slopes, shading but not concealing nature's charms, were circling upwards in fantastic wreaths, and gradually dissolving before the sun's increasing power.

Buxton was evidently not yet up, for all without was still and silent, and, with the exception of the gleeful chirruping of the sparrows that flitted to and fro about the chimneys, or the echoing footsteps of some stable-helper, or swarthy-hued labourer whistling on his way through the sunshine to his daily toil, there was nothing to disturb the sleepy morning quietude.

When we strode forth into open day the shadowy mists had lifted from the landscape, and the warm mellow haze of an unclouded summer morn suffused the air. The dew lay heavy upon the grass, and every leaf, and bough, and twig, loaded with the clear crystal drops, gleamed and sparkled in the glistening rays. There were but few people a-foot : now and then we met an early bird enjoying a morning constitutional, and a few pale and sickly-looking invalids—most of them attended by some anxious friend—might be seen slowly hobbling along the covered walk in front of the Crescent in the direction of the pump-room, or supporting themselves against the iron palisades between the archways, but the early walkers were few, comparatively, in number. The *beau monde* of Buxton, we imagine, are not much given to early rising, for when we returned through the town an hour later there was then very little of life or stir apparent, and many of the hotels and boarding houses had the windows of their principal rooms closed and curtained.

If, as an auxiliary to the use of the waters, people intend to derive any advantage from breathing the pure exhilarating mountain air, they should rise betimes for the purpose, and not keep town hours. Whether it is true, as Boswell observes in his life of Dr. Johnson, that the effort of rising early is one of a very serious nature, we shall not stop to inquire, but certain it is, there is no exertion that is more richly rewarded.

> " Falsely luxurious, will not man awake,
> And, springing from the bed of sloth, enjoy
> The cool, the fragrant, and the silent hour,
> To meditation due, and sacred song ?
> For is there aught in sleep can charm the wise ?
> —— Who would in such a gloomy state remain
> Longer than nature craves, when every muse
> And every blooming pleasure wait without
> To bless the wildly-devious morning walk ?"

Whilst deprecating the practice of late rising it must not, however, be supposed that we advocate the opposite extreme. We have heard of some peripatetics who boast of having accomplished their ten or fifteen miles before breakfast. This sounds like doing great things, but the practice is a very foolish one, and is often attended with depression and other unpleasant sensations during the remainder of the day ; it, in fact, destroys the energies and capabilities of endurance at the time when the reactionary powers of the system are at their lowest, and instead of creating an appetite, as some imagine, it only tends to destroy the natural relish for the anxiously-expected morning meal. Under such a state of lassitude and exhaustion the mind is too much occupied with other sensations to take delight in either scenery or any other object of interest. What we would recommend to health-seekers, especially those who are always on the move, and changing their location day by day, is a leisurely saunte of half-an-hour or an hour's duration. This will enable them to enjoy the welcome country breakfast, which should always be finished so as to allow of their being "upon the road" by eight o'clock.

St. Ann's Cliff is a sloping hill or mound, about 100 feet high, which rises directly in front of the Crescent. The surface is laid out in a succession of terraces, with intervening grass banks adorned with urns, vases, &c. ; broad gravelled paths, rising one above another, sweep round the bold convex front, and communicate with each other by flights of steps in the centre, and by sloping walks on each side, forming an agreeable promenade. It is also well adapted for invalids, with whom it is quite a favourite resort, the walks rising one above another in regular succession, enabling them to mark the rate of their advancement towards recovery by the progress they make day by day in mounting to the higher terraces. Thus we remember to have seen, on the occasion of a former visit to Buxton, an old veteran, who was suffering from rheumatism, caused by exposure during his military experiences. When we first noticed him he was only able—and that with the aid of a stick, and by dint of great exertion—to reach the lowest walk. A few days after we saw him hobbling on half-way up the hill, and before we left he had so far recovered as to be able to take exercise on the walks and even mount to the summit without assistance.

From the top of the cliff the best panoramic view is obtained of what may be called modern Buxton, in which is centred all the more important buildings, as well as the chief hotels, the old town, with which it is connected by steep ascents on each side of the cliff, having nothing to distinguish it in appearance from the generality of Derbyshire villages— a few stone dwellings standing irregularly in and out along the side of the road, with here and there a modern erection, built as if for the express purpose of showing how primitive and comfortless its neighbours are.

Seats have been placed at convenient intervals along the walks where the enfeebled and wearied invalid may sit and witness much of the gaiety of outdoor life with some of the natural and artificial beauties of Buxton. Selecting a convenient place near the highest point, we sat down whilst we recorded in our notebook the following pen-and-ink sketch of the general grouping of the place. The Crescent, of course, forms the most prominent feature in the scene. At the western extremity of this semi-circular range of building are the Natural Baths, and adjoining them is the *Old Hall Hotel*, so interesting from its historical associations. From the hotel a road leads up by the Hall Bank into Higher Buxton, the further side being skirted by a number of spar shops and lodging-houses, which descend one below the other *en échelons*. More to the left of the Old Hall is the Pavilion, and the New Gardens, with the magnificent avenue of stately sycamore trees, near to which is Cavendish Terrace, or the Broad Walk, bordered on one side by a row of substantial private residences. Carrying the eye to the opposite extremity of the Crescent, we have the Hot Baths which abut upon the Manchester Road, the opposite side being occupied by a fine pile of building, called, from its circular form, the Quadrant, in the rear of which are the stations of the London and North-Western and the Midland Railways, and contiguous to them the *Palace Hotel*, a building of truly palatial proportions, and rivalling in architectural effect the Crescent itself. At right angles with the Quadrant is Spring Gardens, the busiest thoroughfare in the town. Here are located the *Grove*, the *Midland*, and the *Shakspere* hotels, with the electric telegraph and coach and omnibus offices. Standing on a gentle elevation, in the rear of the Old Hall, is the Church, and contiguous to this is that range of building, the Devonshire Hospital, formerly the Great Stables, which rather gains in appearance by contrast with the background of woods and plantations covering the side of Corbar Hill, whilst the more distant view is shut out by a long range of undulating hills and barren moors, that sweep round in an irregular circle towards the east, where they are terminated by the flat tableland about Fairfield, the latter being crowned by the tower of the village church, which forms a not uninteresting feature in the scene.

After breakfast we set out for a stroll, intending to see some of the principal attractions of Buxton and its immediate environment.

On reaching the area in front of the Crescent we were struck with the sudden change that appeared to have come over the place.

An hour before everything was still and silent, now all is life and gaiety and fashion. Visitors are thronging from all points; the lame and the halt are slowly hobbling on towards the baths; others are indulging in their morning draught of mineral water, or aiding the effect by promenading to and fro along the Colonnade; others again are toiling up and down the steep Hall Bank, or sauntering along the walks of St. Ann's Cliff; and here and there you may see a group of laughing merry-eyed youngsters in charge of a coquettish-looking nursemaid disporting themselves upon the turfy slopes. But the number of children is small comparatively, rheumatism and lumbago being among the ills that juvenile flesh is seldom heir to. Gay companies, in equally gay-looking equipages, start every now and then from the doors of St. Ann's and the Old Hall to enjoy a forenoon airing; and people of a less aristocratic class are bargaining with the owners of one-horse chaises for a drive to the Lover's Leap or the Cat and Fiddle, whilst in Spring Gardens knots of eager pleasure-seekers are gathering round the Peverel of the Peak bent upon a ride over the bleak and dreary moors to see the multifarious wonders that Castleton displays. Literature seems to be in favour with the stay-at-homes. The benches and rustic seats invitingly placed upon the gravelled walks are for the most part occupied by elderly gentlemen and their dames, many of whom are leisurely perusing the daily papers, or wading through the *Advertiser's* list of visitors, and noting what new arrivals there have been since the *Herald* issued its long array of names a couple of days before. *Cornhill* appears to be in the ascendant with the beaux—at least such of them as are not occupied in staring unmeaningly at the moving panorama of beauty and fashion —and light fiction has its peculiar charms for the belles—just now a couple of bewitching damsels are tripping away from the Library to seek the shady retirement of the New Gardens, intent upon storing their minds with the rich fund of information to be gleaned from the "Cousin's Courtship" or the "Minister's Wooing." The fine arts, too, have their attractions, as is manifest by the group of loungers who are contemplating the cheap engravings and lithographs of Derbyshire scenery exposed to view in the stationer's window, whilst close by a country couple are expressing in plain blunt phraseology their opinions of the personal appearance of the noble, knightly, and scientific personages with whose portraits Mr. Bentley, the photographer, has liberally adorned the entrance to the Hot Baths. As eleven o'clock—the hour when the band plays—approaches the throng every moment increases, bustle and animation are everywhere apparent, clouds of muslin, silk, and lace pass continually before the eye, and the unclouded sun pours down a flood of brilliance that adds immensely to the gaiety of the scene ; even the spar shops seem to experience the cheering influence, and their owners look more than ever determined to inveigle the money out of the pockets of visitors.

Buxton, like Matlock, has quite a trade in the manufacture and sale of marble and spar ornaments, and for these, as also for its fossils, it is dependent upon the limestone beds in the vicinity. The material is worked into vases, tables, obelisks, chains, rings, brooches, and a variety of useful and ornamental articles.

Poole's Hole—which has the honour of being classed among the wonders of Derbyshire, whose praise has been celebrated by Hobbes in Latin hexameters, and by Cotton, the poet of the Peak, in English iambics—stands pre-eminent among the natural curiosities of Buxton, and well deserves the reputation it has acquired. It is one of the principal caverns of the limestone formation which extends over so large a portion of the country, and though inferior in some respects to Peak's Hole, and the Blue-John Mine at Castleton, it nevertheless merits a visit from those who take an interest in exploring such subterranean cavities. The name is said to be derived from a famous outlaw named Poole, who in the reign of Henry IV., tradition asserts, made these recesses his retreat and the depository of his plunder.

On leaving the Crescent we passed along the Broad Walk and thence by a field path which soon brought us to the foot of Grin Low, a steep eminence covered with a thick plantation of firs.

Standing in a sheltered hollow close by the mouth of the cavern, with a flower garden in front screened by trees, is the pretty little Swiss-like cottage of Mr. Redfern, the guide, in which is preserved an interesting collection of antiquities that have been found at different times in the immediate locality. A party of excursionists happened to be in the cavern at the time, so that we had to wait here, with some half-dozen other visitors, until their return.

On entering we pass through a low archway in the cliff, and proceed along a tortuous path that narrows as it recedes into the gloom; the darkness, however, is not so apparent as in the other caverns of the Peak, the interior being lighted with gas—a modern innovation which but ill accords with the natural features of the place, and detracts somewhat from the effect, for every hollow and recess being illuminated there is no room for the imagination to wander, and we lose that idea of vastness and profundity which a shadowy obscurity is so calculated to convey. The path winds through narrow apertures and rocky fissures, the sides of which are covered with brown incrustations of calcareous matter; then we come to a natural ledge, called Poole's Shelf, where the cavern widens, and a capacious opening high overhead is pointed out by the guide as one of Poole's closets. A singularly-striking scene here meets the eye— masses of rock are thrown about in every direction, and piled one upon another in a diversity of forms, rugged as chaos. A few yards further on a crystalline stream is seen channelling its way through the gloomy chasm, twisting and twining among the rude blocks of limestone as it courses on; the water is strongly impregnated with lime, and leaves a deposit upon the birds' nests and other objects which are placed in it to undergo the process of incrustation. Huge masses of stalactite adhere to the walls, their surfaces roughened with countless crystallised conformations where the moisture has trickled over them for successive ages. Curious growths of icicles hang pendant from the roof and from every jutting fragment and inequality, and you pause to witness the effect as the light flashes and glitters upon their snowy shapes. The damp trickles through in places, and falls to the ground with a continuous patter that awakens the sullen echoes of the mountain and adds to the impressiveness of the scene. Stalagmites grow up from the floor and ledges of the rock, fashioning themselves into various grotesque and uncouth shapes, which fancy has endeavoured to liken to the several objects whose names they bear, though it must be confessed that the resemblance is oftentimes remote indeed. A curious mass of stalactite is pointed out on the right called the Flitch of Bacon, and near to it is Poole's Chair. Then we

POOLE'S HOLE.

come to another formation bearing the name of the Font— an extraordinary specimen, seven feet in height, which occasions food for wonder when we remember that it is the fairy work of nature produced by the constant dripping of the moisture through a fissure in the mighty bed of limestone overhead for hundreds, it may be for thousands, of years. Here the pathway has been raised and levelled for the convenience of explorers ; masses of rock lie strewn about in the wildest confusion ; and here and there a loose block is

seen balanced on a mere point, so that you fancy it ready to
tumble down at any moment into the stream that gurgles
over the stony fragments in the gully beneath.

We next enter a spacious vaulted chamber, where the roof
is lofty and the dripping walls are in part adorned with beads
and mouldings, and draped and festooned with crystallised
incrustations of unsullied whiteness. Stalactites of various
shapes and dimensions depend from the jutting rocks, each
dignified by a particular name ; some are clustering together
in groups, others hang in spiral convolutions from the roof,
and others again assume all sorts of fanciful and picturesque
forms, their filmy sides resplendent with the brightness that
gleams and sparkles upon every rippling curve and inequality.
The guide calls each by name—the Rhinoceros, the Beehives,
the Oyster Beds, and so on through the entire catalogue.
Then he explains the process of formation, and tells you
that for variety and beauty of decoration there is no cavern
in the kingdom can compare with this subterranean temple,
in confirmation of which statement he points exultingly
to what he calls "the lion couchant guarding the entrance
to my lady's chamber"—a crystallised mass in which the
imagination would be sorely taxed to trace the faintest
resemblance to the noble monarch of the brute creation.
The subject and the comparison naturally provokes a
little amusement—the ladies giggle ; and one young gentleman, anxious to display his wit, facetiously inquires
if it ever shows its teeth; to which Mr. Redfern replied,
with an air of offended dignity, "Only when it hears a
braying ass."

Onwards the cavern narrows, and we continue along a
gloomy passage where the moisture oozes from above in a
perpetual shower, forming little cup-like hollows in the
ground, in which the water falls with a never-ceasing splash.
In places huge cracks and openings appear in the limestone,
leading to cavities and ante-chambers that extend far into
the inner part of the mountain, rude masses of rock bulge
out, and the farther you penetrate the more wild and rugged
the scene becomes. A few yards beyond you come to Mary
Queen of Scots' Pillar—a pendant column of stalactitic or
calcareous matter which, tradition says, marks the point to

which that unhappy princess ventured in one of her visits to Buxton..

The cavern may be explored for a distance of about 200 yards further, beyond which visitors seldom venture. Here the passage seems to terminate in a *cul de sac;* but, on looking round, a steep and rugged incline is seen leading up over disjointed rocks and slippery crags to a considerable altitude, and terminating in a narrow opening, through which a person may contrive to pass by crawling on his hands and knees. This opening forms the entrance to a range of caverns that are believed to ramify and extend in various directions. The guide clambers up and puts his head through, but having already satisfied our curiosity we feel no inclination to follow his example.

Retracing our steps we pass by the Queen of Scots' Pillar, and continue along the path by which we came, pausing now and then to admire the brilliant and delicate incrustations, and the extraordinary stalactitic formations.

The length of the cavern, from the entrance to the furthest point usually visited, is estimated at 770 yards. Throughout the entire distance the pathways are smooth and firm to the tread, so that it may be explored without inconvenience; in fact there is nothing that need deter the most delicate female from witnessing the subterranean wonders of Poole's Hole.

The cavern is believed, from remains that have been recently found, to have been originally the dwelling-place of an ancient race of men. An account of these discoveries is given in a paper by Mr. Dennis Crofton, read at a meeting of the Royal Irish Academy, from which we make the following extracts: " The proprietor having determined upon making explorations, set men to break up the surface at the distance of a few feet from the side of the cavern, in the before-mentioned recess. As this operation was at the top of both gravel and clay, it was at the height of some seven or eight feet above the natural limestone floor of the cave. Not far from the surface the workmen came on a layer of stalagmite of various thickness, but averaging about three-quarters of an inch. After this had been broken through there came a layer of the brown clay about ten inches or a foot deep. Below this

2D

was another layer of stalagmite, thinner than the upper one, and averaging perhaps a quarter to half an inch thick. When this in its turn had been broken up there came again about ten inches or a foot more of the brown clay, then a quantity of bones compacted within a small space and mingled with fragments of broken pottery and charcoal, but without flint implements. I was not myself present during the excavation, but upon hearing it went into the cavern and made a personal examination of the place, when I found no reason to doubt of the facts having been as described. I also disinterred *in situ* with my own hands some pieces of bone which had escaped the first explorers, and brought away some of the charcoal. I further procured a selection of the first-found bones and pieces of pottery. All of stalagmite, you may now see before you. One of these, as well as specimens of the two layers of the pieces of pottery discovered, which I was unable to get, had a sort of rhomboidal ornamentation, figured on what had been the outside of the vessel. The bones are all of animals such as would be used for human food, and there are none human—of carnivora—or extinct species. They comprise remains of the cow, goat, and pig tribes. The gelatine has nearly disappeared from them, and, in some cases, a portion of it appears to have been replaced by a heavy infiltrated substance—probably, in these instances, carbonate of lime, or iron in some form derived from the enveloping clay. One, an astragalus, has an adherent layer of stalagmite. On the whole, the condition of these remains, as to the absence of animal matter, does not appear to be very different from that of the bones in the Museum of the Academy, brought from the French caves of La Madeleine and Laugerie Haute, in the department of the Dordogne, which have been investigated by Messrs. Lartet and Christy. From the existence of the charcoal and pottery along with the remains there can be little doubt that the place in which they were found was used for cooking by the ancient troglodites; and, upon the whole, I am inclined to consider the deposit in the light of what the Danish antiquarians have designated as a 'kjokkenmodding,' or refuse food heap. As to the antiquity of the bones, it is very hard to give a conjecture and opinions on these matters, where there is little proof, should always be formed with great caution, and put forward with diffidence. There is, however, one thing which may possibly throw some light on this point, as a matter of circumstantial evidence, and it is—that about four years ago, a fibula, and two coins of the reign of Trajan, were found at the opposite side of the cavern, a little further on in it than the bone deposit, at the height of about four inches above the gravel, and in the clay. These I have seen, and have no reason to doubt their genuineness. But there is no evidence as to when, or how, they got to the place in which they were discovered, nor, as far as I am aware, anything, such as the overlaying of stalagmite, which would be determinative of at least a certain degree of antiquity for their imbedding. I have, however, mentioned the circumstance, from its possible bearing on my subject. It is an interesting fact to find that one of the great Derbyshire caverns, like several others which have recently come to light both in England and on the Continent, was anciently appropriated as a place of human habitation."

A great portion of the summit of Grin Low is covered with dross and slag, the refuse of the neighbouring limekilns. Many of these mine hillocks have been excavated, and were formerly the habitations of human beings—generally a small aperture in the side answered the purpose of a window, and an opening through the roof served to carry off the smoke from the interior. Through the exertions of the late Mr. Wilmot, the agent of the Duke of Devonshire, these wretched hovels have been destroyed, and in their stead a number of neat and comfortable dwellings have been erected at Burbage, a hamlet close by, for the poor lime-burners who formerly located here. The former unsightly heaps are now covered by a thriving plantation of firs which adds to the interest of the surrounding landscape.

From the further side of this plantation a path leads through two or three enclosures to the highest point of the hill on which a mass of loose stones have been built up so as to resemble at a distance a ruined tower. This tower, which bears the name of Solomon's Temple, affords a fine view of the valley of Buxton and the surrounding elevations, including Axe Edge, Kinder Scout, Lord's Seat, and Chelmerton Low. The tourist may, if he feels so disposed, extend his walk from this point to the so-called Cottage of Content, a quaint little dwelling with a fancifully laid out garden, where there resided for many years what Cotton, if he had been living, would have immortalised as another wonder—a contented man, one Brandrith Bagshaw. There is a rustic summer-house in the garden, furnished with every accommodation for enjoyment *al fresco*. A field road from the cottage leads to the celebrated Diamond Valley, the soil of which is pro-ductive of those detached crystals known as Buxton diamonds, and which are often found aggregating in clusters in the dark ferruginous earth. The place has lately been closed against the public, and a notice-board now conveys a warning to acquisitive intruders.

On leaving Solomon's Temple we walked over the edge of Grin Low to the limeworks, a vast excavation, or rather series of excavations, which extend over a large portion of the hill-side. The scene here is wild and barren in the extreme, and the effect is rendered more striking by the clouds of smoke which issue from the adjoining kilns and roll in heavy masses about the shattered cliffs and misshapen fragments that lie scattered about. There is not a vestige of green to be seen upon the parched surface, vegetation being entirely precluded by the sulphureous fumes which arise from the smelting furnaces. Havoc and destruction are everywhere apparent, the bowels of the mountain seem literally torn out, and the rocky ruin spread before the eye excites in the mind the idea of nature returned again to universal chaos. There is no lack of animation, however, for amid the striking scene may be observed numbers of miners, quarrymen, and lime-burners industriously pursuing their curious but perilous occupations with a degree of fearlessness and indifference that seems hardly compatible with perfect safety. Some are boring the rock preparatory to a blast, some are seated in hollows and on narrow ledges breaking up the disrupted masses, and others are busily employed in loading the wagons with the stony fragments, or pushing them along the tramways which spread out in various directions; and ever and anon the echoes are awoke by loud explosions, followed by a rumbling crashing sound, which tells that some mighty pile of rock has been torn away from the parent mass.

The limestone is of a bluish gray colour, and it is said that when burned it produces lime of the best quality, which is transported to various parts of the country—the Cromford and High Peak Railway, which passes close by the furnaces and crushing-mill, affording a ready means of transit. The soil belongs to the Duke of Devonshire, to whom a royalty is paid by the company of proprietors who carry on the works.

Contiguous to the quarries is Burbage, a picturesque hamlet, inhabited chiefly by lime-burners and quarrymen, which appears to have lately risen into existence, its present improved condition being mainly due to the exertions of the late Mr. Wilmot, the agent of the Devonshire estates. A pretty little church in the Norman style has been erected, the seats of which are entirely free ; in the tower, at the south-west angle of the nave, a peal of bells, five in number, have been placed, and several of the windows have been filled with stained glass, at the expense of different benevolent individuals ; schools have also been established, and every care seems to be taken to improve the condition of the poor and scattered population.

From Burbage we continued for some distance along the Macclesfield Road, and then turned off to the left, and scaled the trackless moorland slopes of Axe-Edge, a commanding elevation which is reckoned one of the highest hills in the Peak.

There is no beaten path, so we have to stride through heath and bog, over miry patches and beds of peat moss, and across narrow channels where dark-coloured rills come gurgling over the gritstone ledges. At every step the prospect widens, and the horizon spreads further and further ; by-and-by the ascent becomes less toilsome, and we are enabled to make better progress, notwithstanding the spongy nature of the soil ; then we have more heath and bog, another climb, and the summit is reached, on which a little cairn has been erected by the Ordnance Sappers, who, it is said, saw from hence the signals exhibited on Lincoln Cathedral and the top of Snowdon at the same time, though the distance between is more than 150 miles.

The view from this point is very imposing, and on a clear day the eye is enabled to travel over a vast extent of country.

The time, however, was not very favourable to our purpose, a vapoury haze obscured the distant landscape, whilst the nearer foreground was bathed in a flood of light, in which the almost total absence of shadow rendered the prospect less beautiful than it would have been if seen under more favourable circumstances.

Axe-Edge attains an elevation of upwards of 2,100 feet; it forms part of a gritstone ridge, covered for the most part with a stratum of peat moss, from which issue numerous springs, whose waters uniting give birth to four rivers, the Dane, the Goyt, the Dove, and the Wye, the two former tending to the Irish Sea, and the two latter to the German Ocean.

A short descent brought us again to the turnpike road, after a couple of miles' walk along which we reached the far-famed *Cat and Fiddle*, the highest public-house in the Peak district, and, it is said, the most elevated house of entertainment in the kingdom. Here we rested awhile, and then returned by the Macclesfield Road to Buxton, passing on the way the head of Goyt's Clough, a deep wooded dingle, and Edgemoor House, where resided the late Right Reverend Bishop Spencer.

In the afternoon we made a short excursion to Fairfield, a quiet little village about a mile from the town, which, from its elevated position and the extensive views it commands, is much frequented by sojourners at Buxton.

Proceeding along Spring Gardens to Wye Bridge, we there leave the Bakewell Road, and turning to the left pass beneath the railway, and, after crossing Hogshaw Brook, ascend by a steep path that leads up by the grounds of Wye Bridge House, until we reach the tollgate, where the village may be said to commence. It is a plain and homely-looking place, with one or two inns, and a few lodging-houses smartened up in expectation of visitors; modern erections springing up in different parts tell of innovation, and these mingling with the quaint and unpretending structures of former days give it a somewhat incongruous appearance. What it lacks in appearance, however, as compared with its aristocratic neighbour, is more than compensated for by the beauty of its situation. From the upper end of the village a fine panoramic view is obtained of Buxton, with the lower town, the Crescent, the Church, the Palace Hotel, and the Devonshire Hospital, and the lofty eminences that environ it, including Grin Low, Axe-Edge, and the hills bordering the western side of the Goyt.

The church is a plain unpretending erection, occupying the site of a more ancient structure which was taken down in 1838; there are a few marble tablets and sculptured memorials in the interior, and several monumental tombs in the churchyard, among them one to the memory of Stephen Edward Rice of Mount Trenchard, Ireland, the father of Thomas Spring Rice, afterwards Lord Monteagle. Near the west end of the church there is an elevated mound of limestone, surmounted by a pedestal that appears to have formerly had the addition of a sun-dial.

On the summit of the hill beyond the village is an extensive tract of common called the Barms, on which the Buxton races were formerly held. A road, following the old Roman Bathomgate, leads across and continues thence to Chapel-en-le-Frith and Castleton, and another branching off on the right, passes over the moors to Tideswell. On the north side of the common is a farmstead, surrounded by trees, which tradition says occupies the site of an ancient religious house or nunnery. It is known as the Nun Farm, and some neighbouring fields and a brook that runs below still bear the names of the Nun Fields and the Nun Brook.

Returning from Fairfield we struck into a foot-track which leads over some fields on the right and soon afterwards came upon a path that brought us out upon the Manchester Road near the Devonshire Hospital.

There are many other pleasant walks in the immediate vicinity of Buxton which our limited stay necessarily prevented us making acquaintance with.

Now evening draws on, and with it the time when we must bid farewell to the hills and dales of the Peak; the last hour we spent in social chat, recounting the scenes and actions and vicissitudes of our wanderings. Then, having arranged our compact necessaries for a homeward journey, we bade a hearty good-bye to our hospitable friends, and a few minutes later had turned our backs upon the most fashionable of the northern spas.

Here, reader, we bring our narrative to a close, and, for the present, we part company, but a word or two ere we separate. In endeavouring to describe the natural beauties of Derbyshire we have not sought to gain interest by relating any imaginary adventures or visionary "incidents by the way." Our aim has been to portray the different scenes as they appeared to us at the time we beheld them, avoiding, on the one hand, the dry matter-of-fact details of the topographer, and, on the other, the superlatives of guide-book exaggeration. If we have been at any time diffuse it has arisen from a desire not to omit anything which might be interesting or useful to the future tourist. A glance at the map will show what portion of the Peak district has been traversed ; the sum total of our walkings through the mountainous region is 120 miles, but with two exceptions they have not exceeded twenty miles in one day, so that our steps may be followed without risk of over fatigue. The inns we have named are those at which we have stayed, and which we can with confidence recommend to parties visiting the different localities ; the accommodation is good, the fare ample, and the charges moderate.

Our excursion was made during a period of temporary relaxation from the cares of business occupations, to cultivate acquaintance with the charms of nature, with the expectation that a change of scene would prove a stimulus to wholesome excitement, and be productive of much rational amusement, and with the further hope that the health-inspiring winds which blow from the summits of the heathy mountains might be found not less invigorating than the saline breezes which

" Kiss fair ocean's curls."

We stated at the outset that our journey lay through a country almost unexampled for the many and varied objects of interest and curiosity which it possesses ; and if we should be the means of inducing any studious book-worm, any bilious clerk, or toiling artisan, to leave his library, his desk, or his workshop, and follow in our steps, our object will have been accomplished.

*The following Catalogue of Mosses and Ferns found in Castleton and the immediate neighbourhood has been kindly furnished by Mr. John Tym, of the Museum, Castleton.*

## MOSSES.

Anomodon Viticulosus, (*Tall Anomodon.*)
Bartramia Fontana, (*Fountain Apple Moss.*)
Bartramia Pomiformis, (*Common Apple Moss.*)
Bryum Caespititium, (*Lesser Matted Thread Moss.*)
Bryum Capillare, (*Greater Matted Thread Moss.*)
Bryum Hornum, (*Swan's Neck Thyme Thread Moss.*)
Bryum Ligulatum, (*Long-leaved Thyme Thread Moss.*)
Bryum Palustre—Aulacomnion, (*Marsh Thread Moss.*)
Bryum Punctatum, (*Dotted Thyme Thread Moss.*)
Bryum Roseum, (*Rosaceous Thyme Thread Moss.*)
Bryum Rostratum—MINIUM, (*Long-beaked Thyme Thread Moss.*)
Bryum Ventricosum, (*Swelling Bog Thread Moss.*)
Cladonia Burcata.
Cladonia Rangeterina, (*Reindeer Moss.*)
Diacranum Bryoides—Fissidens, (*Lesser Pennate-leaved Fork Moss.*)
Diacranum Glaucum, (*White Fork Moss.*)
Diacranum Heteromallum, (*Silky-leaved Fork Moss.*)
Diacranum Pelucidum, (*Pelucid Fork Moss.*)
Diacranum Scoparium, (*Broom Fork Moss.*)
Diacranum Squarrosum, (*Drooping-leaved Fork Moss.*)
Diacranum Undulatum—Palustre, (*Wave-leaved Fork Moss.*)
Diacranum Varium, (*Variable Fork Moss.*)
Didymodon Flexicaule—Trichostomum.

Didymodon Purpureus, (*Purple Didymodon.*)
Didymodon Rubellus.
Diphyscium Foliosum, (*Leafy Diphyscium.*)
Fissidens Adiantoides, (*Adiantum-like Fork Moss.*)
Fontinalis Antipyretica, (*Greater Water Moss.*)
Grimmia Apocarpa—Var Stricta.
Grimmia Apocarpa, (*Sessile Grimmia.*)
Grimmia Pulvinata, (*Grey-cushioned Grimmia.*)
Gymnotomum Viridissimum—Zygodon, (*Green-tufted Beardless Moss.*)
Hedwigia Aestiva, (*Summer Hedweigia.*)
Hookeria Lucens, (*Shining Hookeria.*)
Hypnum Alopecurum, (*Fox-tail Feather Moss.*)
Hypnum Complanatum, (*Flat Feather Moss.*)
Hypnum Comutatum, (*Curled Fern Feather Moss.*)
Hypnum Cupressiforme, (*Cyprus-leaved Feather Moss.*)
Hypnum Curvatum—Isothecium Myurum, (*Curved Feather Moss.*)
Hypnum Cuspidatum, (*Pointed Bog Feather Moss.*)
Hypnum Dendroides, (*Tree-like Feather Moss.*)
Hypnum Denticulatum, (*Sharp Fern-like Feather Moss.*)
Hypnum Molluscum, (*Plumy-crested Feather Moss.*)
Hypnum Praelongum, (*Very Long Feather Moss.*)
Hypnum Proliferum, (*Proliferous Feather Moss.*)
Hypnum Purum, (*Neat Meadow Feather Moss.*)
Hypnum Riparium, (*Short-beaked White Feather Moss.*)
Hypnum Ruscifolium, (*Long-beaked Water Feather Moss.*)
Hypnum Rutabulum, (*Common Rough-stalked Feather Moss.*)
Hypnum Schreberi, (*Schreberian Feather Moss.*)
Hypnum Sericeum, (*Silky Feather Moss.*)
Hypnum Serpens, (*Creeping Feather Moss.*)
Hypnum Splendens, (*Glittering Feather Moss.*)
Hypnum Squarrosum, (*Drooping-leaved Feather Moss.*)
Hypnum Stramineum, (*Straw-like Feather Moss.*)
Hypnum Triquetrum, (*Triquetrous Feather Moss.*)
Hypnum Undulatum, (*Waved Feather Moss.*)
Hypnum Velutinum, (*Velvet Feather Moss.*)
Jungermannia Asplenioides, (*Spleenwort Jungermannia.*)

Jungermannia Emarginata, (*Notched Jungermannia.*)

Jungermannia Platyphylla, (*Flat-leaved Jungermannia.*)

Jungermannia Trilobata, (*Three-toothed Jungermannia.*)

Lycopodium Alpinum, (*Savin-leaved Moss.*)

Lycopodium Clavatum, (*Stag Horned Moss.*)

Lycopodium Selago, (*Fir Club Moss.*)

Neckera Crispa, (*Curled Neckera.*)

Orthotrichum Anomalum, (*Anomalus Bristle Moss.*)

Polytrichum Aloides, (*Dwarf Long-headed Hair Moss.*)

Polytrichum Commune, (*Common Hair Moss.*)

Polytrichum Piliferum, (*Bristle-pointed Hair Moss.*)

Polytrichum Urnigerum, (*Urn-bearing Hair Moss.*)

Sphagnum Acutifolium, (*Slender Bog Moss.*)

Splachnum Sphæricum, (*Globe-fruited Splachnum.*)

Tortula Muralis, (*Wall Screw Moss.*)

Tortula Ruralis, (*Great Hairy Screw Moss.*)

Tortula Subulata, (*Awl-shaped Screw Moss.*)

Tortula Tortuosa, (*Frizzled Mountain Screw Moss.*)

Trichostomum Aciculare—Racometrum, (*Dark Mountain Fringe Moss.*)

Weissia Contraversa, (*Green Cushioned Weissia.*)

Weissia Curvirostra '*Curved Beaked Weissia.*)

---

## FERNS.

Asplenium Adiantum Nigrum, (*Black Spleenwort.*)

Asplenium Ruta-Muraria, (*Rue-leaved Spleenwort.*)

Asplenium Trichomanes, (*Maidenhair Spleenwort.*

Asplenium Viride, (*Green Spleenwort.*)

Athyrium Filix-Fœmina, (*Lady Fern.*)

Athyrium Filix-Fœmina, (*Var Irriguum.*)

Blechnum Spicant, (*Hard Fern.*)

Botrychium Lunaria, (*Moonwort.*)

Ceterach Officinarum, (*Scaly Spleenwort.*)

Cystopteris Fragilis, (*Brittle Bladder Fern.*)

Lastrea Dilatata, (*Broad Buckler Fern.*)

Lastrea Filix-Mas, (*Male Fern.*)

Lastrea Montana, (*Mountain Fern.*)

Lastrea Spinulosa.

Ophioglossum Vulgatum, (*Adder's Tongue.*)

Osmunda Regalis, (*Royal Fern.*)

Polypodium Calcareum, (*Limestone Polypody.*)

Polypodium Dryopteris, (*Oak Fern.*)

Polypodium Phegopteris, (*Beech Fern.*)

Polypodium Vulgare, (*Common Polypody.*)

Polystichum Aculeatum, (*Common Prickly Shield Fern.*)

Polystichum Angulare, (*Soft Prickly Shield Fern.*)

Pteris Aquilina, (*Common Brake.*)

Scolopendrium Vulgare, (*Hart's-tongue.*)

# ITINERARY.

| ON THE LEFT FROM CHAPEL-EN-LE-FRITH. | CHAPEL-EN-LE-FRITH. (Inn: King's Arms.) | ON THE RIGHT FROM CHAPEL-EN-LE-FRITH. |
|---|---|---|
| | A market town in the High Peak, deriving its name from a chapel erected between the years 1224 and 1238. | |
| Old Slack Hall, a stone building erected in 1727. | | Slack New Hall, a modern residence, standing on the slope of a hill, the seat of Thomas Slack, Esq. |
| Ford Hall, a castellated residence pleasantly situated at the bottom of the valley, belonging to W. H. G. Bagshawe, Esq. | | Road to Perry Foot and Peak Forest. |
| | Rushup Edge. | Eldon Hill, a lofty eminence on the further side of the valley, on the slope of which is Eldon Hole, one of the wonders of the Peak, a deep vertical fissure formerly supposed to be fathomless. |
| Road to Edale, passing over the side of Mam Tor. | At the turn of the road a magnificent view is obtained of Hope Dale, with Lose-Hill and Winbill in the distance. | |
| Mam Tor, or the Shivering Mountain, on the summit of which are the remains of a Roman encampment. | | Road to Buxton, from which branches off the old Sheffield Road leading through the Winnats. |
| Odin Mine, an ancient lead mine believed to have been worked by the Saxons. | | Fluor Cavern or Blue-John Mine. Tray Cliff, in which is found the amethystine or topazine fluor spar. Road to the Winnats, a narrow mountain defile, near the entrance to which is the Speedwell Mine. |
| | CASTLETON. 6 miles from Chapel-en-le-Frith. (Inns: Castle, Bull's Head, and Nag's Head.) The church is a modernised structure, but an archway of the Norman period still remains. ⌢ cr. Peak's Hole Water, a stream that issues from the mouth of the Peak Cavern. | Peverel's Castle, a ruined fortress crowning a precipitous rock, at the foot of which is the entrance to Peak Cavern. Cave Dale, a narrow secluded dell, near the further end a basaltic column of regular hexagonal form is seen cropping out. |
| Cupola Smelting Furnace. | HOPE. (Inn: the Hall Hotel.) ⌢ cr. River Nowe. | |
| Winhill and Losehill. Tradition asserts that a battle was fought in the valley between these two eminences, and that the contending armies encamped upon their summits. | Brough. | The Halsteads, an elevated piece of ground in the angle formed by the confluence of the river Nowe and the Bradwell Brook, is the site of a Roman station. |
| Road to Thornhill. | ⌢ Mytham Bridge, spanning the Derwent, which here joins the Nowe. | Road to Bradwell and Hazelbadge. |
| Bamford Mills. | BAMFORD. Church dedicated to St. John, a neat Gothic structure. | Bamford Edge, a lofty gritstone ridge. |
| Wood Lane, leading to Ashopton, and thence through Woodlands to Glossop. | Hurst Clough. Nether Hurst. Ridgeway. Brookfield. ⌢ cr. Hood Brook. | Road to Sheffield through the Ladybower, a deep wooded dingle watered by the Ladybower Brook. |

| ON THE LEFT FROM HATHERSAGE. | HATHERSAGE. 6 miles from Castleton. (Inns : George, Ordnance Arms.) | ON THE RIGHT FROM HATHERSAGE. |
|---|---|---|
| | The Church, a handsome Gothic structure of the perpendicular period. Near the church is the cottage in which "Little John" is said to have been born, and on the south side of the churchyard the grave in which he is believed to have been buried. | |
| | Camp Green, an earthwork of Danish origin, on the north side of the church | |
| | Higgar Rocks, a sombre mass of gritstone blocks piled confusedly together in one chaotic heap, and believed to be of Druidical origin. | |
| | Carl's Work, an ancient British fort consisting of an irregular mound of rough unshapen stones, with walls, fences, and enclosures opening one into another, built on the brow of the hill. | |
| | Millstone Edge, a precipitous cliff commanding an uninterrupted view of the Hope Dale and the valley of the Derwent. A quarry has been opened on the side of the rock, the stone from which is fashioned into millstones. | |
| | Return to Hathersage. | |
| | | Nether Hall, an embattled Gothic structure, the residence of Joseph Bright, Esq. |
| Hog Hall. | ⌒ Hazleford Bridge. crossing the Derwent. | |
| From the Moor is obtained a fine view of the valley through which flows the Derwent, with the town of Hathersage, and the woods of Leam, Sheriff and Padley, backed by the lofty eminences of Bore Edge, Millstone Edge, Booth's Edge, Froggatt Edge, Baslow Edge, and Curbar Edge, and the plantations environing the stately palace of Chatsworth. | Eyam Moor. | Wet Withins, near to which is a Druidical circle.

Sir William, an eminence attaining an elevation of 1418 feet. |
| Road to Grindleford Bridge.

Ladywash Lead Mine. | Sir William Road. | |

| ON THE LEFT FROM EYAM. | EYAM. | ON THE RIGHT FROM EYAM. |
|---|---|---|
| | **EYAM.**<br>5 miles from Hathersage.<br>(Inns: Bull's Head, Miners' Arms.)<br>A little mountain village, pronounced locally Eem, ravaged by the plague in 1666.<br>The Church, an ancient structure, recently restored, contains numerous architectural details worthy of notice. In the churchyard is a Runic Cross and near to it the tomb of Mrs. Mompesson, the wife of the Rector of Eyam, who died of the plague.<br>Riley Graves—a tomb and six headstones within a walled enclosure on the side of the hill, the last resting-place of a family who, with one exception only, were swept away by the plague. | |
| Eyam Dell, a narrow defile shut in by craggy steeps, between which the road winds up from Middleton Dale to Eyam village.<br>Castle Rock, a curiously-formed mass of limestone, with craggy pinnacles and regular bastion-like projections resembling a castellated structure.<br>Lovers's Leap, a perpendicular cliff, from the summit of which a love-stricken damsel precipitated herself in 1760. | The Delph or Cucklet Dell, At the further end of which is<br>**Middleton Dale,**<br>A rocky chasm, through which winds the road from Tidswell to Stoney Middleton. | The Pulpit Rock, a limestone crag, in which is a naturally excavated archway, from whence the pastor of Eyam was wont to address the people during the visitation of the plague. |
| Middleton Hall, a gabled stone mansion, the residence of Lord Denman. | **STONEY MIDDLETON.**<br>(Inn : The Moon.)<br>A little country village romantically situated on the side of the limestone cliffs. | |
| Calver Cotton Mills.<br>Calver Church. | **CALVER.**<br>A little straggling hamlet abounding in limekilns.<br>⌒Calver Bridge crossing the Derwent. | |
| | | Bubnell Hall, an antiquated structure partially surrounded by trees, is seen rising from the slope on the opposite side of the river ; the mansion is now occupied as a school. |
| | **BASLOW.**<br>(Inns : Peacock, Wheat Sheaf.)<br>A pleasant rural village, standing on a slope that rises from the eastern bank of the Derwent. | Looking up the valley of the Derwent from the bridge, some pleasing views occur— an old-fashioned corn mill, Bubnell Hall, and a few cottages form the foreground, and a succession of wooded eminences and lofty moorland hills fill in the distance. |

| ON THE LEFT FROM STONEY MIDDLETON. | The church, an ancient structure with tower and spire, stands on the edge of the river; in the church-yard are some stone coffins. | ON THE RIGHT FROM STONEY MIDDLETON. |
|---|---|---|
| | | Peacock. |
| Wheat Sheaf. | Chatsworth Park. | Entrance Lodge to Chatsworth Park. |
| Hunting Tower. Stables. | CHATSWORTH HOUSE. 5 miles from Eyam. | Queen Mary's Bower, a low square tower surrounded by a moat, where it is said the Queen of Scots passed many hours during her captivity at Chatsworth. |
| | ⌢ cr. the Derwent by a bridge of three arches said to have been built from designs by Michael Angelo. | |
| | Edensor. (Inn : Chatsworth.) A picturesque village composed principally of villa residences. Church: An ancient structure standing on the side of a hill; in the churchyard is the tomb of the late Duke of Devonshire. On leaving the village follow the road that leads up to Ball Cross, An eminence commanding some fine panoramic views of the country around Chatsworth. A quiet rural lane is continued over the top and then descends to BAKEWELL. 4 miles from Chatsworth. (Inns :   Rutland   Arms,            Devonshire   Arms,            Castle, Wheat Sheaf,            Red Lion.) An important market town situate on the banks of the Wye. The church is a handsome cruciform structure with a lofty tower and spire.   In the interior are   several monuments of the Vernon and Manners' families. | |
| | Mineral Water Baths and Bath Gardens. | Burton Closes, an ornamental residence on the slope of the hill. the seat of Mr. Allcard. |
| Manners Wood, a lofty eminence rising from the opposite bank of the Wye, clothed with plantations. | | |

| ON THE LEFT FROM BAKEWELL. | HADDON HALL. | ON THE RIGHT FROM BAKEWELL. |
|---|---|---|
| | The old manorial residence of the Vernons, Kings of the Peak, and now the property of the Duke of Rutland. | Road to Youlgreave and Winster. |
| | cr. the Wye at Filly-ford Bridge. | |
| Approaching Rowsley, a fine view opens into Darley Dale. | ROWSLEY. 3½ miles from Bakewell. (Inn : Peacock.) | |
| | Leave the highway, and follow the road that ascends by Peak Tor to Stanton. | From Peak Tor a very pretty view is obtained up the valley of the Wye towards Bakewell, Haddon Hall forming a prominent object in the middle distance. |
| | On leaving Stanton enter plantation on the left, in which are several supposed Druidical remains, including three large upright stones, called respectively the Heart Stone, the Gorse Stone, and the Cat Stone ; and a Druidical circle called the Nine Ladies. | |
| Brimsbury House. | Birchover. | Andle Stone, a large monolithic block standing in a field a short distance from the road. |
| | On reaching the highway a little below Birchover turn to the left and continue to | Rowtor Rocks, a picturesque group of gritstone blocks rising to a considerable elevation, and on the summit of which there formerly existed a rocking stone. At the point where the roads meet some curious examples of rock scenery are observable: Bradley Rocks, Graned Tor or Robin Hood's Stride, sometimes called Mock-Beggar's Hall, Durwood Tor, and Cratliff Tor, at the foot of which latter there is an anchorite's cell, with a crucifix sculptured in stone still remaining. |
| Winster Hall, the residence of Llewellynn Jewitt, Esq., F.S.A. | WINSTER. 5½ miles from Rowsley. A small market town occupied chiefly by miners. | Road leads up to Elton. |
| | Wensley. A little rural hamlet, beyond which the prospect opens into Darley Dale and the valley of the Derwent. | |
| | Oker Hill, A lofty eminence, rises from the plain, the site of a Roman Station or intrenched fort. On the summit are two trees which tradition asserts were planted by two brothers, who here took a final farewell of each other. | |

2E

| ON THE LEFT FROM WINSTER. | Beyond Oker follow the pathway on the right bank of the river to | ON THE RIGHT FROM WINSTER. |
|---|---|---|
| Matlock Bath, a thriving hamlet on the side of the hill, prominent in the midst of which is the large Hydropathic Establishment erected by the late Mr. Smedley. | Matlock Bridge. | May Dale Mine. Market Hall and Assembly Room. New Hotel in course of erection. |
| Matlock Church stands on the edge of a curiously-shaped rock. High Tor, an immense perpendicular rock, 350 feet in height. | | |
| High Tor Grotto, a cavern, the roof and sides of which are covered with crystallisations of calcareous spar; approached by a foot-bridge over the Derwent. | MATLOCK BATH. 5 miles from Winster. (Inns: New Bath, Walker's, Hodgkinson's, Temple, Prince of Wales, Rutland Arms, Devonshire Arms.) | Masson and the Heights of Abraham, a lofty eminence, on the summit of which is the Victoria Prospect Tower. |
| Road to Matlock Bath Station. | An inland Spa, named, on account of the magnificent scenery environing it, the Anglo-Saxon Switzerland. The mineral waters are slightly tepid, and considered efficacious in cases of chronic rheumatism, gout, and other diseases. | Old Bath Hydropathic Establishment. |
| On the opposite side of the Derwent a long line of battlemented cliffs is seen, partially covered with trees and a profusion of ferns and ivy. | Rutland Cavern. Speedwell Cavern. Cumberland Cavern. Devonshire Cavern. Romantic Rocks. Petrifying Wells. | Royal Petrifying Well. Church. |
| Bounding the eastern side of the river are the Lovers' Walks, access to which is gained from the Boathouse. | | Road to Walker's Hotel. Road to New Bath Hotel. |
| Paper Mills. Glenorchy Chapel. Willersley Castle, an embattled structure belonging to Peter Arkwright, Esq. Scarthin Nick. A narrow opening in the rocks. On the opposite side of the river is seen Riber Hill and Wild Cat Tor. | | Cromford. |
| Cromford Church, built by the Arkwrights in 1797. Cromford Cotton Mills. Entrance Lodge to Willersley. | ⌒ Cromford Bridge, crossing the Derwent, close to which is Cromford Station. Follow the road on the right, passing under the railway and along the side of the river. | |
| Brough Wood. | About 2 miles from Cromford Bridge quit the open valley and follow the road that ascends on the left between steep wooded acclivities. | Lea Woods. |
| | Lea. Holloway. Return to Matlock Bath. | Entrance Lodge to Lea Hurst, the home of Florence Nightingale. |

| ON THE LEFT FROM MATLOCK BATH. | Thence to CROMFORD. | ON THE RIGHT FROM MATLOCK BATH. |
|---|---|---|
| | 1 mile from Matlock Bath. (Inn : Greyhound.) A small market town, in which Sir Rich. Arkwright built the first cotton mill, 1771. | |
| Road to Wirksworth. | Leaving the Wirksworth road near the upper end of the town, enter Bonsall Hollow, A deep narrow dell shut in by precipitous rocks. At the "Pig of Lead," a small public-house, turn to the left and enter Via Gellia, A picturesque road through the dales. | Road to Bonsall, a quaintly picturesque village with an ancient church and cross. |
| Road to Hopton and Carsington. | | Dunsley Spring, a cascade that descends from the wooded cliff. |
| Griff Wood. | Griff Dale. A narrow mountain glen threaded by a winding stream. | |
| | | Road to Ible. Valley Mill. |
| | Grange Mill. Here turn to the left, and follow the road to Long Cliff Wharf, where it is crossed by the Cromford and High Peak Railway. | Road to Winster and Bakewell. Road to Buxton by Newhaven. |
| Hoe Cliff and Brassington Rocks. Hipley Rock. Bradbourn Church is seen peeping above the umbrage on the top of the hill. Bradbourn Mill. | At the railway arch some pretty views occur of the rocks about Brassington. At the bottom of the valley turn to the left and keep the road for a distance of half-a-mile, then cross the Schoo by a little foot-bridge opposite Bradbourn Mill, and ascend by a field path continuing along to the top of the hill to | White Edge. |
| | TISSINGTON. 10 miles from Cromford. Tissington Hall, a fine old Gothic mansion, the seat of Sir H. Fitzherbert. Cross the Park, and on reaching the highway turn to the left. Fenny Bentley. ⌢ cross river Schoo. | Opposite Park gates road by Spend Lane to Dovedale. |
| Sandybrook Hall. | | |

| ON THE LEFT FROM ASHBOURN. | ASHBOURN. | ON THE RIGHT FROM ASHBOURN. |
|---|---|---|
| | **ASHBOURN.** | |
| | 4 miles from Tissington. | |
| | (Inns : Green Man and Black's Head, White Hart, Wheat Sheaf, George and Dragon.) Church, a fine cruciform structure of the early English and decorated periods, with an elegant spire, familiarly known as "The Pride of the Peak." Ashbourn Hall, the seat of Captain Holland, R.N. | |
| Okeover Church. Okeover Hall, a substantial brick mansion, the seat of H. C. Okeover, Esq. | On leaving Ashbourn cross the Schoo and proceed to Mappleton, thence along Spend Lane and by a bypath across the fields to Thorp, A picturesque village, with an old-fashioned Norman church standing near the edge of a precipice. Further on Thorp Cloud, a high mountain, is seen guarding the entrance to Dovedale, and beyond is Ilam Hall, A fine Tudor-Gothic mansion, the seat of Mr. Watts Russell. Return across the slope of Bunster Hill and by the "Izaak Walton" to | |
| | **DOVEDALE.** | |
| | 4 miles from Ashbourn. | |
| Dovedale Church, an insulated pile of limestone surmounted by numerous crags and pinnacles. | Cross the river by the foot-bridge and keep the Derbyshire side. | Reynard's Hall, a naturally formed opening or cavernous chamber in the limestone. Dove Holes, two cavernous openings in the rock. |
| Mill Dale. Road to Alstonfield. Hanson Toot. | | ⌒ Cold Eaton Bridge. |
| | **Narrow Dale.** Cross the river by the stepping stones to the Staffordshire side. **Pike Pool.** Cotton's Fishing House. | |
| Beresford Hall. | Beresford's Glen. | |
| | **HARTINGTON.** 7 miles from entrance to Dovedale. (Inn : Sleigh Arms.) Church, an ancient structure of the thirteenth century. | |

| ON THE LEFT FROM HARTINGTON. | | ON THE RIGHT FROM HARTINGTON. |
|---|---|---|
| | On reaching the high ground above Hartington, leave the road and cross the hill to Parsley Hay Wharf, and then proceed to | |
| | Arbor Low. A Druidical circle standing in a field near to a farm-house called Bunker's Hill. | |
| | Cross the field to One Ash Grange and then descend into Ricklow Dale, a wild, secluded ravine. At the bottom turn to the right, and follow the little river Lathkill to | |
| Sough Mill. Over Haddon. | Lathkill Dale. A picturesque dell shut in by lofty rocks and hills. | Road to Meadow Place, a farm house, formerly a monastery. |
| | ⌒ Conksbury Bridge. At this point quit the river and ascend by the path on the left, and thence across some enclosed pastures to | |
| | BAKEWELL. 10 miles from Hartington. | |
| | | Holme Hall, an embattled mansion, half-hidden in wood, stands on the further side of the Wye. Lumford Mill. Ashford Hall, the seat of the Hon. G. H. Cavendish. |
| The Rookery, an old-fashioned residence overgrown with ivy. Ashford Marble Works. | ASHFORD-IN-THE-WATER. 1½ mile from Bakewell. (Inn : Devonshire Arms.) | Road to Hassop and Chats-worth. Road to Wardlow Miers and TideswelL |
| | A mile and a half from Ashford quit the highway and follow the river, keep-ing the northern bank, to | |
| Brushfield. | MONSAL DALE. 2½ miles from Ashford. After passing beneath the railway viaduct cross the river by the lepping stones. | Fin Cop. Edge Stone Head. |
| | Cressbrook Dale. Here leave the river, fol-low the ascending path to Cressbrook, then descend by Slack Side to Litton Mill and | |
| Tideswell Mill. Road to Taddington. | MILLER'S DALE. Miller's Dale Station. 3 miles from Monsal Dale. | Road to Tideswell. Monk's Dale. |
| Chee Tor, a perpendicular wall of limestone rock, present-ing a convex front 300 feet in height. | Chee Dale. | Great Rocks Dale. Midland Railway Company's line to Marple and Manchester. |

| ON THE LEFT FROM MILLER'S DALE. | | ON THE RIGHT FROM MILLER'S DALE. |
|---|---|---|
| | Blackwell Dale. 2 miles from Miller's Dale. | |
| Topley Pike, a lofty eminence, along the upper acclivities of which the highroad is carried. Sherbrook Dell, a deep secluded glen, at the entrance to which is the Lover's Leap, a lofty perpendicular rock. | Ashwood Dale. | Pig Tor, a high barren rock projecting into the roadway. |
| | BUXTON. 4 miles from Blackwell Dale. (Inns: Palace, St. Ann's, Crescent, Old Hall, Lee Wood, Midland, Shakspere, Grove, George, Burlington, Eagle, Cheshire Cheese, King's Head.) Baths and Pump Rooms. St. Ann's Cliff. New Gardens. Corbar Wood. Poole's Hole. Devonshire Hospital. | Road to Fairfield and Castleton. |
| Lime Works. Road through Flash to Leek. | BURBAGE. 1 mile from Buxton. | Road to Edgemoor. |
| Axe Edge, one of the loftiest eminences in Derbyshire. On the summit is a small cairn erected by the Sappers, who, it is said, saw from hence the signals on Lincoln Cathedral and the top of Snowdon, the intervening distance being upwards of 150 miles. | Half-a-mile from Burbage cross the Cromford and High Peak Railway and continue to the head of Goyt's Clough. Enter Cheshire. | Valley of the Goyt, one of the four rivers that issue from Axe-Edge. |
| | Cat and Fiddle, a roadside inn on the top of the moor, reputed the highest public-house in England. A mile beyond, some fine views are obtained in the direction of Manchester. Return to Buxton. | |

# INDEX.

# EXTRACTS FROM REVIEWS.

"The natural beauty and variety of the scenery in the Peak of Derbyshire is fully described in Mr. Croston's little volume, which will be found a serviceable handbook for the tourist."—*Westminster Quarterly Review.*

"It is unpretending, full of minute details, and produces a succession of agreeable pictures. The book is, in short, a good, gossiping book, with nothing at all 'sensational' in it—an omission, in these highly-spiced times, which amounts to a virtue, and may be recorded as a recommendation."—*Athenæum.*

"Mr. Croston—who evidently knows the Peak district well, and who also knows what kind of imformation to impart to the visitor—has done wisely in issuing his work, which describes, in a pleasant manner, the entire district comprised in his 'Saunter,' and shows how observant he must have been of every object and every place which came under his notice. It is a charming book, and just what a visitor would wish to have with him as a companion during his saunter among the hills and dales of Derbyshire."—*Art Journal.*

"We assure our readers that—be they residents in or strangers to Derbyshire—they cannot do better than secure a copy of 'On Foot through the Peak,' which they will find not only a pleasant, chatty, and eminently-agreeable companion, but one which will give instruction on every page. The present edition is considerably enlarged, and has the additional attraction of being illustrated with a number of admirable wood engravings representing various places and objects of interest within the district, which Mr. Croston so ably and with such a masterly hand describes. The book cannot be too widely known, for it is one of the pleasantest of its kind that has ever been issued from the press."—*Reliquary Quarterly Archæological Journal and Review.*

"We are glad to see this book, which strikes us as one of the most complete and entertaining guides through one of the most delightful and historical parts of England. As a tourist's companion to Derbyshire we know of no volume we can so warmly recommend."—*The Bookseller.*

"The book itself is so well known that it is unnecessary to say anything in its praise in this place beyond reminding the intending tourist of its existence, and of the fact that for extent, variety, and fulness of information, there is no volume which can compare with Mr. Croston's interesting work. To the general reader it will be of scarcely less interest. Mr. Croston is a genial and gossiping companion, and has something amusing or instructive on every page."—*Manchester Courier.*

"This book is a second edition of an already popular work, and a brief reference to it is, therefore, all that is required. The latest issue has been improved, in some instances rewritten, and the pedestrian cannot have a more interesting companion in his walks through the charming and romantic hills and dales of Derbyshire than this book of Mr. Croston's."—*Manchester Examiner and Times.*

"One of the pleasantest and most agreeable books on our glorious county which have as yet been issued—a work that will please all and offend none. The title is a truly pleasant one, and augurs well for the contents of the volume ; and the volume well supports the favourable impression which the title produces. The author describes the places we have named, and also glances at many others by the way—describing scenery, giving insight into the history of the places, sketching the 'worthies' connected with them, and dotting down anecdotes and gossip which he has heard on the way. We give our hearty commendation to Mr. Croston's book, and recommend it to tourists who may seek to visit the Peak, whether 'on foot' or not."—*Derby Telegraph.*

"An agreeable and unpretentious description of an extensive and well-arranged 'Saunter among the Hills and Dales of Derbyshire,' in which—adding to his own considerable power of observation an extensive knowledge of what other writers have said upon the subject—we get sufficient of history to give a living interest to many of the scenes visited, without becoming antiquarians, and sufficient of the 'ologies' to indicate to the student where he may find food for observation and inquiry without such dry technicalities as might frighten or deter the non-scientific reader. Evidently of an agreeable gossiping turn, our author has elicited and recites many of the tales and legends which lurk among the rustic population of the Peak ; bits of traditionary lore crop up in various parts of the work, and are usually introduced with judicious effect. We feel sure many at a distance who read these pages will be tempted to visit the scenery so well described, and those already in the neighbourhood who look into this delightful book will find much to tempt them to extend their rambles and their sojourn among the hills and dales of the Peak."—*Buxton Advertiser.*

" Mr. Croston is evidently a most intelligent man ; his narrative is familiar and entertaining, his observations shrewd and accurate. He has well and candidly described the various objects of interest he met with and the general impression made upon him. It is always agreeable to find a gentleman who can describe natural objects and scenery as Mr. Croston does without being either prosy or tiresome. Of this natural ingenuity and keen observation our Manchester man possesses a considerable share ; and in reading his pages we have constantly felt that it would not be possible to accompany him on a visit to any place, be it ever so hackneyed or familiar, without hearing from him some observation either in itself original or presented in an original form—a circumstance indeed which affords perhaps the best proof of our author's being an agreeable, learned, and intelligent tourist, or at all events of his possessing the necessary qualities, in a very high degree, of a lively and descriptive writer. Moreover, there is so much good nature, candour, and unmistakable natural sense in Mr. Croston, that the reading of 'On Foot through the Peak' has proved to us a most agreeable and pleasant recreation. In a word, we highly commend the work to our readers, and feel sure that, as it gets more generally known, it will become the standard work on the hills and vales of our beautiful Derbyshire."—*Buxton Herald.*

" 'On Foot through the Peak' is a book which claims at the hands of Derbyshire men more attention than is usually awarded to guide books. Mr. Croston is always interesting, and his work has little in it to remind us of the stilted exaggerated style of ordinary guides. The journeying on the way is lightened with quaint traditions and stories, which are told in a plain and entertaining way."—*Derby Mercury.*

" The work is written in a free, homely, and lively style ; is never diffuse or stale, but maintains its interest and attractiveness throughout. The author has ably fulfilled his task—a task undertaken purely *con amore ;* and we shall be much surprised if the book does not command a ready sale, and cause Derbyshire to become the favourite resort of sightseers, as it deserve to be. The work is beautifully printed and elegantly bound ; and though the price may not be within the means of all, yet it is very reasonable for a work of such sterling merit, originality, and genius."—*Stockport Advertiser.*

" 'On Foot through the Peak' is a pleasantly-written, gossiping account of a ramble through the Peak of Derbyshire, by a Manchester man. Mr. Croston has succeeded in producing a very readable book, which will be enjoyed by those who are well acquainted with Derbyshire, and may induce others to explore its diversified and beautiful scenery."—*Sheffield and Rotherham Independent.*

---

John Heywood, Excelsior Printing and Stationery Works, Hulme Hall Road, Manchester.